About the Author

When Nikki Giovanni's poems first emerged during the Black Arts Movement in the 1960s, she immediately took a place among the most celebrated and influential poets of the era. Now, more than thirty years later, Nikki Giovanni still stands as one of the most commanding, luminous voices to grace America's political and poetic landscape.

Poet, activist, mother, and professor, Nikki Giovanni was born June 7, 1943, in Knoxville, Tennessee. While a student at Fisk University, she re-established the campus's Student Nonviolent Coordinating Committee (SNCC) chapter. In 1968, after studying at University of Pennsylvania's School of Social Work and Columbia University's School of Fine Arts, Giovanni self-published her first volume of poetry, the seminal *Black Feeling, Black Talk*.

Over the span of thirty years as a poet, Ms. Giovanni has received more than twenty honorary degrees from national colleges and universities. Her numerous awards include Woman of the Year from *Ebony, Mademoiselle, Essence,* and *Ladies' Home Journal* magazines; YWCA Woman of the Year, Cincinnati Chapter; Outstanding Woman of Tennessee Award; Ohio Women's Hall of Fame induction; Distinguished Recognition Award, Detroit City Council; McDonald's Literary Achievement Award for Poetry, presented in the name of Nikki Giovanni in perpetuity;

Outstanding Humanitarian Award, the House of Representatives of the Commonwealth of Kentucky; two Tennessee Governor's Awards in the Arts and in the Humanities; the Virginia Governor's Award; the Black Caucus of the ALA Honor Award for Nonfiction; and three NAACP Image Awards for *Quilting the Black-Eyed Pea, Blues: For All the Changes,* and *Love Poems.*

Ms. Giovanni has been given the keys to more than a dozen cities, including New York, Los Angeles, Dallas, Miami, New Orleans, and Baltimore. She was named the first recipient of the Rosa Parks Woman of Courage Award and holds the Langston Hughes Medal for Outstanding Poetry.

Nikki Giovanni is the author of more than twenty books of poetry and prose for adults and children. She is University Distinguished Professor of English at Virginia Tech and has been published by William Morrow, an imprint of HarperCollins Publishers, for over thirty years. Ms. Giovanni continues to read her work all over the country.

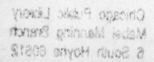

THE PROSAIC
SOUL OF
NIKKI
GIOVANNI

BOOKS BY NIKKI GIOVANNI

POETRY
Black Feeling, Black Talk/Black Judgement
Re: Creation
My House
The Women and the Men
Cotton Candy on a Rainy Day
Those Who Ride the Night Winds
The Selected Poems of Nikki Giovanni
Love Poems
Blues: For All the Changes
Quilting the Black-Eyed Pea

PROSE
Gemini: An Extended Autobiographical Statement on My First Twenty-five Years of Being a Black Poet
A Dialogue: James Baldwin and Nikki Giovanni
A Poetic Equation: Conversations Between Nikki Giovanni and Margaret Walker
Sacred Cows . . . and Other Edibles
Racism 101

EDITED BY NIKKI GIOVANNI
Night Comes Softly: An Anthology of Black Female Voices
Appalachian Elders: A Warm Hearth Sampler
Grand Mothers: Poems, Reminiscences, and Short Stories About the Keepers of Our Traditions
Grand Fathers: Reminiscences, Poems, Recipes, and Photos of the Keepers of Our Traditions
Shimmy Shimmy Shimmy Like My Sister Kate: Looking at the Harlem Renaissance Through Poems

FOR CHILDREN
Spin a Soft Black Song
Vacation Time: Poems for Children
Knoxville, Tennessee
The Genie in the Jar
The Sun Is So Quiet
Ego-Tripping and Other Poems for Young People

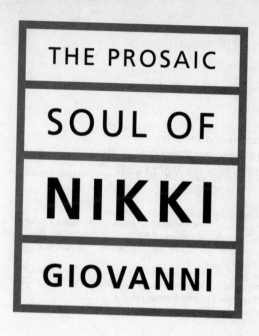

THE PROSAIC
SOUL OF
NIKKI
GIOVANNI

Nikki Giovanni

Perennial

An Imprint of HarperCollins*Publishers*

Library of Congress Cataloging-in-Publication Data
Giovanni, Nikki.
  The prosaic soul of Nikki Giovanni / Nikki Giovanni.—1st ed.
    p. cm.
ISBN 0-06-054134-2 (alk. paper)
    I. Title.

PS3557.I55A6 2003
818'.5408—dc22   2003058224

07 08 09 ❖/RRD 10 9 8 7 6 5 4 3 2

Contents

CONTENTS

GEMINI

An Extended Autobiographical
Statement on My First Twenty-five
Years of Being a Black Poet

1971

To my son Thomas and
Barb's son Anthony and their
fathers, who probably never
thought they could produce
anything as lovely as them

Introduction
by Barbara Crosby

Dear Anthony,

Your Aunt Nikki is my best friend, Chris's favorite aunt, Tommy's mommy and Louvenia's representative on earth. Maybe Louvenia is one of the best explanations for all of the apparent contradictions which ultimately always fit. Louvenia was one of the last strong Black Southern ladies who would bash you over the head with an umbrella if you didn't give MLK proper respect. She was also Nikki's grandmother.

If one believes that genes move toward perfection of characteristics then Nikki, with the added props of being born a Gemini seven, fell into an advanced stage of double realities, functioning consistently within two seemingly contradictory realms simultaneously. Like she begs a nonpaying company to take a best-selling work and refuses a company offering good advances. Or wears a threadbare sweater ("But my sister made it for me") over an expensive velvet jumpsuit. Or develops a readership and following among a group of people who have been traditionally considered nonreaders, and then has her writings rejected by slick, sophisticated magazines because they can't understand it. Could these be the regular conflicts of an Eastern nature living in a Western culture?

Being a Gemini only partially explains the difficulties inherent in the existence of this small, quick, harsh, gentle girl-woman. Another part is genius. Are geniuses known from birth or must they grow with their secret and maybe never even realize it themselves? The weird housewife or that scatterbrain sales clerk just might be nonfunctioning because of a million million thoughts which fall into emptiness. One must have a way of communicating, a way of organizing and sharing, for genius can be very lonely. Luckily Nikki realizes it, maybe through the results of white folks' tests or maybe because Louvenia told her, or maybe she just knew. At any rate she was left with the simpler task of figuring out how to use it.

When she was little she read Ayn Rand, cheap novels, books about the formation of clouds and fairy tales. She listened to Yolande and Gus, Flora and Theresa at the table and watched Gary's adventures into the big real world. She saw every B movie she could squeeze from her Sunday money after bus fare from the Valley to Cincinnati. Then she would secrete herself and write stories—only to hide them. One of a genius' earliest lessons is that her consciousness is considered bizarre by others so she hides away for fear of being misunderstood, and for fear.

As if she didn't have enough trouble already, poor Aunt Nikki was also blessed with a spiritual/emotional nature reaching back to her African roots. Dogs love her though she says that she is afraid of them. Cats have such a hold on her that she feels in direct conflict with them: she says they sit and stare and dare her to work. Her strongest affinity is to turtles, with which she has fantastic luck. They live for years unless she takes them out for air and loses them in the tall grass. Her idea of winter fun is a trip to the zoo with Chris, though I have never understood and neither did Louvenia why she hates parades.

She has a special ability and need to function with old ladies, and many of her girlfriends—from stars through social workers of various sizes—are over fifty. But her magic trick is communication with adolescents. I've sat in on her college classes and not understood a word she has said while all her students seemed to understand perfectly. Maybe I was listening with the wrong part. Maybe she was just communicating love to the Black soul and I was using Western-trained ears.

To me Nikki has been a friend. But the relationship has required energy and movement. Some great cracker once said that the greatest sin was being a bore. Nikki's personal growth has required that all around her grow. As she moves she pulls us all with her to new positions of intellectual and spiritual understanding. She is rejecting of weakness, which saps the strong. Ellis says that there are a few centripetal forces who draw others to them, artist-suns who form creative universes with the others as planets. Nikki is one of these.

Nikki is at this point in time a superstar in a remote area, a Black female poet with a television following that includes both the New York fly set and the Knoxville church ladies. She is pretty and eccentric—some would call her wild; this depends on your point of identification. She curses with a style and sense of the genteel, a freedom and control in an admirable balance that is impossible to imitate. Those who are attracted by her glamour and try to copy it find that the shoes pinch awfully. I would warrant there is only one human being who takes Nikki for granted: her son, Thomas, who came to give love and break up chairs, who came to say, "You are not alone."

So now, with the category of Black motherhood to add to her definition, she is sailing through adulthood like a flying fish jumping to bait or an egret heading for the elephants, touching all elements—land, water and air. The fire is within. The fire from which the phoenix emerges.

At this writing she is still growing, and I wouldn't presume to understand her. All I know is that she is the most cowardly, bravest, least understanding, most sensitive, slowest to anger, most quixotic, lyingest, most honest woman I know. To love her is to love contradictions and conflict. To know her is never to understand but to be sure that all is life.

And when I asked Nikki what *Gemini* was all about she said proudly and definitely, "A fictionalized autobiographical account of my first twenty-five years." I asked her, "What does that mean?" And she looked up from her desk with the kind of impatience she has with me to say, "Barbara, how would I know?"

1

400 Mulvaney Street

I was going to Knoxville, Tennessee, to speak. I was going other places first but mostly to me I was going home. And I, running late as usual, hurried to the airport just in time.

The runway is like an aircraft carrier—sticking out in the bay—and you always get the feeling of drunken fly-boys in green airplane hats chomping wads and wads of gum going "Whooooopie!" as they bring the 747 in from Hackensack to La Guardia. It had been snowing for two days in New York and the runway was frozen. They never say to you that the runway is frozen and therefore dangerous to take off from, and in fact you'd never notice it because all the New York airports have tremendous backups—even on clear days. So sitting there waiting was not unusual but I did notice this tendency to slide to the side with every strong wind, and I peeked out my window and noticed we were in the tracks of the previous jet and I thought: death has to eat too. And I went to sleep.

The whole thing about going to Knoxville appealed to my vanity. I had gotten a call from Harvey Glover about coming down and had said yes and had thought no more of it. Mostly, as you probably notice, artists very rarely have the chance to go back home and say, "I think I've done you proud." People are so insecure and in some cases jealous and in some cases think so little of themselves in general that they seldom think you'd be really honored to speak in your home town or at your old high school. And other people are sometimes so contemptuous of home that they in fact don't want to come back. This has set up a negative equation between the artist and home.

I was excited about going to Knoxville but I didn't want to get my hopes up. What if it fell through? What if they didn't like me? Oh, my God! What if nobody came to hear me? Maybe we'd better forget about it. And I did. I flew on out to Cleveland to make enough money to be able to go to Knoxville. And Cleveland was beautiful. A girl named Pat and her policeman friend couldn't have been any nicer. And he was an intelligent cop. I got the feeling I was going to have a good weekend. Then my mother met me at the Cincinnati airport, where I had to change over, and had coffee with me and had liked my last television appearance. Then they called my flight, and on to Knoxville.

When we were growing up Knoxville didn't have television, let alone an airport. It finally got TV but the airport is in Alcoa. And is now called Tyson Field. Right? Small towns are funny. Knoxville even has a zip code and seven-digit phone numbers. All of which seems strange to me since I mostly remember Mrs. Flora Ford's white cake with white icing and Miss Delaney's blue furs and Armetine Picket's being the sharpest woman in town—she attended our church—and Miss Brooks wearing tight sweaters and Carter-Roberts Drug Store sending out Modern Jazz Quartet sounds of "Fontessa" and my introduction to Nina Simone by David Cherry, dropping a nickel in the jukebox and "Porgy" coming out. I mostly remember Vine Street, which I was not allowed to walk to get to school, though Grandmother didn't want me to take Paine Street either because Jay Manning lived on it and he was home from the army and very beautiful with his Black face and two dimples. Not that I was going to do anything, because I didn't do anything enough even to think in terms of not doing anything, but according to small-town logic "It looks bad."

The Gem Theatre was on the corner of Vine and a street that runs parallel to the creek, and for 10 cents you could sit all day and see a double feature, five cartoons and two serials plus previews for the next two weeks. And I remember Frankie Lennon would come in with her gang and sit behind me and I wanted to say, "Hi. Can I sit with you?" but thought they were too snooty, and they, I found out later, thought I was too Northern and stuck-up. All of that is gone now. Something called progress killed my grandmother.

Mulvaney Street looked like a camel's back with both humps bulging—up and down—and we lived in the down part. At the top of the left hill a lady made ice balls and would mix the flavors for you for just a nickel. Across the street from her was the Negro center, where the guys played indoor basketball and the little kids went for stories and nap time. Down in the valley part were the tennis courts, the creek, the bulk of the park and the beginning of the right hill. To enter or leave the street you went either up or down. I used to think of it as a fort, especially when it snowed, and the enemy would always try to sneak through the underbrush nurtured by the creek and through the park trees, but we always spotted strangers and dealt. As you came down the left hill the houses were up on its side; then people got regular flat front yards; then the right hill started and ran all the way into Vine and Mulvaney was gone and the big apartment building didn't have a yard at all.

Grandmother and Grandpapa had lived at 400 since they'd left Georgia. And Mommy had been a baby there and Anto and Aunt Agnes were born there. And dated there and sat on the swing on the front porch and fussed there, and our good and our bad were recorded there. That little frame house duplicated twice more which overlooked the soft-voiced people passing by with "Evening, 'Fessor Watson, Miz Watson," and the grass wouldn't grow between our house and Edith and Clarence White's house. It was said that he had something to do with numbers. When the man tried to get between the two houses and the cinder crunched a warning to us, both houses lit up and the man was caught between Mr. White's shotgun and Grandfather's revolver, trying to explain he was lost. Grandpapa would never pull a gun unless he intended to shoot and would only shoot to kill. I think when he reached Knoxville he was just tired of running. I brought his gun to New York with me after he died but the forces that be don't want anyone to keep her history, even if it's just a clogged twenty-two that no one in her right mind would even load.

Mr. and Mrs. Ector's rounded the trio of houses off. He always wore a stocking cap till he got tied back and would emerge very dapper. He was in love with the various automobiles he owned and had been seen by Grandmother and me on more than one occasion sweeping the snow from in front of his garage before he would back the car into the street. All summer he parked his car at the bottom of the hill and polished it twice a day and delighted in it. Grandmother would call across the porches to him, "Ector, you a fool 'bout that car, ain't cha?" And he would smile back. "Yes, ma'am." We were always polite with the Ectors because they had neither children nor grandchildren so there were no grounds for familiarity. I never knew Nellie Ector very well at all. It was rumored that she was a divorcée who had latched on to him, and to me she became all the tragic heroines I had read about, like *Forever Amber* or the *All This and Heaven Too* chick, and I was awed but kept my distance. He was laughs, though. I don't know when it happened to the Ectors but Mr. White was the first to die. I considered myself a hot-shot canasta player and I would play three-hand with Grandmother and Mrs. White and beat them. But I would drag the game on and on because it seemed so lonely next door when I could look through my bedroom window and see Mrs. White dressing for bed and not having to pull the shade anymore.

You always think the ones you love will always be there to

love you. I went on to my grandfather's alma mater and got kicked out and would have disgraced the family but I had enough style for it not to be considered disgraceful. I could not/did not adjust to the Fisk social life and it could not/did not adjust to my intellect, so Thanksgiving I rushed home to Grandmother's without the bitchy dean of women's permission and that dean put me on social probation. Which would have worked but I was very much in love and not about to consider her punishment as anything real I should deal with. And the funny thing about that Thanksgiving was that I knew everything would go down just as it did. But I still wouldn't have changed it because Grandmother and Grandpapa would have had dinner alone and I would have had dinner alone and the next Thanksgiving we wouldn't even have him and Grandmother and I would both be alone by ourselves, and the only change would have been that Fisk considered me an ideal student, which means little on a life scale. My grandparents were surprised to see me in my brown slacks and beige sweater nervously chain-smoking and being so glad to touch base again. And she, who knew everything, never once asked me about school. And he was old so I lied to him. And I went to Mount Zion Baptist with them that Sunday and saw he was going to die. He just had to. And I didn't want that. Because I didn't know what to do about Louvenia, who had never been alone in her life.

I left Sunday night and saw the dean Monday morning. She asked where I had been. I said home. She asked if I had permission. I said I didn't need her permission to go home. She said, "Miss Giovanni," in a way I've been hearing all my life, in a way I've heard so long I know I'm on the right track when I hear it, and shook her head. I was "released from the school" February 1 because my "attitudes did not fit those of a Fisk woman." Grandpapa died in April and I was glad it was warm because he hated the cold so badly. Mommy and I drove to Knoxville to the funeral with Chris—Gary's, my sister's, son—and I was brave and didn't cry and made decisions. And finally the time came and Anto left and Aunt Agnes left. And Mommy and Chris and I stayed on till finally Mommy had to go back to work. And Grandmother never once asked me about Fisk. We got up early Saturday morning and Grandmother made fried chicken for us. Nobody said we were leaving but we were. And we all walked down the hill to the car. And kissed. And I looked at her standing there so bravely trying not to think what I was trying not to feel. And I got in on the driver's side and looked at her standing there with her plaid apron and her hair in a bun, her feet hanging loosely out of her mules, sixty-three years old, waving good-bye to us, and for the first time having to go into 400 Mulvaney without John Brown Watson. I felt like an impotent dog. If I couldn't protect this magnificent woman, my grandmother, from loneliness, what could I ever do? I have always hated death. It is unacceptable to kill the young and distasteful to watch the old expire. And those in between our link commit the little murders all the time. There must be a better way. So Knoxville decided to become a model city and a new mall was built to replace the old marketplace and they were talking about convention centers and expressways. And Mulvaney Street was a part of it all. This progress.

And I looked out from a drugged sleep and saw the Smoky Mountains looming ahead. The Smokies are so called because the clouds hang low. We used to camp in them. And the bears would come into camp but if you didn't feed them they would go away. It's still a fact. And we prepared for the landing and I closed my eyes as I always do because landings and takeoffs are the most vulnerable times for a plane, and if I'm going to die I don't have to watch it coming. It is very hard to give up your body completely. But the older I get the more dependent I am on other people for my safety, so I closed my eyes and placed myself in harmony with the plane.

Tyson Field turned out to be Alcoa. Progress again. And the Alcoa Highway had been widened because the new governor was a football fan and had gotten stuck on the old highway while trying to make a University of Tennessee football game and had missed the kickoff. The next day they began widening the road. We were going to the University of Tennessee for the first speaking of the day. I would have preferred Knoxville College, which had graduated three Watsons and two Watson progeny. It was too funny being at U.T. speaking of Blackness because I remember when Joe Mack and I integrated the theater here to see *L'il Abner*. And here an Afro Liberation Society was set up. Suddenly my body remembered we hadn't eaten in a couple of days and Harvey got me a quart of milk and the speaking went on. Then we left U.T. and headed for Black Knoxville.

Gay Street is to Knoxville what Fifth Avenue is to New York. Something special, yes? And it looked the same. But

Vine Street, where I would sneak to the drugstore to buy *Screen Stories* and watch the men drink wine and play pool— all gone. A wide, clean military-looking highway has taken its place. Austin Homes is cordoned off. It looked like a big prison. The Gem Theatre is now some sort of nightclub and Mulvaney Street is gone. Completely wiped out. Assassinated along with the old people who made it live. I looked over and saw that the lady who used to cry "HOT FISH! GOOD HOT FISH!" no longer had a Cal Johnson Park to come to and set up her stove in. Grandmother would not say, "Edith White! I think I'll send Gary for a sandwich. You want one?" Mrs. Abrum and her reverend husband from rural Tennessee wouldn't bring us any more goose eggs from across the street. And Leroy wouldn't chase his mother's boyfriend on Saturday night down the back alley anymore. All gone, not even to a major highway but to a cutoff of a cutoff. All the old people who died from lack of adjustment died for a cutoff of a cutoff.

And I remember our finding Grandmother the house on Linden Avenue and constantly reminding her it was every bit as good as if not better than the little ole house. A bigger back yard and no steps to climb. But I knew what Grandmother knew, what we all knew. There was no familiar smell in that house. No coal ashes from the fireplaces. Nowhere that you could touch and say, "Yolande threw her doll against this wall," or "Agnes fell down these steps." No smell or taste of biscuits Grandpapa had eaten with the Alaga syrup he loved so much. No Sunday chicken. No sound of "Lord, you children don't care a thing 'bout me after all I done for you," because Grand- mother always had the need to feel mistreated. No spot in the back hall weighted down with lodge books and no corner

where the old record player sat playing Billy Eckstine croon-
ing, "What's My Name?" till Grandmother said, "Lord! Any
fool know his name!" No breeze on dreamy nights when
Mommy would listen over and over again to "I Don't See Me
in Your Eyes Anymore." No pain in my knuckles where
Grandmother had rapped them because she was determined I
would play the piano, and when that absolutely failed, no
effort on Linden for us to learn the flowers. No echo of me
being the only person in the history of the family to curse
Grandmother out and no Grandpapa saying, "Oh, my," which
was serious from him, "we can't have this." Linden Avenue
was pretty but it had no life.

And I took Grandmother one summer to Lookout Moun-
tain in Chattanooga and she would say I was the only grand-
child who would take her riding. And that was the summer I
noticed her left leg was shriveling. And she said I didn't have
to hold her hand and I said I liked to. And I made ice cream
the way Grandpapa used to do almost every Sunday. And I
churned butter in the hand churner. And I knew and she
knew that there was nothing I could do. "I just want to see you
graduate," she said, and I didn't know she meant it. I gradu-
ated February 4. She died March 8.

And I went to Knoxville looking for Frankie and the Gem
and Carter-Roberts or something and they were all gone. And
400 Mulvaney Street, like a majestic king dethroned, put
naked in the streets to beg, stood there just a mere skeleton of
itself. The cellar that had been so mysterious was now
exposed. The fireplaces stood. And I saw the kitchen light
hanging and the peach butter put up on the back porch and I
wondered why they were still there. She was dead. And I

heard the daily soap operas from the radio we had given her one birthday and saw the string beans cooking in the deep well and thought how odd, since there was no stove, and I wanted to ask how Babbi was doing since I hadn't heard or seen "Brighter Day" in so long but no one would show himself. The roses in the front yard were blooming and it seemed a disgrace. Probably the tomatoes came up that year. She always had fantastic luck with tomatoes. But I was just too tired to walk up the front steps to see. Edith White had died. Mr. Ector had died, I heard. Grandmother had died. The park was not yet gone but the trees looked naked and scared. The wind sang to them but they wouldn't smile. The playground where I had swung. The courts where I played my first game of tennis. The creek where our balls were lost. "HOT FISH! GOOD HOT FISH!" The hill where the car speeding down almost hit me. Walking barefoot up the hill to the center to hear stories and my feet burning. All gone. Because progress is so necessary. General Electric says, "Our most important product." And I thought Ronald Reagan was cute.

I was sick throughout the funeral. I left Cincinnati driving Mommy, Gary and Chris to Knoxville. From the moment my father had called my apartment I had been sick because I knew before they told me that she was dead. And she had promised to visit me on the tenth. Chris and I were going to drive down to get her since she didn't feel she could fly. And here it was the eighth. I had a letter from her at my house when I got back reaffirming our plans for her visit. I had a cold. And I ran the heat the entire trip despite the sun coming directly down on us. I couldn't get warm. And we stopped in Kentucky for country ham and I remembered how she used to hoard it from us and I couldn't eat. And I drove on. Gary was supposed to relieve me but she was crying too much. And the car was too hot and it was all so unnecessary. She died because she didn't know where she was and didn't like it. And there was no one there to give a touch or smell or feel and I think I should have been there. And at her funeral they said, "It is well," and I knew she knew it was. And it was so peaceful in Mount Zion Baptist Church that afternoon. And I hope when I die that it can be said of me all is well with my soul.

So they took me up what would have been Vine Street past what would have been Mulvaney and I thought there may be a reason we lack a collective historical memory. And I was taken out to the beautiful homes on Brooks Road where we considered the folks "so swell, don't cha know." And I was exhausted but feeling quite high from being once again in a place where no matter what I belong. And Knoxville belongs to me. I was born there in Old Knoxville General and I am buried there with Louvenia. And as the time neared for me to speak I had no idea where I would start. I was nervous and afraid because I just wanted to quote Gwen Brooks and say, "This is the urgency— Live!" And they gave me a standing ovation and I wanted to say, "Thank you," but that was hardly sufficient. Mommy's old bridge club, Les Pas Si Bêtes, gave me beads, and that's the kind of thing that happens in small towns where people aren't afraid to be warm. And I looked out and saw Miss Delaney in her blue furs. And was reminded life continues. And I saw the young brothers and sisters who never even knew me or my family and I saw my grandmother's friends who shouldn't even have been out that late at night. And they had come to say *Welcome Home*. And I thought Tommy, my son, must know about this. He must know we come from somewhere. That we belong.

2

For a Four-Year-Old

For a four-year-old I was a terror. Mostly this was because my big sister, Gary, would wolf all the time, then come running in from school, throw her books down and scream at my mother, "JUST LET ME GO GET THEM—JUST LET ME AT THEM!" And Mommy, digging the whole scene, would say, "Gary, have a glass of milk and some graham crackers and let's talk about your day." And Gary would say, "But Peggy's waiting outside. I gotta go fight." And I, sitting on the top porch waiting for Gary to come home, would already have adequately handled the situation. Since it was a thrice-weekly occurrence at least, I kept a large supply of large rocks on the top porch. And as Gary crossed the front porch I had started pelting Peggy and her gang with my pieces. So by the time Gary put her books down and called out how she had to fight, I had them on the run. For a four-year-old I was beautiful. Peggy and her gang would always run out of my reach and call up, "YOU TELL GARY WE'LL GET HER! YOU AIN'T ALWAYS HOME!" Then they'd leave.

By the time Gary had changed clothes and had her first glass of milk it was all over. Mommy innocently asked where I had been, telling me, "Gary's home." And I said, "Yeah, Peggy chased her again. But I took care of it." "Kim, you've got to quit fighting so much. You'll be five soon and in school yourself. And you've got to control yourself."

"I'm glad Kim got that ole Miss Yella," Gary piped up from her plate. "She's always picking on somebody." "Somebody's always wolfing," Mommy said. "And who are you to call anybody yellow?" "Well, at least my hair don't hang all the way down to the ground." "Doesn't. Doesn't hang. And Kim, you'll have to quit storing those rocks on the porch. Gary can fight her own battles." "Yes, Mommy."

The summer passed rather happily with Peggy and sometimes Skippy chasing Gary from piano lessons. I always thought Gary was tops. She is very smooth, with the older sister style that says I-can-do-anything, you know? And I thought she could. "Kim," she said, taking me aside in the back yard, "you know why I don't fight? It's not that I'm scared or something—but I'm a musician. What if my hands were maimed? What if I were injured or something? Then Dr. Matthews couldn't give me lessons anymore. Then Mrs. Clarke couldn't give me rehearsals anymore. Why, their families would starve. Walter and Charles couldn't wear clothes. The studio would close down. And the world would be deprived of a great talent playing 'Claire de Lune.' You understand, don't you?" And I did. I swear I did. All I wanted from this world was to protect and nourish this great talent, who was not my cousin or best friend or next-door neighbor but my very own sister.

I had turned five at the end of the school year and would be going to school myself in the fall. I had a mission in life. No one must touch Gary. "Kim," Mommy said, "you know Gary says a lot of things that are true but not as true as she makes them sound." And I thought no one, not even our mother, appreciated the mission Gary and I had. She must be free to work. Really! If I hadn't been prepared to deal I don't think Gary would have survived—with her frivolous music and fancy ideas. That's the stuff extinction is made of. In my own little anti-intellectual way I understood a profundity. It is un-American, if not dangerous, not to fight. I felt I stood alone.

We lived in Wyoming, Ohio, which is a suburb of Cincinnati, which some say is a suburb of Lexington, Kentucky. But we liked it. The sidewalks run broad and clear; the grass and mud intertwine just enough to let you be a muddy little lady; and there were those magnificent little violets that some called weeds and that I would pick for Mommy to put in her window vase.

Most of the summer was spent running and swinging and making believe. I did learn the hard way not to make-believe and swing at the same time. I was going way up high. People were standing at the bottom marveling at me. "She doesn't spell or read as well as Gary," they said, "but clearly she's an Olympic contender at swinging." They were amazed. Then I fell out of the swing. I wasn't so hurt as I was hurt. Swinging was my strong point. It's really a cruel life when your strong point falls through. But I had a backup. Gary had taught me how to read and write a little and I could count to ten in French, Okinawan and Pig Latin. I knew no matter what, I was going to knock kindergarten out. When fall finally came I was overprepared. I had even practiced nap time.

I woke up that morning bright and early to a solid cold cereal breakfast. You see, I had early recognized the importance of getting away from the hot-cereal-Father-John's-Tonic syndrome. The older you are the less they—i.e., parents— care what you eat until you get married or something. Then they—i.e., lovers—start the whole parent syndrome all over again. So I had told Mommy in no uncertain terms—*cold cereal, no toast, no Father John's and plenty of coffee.* She at least let me have the corn flakes.

She also insisted on taking me to school. Surely that was an insidious move on her part. I had planned to walk with Gary and let everybody know that just because I was going to school I wasn't going to be no lady or nothing like that. What I had done to Peggy last year I could do again.

You see, the winter before, Mommy had let me go meet Gary from school. That had been right after Christmas. Gary had taken the sled to school because we had finally gotten snow in January. I was going to meet her and ride home. Mommy had bundled me in my brown snowsuit and airplane hat pulled over my ears and mittens (though I had been insist- ing on gloves for some time) and a big scarf. Mommy took her job of mommying quite seriously and never wanted me to catch cold or something. I practically rolled down the stair and, gaining momentum, bounced along Burns Street, making the turn at Pendry past Mrs. Spears's house, just barely turn- ing Oak and managing by the grace of God to stop in front of Oak Avenue school. Gary alighted from the side door with the sled and Peggy on her heels. We put her books on the beauti- ful beige sled with the magnificent red streak and started home, Peggy and the three goony girls a respectful distance behind.

"What will we do if they bother us?" Gary asked. "I'll beat

her up." "Well, it's different when we're home but we've got the sled to look out for." "Don't worry, Gary, I'll beat her up." "Well, she better not hurt you or I'll deal with her myself." "Oh, no, Gary. Don't you get in it. I can beat Peggy all by myself." Even then I couldn't bear the thought of someone's laying uncaring, irreverent hands on her. "I can handle it." We turned the corner.

Pendry is one of those little suburb streets that they always show when they want to convince you Negroes want to live next door. The sidewalks are embraced by cut grass in the summer and a clean blanket of snow in the winter. All the houses have front yards and white steps leading to them. Mostly they are brick houses, except the Spearses had a white frame one. As we turned onto Pendry the gang moved up on us since no one from the school could see. "Look at the stuck-up boobsie twins," they started. "Mama had to send the baby to look out for the coward."

"Don't say anything," I advised. "You always say some-thing to make them mad. Maybe they'll just leave us alone." We made it past the house where we never saw the people and started by Dr. Richardson's. "They walk alike, talk alike and roll on their bellies like a reptile," they chanted. There had been a circus that year and everybody had gotten into the barker thing. "Just look at them, folks. One can't do without the other." And they burst out laughing. "Hey, old stuck-up. What you gonna do when your sister's tired of fighting for you?" "I'll beat you up myself. That's what." Damn, damn, damn. Now we would have to fight. "You and what army, 'ho'?" *Ho'* was always a favorite. "Me and yo' mama's army," Gary answered with precision and dignity. "You talking 'bout my mama?" "I would but the whole town is so I can't add nothing." They sidled up alongside us at the Spears's. "You take it back, Gary." Deadly quiet. "Yo' mama's so ugly she went to the zoo and the gorilla paid to see her." "You take that back!" "Yo' mama's such a 'ho' she went to visit a farm and they dug a whole field before they knew it was her."

Peggy swung and I stepped in. Peggy had long brown hair that she could easily have sat on if she wasn't always careful to fling it out of the way. She said it was her Indian ancestry. She swung her whole body to hit Gary as her goony girls formed a circle to watch. And as she swung I grabbed her hair, and began to wrap it around my hand, then my arm. I had a good, solid grip. Gary stepped back to watch the action. Mrs. Spears went to call Mommy. The next clear thing I remember is Mommy saying from a long, long way away, "Let her go, Kim," and Peggy being under me and me wondering why it was so cold. I, at four, had defeated Peggy Johnson. And she was bad. As Mommy fussed me home that was all I could think about. I had won. Now that that was established the rest would be simple.

So Mommy walked me to school telling me how nice the kids were and how I would enjoy it and I was thinking whether Peggy would remember last year and how I could make sure she knew the same would hold true. She must not, no one must touch my sister. "You must realize Gary is in the fifth grade and can fight for herself. You'll have enough to do just taking care of yourself. Your sister isn't a dummy. She skipped, didn't she? And she's not a weakling. She beats you up when you have arguments and I don't want any repetition of what happened last year. OK?" "Yes, Mommy." "I'm counting on you, Kim. It's very important you give the children a chance. You can't always run around with Gary and her friends. Make some of your own. If you give them a chance they'll just love you as much as your father and I do. OK?" "Yes, Mommy."

"Mrs. Hicks is a wonderful woman." "I remember Aunt Willa, Mommy. I like her and Elizabeth Ann." Sometimes I played with Elizabeth Ann even though she was younger than I. Aunt Willa was super. She played Pekeno at our house and sometimes they let me deal since I was always up and meddling. Aunt Willa would always pay you when you gave her a good hand. Some of Mommy's friends would just say, "Good dealing," and some would say, "Kim, why aren't you in bed?" But Aunt Willa was all right. She was always straight. You could really go to kindergarten with a lady like that. "And remember everybody in class doesn't know her like you do. So what are we going to call her?" "Mrs. Hicks," I pronounced very distinctly, "just like you said I should." "That's my big girl." Mommy squeezed my hand and looked relieved. Adults are certainly strange. They always do things they don't want people to remember but they never remember not to let you see them doing it. I mean, if they cared in the first place, it would have gone down differently. But what the hell—I would call Aunt Willa Mrs. Hicks and be good because I dug the whole game. Even then. From a low vantage point.

I was bouncing up the stairs prepared to knock them dead when Mommy opened the door and I looked at all those little faces. I broke down. I didn't know these people. They didn't look like they were seeing a woman with a mission. My God!! They might not even care. I started crying. Mommy, in the usual vanity that mothers possess, thought I didn't want to leave her but that wasn't it at all. I was entering a world where few knew and even fewer would ever understand my mission. Life is a motherfucker. Mommy—four eleven, ninety pounds after Christmas dinner—walked out of that kindergarten room a little taller, a bit prouder . . . her baby girl really cared. The kids, in their usual indifferent way, stated, "Kim is a cry-baby." I wanted to shout at them all—"*You dumbbumbs*"—but I restrained myself by burying my head in Aunt Willa's lap and softly pleading, "What shall I do?" Aunt Willa hit upon the saving idea: Go get Gary.

In She strode—like Cleopatra on her barge down the Nile, like Nefertiti on her way to sit for the statue, like Harriet Tubman before her train or Mary Bethune with Elenora; my big sister came to handle the situation. You could feel the room respond to her presence. It could have been San Francisco at the earthquake, Chicago as Mrs. O'Leary walked to her cow, Rome as Nero struck up his fiddle, Harlem when Malcolm mounted the podium; Gary came to handle the situation. Looking neither right nor left she glided from the door, her eyes searching for the little figure buried in Aunt Willa's skirt. "Kim"—her voice containing all the power of Cicero at the seashore, Elijah at the annual meeting—"Kim, don't cry." And it was over. Tears falling literally pulled themselves back into my eyes. In a gulp, with a wipe of the hand, it was over. "I'll walk you home for lunch. Come on, now, and play with the other kids. There's Donny, Robert's brother, and Pearl. They want to play with you." The pain, the absolute pain of wanting to be eight years old and in the fifth grade and sophisticated and in control. I could have burst! "I'm sorry." "Don't worry about it. Mommy just wouldn't want you to cry." She turned her full gaze on me. "I've got to go back to class now." She paused. Of course I understood. Oh, yes. I understood. "See you at lunch," she whispered. And as majestically as she had come—red turtleneck sweater, white short socks and yes, sneakers (I still had to wear high-top shoes)—she vanished through the door. And I had been chosen to nourish this great woman, to protect her and perhaps, should I prove worthy, guide her.

For some reason, probably a blood thing, I was always good with my hands . . . and feet . . . and teeth . . . and I had a very good eye. If this wasn't the age of Black Power I would possibly attribute that to my Indian blood, but now I'm sure it goes straight to my Watusi grandfather and Amazon great-grandaunt. Skippy, an old enemy who I later learned planned to marry Gary, was pulling her hair and marking her knees up with his ballpoint. Gary would tell me of these things laughingly and I would exclaim, "*It's so wrong of him to abuse you,*" not to mention, in such a white way, "I will take care of it." She assured me, "It's all right, Kim. He's just teasing." But mine was not a world of frivolity. He was disturbing the genius. He was, in fact, not just disrespectful, because that at least means you understand the position; was not in reality just insolent, because that just means you are jealous—he was common! I had no choice. I called him out.

I would imagine no boy likes to be called out by a kindergartner, especially on the playground . . . especially to a marble duel. Plus he recognized what I didn't—he was in a trick. If he defeated me, he was supposed to. If he lost—my God! A nine-year-old boy losing? To me? My God! In deadly calm I drew the circle.

Now, our family was never what anyone could call well off. Mommy didn't work, but that was because the money would have been spent in babysitting fees. Gus, our father, held down a couple of jobs, which meant we rarely saw him. Grandmother had never actually worked either, but we're from a small town and Grandpapa was a schoolteacher—of Latin actually—which says a lot about our pretensions. But despite hard times, depressions, lack of real estate, we had passed, from generation to generation since we had first been brought to these shores, a particular semiprecious jewel that was once oblong in shape. It was originally brown with a green tint. In order to conceal it successfully through several hundred years of slavery we had worn it in odd places. It had been rounded off through the sweat and kisses of generations of Giovanni-Watson ancestors. We consulted it for every important and quite a few unimportant events and decisions.

When I decided to challenge Skippy I snuck the jewel from my mother's hiding place. As I drew the circle and stood back I was all confidence. There was no chance for the poor fellow. "You go first," I generously offered with the assurance of Willy McCovey at third base nodding to the pitcher to play ball. A sure winner. "No, you go first." Quietly, with a Huey Newton kind of rage. "You can go on." Smiling, prancing like Assault at the Derby. "You go on, Kim. You should get at least one chance." "One chance!" I knelt and spotted. There was no stopping me. I shot marbles from between my legs and over my back. I put a terrible double spin on my shot that knocked his cat's-eye out and came back for his steelie. I was baaaaad. I shot from under my arm and once while yawning. Good God! There was no way to defeat me! I rose from the earth brush-

ing off the little specks that clung to my dress, tip chest two
miles out. "And if you mess with my sister again I'll deal with
you on a physical level." I was ready for anything. He squared
off. "You keep it up, Kim, and somebody's gonna really get
you." I half stepped back. "You, Mighty Mouse? You?" Sure,
all the kids knew I could handle myself but teachers never
know anything. I had him in a double bind. All the grown-ups
ever saw was big brown eyes, three pigtails and high-top white
shoes. He would really catch it if they saw him fighting—me
especially. My stock in trade was that I looked so innocent. So
he backed down. I understand his problem now, but then—a
chicken at the top of the pecking heap—I ruled the roost. And
as I sauntered happily up Oak Avenue, turned on Pendry,
passed the Spearses' house and headed for Burns Avenue I
was feeling *très* good. Plus Mommy gave me my very favorite
cold lunch—liverwurst with mayonnaise dripping from the
raisin bread. Too much! I was prepared to take a long nap. I
was prepared to work the number problems Gus had left for
me. I was ready for everything . . . but Gary's reaction at 3:30.
     "HOW COULD YOU DO THAT TO HIM?" "Who?"
"HOW COULD YOU? MOMMY, KIM'SPICKINGON-
MYFRIENDS!" "Who, Gary?" My God! Her absolute displea-
sure. No "Hi." No "How'd it go today?" No approving smile.
"Who, Gary?" "MOMMY, SHE MADE SKIPPY LOOK LIKE A
FOOL!" "Skippy?" "YOU SHOULD HAVE SEEN HER!" "But
he was picking on you." "I AM MORTIFIED!" "Mortified?"
     My world was coming to an end. And all because of
Skippy. I would handle this right away.
     I ran out of the house like a pig runs when a Muslim
comes, near rage. Absolute rage. "SKIPPYYY!" All the way

down to his house. With just a brief stop for some sort of weapon. I don't actually remember picking up that piece of cement but it was there—along with my trusty broomstick that Flappy had made for me. I flew down to the corner, though of course being careful to stay on my side of the street. "SKIPPYYY! COME OUT! I WANT TO FIGHT YOU!" And there he was. Buck teeth, pants hanging off, sneakers and all. "COME ON OUT." He was ready. I could see he had been building his supply of rocks. He threw. But missed. I ducked and started running back and forth. "COME ON OVER." "YOU KNOW I CAN'T CROSS THE STREET." My father and Skippy's father had made an agreement that I couldn't cross the street since I fought and beat Skippy a lot. But he was in a rage. "TRY TO MAKE ME LOOK LIKE A FOOL, OLE SILLY GIRL. I'LL GET YOU." "COME ON OVER." I was a streak of energy. I was the fire after the A bomb fell. All heat and light. "COME ON OVER." And he did. I wanted to devour him. To kill him slowly. To punish him beyond words able to describe the emotion. He looked both ways and was on my territory. Like the Black panther I leaped. And he feinted and landed a solid blow. I never felt it. I clawed at his face and pulled his shirt loose. *"YoutoremyshirtI'llkillyou!"* And he bit me. We fell onto the lawn and people were all around. We squared off and I heard Mommy say, "I hope he gets her." It crushed my will. I had been prepared to draw blood. Gary was mad and Mommy was rooting for the opposition. He swung and landed flat on my nose. Blood spurted, as blood is wont to do. I didn't cry or even really feel hurt. I just looked at him, then picked up my broomstick and set off for home. People started consoling Mommy but she was just saying, "I'm glad.

Maybe Kim'll learn she can't fight Gary's battles." And I was crushed. I walked from Mrs. Williams' house to mine without family, friends or loved ones. No one understood what I had tried to do. No one. I thought of *Beautiful Joe* and *Mistress Margaret, Heidi* and the *King of the Golden River.* And conceived of myself in that league. I think I smiled as I opened the door.

On Being Asked What
It's Like to Be Black*

I've always known I was colored. When I was a Negro I knew I was colored; now that I'm Black I know which color it is. Any identity crisis I may have had never centered on race. I love those long, involved, big-worded essays on "How I Discovered My Blackness" in twenty-five words more or less which generally appear in some mass magazine—always somehow smelling like Coke or Kellogg's corn flakes—the prize for the best essay being a brass knuckle up your head or behind, if you make any distinction between the two.

It's great when you near your quarter-century mark and someone says, "I want an experience on how you came to grips with being colored." The most logical answer is, "I came to grips with Blackdom when I grabbed my mama"—but I'm told on "Julia" that we don't necessarily know our mothers are colored, and you can win a great big medal if you say it loud. If

*Reprinted from US (New York: Bantam Books, October 1969), pp. 94–101.

your parents are colored we have found—statistically—the chances are quite high that so are you. If your parents are mixed the chances are even higher that you'll grow up to be a Nigger. And with the racial situation reaching the proportions that it has, the only people (consistent with history) able to discover anything at all are still honkies. Or if you haven't gotten it together by the time you go to preschool, then you're gonna be left out. Now, that's only on the subconscious level.

My father was a real hip down-home big-time dude from Cincinnati who, through a screw-a-YWCA-lady or kiss-a-nun program, was picked up from the wilds of the West End (pronounced deprived area), where he was wreaking havoc on the girls, and sent to college, mostly I imagine because they recognized him as being so talented. Or if not necessarily talented, then able to communicate well with people. He was sent to Knoxville College in Tennessee. Nestled lovingly in the bosom of the Great Smoky Mountains in the land of Davy Crockett and other heroes of Western civilization is Knoxville, Tennessee. Knoxville, in those times, was noted for *Thunder Road* starring Robert Mitchum and/or Polly Bergen of Helen Morgan fame; but when my father boarded the train to carry him back to his spiritual roots (it was just like my great-grandfather to be the only damned slave in northeastern Tennessee) all he saw were crackers—friendly crackers, mean crackers, liberal crackers, conservative crackers, dumb crackers, smart crackers and just all kinds of crackers, some of whom, much to his surprise, were Black crackers. He hit the campus, "the Nigger the world awaited," shiny head (because Afros were not in vogue), snappy dresser with the one suit he had and a big friendly smile to show them all that just because he was in the South he wasn't going to do like a lot of people and cry all the time and embarrass the school. In walks the fox.

Swishing her behind, most likely carrying a tennis racket and flinging her hair (which at that time hung down to what was swishing) was the woman of the world, the prize of all times—Mommy. Mommy has an illustrious background. Her family, the Mighty Watsons, had moved to Knoxville because my grandmother was going to be lynched. Well, the family never actually said she was going to get lynched. They always stressed the fact that traveling late at night under a blanket in a buggy is fun, and even more fun if a decoy sitting in a buggy is sent off in another direction with Uncle Joe and Uncle Frank carrying guns. They told us the guns were to salute good-bye to Louvenia, my grandmother, and John Brown ("Book") Watson, my grandfather.

If I haven't digressed too much already I want to say something about Grandpapa. He was an extremely handsome man. Grandmother got the hots for him and like any shooting star just fell and hit *splash*. Now, we in the family have always considered it unfortunate that Grandfather was married to another woman at that time. And Grandmother, to make matters even more urgent, would not give him none. Grandfather considered that more unfortunate than his marriage. And since he was the intellectual of the family, hence "Book," he assessed the situation and reached the logical conclusion that he should marry my Grandmother.

The Watsons were quite pleased with Louvenia Terrell because she was so cute and intelligent, but what they didn't know and later learned to their chagrin was that she was terribly intolerant when it came to white people. The Watson clan

was the epitome of "Let's get along with the whites"; Grand-
mother was the height of "We ain't taking no shit, John
Brown, off nobody." So the trouble began.

First some white woman wanted to buy some flowers
from Grandmother's yard, and as Grandmother told it they
were not for sale. She didn't make her living growing flowers
for white people. The woman's family came back later to settle
it. "John, yo' wife insulted ma wife and we gotta settle this
thang." Grandpapa was perfectly willing to make accommoda-
tions but when the only satisfactory action was Grandmother's
taking twenty-five buggy-whip lashes, he had to draw the line.
"Mr. Jenkins, we've known each other a long time. Our fami-
lies have done business together. But this is too much." "John,
we've gotta settle this thang." And about that time Uncle Joe,
who always liked to hunt, came out of Grandpapa's house with
his gun and powder and asked if he could be of any help. The
Jenkinses left. The Watsons stayed up all night with a gun
peeking from every window. The guns in those days were not
repeaters so the youngsters in the family had been given com-
plete instructions on how to clean and load in the shortest
time possible. I'm told by my granduncles there was a general
air of disappointment when nobody showed. After almost a
week of keeping watch things reverted to normal. Grandpapa
says the white dude told him later they didn't need the flowers
anyway.

Then one Sunday afternoon Grandmother and Grand-
papa were out strolling when a Jewish merchant asked them
to come look at his material. He owned one of those old stores
with bolts and bolts of material because most clothes were
made, not store-bought. Well, they looked and looked. Grand-

mother had him pull bolts from way up high to way down low. Then she got bored and told Grandpapa she was ready to go.

MERCHANT: You mean you're not going to buy anything?

GRANDMOTHER [*innocently*]: No.

MERCHANT: You mean you had me pull all this material out and you're not going to buy anything?

GRANDMOTHER [*a little tired*]: My husband and I were walking down the street minding our own business when you asked us to come in. We did not ask you.

GRANDFATHER [*wary of the escalation in the exchange*]: Let's go, Louvenia.

GRANDMOTHER [*as she generally did when she was in an argument*]: Hell, it's his own fault. [*To the merchant*] Nah, we don't want none of your material.

GRANDFATHER [*pinching and kicking at her*]: Let's go, Louvenia.

MERCHANT [*in the background screaming obscenities*]: I'll have you horsewhipped for talking to me this way.

GRANDMOTHER [*really wolfing now*]: You and which cavalry troop? My husband will kill you if you come near me!

GRANDFATHER [*almost in tears*]: Let's go, Louvenia.

They hurried to spread the alarm of impending danger. A woman in the next county had recently been lynched and her womb split open so there was no doubt in Grandfather's mind that the whites might follow through this time. A family meeting was called and all agreed that Grandmother and Grandfather (most especially Grandmother) had to leave Albany,

Georgia. The sooner the better. When night came they climbed into a buggy, pulled a blanket over themselves and slept until they reached the Tennessee border. Having no faith in southern Tennessee they began again by public transportation to head North. The intention was to go to Washington, D.C., or Philadelphia, but when they found themselves still in Tennessee they agreed to settle at the first reasonable-sized town they came to—Knoxville. Grandfather settled Grandmother in a good church home and went back to Albany, where he taught school, to finish the term out. Grandfather was like that.

Three lovely daughters were born in four happy years. Grandmother settled down to play house. The girls were all right with Grandpapa but, as Grandmother always said, "John Brown always had plenty of toys," so naturally she had more fun than he did. The oldest child was my mother.

Now, Mommy was an intellectual, aristocratic woman, which in her time was not at all fashionable. She read, liked paintings, played tennis and liked to party a great deal. Had she been rich she would have followed the sun—going places, learning things and being just generally unable to hold a job and be useful. But Mommy made just one bad mistake in the scheme of things—she sashayed across the Knoxville College campus, hair swinging down to her behind, most probably carrying a tennis racket, and ran into a shiny-head Negro with a pretty suit on. He, being warm and friendly and definitely looking for a city girl to roost with, introduced himself. I have always thought that if his name hadn't been exotic she would never have given him a second thought; but Grandfather, whom my mother was so much like, had a weakness for

Romance languages and here comes this smiling dude with Giovanni for a name. Mommy decided to take him home.

From the resulting union two girls were born: typical of me, I was the second. Gary, my sister, is what is commonly known to white people as a smart Nigger. In the correct tradition of we-don't-take-no-shit-off-nobody, she could wolf away for hours. I'm still amazed she hasn't risen to national fame for her sheer ability to rap. Me—I'm different. I generally don't like to get into arguments, but I did like to fight. Many's the night if I hadn't remembered my Grandfather's patrician blood I'd have been swinging a blade on the street—that is, until I became a Black and decided Black people should not fight each other under any circumstances. Gary would go out and blow off about what was going to happen if she didn't get what she wanted and, not getting it, would come in and tell me, "You've got to go fight Thelma [or Barbara or Flora] 'cause she's been messing with me." Folks in my home town still have a lot of respect for me dating back to those days.

How and why I became a fighter is still a mystery to me. If you believe in innateness, then I guess the only logical conclusion is that it's in my blood. But most of us have a history of fighting unless you are Whitney Young's daughter or Roy Wilkins's mother. And I'll even bet Roy's mother was a real scrapper. Through a series of discussions I was having with a social worker, I discovered I am not objective. Any feeling I may have for someone or something is based on how he or it relates to me. Like I don't go for people because they are rich or famous or everybody thinks they are so hip. I don't support institutions because they are successful, democratic and said to be the best in the world. If something is good to me I like it; if it hurts me I don't. This feeling is extended to my friends. If someone or something abuses my friends then it has in effect hurt me, and I don't go for that even if the *New York Times* says it is the hippest thing going. Like I wasn't impressed with James Earl Jones as an actor because though he may have done a beautiful job as Jack Johnson, the role is an insult. I'm not impressed with America. It acts well, too. There are no objective standards when it comes to your life; this is crucial. Objective standards and objective feelings always lead to objectionable situations. I'm a revolutionary poet in a prerevolutionary world.

And dealing with Blackness as a cultural entity can only lead to revolution. America, as Rap Brown pointed out, has always moved militarily because it has no superior culture. We, as beginning revolutionists, ought to understand that. Great cultures have always fallen to great guns. They always will. That's not a subjective thought; it's a fact. Facts are only tools to gain control over yourself and other people. So white folks develop facts about us; we are developing facts about them. In the end it's always a power struggle.

I've been taught all my life that power is an absolute good, not because I'm objectively more fit to wield power but because subjectively if I don't wield it it will be wielded over me. Trade white racism for Black racism? Anytime, since I'm Black. But facts show that Black people by the definition of racism cannot be racist. Racism is the subjugation of one people by another because of their race, and everything I do to white people will be based on what they did to me. Even their Bible, the Christian one, says, "Do unto others as they have done unto you." And Black Christians are becoming more aware of the meaning behind the Golden Rule. It's only logical.

I believe in logic. Logic is not an exercise to prove "*A* implies *B*" but a spiritual understanding of the subjective situation and the physical movement necessary to place life in its natural order. Black people are the natural, hence logical, rulers of the world. This is a fact. And it's illogical for me to assume any other stance or to allow any other possibility. It's self-negating. If you don't love your mama and papa then you don't love yourself. Fathers are very important people.

Black people have been slaves in America and the world. Some slaves cleaned, some cooked, some picked cotton, some oversaw the others, some killed slavemasters, some fucked the slavemaster (and his mama) at their demand. A slave has no control over whom he fucks. Check it. But that's not your father because some beast raped your mother. Neither is it your mother because some beast sneaked down to Uncle Tom's cabin. White folks with degrees in sociology like to make generic judgments about political situations. If your father was drafted and killed in World War I, World War II, the Korean conflict, or the Vietnam advisoryship, they don't tell you he deserted your mother (which he logically did if he went off to fight the enemy's wars). They tell you what a good dude he was and "Ain't you proud of that shiny new medal?" And you are proud of him and say, "My father was a great man," even though he was never around to be anything to you. If the same man had been run out of town or was not allowed to hold a job, or your mother couldn't get relief with him in the household, then you should look upon his leaving home with the same loyalty as if he had gone to fight a war (which he really did). Or look at them both with the same disdain. Neither was there to love you and your mother when you needed to be loved and protected. One of the jobs of a father it to protect and provide, as best he can, for his family. This is related to power.

All Black men in the world today are out of power. Power only means the ability to have control over your life. If you don't have control you cannot take responsibility. That's what makes that latter-generation Irishman's report on the Negro family so ridiculous. How can anyone be responsible without power? Power implies choice. It is not a choice when the options are life or death. It's against the law of nature to choose death. That's why suicides and soldiers make such interesting subjects. They are going against the laws of nature.

If, however, your father is part of the power group and he does not associate with you then he has chosen not to be your father (and the power group does have this choice). It is then up to you, for your own mental health, to put any ideas of generative father out of your mind and function with your father surrogate. That is, if your Uncle Bill is the one who takes you to the zoo, Uncle Jimmy the one who is there at Christmas and Uncle Steve the one who spends your birthdays with you, then you pull from them the composite father—and though Uncle Albert only loves your mother and doesn't pay much attention to you he should be a part of the composite also. Same with mothers.

If people treat you like a child then you pull together the composite feeling of being mothered. It's illogical to hunger after the love of someone who doesn't love you when there are plenty of people who would love you—if you believe in love—because feeling is a tool that can be used to keep you from having the necessary substance for being a healthy person. As long as we as a people must deal with the no-good-man-loses-a-woman syndrome as an objective reality we will never be able to gather unto ourselves the subjective feelings essential for propelling the actions needed to place the world in its natural order. I have learned these things by living in the world for a quarter-century.

Gus, my father, has always been a fascinating man to me. I haven't always liked him, but then I haven't always liked myself. The two are related. Gus just sort of believes in himself and thinks everything he's done has needed to be done so that he could be the really groovy person he is. My mother usually agrees with him about that. He has functioned as a father, which doesn't mean we always had nifty toys or the latest clothes, but to his mind if he couldn't get it for us we didn't need it anyway. There may be more validity to that than meets the eye. Ultimately my mother took a job which led to many quarrels. They still fuss about it now—only because she wants to quit and he won't let her. Gus, being a great believer in Freud, will probably always have some conflict around him. He'd be lost without it. How can you eliminate conflict without changing the system? Most people want to be comfortable, which is illogical if you're not free. Which is maybe why folks still cut each other up. Conflict is active and must be kept near the surface.

Life/personality must be taken as a total entity. All of your life is all of your life, and no one incident stands alone. Most people evolve. The family and how it's conceptualized have a great effect on anyone. No matter what the feelings, the effect is still there. Like James Baldwin in *Tell Me How Long the Train's Been Gone* still has to negate God and the God influence. God still means something to him. The feeling is still there. Base experiences affect people; before they are born, events happen that shape their lives. My family on my grandmother's side are fighters. My family on my father's side are survivors. I'm a revolutionist. It's only logical. There weren't any times I remember wanting to eat in a restaurant or go to a school that I was blocked from because of color. I don't remember anyone getting lynched. And though I had friends who went to jail during the sit-ins, we were committed to action anyway, so there must have been something deeper. Beliefs generally come through training, and training is based on feeling.

I was trained intellectually and spiritually to respect myself and the people who respected me. I was emotionally trained to love those who love me. If such a thing can be, I was trained to be in power—that is, to learn and act upon necessary emotions which will grant me more control over my life. Sometimes it's a painful thing to make decisions based on our training, but if we are properly trained we do. I consider this a good. My life is not all it will be. There is a real possibility that I can be the first person in my family to be free. That would make me happy. I'm twenty-five years old. A revolutionary poet. I love.

4

A Revolutionary Tale*

The whole damn thing is Bertha's fault. Bertha was my room-mate and a very Black person, to put it mildly. She's a revolu-tionary. I don't want to spend needless time discussing Bertha but it's sort of important. Before I met her I was Ayn Rand–Barry Goldwater all the way. Bertha kept asking, how could Black people be conservative? What have they got to con-serve? And after a while (realizing that I had absolutely noth-ing, period) I came around. But not as fast as she was moving. It wasn't enough that I learned to like the regular mass of col-ored people—as a whole, as it were; she wanted me to like the individual colored people we knew. I resisted like hell but eventually came around. Bertha is the sort of person you eventually come around.

Now, just be patient; you want to know why I'm late, don't you? So I got an Afro and began the conference beat and did all those Black things that we were supposed to do. I even gave up white men for the Movement . . . and that was no easy sacrifice. Not that they were that good—nobody comes down with a sister like a brother—but they were a major source of support for me. I agreed that they shouldn't be allowed to support the Movement, but I believe in having income passed around, and if anyone has income to spare, whiteys do. So I cut myself off from a very important love of mine—money—and that presented a problem. No, I'm not going round Robinhood's barn; this is a part of it.

So when my income was terminated for ideological reasons you'd think Bertha would say something like "I'll take over the rent and your gas bill since you've sacrificed so much for the Movement." You'd really think that, wouldn't you? But no, she asked me about a job. A job, for Christ's sake! I didn't even know anybody who worked but her! And here she was talking about a job! I calmly suggested that I would apply for relief. You see, I believe society owes all of its members certain things like food, clothing, shelter and gas, so I was going to apply to society since individual contributions were no longer acceptable. She laughed that cynical laugh of hers and offered to go down with me. "No," says I, "I can do it myself." So I went down at the end of the week.

Now, I'm a firm believer in impressions. I think the first impression people make is very important, and since I would have to consider welfare my job from now on, for Bertha's sake at least, I got dressed up and went down. I'm sure you've applied for relief at least once so you know the procedure. I went to Intake and met an old civil servant, the kind who's been on the job since Hayes set the system up. She asked me so many questions about my personal life I thought she was interviewing me for a possible spot in heaven. Then we got to my family. I told her Mommy was a supervisor in the Welfare Department and Daddy was a social worker. She shook her head and looked disgusted—just plain disgusted with me— huffed up her flat chest and said, "Young lady, you are not eligible for relief!" And stormed away.

I started after her. "What the hell do you mean, 'not eligible'?" I asked. "I'll take somebody's job who really needs it, somebody with skills or the ability to be trained, with a wife and kids, or maybe just an unwed mother will be put out of work! What kind of jive agency are you? You sure don't give a damn about people!" As she turned the corner I had to run to keep up with her. "And who are you to decide what I need? You're nothing but a jive petty bourgeoise bullshit civil servant." Yes, I did. I told her exactly that. I mean, that's what she was. "Going 'round deciding people's needs! You got needs yourself. Who decides how your needs are gonna be filled? You ain't God or Mary or even the Holy Ghost—telling me what I'm eligible for." I was really laying her out. The nerve! I'd come all the way down there and didn't have on Levi's or my miniskirt but looked *nice*! I mean really *clean*, and she says I'm not eligible. Really did piss me off.

At the end of the corridor she was hurrying along I saw this figure. It looked small and pitiful. It was Mommy. I guess someone had recognized me and called her to come down. I went over to put my arms around her. "Don't cry, Mommy. It'll be all right." But she just cried and cried and kept saying, "Oh, Kim, why can't you be like other daughters?" I got so involved with soothing her that the servant got away. "Mom," I said as I walked her to her office, "there's going to be a Black Revolution all over the world and we must prepare for it.

We've got to determine our own standards of eligibility. That's all." She quit crying a little and just looked at me pitifully. Then she put her arms around me and said, "Oh, Kim, I love you. But why can't you just get married and divorced and have babies and things like other daughters? Why do you have to disgrace us like this? I didn't mind when you got kicked out of school for drinking and I even got used to all those men I didn't like. And remember the time you made the front page for doing that go-go dance at the Democratic Convention? I've been a Democrat all my life! You know that. But I was proud that in the middle of Johnson's speech you jumped on the table, shoes and all, to dance your protest to the war in Vietnam. But this is my job! Your father and I have worked very hard to give you everything we could."

"Mom," I cut her off, "I'm not against your job." I tried to explain it wasn't personal even when I'd had to throw that rock through her window that time. "We didn't firebomb, did we? 'No,' I told the group, 'don't firebomb the Welfare Department.' And when we had to turn the director's car over, you noticed that he didn't get hurt? I told the group, 'Be sure not to hurt the director.' That's what I told them. But Mom, I'm broke now. All my savings are gone and if I don't get on relief I'll have to take a job. Oh, Mommy, what will I do if I take a job? Locked up in a building with all those strangers for eight hours every day. And people saying, 'Good morning, Kim. How's it going?' or 'Hey, Kim, what you doing after work?' I mean, getting familiar with me and I don't even know them! How could I stand that?"

Then, for the first time in the twenty-three years I'd known her, she looked me dead in the eye—I mean exactly straight—and said, "You'll either have to work or go to grad school." It floored me. I mean, she's never made a decision like that all the time I've known her.

"Mom," I said, "you don't mean it. You've been talking to Bertha. You're angry with me for what I told that civil servant. I'll apologize. I'll make it up somehow. I swear! I'll get my hair done!"

But she would not budge. "Kim, it's school or a job."

"Mom, 'member when I went back and graduated from college? Magna cum laude and all. 'Member how proud you and Daddy were that I had the guts to go back after all they did to me in college? 'Member what you said? 'Member how you said I had done *all* you wanted me to do? 'Member how you kept saying you wouldn't ask me for anything else? 'Member, Mom? Mommy? 'Member?"

She still wouldn't budge. I tell you it's something when your own mother turns against you. She knew I was working for the Revolution. "What would happen to the Revolution if I quit to take a job? What would my people do?" I asked her. And she looked at me and said, rather coldly if I recall, "Your people need you to lead the way. Not just toward irresponsible acts but toward a true Revolution."

"There's nothing irresponsible about chaos and anarchy. We must brush our teeth before eating a meal."

"Kim, I've read everything you have written. I've heard all your speeches on tape. And what are you talking about now? Program. I've read Frantz Fanon and Stokely Carmichael. I especially enjoyed *Burn the Honky* by H. Rap Brown—he's got an amazing sense of humor. I've read Killens and Jones and Neal and McKissick. I've read most of the books on those lists you gave us. Haven't I always tried to understand and sympathize with you? When I was going to get Mother a cookbook, did I buy the *Larousse Gastronomique*? No! I bought the *Ebony Cookbook*, even though Mother has forgotten more than Freda DeKnight could ever have known. When your father and I went to the social work convention in Detroit last year, did we stay with the other delegates at the Hilton? No! We stayed at the Rio Grande. I've done all I could for the Revolution and I'll probably do more. But I'm not going to allow this behavior. You will get a job or you will go to school."

"Aw, Mommy," I protested, "you just don't understand. . . ."

"Kim, that's all there is to it. I'll give you a surprise when you tell me something definite."

I was crushed. Absolutely crushed. My own mother turned against me. I must have looked terribly hurt because she kissed me again and said, "Oh, Kim. It's best—really it is. If I can read your people and try to understand your way, you can try mine."

I called my father. I asked him to take me to lunch. I think he knew. He didn't know when I called him but by the time we met for lunch—he knew. Of course, being a social worker and relating to people and all for a living, he didn't just burst in and say, "I agree with your mother." No. He sat down and ordered me a drink. He doesn't drink anymore since he and his liver made an intellectual decision that Negroes shouldn't get high. This is his sacrifice for the Movement. He'd quit five years earlier when he was in the hospital; he considered it a religious conversion thing. His own special sacrifice to Jesus. We used to ask about it but he always just said Jesus had spoken to him through his liver. And nothing would shake him. He quit church after a couple of months but he continued to tithe every month faithfully and never drank again. His tennis game improved and he got to be a good swimmer again. He took up golf and, to tell the truth, had gotten so damn clean-cut American that Mommy began sneaking gin into his eggs every morning just to keep him from becoming a real bastard. He doesn't know that, however. So we sat down and I had a drink and we ordered lunch.

"What's on your mind, chicken?" (He always calls me some sort of animal or inanimate object. I'm not sure what his message is.)

I didn't want to throw it on him right away. "DaddyMommysaysI'vegottogotoschoolortakeajobandIdon'tthinkthat'sfair," I said.

"Uhmm. Would you say that again in English . . . I mean American?"

"Mommy says I have to go to school or get a job."

"Good, lambie pie. Which one is it?"

"Daddy, you don't understand. I don't think it's fair."

"Of course not, sugar lump. She shouldn't have said it like that. You just get yourself a nice job. You don't even have to consider school. I'll call up Harry White and see what he can do for you. Or you can get one on your own. . . . You just let me know what you would like."

"Oh, Daddy," I said, "you're on her side and she's been talking to Bertha and nobody even understands me."

"I try to understand you, angel cake. I've read almost all those books on your lists and everything you've written and I've heard all your speeches. I think you're doing fine work but you must set an example, too. You just show your people that new systems can be created. If you want to destroy something, you must first learn how it works and what need it's filling. After the—how do you say—Black Flame encases the world, you'll want your people to work for the Black Nation. How can you encourage that if you have no idea what you're asking of them? That's one thing I noticed about everyone from Nkrumah to Ben Bella to Brown. They don't really know what they're asking everyday people to do. Not that they don't work—and hard—but do they punch a time clock? Do they have a thirty-minute lunch break? Do they dig ditches? Work in a mine? Not that they have to do every one of those; but have they labored? It's important that they do. And all the reading and writing in the world doesn't give a true understanding of time clocks. Maybe they'll do away with time clocks but they must first understand what purpose they serve before they do."

"Oh, Daddy, not that many Black folks ever punch a clock!"

"I'm not talking about a clock and you know it. I'm talking about going to work on time, eating lunch on time, getting off on time, going home on time. All those meetings, conferences and rallies—even if they are on time—are scheduled to your and their convenience, not the people's. Get up at six-thirty or seven, go downtown, eat lunch with a couple of thousand people, relate to your supervisor, relate to your clients, relate to the people in your office or sewer, get off at four-thirty or five, rush home, read your paper while your wife cooks dinner, talk to your children, listen to their troubles, put them to bed; talk to your wife, listen to her troubles, take her to bed; and in your spare time watch TV, say hello to your neighbor, run to the store, go to a rally, try to read a book. Try that and you might understand why the Revolution, as you call it, moves so slowly."

"Oh, Daddy, I didn't want a lecture. I just wanted you to be on my side."

"Is that my name now? Ohdaddy? I am on your side, brown sugar. That's why I'm telling you this. Get yourself a job, then do all the things you're doing. You may readjust your methods."

"I won't change! I won't let the bourgeois system get me!"

"I didn't say your *thinking*, Kim. I didn't say you would readjust your thinking. I said you may change your *methods*."

Lunch was ruined for me. I went home to type a résumé and that wasn't easy. It had been that kind of day.

I have this really neato pink IBM—it was a gift, though when I got it it was a down payment. It's always worked right: I've never had a bit of trouble with it. Once a year I call the people and they clean and service it—that's it. It's a dream. But that day, of all days, it just wouldn't work right. The *s* was skipping and the *a* was hitting twice, plus the magic margin wouldn't click in, and it was just a fucky day. I quit and stretched out on the floor. I fell sort of half-asleep. I couldn't decide between school and an agency job and it must have been on my mind because I had a really terrible dream. There was a university chasing me down the street. I turned the corner to get away from it and ran right into the mouth of an agency. It gobbled me up but it couldn't digest me. When it tried to swallow me I put up such a fight that it belched me back into life. As I hit the street there was the university again, waiting for me like a big dyke with a greasy smile on her lips who has run her prey into a corner. I woke up screaming. Both of them would destroy me! And furthermore, what did I need with a master's degree?

As I brooded on my future the image of educational institutions kept coming back. Going to school is like throwing a rabbit into a brier patch. There would be scores of students I could convert. And because of "academic freedom" the school would have to accept and support me or at least leave me alone unless I flunked out, drank a lot or smoked in public. And if I applied for a job in social work both Mommy and Daddy would be pleased because I'd get a degree and agency training and an inadequate paycheck to boot. So I sat down at my pink IBM to type a letter for an application blank. Surprisingly enough the typewriter was fixed. I mailed it immediately and sat back while others stronger and wiser than I determined my fate.

Geez, you've got a one-track mind! I'm trying to get around to explaining about the delay. I was, you know, accepted in school. I thought everyone would be happy and leave me alone. That was February and I had nine months of Freedom before enrollment day. And I fully intended to use them. I got my acceptance letter on a Tuesday. That was so upsetting that all I could do for a long time was just gnash and growl. It didn't bother Bertha a bit. She just started running around the house singing, "Kim's going to school. . . ." You know, like she was happy. My mood wasn't too positive so I told her, dead calmly, that if she didn't get the hell out of my half of the apartment I'd kill her. She laughed one of those grand ha-ha-ha-type things, then spread her arms and pirouetted out the door.

It was hard to take. After these years of freedom of choice and movement I was going back to school. I just cried and cried.

Then I thought: what the hell! Hadn't I survived the time we were playing "The Prince of Wales"? Hadn't I survived the Wisconsin Sleeper? Hadn't I been to Harlem? Hadn't I refused to lay a white boy when we were in Mississippi on the big march? Why wouldn't I survive now? I was really talking it up to myself. Much worse things had happened to me and here I was acting like a crybaby. Why wouldn't I survive, I asked myself bravely, boldly—perhaps brazenly! Why would I not survive? BECAUSE! came the answer and I cried and cried.

I've got to tell you this. No, don't be that way—listen. If ever something happens to you that makes you really unhappy and you've just got to cry about it, don't cry in the same spot. Move around. That's what I learned. After I cried and cried, there was this shiny puddle around my feet and there were these blood-red eyes looking up at me. I learned then, never cry in one spot. But I was cool with it. I never really got emotionally involved in it. I cleaned up the mess, took a shower, got dressed to a T, then went out walking the streets.

I stopped by a bar I know and had a drink. One of my brothers, soul brothers, bought me a drink and we started discussing what would have to come down. He and I got into a real deep thing and we talked until the bar closed. He kept wanting to kill Toms and I still think that's not who we have to kill. Toms, I told him, only have power if we let them have power. I mean, if a Tom says get off the streets and you get off the streets, then that's your fault, not his. If on the other hand a Tom tells you to get off the streets and you don't—well, then the power structure has no use for him. Plus if you can encourage him in a physical way to come on over to your side, you've made a friend. I mean, you can beat a brother or boycott him or something besides killing him to get him to either help you or get out of the way. There are too few brothers on this shore already for them to be killing each other off. We need to get rid of whitey. I mean, if we can't kill a whitey, how can we ever justify killing a brother? That's a hell of a copout to me. Talking about killing brothers—and sisters too—and not being able to kill a whitey. We can only justify offing a brother if we have already offed twenty whiteys—that's the ratio, I told him, for offing a brother. So we went to his place to talk further.

The next morning all my problems were solved, I thought. I had figured it all out. Now, this much I knew about social work school—they will put up with anything at all except heterosexual relations. I mean, anything at all. And the school where I was accepted was founded by two ladies who had adopted children. I just knew if I wrote them and explained that I had not only been screwing but had enjoyed it—well, I thought, they'd write a nice letter explaining the mistake in accepting me and that would be the end of that. So I jumped up and dashed home to compose a letter. Then I thought, that won't get to them soon enough—I'd better send a wire. So I did.

PLEASE BE ADVISED STOP I HAVE SCREWED STOP IT WAS GOOD STOP SO THERE EXCLAMATION POINT YOURS IN FREEDOM

                                    KIM

I thought they would really be sick of me the minute they received that. I got a long, involved letter explaining how proud they were that I was open to new things and that they were very pleased at my level of honesty. I tell you I was p.o.'ed. That's the only way to describe it. And what the hell did she

mean, "new things"? I'd been screwing since I was twelve—
ten if you want to count the times before it was serious. And
he wasn't new anyway. I was truly indignant, but Bertha dis-
couraged me from expressing my feelings to the school by just
demoralizing my whole intellectual thing.

Well, yes, it was a calculated intellectual involvement. You
see, I never act on my unbridled emotions. Emotions are to be
controlled by the intellect. Even when I act in what could be
considered an emotional manner, I have thought it out before
and have *decided* this will be the way I act. So to have my whole
intellectual bag blown sky high right before my eyes—well,
that was frightening. I started to give Bertha a quick punch in
the gut but my whole action-reaction syndrome began to reek
of emotion so I just cooled it a bit and dropped a half-teaspoon
of Drano in her coffee later during the day.

Strange about that. I was only playing a little joke and
there was plenty of milk on hand, you see, to help offset the
effects. So Bertha drank her coffee and went to the john and
never once indicated that anything was wrong. Later, when I
asked, she did say it had been awfully runny, but that was all.
I'm a failure, I told myself—a failure. Oh, goody! I'm a failure.
I don't have to deal with it anymore. I dashed another tele-
gram off to the director of placement.

PLEASE BE ADVISED STOP HAVE PUT DRANO IN ROOM-
MATES COFFEE STOP SHE LIVES STOP I AM A FAILURE
STOP YOU MUST REJECT ME STOP

Those ridiculous people up there just considered it a bid
for attention. I got a nice, long letter explaining how they real-

ized I hadn't received an answer to my application yet and they were sorry but they had a lot of work and sometimes even the best of us get tied up, etc. Plus, if you can dig it, they thought I had ingenious ways of letting them know my needs. I mean, really! Ingenious! Goddammit, I was a failure. If I didn't find a quick way out of this, why I'd end up in an institution, a part of an agency, being decent, responsible—all those ugly, sick things that I hated. I'd really have to think of a scheme.

It was way in the middle of April before it even dawned on me. I mean, it was so simple; I was overlooking the obvious. What is the one thing we know for damned sure about white people? I mean, you know, besides the fact that they hate Negroes, children and sex. . . . What is the one thing we know absolutely and positively about any honkie anywhere in the world? That he worships money. He's got such a case about money he's transferred it to anything green. That's why you see those goddamn KEEP OFF THE GRASS signs. Not that he cares about grass, but it's green. What's the quickest way to turn a honkie off? Ask him for money. He's as nice as he can be as long as he thinks he'll get your money—but the minute you ask him for some, well, that's like asking a hippie for his pot or a Negro for his knife. I mean, they get *hostile*. You don't believe it? Go into any bank and deposit five bucks. Then go back in a week and withdraw it. When you go to deposit it they're all smiles. A V.P. will come out and shake your hand. The teller smiles and welcomes you to the family. And that's only five bucks I'm talking about. When you go to withdraw it, the first thing the teller will say is, "You realize this will close your account." Just like you didn't know that if you deposit five bucks and you withdraw five bucks you are closing your account. And you just smile at him and say, "Yea, groovy." He'll frown and say, "This will cost you one dollar." And you say, "Cool. Gimme my four bucks." Then he says, "This will take a minute." That's when you look at him very menacingly and say, "I should surely hope the hell not." Then he'll slam your money down and scream, "NEXT," or he'll slap the NEXT WINDOW PLEASE sign up and turn his back on you. And this is a Black teller I'm talking about.

So, knowing this, I wrote the director of placement and told her I had no money and needed a stipend and a tuition grant. I just knew, whatever my charm or what not, they weren't going to pay me to go to their school. I mean, as tight as they are, they are not about to give me any money. I was as happy as a ten-year-old turkey the day before Thanksgiving. I knew I now had them by the ass—I was just naturally too tough to handle. I walked a little taller, breathed a little deeper, felt a little prouder. I was so happy that I went back to my Revolution work. Not that I hadn't been working for the Revolution all along, but I had really been hung up on this thing about a job.

We set up a Black Arts Festival and I was working my you-know-what off. You may have heard about me being on the radio telling all the honkies not to come. I'm sure you heard about Lonnie going into the honkie neighborhood with his sign saying, YOU'RE NOT READY. It was great advertising for us and we were all really sorry about that kid. However, though the papers played it down after the first day it is not true that Lonnie tore his leg from the joint—he only fractured it. And contrary to first reports the kid will walk again. I personally tell all the brother Black Belts I know that they shouldn't provoke white kids, then beat on them. But, well, you're not always able to control folks, even if they do take a lot of your advice. But that was the only incident that could be, in some quarters, considered unfortunate. It was a groovy set. The blue beasts foamed at the mouth but it was our day! I say again, it was revolutionary! Slavetown, U.S.A., was back in the Movement 'cause the Kim was back into her thing.

I really forgot all that crap about school and jobs and do. I just put it out of my mind. Our underground press, yes, it does have something to do with why I'm late. You see, we were putting out a magazine called *Love Black*. It was a group thing, you know, but it really belonged to all the people. We had learned the secret of why the folks don't read. C'mon, see do you know. You jive, they can *too* read. But nobody ever writes for them or writes anything they can relate to. So, having figured that out through the very difficult process of stopping every brother we could on the corner one day and asking him what he would enjoy reading, we went about getting *Love Black* out. See, most folks don't read, honkies especially, but people too. You think they really read *Good Housekeeping* or *Time*? They look at the pictures and will scan an article they can see the end of. Most people like to read what they can see the end of. So we started a Black mag on 8½-by-11-inch paper, with articles that took up a page or less. Also, it didn't run more than twenty pages all toto. Therefore, a brother could read the whole damned mag and really do two things: learn something positive about himself, and complete something he started.

Now, don't start breaking into my explanation. It may well have been propaganda but all pieces of paper with writing are propaganda, and if I have to deal in mind control it's much better to be Blackwashed. I mean, the honkie press just naturally screws with any Black man's mind because it doesn't recognize that there is a Black mind. It does what it can to a Black mind—it whitewashes it, it flushes it out of his head. That's what it does. But we were giving the people something and we were getting a lot. One issue we were late and all kinds of soul stepped up and told me if I didn't get my thing together and get the mag out, well, they would look upon that with disfavor. And they also sent articles in. Like we'd get slightly used toilet tissue with an article on it, or brown paper bags with short sayings, or just a note to say the writer dug us. Some of it looked like our ancestral writing and we really had to work at deciphering it, but when you saw how the man changed after he had "published," well, it would really hit you. You see, the brother will read if he's writing it or if he knows people who are, and *Love Black* was strictly ours. It wasn't the prettiest thing in the world and sometimes it wasn't too clear. I've always maintained that if the Revolution fails it'll be because we know nothing about machinery. But it was ours. It talked about Slavetown and what the brother thought and felt, and the brother was digging it. You got to understand the whole concept of writing.

On the East Coast everything is dishonest. They do a lot of things but mostly it's 3,000 percent bullshit. The people are so used to talking Black, buying Black and thinking Black they don't get shook anymore. Every hustler (why is it a Black capitalist is called a hustler?) and every panhandler is Black, so Black doesn't mean anything. It's taken for granted. And one Black thing is like another. They've been saturated with a program that has never come off. Between Garvey and Malcolm, Harlem should be owned lock, stock and barrel by us—but we are still trying to get rat control and jobs, and paying rent to honkies.

In the DuPont plantation state they even passed a law that said if building codes aren't lived up to you can deposit your money in one of the company banks and leave it there till the cat comes around. Ain't that the jivest crap you ever heard of? I mean, paternalism with a capital WHITE. No, wait a minute. If you live in a house or apartment and something is wrong with it, and you are living there every day the good Lord makes you Black, well, you should fix that place up and what's left over from rent should go in your pocket. So the old witch from the Welfare Department comes down and tries to explain that she'll have to hold your check if you don't pay your rent to the rightful owner. And that's when you come out of your thing so righteously and whip it on her so beautifully. You just light up a joint and calmly explain that "Honkies have made women, bombs and Kellogg's corn flakes, but they have never made a piece of land. The land is one bitch that is every-body's woman and I, being a man and all, have got a right to a piece of her."

You see, the honkies' whole sex thing is tied up to land. No lie. Land is their love. All land, except Germany, is female. The motherland, her, she—all land is woman. And they do anything to prove that they are worthy to be land's man. Only land doesn't give a crap about white people. See, land has this memory thing. Land remembers God stepped out in space and looked around and said, "I'LL MAKE ME A MAN." God reached down into land, a woman, and formed this thing—

you know, a man. Now, land has always been Black. And you know God well enough to know that he goes first class. So God got the best land he could find, which had to be the Blackest land he could find. You just don't know about any white land. Snow, maybe, some white sand, maybe; but you just don't know about any white land. And land is hip to that. Land is very put out that we are making her prostitute herself for the beast. You didn't hear about any land being raped until the beast came along.

We live in harmony with land because we are part of land and we are out of land. The honkie came from sand and snow. Now, what are they? They're nothing. They have a place on earth but they're nothing. Snow freezes land and sand dries her up; both destroy land and land wants to live and re-create. You run it on down to where you are going to free land so that she can go about woman's work of taking care of her children— the Black people of the earth. Now, she'll send the law out but that doesn't mean anything either. The law only means something if you think it does. So she'll send out the law to make you pay and you smile sincerely and promise to get it in next week. After you're alone with your piece of land you remove very carefully anything that cannot be replaced, like pictures of your first lay, your joints, etc., and you throw kerosene on everything else. You see, it's yours, and if you can't enjoy it in freedom and peace, then land wants you to destroy it.

You can't destroy land because she'll always be there, but you can destroy the rapist's claim. The only thing about land that makes the beast think he owns her is the stake he's put up to clinch his claim—a house, a building, a fence—so you destroy that. That's when you burn. You don't burn to get the thief to fix it up; you burn when you've staked your claim and they try to steal it from you. And I really believe that after you've fixed it up and made it yours, you'll kill for it.

That's the thing we've got to understand. The Revolution isn't to show what we're willing to die for; Black people have been willing to die for damned near everything on earth. It's to show what we're willing to kill for. Yes, it is! Do we love life enough to deal righteously with key honkies? We don't have to deal with King and Young and those other three or four if we don't want to. We have got to deal with the folks who sent them up. Which means we have to control ourselves. I have got to control me and you have got to control you. If I see something that needs to be done and you see something else, we don't have to argue about what to do. You do yours and I'll do mine. It's like we're on a road that forks and then comes back together. We just had different priorities, and that don't make one right or wrong—just different. But if I use the fact that you want to do something I don't want to do to keep from doing what I have to do, then I'm not together. I'm bullshitting and I know it.

You and I are never in a conflict situation because we're after the same thing—we're after the same honkie—and however we get him is our business. All that jive about coordination and keeping people in line and élites is crap and doesn't really mean anything. That's no Revolution—that's not anarchy! And anarchy is what we want. This country doesn't even have anything that we can't build again if we need it. Even to try to think of taking over and preserving General Motors—what for? Nobody's trying to make the system Black; we're trying to make a system that's human so that Black folks can live in it. This means we're trying to destroy the existing system. It's not even a question of whether Black folks can run it better than white folks. We don't have to prove to whiteys that we can—and if we took over their system it would be for that reason. We haven't got to prove anything to honkies because they are nobody's authority on anything.

But the whole damn thing I do blame on Bertha, because I was just happy sitting at home twiddling my toes and masturbating every now and then. I didn't even know that I was colored, let alone anything about Blackness. But she kept bringing those beautiful Black people home and they kept talking that talk to me, and as I moved I moved toward Black Power. And I recognized the extent of white power, which is so pervasive that the American solution cannot be Black Power at all, though as a world solution it is a possibility. It must be Revolution—anarchy, total chaos—and this should not be so hard for us since we have worked so diligently in every other cause; we can now work for our own. We have sacrificed our lives and interests for white power; now we can save ourselves through Revolution—our baptism by fire.

But as I worked this out, people kept calling me a hater, and really I'm a lover. No one knows how much I do love all that is lovable. Then Bertha chimed in to ask whether I love Black folks enough to trust them to TCB, and whether I trust black people to do those things necessary by any means necessary, recognizing that the means are in fact the ends. She kept saying that if they and I are one then I should get out of the way and see where they would go without me. And since Revolution ages you so quickly, and having watched the summer, I had to admit that I was old and tired, and I recognized that already we were moving beyond my vision. Maybe I should step aside and regroup.

So I packed and made arrangements to come to school, and everybody cheered and was really pleased with my decision. And I kept telling myself that it would be good and that I was dealing with the best the system had to offer and that, if I couldn't relate meaningfully enough to them to accept them, then I could easily go back to destroying it in a very real manner.

Having made my decision, I decided to walk. I mean, it would have been much too easy to hop a flight or thumb a ride. And though physical punishment of myself didn't span the whole import of my act, it did serve as a human extension of myself to help offset my total feelings of wasting my time. Then or now.

And I had no idea you are so far away from Uncle Tom's Cabin in Slavetown. I thought I could make it in a day or two but it's taking much longer. I'm really sorry about holding you up and all, but it's done now and here I am. See can you handle it.

5

Don't Have a Baby till You Read This

Well, you see, I hadn't talked with you, that is, you weren't born and I wasn't expecting you to be. So I decided to spend Labor Day with my parents in Cincinnati. Now, when I told my doctor, because you didn't have a doctor yet, that I was going, he thought that I was going to fly, he told me later, though he couldn't have really thought that because airlines won't let you fly in the last month. But anyway he wasn't thinking and neither to tell the truth was I. So I started out in Auntie Barb's new convertible Volkswagen and we all know how comfortable they are when you plan to drive 800 miles. But that's really not important.

We actually got started about 7:00 A.M. so that we could beat the morning traffic. When we hit the Pennsylvania Turnpike, I thought that was the turning point. We had stopped for lunch before the long stretch into West Virginia when this big black car went zoooooming past us and this thing fell out. I thought, how awful that those white people in the *passing lane* would be throwing out garbage. Then it became obvious that it wasn't and I said, God, I'm gonna hit that dog that fell out of that car, and just as I was adjusting to that Barb said, "IT'S A CHILD!" and I hit the brakes and luckily so did the truck driver in the middle lane and I hopped out of the car while the truck stopped. And the father ran back saying, "Oh, my God! Oh, my God!" but the mother just sat in the car and didn't even turn around and the other small child, another little girl, just looked back to see and maybe there was a glint in her eye, but it's hard to tell under excited circumstances. And Barb said, "What cha doing getting out of the car? What if that truck hit you?" And I thought it would be a terrible thing for an evil militant like me to be hit on the turnpike because some white people threw their child out the window the way they throw their cats in the lake and I vowed it would never happen to me again. But you were inside and you stirred and I said, "Emma," because I called you Emma, thinking that you were going to be a girl, and I was naming you after your great-grandmother, "I'll never throw you out the car 'cause we don't treat our children that way."

And Barb was so upset by the whole thing that she asked me if I wanted her to drive. Barb was always that way. She figures if she's upset then everybody is more upset than she is because she thinks she's so cool and all. But knowing that about her I drove until we hit Athens, Ohio, and she brought us in into Cincy.

When we walked into the house my mother—since you weren't born she was still just my mother—said, "When you gonna have that thing? You look like you're gonna have it any minute!" And being modern and efficient and knowing she doesn't know anything about having children, I said, "Oh,

Mother, the baby isn't due until the middle of September. And I don't look like that." She was walking around the house all bent over backwards with her flat tummy poking out and laughing at me. Your Aunt Gary laughed at me also but I reminded her she hadn't had a baby in ten years and things had changed since then. Plus I was tired so I said I was going to bed and Gary said, "Why not spend the night with us since we'll have to go to the store tomorrow for the weekend?" And I said the way Mommy was treating me I should go some-where because it was obvious she wasn't going to let up, so I said, "Emma and I will spend the night with Gary."

At which Gary said, "You're having a boy and we ought to decide on a name for him." You know how group-oriented Gary is. So she called everyone and said, "We have to name Nikki's baby." I said, "Her name is Emma. But I don't have a middle name for her." And we kicked that around. Then Gus came upstairs—he always goes downstairs when all his women come home for some reason—and said, "You know, my father's name was Thomas." And I said, "Well, if it's a boy we'll name him Thomas." And the reason I could be so easy about saying I'd name a Black child in 1969 Thomas was that I knew you'd be a girl. So we settled the name thing and I went and had an extended B.M., and I thought, that junk on the turn-pike really shaped my constipation up. And really, which you may remember, I thought you were constipation all through the first four months, so it wasn't unusual that I still thought that. Your very first foods were milk of magnesia and Epsom salts because I kept thinking I was a little stopped up. And when I didn't get regular I started the sitting-up exercises because I thought I was in bad shape and getting too fat for the laxatives to work. And to tell the truth I didn't think of being pregnant until we were in Barbados and the bikini suit stretched under my tummy and I told Barb, "I think I'm going to have a baby, Barb." And she said she had suspected as much.

So we went out to Gary's to spend the night and Barb went to Grandma Kate's and Mommy and Gus had to stay all by themselves. And the next morning I was tired but I had been tired so long I hopped out of bed with Chris, who offered to fix me one of those good cheese, dried ham and turkey sandwiches that he fixes for breakfast, and I had to turn the little guy down and settle for tea. Chris asked, "Are you really gonna have a baby?" and I said, "It looks like that." And he said, "Is it hard?" And I said, "I don't know much about it but Emma probably knows what to do." And he said, "Well, I'm glad to have my own first cousin 'cause everybody else has first cousins. But I wish you'd have a boy." And I said, "It's really out of my hands, Chris." And he smiled that Chris smile that says you-really-could-do-it-if-you-wanted-to-but-you-don't and said, "If you have a boy I can give him all my old clothes and teach him how to swim and give him my football helmet." And I said, "I think it's going to be a girl. But we don't have to worry about that now." So he went to wake his mother up so we could go to the grocery store. Gary came to breakfast saying, "Chris really wants you to have a boy 'cause most of his friends have brothers and since he doesn't he's got nobody to fight with him." And I said, "Gary, why don't you have a baby or talk to Barb or Mommy? Because I'm going to have a girl." And she gave me that Gary smile that says you-really-could-do-it-if-you-wanted-to-but-you-don't and said,

"Well, I don't see why Chris never gets anything he wants from this family. He's part of it like anyone else." And we went to the store.

You know Gary's sense of organization, so all her friends and Mommy and Gus came over that night to fix the food for Labor Day. And we were up late playing bid whist because I love bid whist and since most of my friends are ideologists we rarely have time for fun. But I was winning when I told A.J., my brother-in-law, "I think I'll call it a day." And I went to lie down. Gary came back and said, "Are you in labor?" And I said, "Of course not. The baby isn't coming until the middle of September." And I stretched out. Then Barb came back and said, "Are you having pains?" And I said, "No, I'm not, 'cause the baby isn't coming until the middle of September and that's two weeks away and I'm just tired and a little constipated. Maybe I should take a laxative." And she said, "Just stretch out." Then I heard Gus tell Mommy, "You better go see about Nikki. Those children don't know anything about babies." And Mommy, who usually prefers not to be involved, said, "They know what they're doing." But he prodded her with "*What kind of mother are you?* The baby's back there in pain and all *you* care about is your bid!" So she came back and tenderly said, "Your father thinks you're going to have the baby. Are you all right?" And I said, "Of course. I'm just a little constipated." And she asked if I wanted a beer. "When I was pregnant with Gary I drank beer a lot and it helped." So I said yes to pacify her and I heard Gus say, "You're giving the baby a *BEER?* Lord, Yolande! You're gonna *kill* the child!" And she said something real soft and everybody laughed and Mommy didn't come back.

Then the house was quiet and I still didn't feel well and I kept thinking if I could just use the bathroom it would all be OK, but I couldn't use the bathroom. So I was pacing back and forth and Chris came out and said, "Are you having the baby?" and I said no. And Gary came out and said, "It may have been ten years but I think you're having the baby." And I said, "Don't be ridiculous. I paid my hospital bill in New York and I'm not having the baby here." And she said, "OK, but I'm going to call Barb 'cause you've been up all night." And I said, "It's only 3:00 A.M. and don't wake anybody up. I'm not having the baby. It's the junk I ate on the turnpike." But she called Barb, who said, "Maybe we better call Dr. Burch in New York because he would know." And I said, "Don't call him and wake him up. I'm not having any baby." But she did. Dr. Burch said I wasn't having the baby until the first of October according to his calculations but to take me to the hospital anyway to be sure and to let him know no matter what time. And that was when I first realized that he really cared and he said to tell me not to worry because it's a simple thing and I thought, uh-huh. And poor A.J. was awakened to take me. They said I wouldn't be in labor until the water broke but to keep an eye on it. So everybody went back home to bed and Barb slept on the couch.

Around six I noticed I was still up and I was really tired and I started crying and saying, "If I just understood what's wrong I would feel better!" And Barb said, "You're probably going to have the baby." And I said, "No, Barb. You know I'm not until the middle of September." And she said, "Burch says the first of October so you both may be off." "Emma," I said, "you wouldn't do this to me." But you didn't move. I had started to the toilet for the umpteenth time when I wet on myself and I was so embarrassed that I felt like a Fudgesicle on a hot day or a leaf in autumn. I just wanted to get it over with. So Barb whispered something to Gary who told A.J. and the next thing I knew I was on my way to the hospital again. This time they said, "Take her right on in." And the doctor came to check me and said, "Take her right on upstairs." Then he smiled at me: "You're going to have a baby."

"A BABY? BUT I DON'T KNOW ANYTHING ABOUT HAVING A BABY! I'VE NEVER HAD A BABY BEFORE." And I started crying and crying and crying. What if I messed up? You were probably counting on me to do the right thing and what did I know? I was an intellectual. I thought things through. I didn't know shit about action. I mean, I could follow through in group activities, I could maybe even motivate people, but this was something I had to do all by myself and you were counting on me to do it right. Damn, damn, damn. Why me?

When in doubt, I've always told myself, be cool and positive. Like when they said God was dead and Forman asked for his money back, I said, "God was a good fellow when he was around." You know what I mean—the moderate statement. When L.B.J. decided not to run for president again I said, "That's good." You know? There's something positive in everything. We've got to keep things balanced. So when they wheeled us upstairs and I immediately understood it was you and me and I wasn't going to be much good crying, I stopped and went to sleep.

"SHE WENT TO SLEEP? IN THE MIDDLE OF LABOR?" my mother said. And she came right out to the hospital. But there wasn't anything she could do so she just sat down and had a beer with one of the ambulatory patients. The nurse woke me up and asked how I felt and I said fine because I didn't want to upset her with my troubles. And I tried to go to sleep again. I had been up all night and was quite tired. Then the doctor came and said, "Bear down when you have pain." So I grunted. And he said, "Are you in pain now?" And I said I didn't want him to think I was being negative but I wasn't in pain until he stuck his hand up there. And he told the nurse, "Maybe we better take the baby. Get her doctor on the phone." So they called Burch and he said, "You better take the baby if she's sleeping because that is a bad sign." And they told me what he'd said. Then this cherubic woman came in and said, "I'm your anaesthesiologist and I'm going to give you a spinal." Then she began explaining all the various things about it and I said, "Under more normal circumstances I'm sure this would be very interesting. But right now if you'd just like to go ahead and do it it would be fine with me. I mean, I really trust the hospital a lot right now and I'm sure you're more than qualified." She looked at me rather perplexedly and I was going to suggest we meet in the cafeteria the next day when I don't remember anything more. Then there was this blinding light and the doctor said, "We'll have to give you a Caesarean," and I said I knew that when I realized I was pregnant or at least I wanted to. And he said, "We'll give you a bikini cut," and I tried to explain that I didn't GIVE A DAMN what they gave me, just get the baby. And the bikini cut didn't work because then I heard, "Nurse, he won't come out this way. We'll have to give her. . . ." I decided: when in doubt. . . . Then he said, "I think we've got him," and I opened my eyes because I wanted to know what you looked like in case they misplaced you or something and there you were, butt naked and really quite messy, and they said, "Mother"—why do they call people that?—"you've got a boy." And I thought, but I was having a girl. Then I went to sleep for a good rest.

When I woke up I thought it was the next day, only it was the day after that. And people kept coming around saying, "She looks much better." I thought, God, I must be really fine, so I asked the floor nurse for a mirror and she said, "Be right back," but she wasn't. Then I noticed a line running into my arm and one out of my leg and it dawned on me I must look like hell on a stick. And I thought it behooved me to ask about my condition. The nurses all said, "You're fine now, Mother," and I said, "My name is Nikki," and they said, "Yes, Mother." So when Gary came I was interested in how I had done. And she, typical of hospital personnel, said, "You're much better now." So I said, "How was I then?" "A good patient." And I said, "Gary, when I get up I'm gonna kill you if you don't tell me." "Well, you would have come through with flying colors if your heart hadn't stopped. That gave the doctors some concern for a while. Then the baby—he's cute; did you know he was sucking his thumb in the incubator? The smartest little guy back there. Well, he was lying on your bladder and a piece of it came out. But other than that you're fine. Mommy and Gus and Barb and I were with you all the time." And I thought, uh-huh. "And Chris is really glad you had a boy. He said he knew you could do it if you wanted." And I thought, uh-huh.

Then she had to leave the floor because the babies were coming. I pulled my gown straight and worked my way into a sitting position and smiled warmly like mothers are supposed to do. And the girl next to me got her baby. Then all the people on my side. Then all the people on the other side. And I started to cry. The floor nurse said, "What's the matter, Mother?" and I cried, "Something has happened to my baby and nobody will tell me about it." And she said, "No. Nursery didn't know you were well. I'll go get it for you." And I said, "Him. It's a boy." So she brought you to me and Gary was right. Undoubtedly the most beautiful, intelligent, everything baby in the world. You had just finished eating so we sat, you in your bassinet and me in my bed, side by side. Then the nurse said, "Don't you want to hold him?" And I started to say, bitch, holding is to mothers what sucking is to babies what corners are to prostitutes what evasion is to politicians. But I just looked at her and she looked at the lines into and out of me so she put you in the bed, and you were very quiet because you knew I didn't feel too swell and if you did anything I wouldn't be able to help you.

The next morning my doctor came by and said his usual and I said, "I guess so I'm alive," and he said, "If you'll eat I'll take the tube out of your arm." Remembering what hospital food had been like when I'd had my hemorrhoidectomy a couple of years back, I hesitated, but he reminded me that I could feed you so I was suckered. And I was glad because I met the dietician, who was really a wonderful woman. But I made the mistake of saying I liked oatmeal and she made the mistake of giving me a lot and I didn't eat it, and they said, "Mother, if you don't eat we'll have to put the tube back in." So I had to tell her to keep my diet thing together. Institutions make it hard for you to make friends. Then someone asked if I wanted you circumcised and I said yes and they brought you back and you were maaaad. And I loved it because you showed a lot of spirit. And I snuck you under the covers and we went to sleep because we'd both had a long, hard day. They said you wouldn't let the nurse in white touch you for a good long time after that, which is what I dig about you—you carry grudges. And that was a turning point. I decided to get you out of there before they got your heart.

It's a funny thing about hospitals. The first day I was really up and around they were having demonstrations on how to avoid unwanted pregnancies, and I really was quite interested but since I was from New York and in their opinion didn't belong on the ward they called everyone who was ambulatory together and left me in the bed. Then they privately visited the catheterized patients, of whom I was still one, and they passed me by with one of those smiles nurses give you. And the aides came over and one said, "I understand you teach school. What are you doing on the ward?" And I said, "I teach school and I'm here to have the baby." "But you're from New York." And failing to see the connection I said, "I'm Gary's little sister," and they said, "Oh." But since they never thought of me as being a poor Black unwed mother I didn't get any birth control lessons. Hospitals carry the same inclinations as the other institutions.

That Wednesday they brought you to me for the morning feeding and you, being impatient and hungry, were crying all the way. When I heard the wail, I knew it was you and it was. You cried and cried and I was struggling to get you up in the bed and you didn't care anything at all about the problems Mommy was having. Finally I got you in and fed you and you smiled. I swear you did, just before I put the bottle in. Well, I had pulled the curtain so we could be alone and I guess they forgot about us because when they came to get the babies they left you. And I sat and watched you sleeping. Then I started crying and crying and Gary came in and caught me. "What's the matter with you?" she sympathetically asked and I said, "He's so beautiful," and I cried a little longer and she said, "You sure are silly," looked at you and then said, "He really is beautiful, almost as pretty as Chris," and I thought, uh-huh.

She left to get me some cigarettes and I decided to sit all the way up so I could cuddle you, and for some reason I started feeling real full but I knew I didn't have to use the bathroom because I was catheterized, so I paid it no mind. Gary brought the cigs back and I lit up my first cigarette since coming to the hospital. Then it happened. The bed was flooded with urine. And I with great exactitude said, "NURRRSE," and she came running. "What's the matter, Mother? What are you doing with the baby still here?" *"Never mind that! I've wet the bed."* And she laughed and laughed. "You're the only catheterized patient in my knowledge who ever wet the bed." Then she called someone to change it. The aide laughed too and said, "What's the baby doing still in here?" And I made up my mind to ask the doctor as soon as he came.

"What do I have to do to get out of here?" "What's the rush? You can take your time." "I wanna go home." "To New York? That'll be a long time." "To my mother's." "Well, if you can walk and use the bathroom, we'll let you out Sunday. But I don't think you should worry about that." "I'll be ready."

So the first thing I had to do was get out of bed. I hadn't been out of bed since I got in because I had peeped a couple of days before that the position I was in was the critical position. The woman on the other side in number 1 had been moved but I had stayed. People had moved into number 2 but I was still in 1. And I guess if they had told me how sick I was when I was that sick, I would have died. So in the interest of not upsetting God I just lay back and did what they told me to. Now I had to get up so I could get you home.

First I got the bag and flung my legs over the side. Then I smoked a cigarette to congratulate myself. Then I stood up. And I must say the world had changed considerably since I had lain. Everything was spinning. But you know me. If there's a challenge, I'll overcome. So I moved on to the chair. I was huffing and puffing like I had just felled a tree or climbed a mountain, and I was scared. What if I fell and they decided to keep me there for another week or so? But I made it into the chair and sat up. My timing was perfect. The nurse who messed with stitches came by and smiled. "Oh, you're sitting up?" And I said sure with a smile, hoping she wouldn't see the sweat I was working up. "Maybe I'd better get back in bed so you can examine me" (rather hopefully put out), and she said it would be better. Well, at least I had done the first thing.

That evening I sat up for a delicious dinner of warm milk (just to room temperature), gray goo and green goo. They smiled and said, "It'll make you strong," and I thought about my mother saying the same thing about Father John's medicine and I thought, uh-huh.

You can tell a lot about a woman from the way she masturbates. Some go at it for a need thing, some because their hand just happened to hit it, some to remember their childhood. Some women turn on their backs, some their stomachs, some their sides. You can peep a whole game from that one set. So in the interest of finding what was left and what wasn't I reached down to this skinned chicken and said to myself, yeah, it's still there but good and tired. And it wasn't in the mood for any games. I felt the necessity to check since every stranger in the world it seemed had looked up my legs. Institutions still haven't found a way to give service and leave the ego intact. Realizing for one that I hadn't needed to be shaved and for two never having been very hairy, I got nervous and wanted my mother. "Will it grow back?" I asked and she said sure, it always does. But it had taken me a good nineteen years of brushing and combing and high-protein diet to get the little I had and maybe it'd take that long to grow back. "Certainly not. It'll be there before you know it," but I still worried. I wanted to get out of there before they shaved my head and took my kidney.

The next thing, since I had so easily mastered sitting up, was walking down to the nursery and back. I made that my goal since I would have you as a reward at the end and the bed at the return. As I stepped lightly from my bed and grabbed my bag, flung my pink robe in grand style over my shoulders and started from position 1 to the nursery, I heard a collective gasp go up in the ward—"Ooooooo"—and I smiled, waved my hand a little and then proceeded. Visions of the old house flew before my face. We lived now in an all-Black city called Lincoln Heights. It wasn't our first real home but it was our first house. When we'd gotten that house we'd all been very excited because I would have a yard to play kickball in, Gary would have a basement to give parties in, Mommy would have a real living room and Gus would have peace and quiet. It was ideal. And we all could make all the noise we wanted to. I have always thought it's very important for people to have their own piece of land so that they can argue in peace and quiet. Like when we had rented an apartment, we hadn't really been able to have arguments and Mommy and Daddy had had to curse each other out on Saturday afternoons so that the landlady wouldn't complain. But now they could fight all day long and well into the night without disturbing anyone. And Gus could throw things and Mommy could call him a motherfucker without appearing to be crude. People need something all to themselves.

I was halfway down the aisle. I passed the fifteen-year-old who had cried, "Help me," because she hadn't known how to feed her baby. I was quickly approaching the thirty-five-year-old who had had the twelve-pound baby. I was going past the girl who listened to "I Can't Get Next to You" all day long on her godawful radio.

We had lived in the old house until I was seventeen; Mommy and I had decided that she and Gus made enough money to have a new house. "I ain't moving" was Gus's reply to our loving suggestion. "I'm happy where I am. A man gets comfortable in his house and the next thing you know they want him to move." And we began looking for houses in Lincoln Heights because we didn't want to lay too much on him at one time. I mean, my father is an old man and it's been proved that old people die earlier when they are uprooted. Like my grandmother would probably have lived another ten or twenty years, but urban renewal took her home that she had lived in for forty-three years, and she was disjointed and lost her will to live. Like a lot of other old folks. I guess nobody likes to see memories paved over into a parking lot. It just doesn't show respect.

So we found a nice little home on the other side of Lincoln Heights and mentioned to my father how we were closing the deal and would be moving in a month. "Nikki, you and your mother can do what you want. She never did listen to me anyway. But I'm staying here." "But you'll be all alone." "Nope. I'll have my radio and I can listen to the ball games. I don't need any of you." "But we need you, Gus. What's a family without you? Who will fuss at us and curse and make us get off the grass? Who will say we can't take the car? Who will promise to build a barbecue pit if you don't come?" "Well, that's different. If you all really need me, I guess I'll go. I thought you didn't want me to." "God, we'd have a dull damn house without you."

So we all prepared to move.

Now, my mother is a very efficient woman, in her mind. And she has a lot to do. So moving day when the movers came we had only packed up the bathroom. But typical of the communal spirit, they all just packed us up and we moved.

The new house was a dream from the git. We were the first and only people to live in it. Gus planted a garden and began to fix up a den and library in the basement. Mommy had a big kitchen and a real living room. We all had a separate bedroom. It was going to be great.

I moved on down to the nursery. You were asleep so I couldn't see you and I headed back.

Yep, I would be good and glad to get home.

The nurse wheeled me down to Gary's waiting car. The nurse carried you and I carried your things. It was the first time you had on clothes and you looked really funny all dolled up and I thought: no doubt about it, the most beautiful baby in the world.

We hightailed it, though I didn't want to go quite that fast, out to Mom and Gus's. I asked Gary to slow down a couple of times but she said the air was polluted and she didn't want you exposed any more than was absolutely necessary. And I thought, that's good logic, so we hit a cruising altitude and before we knew it we were breaking like crazy for exit 19. Your sweet little hand gripped my sweaty big one and we went to sleep for the last half-mile.

When we drove up Gus ran out to grab you but Flora, Mommy's friend, was there and when he set foot in the house she grabbed you. Gary and Chris had run ahead to see if they could hold you and I struggled with your things and my things to get out of the car. Then I had to knock on the door because my hands were full and Gus said, "Come on in, Nikki. Can't I hold the baby? After all, I did name him." And I said, "Can somebody open the door?" and Chris came since he knew he was on the tail end of holding you. Then Flora, who is definitely noted for being proper and Christian and ladylike, said, "I have the baby, Gus, so you may as well go sit down because I'm going to hold him," and she put a double clutch on you and I knew there was nothing I could say. I sat down to smile benevolently at you and then Mommy said, "Why don't you go lie down?" and Gary said, "Yeah, go lie down," and Flora, who is almost always reticent, said, "You may as well go lie down because I'm holding the baby till I leave," and she drew you closer, and I decided there was nothing I could say so I went to lie down.

They had fixed up my old room and had very bright colors on the bed and all kinds of jingle toys for you. They had bought a bassinet, which was of course blue with white lace, and three pairs of jeans. Chris later told me that was his idea since he knew little boys preferred jeans to most other clothes. I felt relatively secure when I lay down because your bassinet and diapers were in my room.

Then I noticed that it was dark and no one had been back in my room for anything. Dogs! I said to myself. They have diapers out front, I'll bet cha. So I struggled into a robe and hobbled outside. "Hi, lady," Gary said. "What cha doing outa bed?" "Yeah, Nikki, go on back to bed," Gus said. "We got everything under control." "Nik, can I hold the baby?" Chris asked and Mommy said, "Would you like a beer? I drank a lot of beer when I had Gary." So I decided to go back to bed.

The next couple of days I spent just getting oriented to being in someone else's home after having had my own for so long. Then I made the grand discovery. THE GRAND DIS-COVERY. *Finnegans Wake* is true. You have got to overthrow your parents but good or you'll live to regret it. Which is not that some parents aren't hip. Or nice. Or loving. But no matter how old you are or what you do you're a baby to your parents. I'll bet you even when Candy Stripe, the famous strip-tease dancer, goes home she's a baby to her mother. My grandmother wouldn't give my mother a key to the house when we visited her and I was old enough to remember that! Even Agnew's mother probably thinks he's still a child. If he ever was. Parents are just like that. So I decided I would have to take complete control of you if I was ever going to get back to my own house again.

First the bath. "Mommy, I think I'll bathe the baby today."
"I can do it. I took off from work so I could look after you
two." "Yeah, but they taught me a new way to bathe him in the
hospital. And you probably aren't familiar with that."

She ambled rather hysterically over to the phone to call
Gary. "I think she's still under the anaesthesia because she
said I don't know how to wash the baby," and Gary said some-
thing and she hung up and called Gus. "I don't know who she
thinks bathed her all that time," and Gus said something and
she hung up and said, "Why don't you bathe the baby and I'll
just watch?" I smiled a sly, sly smile and thought, hurrah for
me! But it wore me out so I went back to bed while Gram got
to play with a clean baby.

Tuesday after the bath, I sat down with my mother, whom
we should hereafter refer to as Gram, for a cup of coffee.
"Nikki," she said slowly, like she always does when she has
true information to impart, "I don't want you to think I'm
meddling in your business. I know you're grown and able to
take care of yourself. But don't you think it's time you learned
to bake? I didn't learn to bake until after you were born and
it's a terrible burden on your child when everyone else has
cakes and cookies homemade and your child is the only one
with sweets from the bakery."

I immediately understood the importance of what she was
saying. It's true, I thought, only I remembered what it was like
having her make lumpy cakes with soggy icing. Maybe she,
being a grandmother and all, could help out now. I didn't
know a single grandmother who couldn't bake. And after all,
who was I to scorn her offer? We younger people should rec-
ognize that the older generation didn't survive all these years

without some knowledge. So I got up to face the blackberries. Then I understood her sneaky grandmother psychology. If I baked the cobbler I would be too tired to feed the baby. The hurrieder I went the behinder I got and I accepted my defeat for the day.

By Wednesday I was worn out. She had won. They—because Gus was definitely a part of it all—started coming in in the morning to get you and I would see you at lunch; then I had to go back to bed and wouldn't see you until it was your bedtime. I somehow felt neglected. Now, it's true that I was tired and it's true that they loved me but I sat all day in my old bedroom and I couldn't play with you and I failed to see going through all that mothers go through to have grandparents take over. I decided I would have to go against my history and my ancestors' way of doing things: "I WANT MY BABY NOW, DO YOU HEAR ME? NOW!" And Gus came in to say I'd wake you up if I kept up that noise. "IF I DON'T GET MY BABY RIGHT AWAY I WILL ROUSE THIS WHOLE NEIGHBORHOOD AGAINST YOU TWO GRANDPARENTS, DO YOU HEAR ME?" And Gus told Mommy maybe they'd better bring you to me and Mommy said real low, "Or put Nikki in the basement," and I sprang at her: "AHA! I KNOW YOUR SNEAKY PLANS. ALL YOU CARE ABOUT IS TOMMY AND I WON'T STAND FOR THAT. I'M YOUR BABY AND DON'T YOU FORGET IT." Then she cuddled me on her lap and said real soothing things and walked me back to my room. I had almost gotten you and I would be more successful at dinner, I vowed. Then I had to admit that they still loved me and that did make it a lot better. Or harder. But anyway, I needed a lot of love and that's what I knew.

Friday I went back to the hospital. I was doing fine. I could go home next week and you could too. They gave me a prescription for something and I asked Gus if he'd stop on the way home and get it filled. "Gary can do it. We'd better get the boy home," he said, and I said all right. Then I realized Gary didn't know what it was and I couldn't get it until she and Chris and A.J. came out, but I thought that'll be all right, so we went on home. Then when Gary came out she took pictures of you and I took pictures of you and Gary and I forgot about it. The next morning I asked again and Gus said, "What's the rush? You'll be here another week or so." And I said, "I'll be here longer than that if I don't get it filled." And he said, "Well, there's always plenty to eat in this house and you know you're welcome to stay," and I dug it. So I said, "Tommy needs alcohol, and while you're there get this filled," and he said, "Why didn't you tell me the boy needed something?" and he flew. I called New York and said Sunday I'd be home. Because I had to come to grips with a very important thing—as I said, *Finnegans Wake* is true.

So everyone began adjusting to the fact that we were leaving. Mommy said, "I'll be glad because I have things to do and I haven't been doing them. Besides, I'm a busy woman and I work and I have a lot to do and won't hardly miss you at all. You know I'm a supervisor and I'm. . . ." And I said, "We'll be back Christmas," and she felt better. Gus said, "Well, it's good that you're going, Nikki, 'cause the boy cries in the middle of the night and sometimes when the ball game is on I can't even hear it, and your mother and I kinda like the peace and quiet when nobody is around," and I said, "We'll be coming in on the twenty-first so you'll have to meet us." And Gary just cried and cried and Chris said, "You shouldn't leave—you should stay and Mommy will go get your things and I'll teach Tommy how to swim," and I said, "You can come visit us, Chris, as soon as school is out and we'll be home for Christmas." And we began packing and piling into the car and Gus said he wanted to go to the airport but it was going to be frost tomorrow so he had better look after the tomato plants and everybody else just openly cried all the way to the airport but you just peacefully slept while the plane took off and we came home.

6

It's a Case of . . .

The case of Angela Yvonne Davis is so close to me—closer than I maybe would care to admit. But lately I have become completely secure in who I am and what that who means and have decided that neither those who love nor those who hate me can define it for me. And I will continue to love and not love those of my choosing. And I fell completely and absolutely in love with the image and idea of an Angela Yvonne, though I never have met her and now probably never shall unless we somehow end in the same camp—or prison, if you don't want to deal with camp.

I remember my first, only, last and evermore trip to California. Because of the fear I had over Colorado that some redneck would come out of the Grand Canyon, a wad of tobacco in his cheek, with his trusty bowie knife and carve the plane from the sky; because of the anticipation of seeing clusters of native Americans riding the plains after the buffalo; because of the image in my mind of the little-engine-that-could huffing across the landscape and the Black and Yellow backs that made that possible, I hated the West. I probably would have hated it if Nixon hadn't been president; I probably would have hated it if Reagan hadn't been governor; I probably would have hated it if it hadn't been winter and giving off the kind of chill that has no relationship to weather. But these things being true, I told Jesus and my juju (to be absolutely on the safe side) that if I got out of California alive, I would never return unless I had â personal message from a burning building. I transferred planes and went on to visit friends in Fresno who were going to show me California.

I couldn't deal with being shown. I just wanted to read my poetry and get out. But I stayed and we started up the coast. "Would you like to meet Angela Davis?" one of them asked and I wanted to know, "Do you know her?" He looked at me in that way a man does when you say something foolish—"I've met her," he said. And I was thinking, if I can leave tomorrow I can get back to Cincinnati, pick up my son and go on to New York, where buildings are piled on each other as they should be; back to civilization, where the air isn't fit to breathe but where one doesn't feel the necessity for carrying a gun, at least above the Delaware Memorial Bridge or maybe just at least where there is asphalt beneath your feet, or whatever rationalization I had. I didn't want to stay just to see some controversial woman—I could check a mirror or my roommate or half the people I know for that. "No, thanks, not this time. Maybe she'll come to New York." And I split, literally. The plane landed in Love Field in Dallas, Texas, and a chill so deep it could have been a beginning orgasm hit me. And I swore, as I closed my eyes to avoid seeing death walk into the plane and touch me from the storm we were flying through, that if I made it alive I would never travel beyond the Mississippi again.

I can deal with the South because I love it. And it's the love of someone who's lived there, who was born there, who lost her cherry there and loved the land—but California? Seeing those whites without the familiar streams and woods, without the familiar dirt roads? Seeing those horrendous whites with all the asphalt and light? My God! A Mississippian on a freeway! I was not prepared to deal. And Love Field should have its name changed. Should maybe be salted over, as should all of Texas—perhaps most of middle America. Terrible vibrations. And we crossed Missouri and Illinois and Indiana and I could breathe again. It was ten or eleven below when we landed in the Greater Cincinnati airport but I was warm again. I mentioned to my mother and sister I could have met Angela Davis and Mommy said, "Why didn't you, Idiot? I think she's on the ball," or something very similar, since mothers are always trying to keep up with the language but usually never quite making it. And Gary, in her informed sort of way, asked, "Who's she?" "Some Communist teacher in California. They say she's brilliant." And Gary, being extremely parochial, said, "She can't be much. I never heard of her." Then the game was on because Mommy likes to keep one up on Gary, whose frame of reference is, "Is she a friend of yours? A friend of a friend's? Then why bother?" So I missed Angela Yvonne and came on to New York and thought little more of it till summer.

I wanted Tommy to be away from these confining shores, not to mention my own needs to be if not free at least more relaxed, so we set out for Haiti in August for sunshine and Black people. Haiti was an awful disappointment. And that's an understatement. I didn't see any more poverty there than I see in Harlem and a lot less than I see in Ruleville, Mississippi. The housing was no more nor much less substandard than in many Northern communities. The health of the people seemed good and there was great love for Duvalier. The people of Port-au-Prince are an urban people, and that is a fact but an ugly one. If I had wanted Boston I could have stayed home. And the games are old ones I rejected in my youth. There is a Puritan attitude I was wholly unready for. And there was the massive game of if you're not Haitian you're foreign and therefore fair prey. I didn't want to feel like a foreigner in Haiti. I wanted to be at home with the brothers and sisters. The island, like New York, had electric generator trouble but they could have left the air-conditioning off and let us deal with the heat. The flickering lights all over the city made me very sad because it seemed the people didn't know what they had and were trying to offer what any European country would offer—only I didn't want to go to a European country. And we could not get around. I would imagine it's wholly possible if you know someone and if you speak the language but I had neither advantage. I wanted to walk the marketplace and see the island but you couldn't walk anywhere because of the unwritten law that tourists must take cabs and the cabbie is your guide, like it or not. We asked to be taken to a Haitian restaurant and the guide took us to a very bad Western restaurant, and when I said, "Well, take us where you eat," he said, "I eat here," but he didn't, and that made me angry because he could have said just no. We ordered lunch anyway and then he said he'd be back in half an hour and we gulped the food and left. We were going to walk the marketplace. We found a darling little ten- or twelve-year-old and asked him to show us the market. "Just stay with me and keep an eye on your purse," he instructed, and baby on my back, I set out.

The market is beautiful: dirty as are all markets from Philly's old market to 110th Street's in New York to Knoxville's new one, but the people were great. The women laughed and pointed at how I held my baby. They would smile at me and I at them. I began to rewarm. The beggars came, pointing to obviously healthy babies to indicate hunger, and I chucked them under the chin and smiled at their mothers. Begging is probably the oldest profession in the world. A good beggar can make more than a good professional anything else. Begging in my mind is a male profession and women aren't as convincing at it as men. Prostitution, its competitor for longevity, is essentially its female counterpart though where white men have gone they have carried male prostitution with them. Signs of it are coming out in the islands as they are in the States and probably it is on the rise in Africa. I have respect for beggars so that didn't color my picture of Haiti either. I'm essentially a hustler because I'm essentially Black American and that carries essentially a hustling mentality (if you can essentially follow that).

As we were crossing the street with our little guide, so earnestly and happily going about his task, a man called him aside and said the police were looking for him. I asked why. "Your driver says I stole you from him." And I thought, that's odd since I don't belong to him; and I felt uncomfortable. A long discussion ensued and then we were on our way through the market again. And I saw the statues being turned out in the mahogany factory and I saw the pictures that look as though they're almost all painted the same day, and I thought, no—no, not Haiti. It's the oldest free Black country in the Western Hemisphere. Not Toussaint's Haiti. So I decided I'd visit the Citadel.

One of the main reasons anyone would visit Haiti is to see the magnificent Citadel. Thousands of men walked to their deaths over the top. This was where the island was defended. This is, if I may, the Statue of Liberty to Haitians or at least Black people or at least me. So I inquired. You would have thought I was asking the Virgin Mary to see her pussy. People got secretive and protective as if one lone Black woman could somehow destroy what the French, Spanish and American crackers could not. Finally I pinned the young mulatto (yes, they really are into that still) down on when I could go and how much it would cost. "One hundred and fifty dollars! It didn't cost that to come here." And the plane only left every Monday and Wednesday so you had to stay overnight. I decided I'd drive . . . only to learn you must get (1) a driver, as the roads are extremely unreliable even in the city, and (2) passes from each district you must go through. I decided to leave. I asked to call the airport for a plane schedule only to be told the phones weren't working. Then when I pulled my ugly American thing I was told the airline ticket office was closed and you couldn't catch a plane unless you had a reservation twenty-four hours in advance. Haitian rum is not among my favorites and I hadn't had a serious drink since I'd been kicked out of college for a semester's binge, but I gave in. While sitting on the veranda I met two ladies from Saint Thomas who were or looked very depressed. "You need a man in Haiti," and that simple statement helped me understand that indeed I was not in a Western country and perhaps I should check myself. Tommy is very masculine and everyone was very kind to him, but he was not a man. Manly—*oui*; man—*non*. I decided to push on to Barbados, which I know and love.

The water was so clear in Barbados that I could stand waist deep and see my funny flat toes. Diamonds sparkled in the sand The faces—the beautiful Bajans. I almost forgot Rap Brown was missing. I almost put aside Featherstone and Che. I read no papers and knew of no other tragedies. "Why do you change so," I asked a Bajan friend, "when you come to the States?" "Change?" he asked. "Yes. You come like immigrants and the first word you learn is *nigger*." "That's not true," he protested. "Why, we go to get ahead so that we can come back and live well." "But you have everything here. You can walk the beaches naked and not only will you not be molested but you won't catch any germs." "Yes, but we want to get ahead. We want to develop." "Develop to what? Air pollution? You'll soon have that with the U.S. Air Force building a base here. Policemen carrying guns. You'll soon have that with all the crazy young whites coming here." "Ah, but you mean Americans. The Canadians are nice, and the British." "To me they are all white." "Ah, but no. The Americans are terrible but the others are nice. We wouldn't be here if it weren't for the British." "But that's not true," I protested, and we walked on down the beach and soon forgot the discussion.

Probably one of the reasons I love Barbados is that I don't swim. All my life I've had a terrible fear of drowning, especially since I read *Titanic*, about a girl who dreamed of drowning and eventually wound up on the *Titanic* and met her death. I never go in more water than I can comfortably sit down in. I never go in boats of any kind and always spill gin before boarding a plane which will fly over water. But Barbados has the most gentle water in the world and I can go all the way out to where it touches my chin and I dream I'm an

Olympic wave-jumper. The announcer is saying, "Now watch Giovanni take this big boy. Is she going to move? No! No! It looks like—yes! She's still standing, she's still standing!" And on the shore they are cheering wildly and I am saying, "I try to move with the wave. I try not to fight it. Now, please excuse me. I've been out there fifty-two hours setting a new record." And I smile beautifully and move through the hands reaching to congratulate me. But that morning I thought of the enigma of West Indians in the United States. They are immigrants no matter what my friend said. And they seem to feel somehow they are more American as they mistreat me. West Indians who own slums in Brooklyn and Harlem are as bad as Jewish slumlords or maybe worse because no one expects his own people to mistreat him and because they pattern themselves after absentee landlords. West Indians holding sensitive jobs that could be of some benefit to Black people always feel extremely loyal to the whites who hire them, and worse—they feel they must somehow protect the system from my insolent and arrogant indifference. They are prone to run the-little-Jew-storeowner game on you, and if you had any initiative, you would own perhaps a store. In a Jewish neighborhood? West Indians can get loans and are supported more than I by the system, and the reason is that the system will do anything to keep them in the States, holding on to their dream of their island, using them to let me know nothing is lower on earth than Black Americans. That's why Poitier could win an Oscar while Jimmy Edwards could not. That's why the great Black movie stars who are making headway are West Indian—Calvin Lockhart, for instance, though not Dick Williams. We Black Americans become resentful of this because we have worked hard and have long thought internationally only to come now to the position that parochialism is nationalism, which is internationalism. We have come now to saying that he who marches should benefit; we have come back to the concept that he who lives in the neighborhood knows that neighborhood, so that before you can organize in it you must ask the people if you are welcome. We have finally—after white folks, responsible Negroes and militants have decried the gang system—come to realize it's our strongest trump. If you're about the world nothing will get done. And we look with a jaundiced eye at those who say we must fight a war in the Congo but not in Mississippi. We worry about the voices that say we must learn Swahili but not necessarily talk to our neighbor who's crying across the room or next door. We are learning not to listen to those who focus on issues and answers in faraway lands while we are still not together among ourselves. We see riots as community control and looting as organization because we recognize that when a people or more specifically when Black people have what they want in terms of televisions and clothes, they/we still have a problem with white people: a basic disagreement concerning life styles.

I bobbed up and down in the water and thought about how beautiful a people is at home. I would have hated West Indians had I not visited Barbados. I fully understood and agreed with Harold Cruse about that. (And the issue isn't which whites are better—there is no appreciable difference between Canadians, Britishers and Americans. They are all whites, period.) While everyone in the universe feels free to fault Black Americans for being uninterested in improving relationships with brothers and sisters around the world, no one has told the brothers and sisters how to treat us. I have learned not to trust the Black immigrants but to look to the people at home before making a judgment. And I would say to West Indians and Africans, you must realize we are still at the bottom of the heap in our native country, and before you let them ship you up from your island (thereby keeping it cool and safe for them to play in) think about us here. Before you accept a job here think too about the Black people who need and deserve that job. And we will try to think about you. Many of us who would like to have not moved to the islands or Africa for that very reason. We don't want to become colonialists. We recognize that if we are serious about nationalism then we must be serious about Black people. It's arrogant of Black Americans and Africans and West Indians to think they know more than the people who inhabit another land. Which is not to say we cannot draw inspiration from each other and not at all to say one cannot make suggestions to another. But on a group scale we have seen Ghanaian resentment of Black Americans, Black American resentment of West Indians, and Lord knows which Black group West Indians hate. The playing off of Black against Black is as divisive as "Help a junkie bust a pusher." We must learn to respect each other, our men and women, our customs and habits. It will not be easy or happen overnight but it must be started. I'd like to live in Barbados, where the police not only don't carry guns but can't even ticket you—they must request that you come to court. I'd like to rear my child in clean air and fresh waters in a land not plagued by starvation and sexual hangups. But the price for that is the displacement of a Bajan. And I have learned and know that I will be easier for the government to deal with than natives as they are easier to deal with here than we are. As a nationalist I am not prepared to be anti-nationalist in my actions. And the sun kissed the water and the warmth carried over to me. I hope I can love you as I would like someday, I said to the beach as I prepared to go home.

Arriving on the West Side of New York and seeing that it was still standing, I checked my phone messages. I picked out "Your mother." And I thought, odd, since she sort of believes the phone is a wonderful, newfangled radio on which you can dial the right combination of numbers and letters and some- how a friend's voice will be there. When my sister and I were home we always did the dialing, then called her to the phone, and she still to this very day thinks we know magic. I dialed with authority and control directly. "What's up? Somebody sick?" "No. They got your girl!" "What girl?" "Angela Davis." Damn, I thought, so it's really gonna start. "What happened?" And she ran it down. "But if they filmed it and she wasn't there I don't understand the charges." "Well, in California, if you're an accessory before the fact, they can hold you equally guilty." "That is some shit. That's like saying if you ever smiled at a Black man and that smile caused him to realize the infre- quency of happiness in his life and incited him to act out his unhappiness, you are therefore guilty of rioting." "You're a writer." "Now, what does that mean?" "You're trying to be log- ical about white folks again." "Watch your tongue, woman. Next thing I know you'll be hopping in bed with that man you're in love with." "If you mean your father, my dear, I do already. And I'm going to hang up if you're going to be disre- spectful." And I had a problem. The two Black people on the ten-most-wanted list in 1971 were/are political prisoners. And I began to think of the reality and try to compress the reality I saw as Angela Yvonne Davis. I had read Richard Wright's story "Bright and Morning Star," and while I identified with the mother I failed to understand why they latched on to communism. Then I got older and recognized that a drowning man will grab a twig. But slowly and deliberately the people were turned against the idea of communism while the two governments came closer together in policy, while Black people and white people split again—because it's been proven over and over from the beginning that white people are white first, people second, and interested in *their* white welfare third. The Communist cause, however, had a certain romance about it and a certain hopelessness that my basic Blackness made me sympathize with. And reading the transcript of the army-McCarthy hearings made me feel, why, of course those people have a right to live! They want a better life for us all. And I even got indignant that the government would try to stop it. But Russian history taught me Russia has always been an ally of the West, including the United States. And a sketchy reading of Chinese history taught me that China has always been outside. Both Russia and the United States have more fear of China than of each other.

Because Angela said she was a Communist they accuse her of being controlled or influenced by Russia. But if that were the case, why didn't she go to Russia? Why didn't the Soviet government protect her? It has a network to handle that. Why didn't the Russian Embassy offer her asylum if she was fighting the Kremlin's cause? Because clearly she was not. International communism is insidious in its moves to compromise

Black people. Gus Hall and all his cohorts will say she's a party member, but how come she's the only one wanted by the FBI? If they were just looking for Communists, they could have gone to the State Department or to the Pentagon or to the CIA. If they were just looking for Communists, they could have gone to the faculty of Harvard or Princeton or any division of the University of California since the overwhelming majority of intellectuals over forty-five were at some point either members of the Communist Party or sympathizers. We've watched the Communist movement father and control the now established and reactionary labor movement. Any group that could be in any way responsible for organized labor is no threat to capitalism. We've watched the organized labor movement support Reagan and Nixon and George Wallace. We've watched Shanker encourage his union members not to teach Black children because their Black parents want control of their Black education. And we've looked with utter disgust at Bayard Rustin marching like the fool he is alleged to be, with Shanker—a lackey of his own destruction for some ideology— when clearly DuBois was right: the problem is the color line.

The world does not move on ideologies; it moves not even on interests, because it would be to the interest of some whites to unite with us. It moves on color. And that must be understood. Angela Yvonne is wanted and may be destroyed because she is Black. Her capture and destruction serve two purposes—to show Black people, most especially the middle class, what will happen if they step out of line; and to raise again the very safe and meaningless banner of the Red scare. Black people, which is to say colored peoples here in the United States, are backing off the Angela Yvonne Davis case, saying let the Communists defend her. But she needs our defense because she involved herself in Black action. This is the tragedy, this is the national shame of Black people. If you move to Black rhythms even your own people will turn against you. Jonathan Jackson and his friends took Black action, and white folks said at that van, no matter how many of us must die we will not let you be successful. Angela Davis was sought because as long as she was on the run, we were successful. The reason is not ideology. We don't even know her involvement with the Communists. But that doesn't matter any more than it matters whether Martin Luther King was screwing another woman because the question put upon us is, are we real or unreal? And we must deliver the answer. We have watched with concern the number of accidents, drug overdoses, and incidents of arrest and harassment over the past ten years, starting with the assassination of Lumumba and going to the overthrow of Sukarno and Nkrumah, the accident of Otis Redding, the prolonged illnesses of Sylvester Stewart and Aretha Franklin, the deaths of Nasser and Jimi Hendrix, the "justifiable" homicides of Sam Cooke and the Jackson State students and the blatant verbal attacks by Agnew on the public media. We have watched with concern the unemployment of Muhammad Ali and the slowing work schedule of Miriam Makeba and Nina Simone, as well as the subpoena of *New York Times* reporter Earl Caldwell for refusal to divulge his sources on a Black Panther story. We feel that these and numerous unlisted complaints, such as the fact that most public and private telephones in the country are tapped and that during "emergency" periods certain people cannot either call out or receive calls, is a part if not an incitement of the pres-

ent hopelessness and fear that pervade this nation and there-
fore this world.

We watched Angela's face as she stepped from the motel.
And she had one of those yes-I-know looks on her face as if to
say, this too must be gotten through; and as if life, which I
think she values, is all that's left and she must hold on to it.
And we feel this is a clear violation of her right to her opinion.
All you people who said, "Bring the oppression on down,"
where are you? It can't get much higher. And all you people
who wanted her to shoot it out with the police ought to quit
watching TV. It's affecting your minds, in a dangerous way.
And all you people who just wish Angela Yvonne Davis had
never existed ought to be glad she does—Black, brilliant and
therefore beautiful—because your turn is coming next. That's
a mean sort of truth no one wants to grapple with. We keep
looking for the music to stop and the lights to go out and the
White House to crumble and a big sign to be put in Times
Square saying, "America has fallen" or maybe "Will the real
Revolution please stand?" We've watched them attempt to
emasculate Huey Newton since there is no revolutionary who
doesn't want children. And we ought to check ourselves when
we say we want more from people who have already given all.
Betty Shabazz probably doesn't sleep at night, and whether
she gets a blond wig and marries a white man in no way alters
the fact that Malcolm's blood runs through her daughters'
veins and that he was with her. Coretta King cannot negate
Martin and Jackie cannot change what John Kennedy meant.
They should all in some way be unbalanced. We make jokes
and say, "Wonder why she did that?" without realizing the
horror of sitting with the brains of someone you loved or

wanted or had in your lap; without ever dealing with the pain of sitting the children down, saying, "Be quiet, Daddy's gonna speak in a moment," and seeing thirty-eight bullets pumped into him; without ever realizing maybe they'd had a quarrel and he said, "I'll talk to you when I get back from Memphis," and he never returned and the last words he heard from you were not so soft. There is a reality to the unbalance, and we're fools if we expect anything near the normal to come out of them—if there is such a thing as normal in an abnormal world run by subnormal people. People keep expecting Angela to be logical. But that's a twenty-six-year-old woman who probably had every reason to feel she could flow through life, find something/someone and be brainy and cute and who suddenly found herself the most wanted woman in the world. Would you come to Harlem if you were on the run? It's easy to say yes, but where in Harlem? Could she stay at the Theresa Hotel? Or maybe the hole that will be an office building? And it's easy to ask, why didn't she leave the country? But when's the last time you left? You're in danger too, and where can you go? Trotsky's enemies got him. Angela's enemies were going to get her. Probably the only person prepared to deal was not allowed out of his hotel room, was allowed no visitors, no press conference, nor a trip to Harlem because the U.S. Government was concerned for his safety. Which is probably its way of saying, "If you see Black people we'll have to kill you." And he did not see Black people. The issue of Angela Yvonne is clear. She's not an enigma; she's a young Black woman who has been thrown in with sadistic dykes, not to make sure that her spirit is broken—it was broken when they turned her in— but to show us all that our spirit can be broken. I am hoping it will have an equal and opposite effect. It will, if we follow natural laws.

The state of the world we live in is so depressing. And this is not because of the reality of the men who run it but because it just doesn't have to be that way. The possibilities of life are so great and beautiful that to see less wears the spirit down. It's like the more you move toward the possible, the more bitter you become of the stumbling blocks. I can really understand why people don't try to do anything. It's not really easy, but if you have to deal with energy it's a much more realistic task to decide not to feel than to feel. It takes the same amount of time but not to feel is ultimately more rewarding because things always come back to that anyway. . . .

You were a fool.

The more you love someone the more he wants from you and the less you have to give since you've already given him your love. And he says, "Prove it," with the same arrogance we show when we say, "Be Black." That's a given. If I say, "I love you," don't ask how I know—move on it. Nina Simone once told me that adulthood for her would be moving on what she knows to be true. Yet to move on the ultimate truth is to sit on the corner and tell lies and bang somebody every now and then, but not too good too often because you won't be able to get rid of him. The truth is that there is this shell all around you, and the more you say, "All right, you can come in" to someone, the more he questions the right of the shell to exist. And if you fall for that and take it away, he looks at your nakedness and calls you a whore. It's an awful thing when all you wanted was to laugh and run and touch and make love and really not give a damn. Aretha said at her Lincoln Center concert, "Tell yourself everything's gonna be/ Allllllllllllllllll right." Sometimes I think the people who walk the streets in their orange pants and striped green shirts, with their Afro wigs and miniskirts, know something so deep the language hasn't been invented to express it. They know more than my political analyzing, more than the Jewish slumlord who collects the rent, more than the white men running the country and the world, more than the ritual and the Koran, more than James Brown or Roberta Flack, more than I know about who's sleeping in my bed, more than my mother knows about me and I her, more than mathematics and the little green apples and all that, because some of the infrequent times when I sit down alone I feel it too and know that that feeling is real. The Bible puts it another way: ". . . as it was in the beginning, is now and ever shall be."

7

A Spiritual View of Lena Horne

"It's a lonely ole world! When you gotta face it/ All alone."*

You start out somewhere, try Brooklyn, as a child—if you're lucky as an innocent child, if not, as a child anyway. Usually Mother and Father and other spiritual ancestors are with you—giving, taking, loving—just a little bit. With proper upbringing and proper care you too could have become an Early American; with impropriety you might have become a Cotton Club girl with a voice somewhere deep inside and *they*, hearing the rumblings of your spirit, call you a singer because *they* have never understood true rhythm. *They* called you pretty. Being pretty has always had drawbacks for Black women; being beautiful is our natural state. *They* knew you had something and *they* couldn't get it—so *they* sought control. And sometimes your life maybe looks like a boxcar of the Scottsboro variety where you sat in a corner and watched the scenes—maybe Georgia was one of them where you were

*From "Lonely World Blues," as sung by Amanda Ambrose.

happy, because your feet were in red clay and you, being part Indian and part Senegalese, were at home with your family.

I say it's a lonely ole world when something needs to be done and you want to do it, only no one tells you what it is. Be a cymbal for our people? Yeah, sing the funeral ditties about happiness being a thing called Joe. Ain't *they* never gonna recognize that *thing* is a five-letter word starting with p——? Or maybe it's up to us and Joe anyway. Ole Black and otherwise, maybe it's really up to us to declare him a man—*they* think men are fruits hanging from trees. Remember Billie singing about it? Lillian Smith wrote a novel about it and then resigned from CORE because she couldn't really face the problem; then she died. Or was it the other way around?

Blues is a phenomenon I once heard when Lena Horne sang "Polkadots and Moonbeams." I was in bed (children being neither seen nor heard after nine o'clock) when the voice came through the television to my antenna. And it sounded as if she meant it, which made me, even in a pre-Black stage, very sad. People aren't supposed to be mean—they can act mean; maybe they have to be that way—but are not supposed to feel something.

And it's strange how things work out—"Everything you do is right/ Everything I do is wrong"—because Lena Horne has been singing a long time not to have a singing voice. I mean, she has a voice—*they* don't understand the melody. It's like living in Delaware and the DuPont factory workers being on the job a decade and someone telling you they are un/ill-equipped for the job. Looks fade. Pepshowitis is easily overcome. The mind in this country is attuned to depreciation. Can't be looks that allow Lena to entertain my mother and me. The Temptations have already said, "Beauty's Only Skin Deep," and J.B. has said, "True brothers, and money won't change you," either. So there is this phenomenon called Lena Horne who has been confused by the phenomenon named Lena Horne and who will say that she can't sing. I can't dig it because I heard her at the Waldorf do "After You" (who was she singing to?). It's like Nina Simone taking the Santa Claus out of Irving Berlin; something was brought to that song. I still think Lena Horne's untouchable.

Maybe if she'd been born in India she would have been in the Untouchables quarter (they call it segregation in reverse now) and the great Bwana would have told Gunga, "That one!" And Gunga, nigger that he was, would have said, "Horne? Can I blow that Horne?" And Bwana, as played by Bob Hope in one of the *Road* shows, would smile down his nose and say, "No, *I* got the itch." Yeah, *they* made Lena's story and starred Marilyn Monroe and Tom Ewell and then redid the sucker with Jayne Mansfield (though the leading male remained the same, which should tell us something) because Hollywood doesn't want to show a Black woman sitting on Billie's bed talking all night long about this "lonely ole world/ When you gotta face it/ All alone." *They* like the quarrels of the old with the young, *they* like division for diversion, but we ain't got time. "Would like to but can't take the time. . . ." *They* like to see you hate and be hateful/hated by husband and son and *they* have no right to see this but you cannot show anyway what is not there. *They* like to see our men go show and tell every day to the garment district, automobile factories, pulpits, bandstands, everywhere really. And as we moved away from that *they* created a poverty show which is a great comedy; we're laughing ourselves to death. *They* also have a Vietnamese and Laotian theater. Same show. Call it cowboy and Indian. Call it Coney Island (hope the Indians get that also). Call it coast-to-coast rolling. It's really all about sex anyway. WANTED: A NEW DEFINITION OF GENIUS.

Innovators are the combined energies of the people. They frequently feel guilty about taking more than they give, which should not be. The innovator who isn't taking more from the people than she is giving has nothing to give. When the people stop giving, the leader is bankrupt. Many people feed into the one person who is/becomes the personification of the people. That's what stars are all about—a collection of mass gravitation. When the moon burned out in 1947 we began looking for bright stars. One's starmanship is based upon the ability to shed light. "It's a lonely ole world."

As Lena steps before a camera and walks to the microphone she's got to know she's not alone. Not only are her ancestors there; mine are too. We are there. Hearing her sing. And it's a funny thing about loneliness. It happens because no one understands and maybe even she doesn't understand we are there. Such is the nature of leader/followership. We were and are there to watch her show *them* and we were hopeful that *they* would see. Then when *they* didn't see she probably thought we didn't see either, but we did. Big Brother and the Grateful Dead may have been there, but so was Aretha. And that's who she sings to, and to me and all the Delta ladies and Omega men. Yeah, and maybe even the partying Kappas because when she sings we sing. And it's a proven fact that if we would all sing one note together our combined energies would turn the moon back on and the Arabs, being moon people, could reclaim their land and she could reclaim herself. Which she will do in the sunlight anyway.

Beauty is a natural wonder. One rarely looks directly at the sun and even less frequently thanks it for being itself. We especially didn't when our mood was antispiritual. But a thousand cats walking in step across the Golden Gate Bridge will break it down, just as twenty-five Black people on a Mississippi plantation doing that old Gospel shuffle, singing "The Circle Will Not Be Broken," could be heard one hundred miles. A people will come into our own. And we don't say it's better for all people, just that it's better for us. We like her better because she likes her better. And we'll like her more as we like us more, relationships being crucial.

It's all so physical, Happiness once told me. AS IT WAS IN THE BEGINNING. The combined price must be paid. IS NOW. We've got an overdue bill to future Black people. AND EVER SHALL NOT BE. "It's a lonely ole world." We've done that. Dinah Washington did that. The earth is the giver of basil, savory, sage and mostly thyme, which should go into everything we do. But Dinah called it "Bitter." Aretha shouldn't have to sing that song. And Lena shouldn't feel guilty because she sang in supper clubs; after all, little Tommy Tucker did and that brother put out some heavy dues. RISE, SALLY, RISE. We have all been lions in a den of Daniels.

It's a question of perspectives. Once we thought everything had to be done yesterday; now we feel most won't get done until tomorrow. They say it's nation time. The ability to prospect old Black (similar to though not quite the same as finding a million-dollar baby in a 10-cent store), because coal is just a diamond that didn't want to go on Jackie's fingers or around Liz Taylor's throat, is crucial. It's about old friends who let you be quiet and new friends who want to hear you talk. And Lena Horne is a spiritual experience, which is "what keeps me Black and *them* white." Lena Horne plays with unicorns and probably had a satyr steal her cherry. And she probably liked it. It's a question of perspectives. The everyday grind of being on stage must be broken. The prospect of happiness without dues is like a cracker without hatred. I mean, *they* may grow bigger tomatoes but they don't taste like anything.

Lena Horne is not a chocolate Hedy Lamarr, she's a Black Lena Horne, just as Uggams isn't a brown Smothers brother. We must come into our own. And "Do you mind?" is destructive, Horne says, because people like to hurt you under the guise of honesty and honesty without love is destructive. And one feels Lena, despite the shields, despite the time, or perhaps because of the woman. One would like to hug her and make everything all right. If one had the world of time it would take. And lacking the proper mixture of necessities some smile and say, "Hey, ain't you Lena Horne?" and walk on down 57th Street, which we did once. To my car. And I waved while she walked away and thought of my grandmother, who always used to say, "Why, my Agnes looks every bit as good as Lena Horne!" and my mother, whom I love, and my father, who loves me, and my son, who gave my life meaning. And driving to Verta Mae's book party I thought: what a shit place America is.

8

The Weather As a Cultural Determiner

The culture of a people is an expression of its life style. What defines a life style and what determines it? A Black man living at the North Pole is still a Black man—with African roots, with a Black, hence African, way of looking at his life, of ordering his world, of relating his dreams, of responding to his environment. And the strangest aspect of this Black man living at the North Pole is that his children, who have never lived anywhere but the North Pole, will retain and manifest this African way. And so will their children. And so will theirs. And even on down until one would think that all things African had been bred out of them. But when someone comes along playing a conga drum it can happen that one of these descendants will fall right into the rhythm, or he will see a Black woman and find her most beautiful, or he will sit and long for the sun, or he will meditate on his life and conjure dreams a man living at the North Pole could not conceive unless at one point Africa had been in his blood. The same with white people. A white man in Africa never becomes an African. His children never become African; they are white people living in Africa. The sight of snow brings feelings of nostalgia to them.

One of the things white people say about us is that we have no ability to delay gratification. This is in my opinion not only true but good. We came from a climate that immediately gratified us, that put all the necessities of life at our fingertips: the weather was warm; food was available from the sea and the air and the land; we could sleep outside; we could, in other words, complement our environment and survive. The very color of our skins shows that; we complemented our environment, we blended with it. On the other hand, the white man could not survive outside in Europe. To be exposed to its winters would be to perish. His home was built to protect him from the cold. His eating habits were based on his ability to measure his appetite. His survival was based on his ability to measure his appetite for life. An African who had a jones about some chick could start out walking, find her, run off to the bush and be gratified. A white man had to control his sexual urge because the nearest nonrelative might have been and most likely was miles away. In the winter months he couldn't take a chance of striking out for her. He had to wait until the weather would allow him to go. That's maybe one reason incest is more prevalent among white people than Black. That's also one reason Black people marry more than one woman. If you were cooped up in a cabin/castle with two or three women and you had a poor hunting season you were in trouble. Somebody would starve.

And I mention this because white people in America still manifest that urgency about meeting necessities despite their so-called affluence: they still hoard, they still are the ants, and we are the grasshoppers. It almost appears to be genetic. A Black man today with a million dollars will spend it and have a ball. A white man will invest and save. And one will never understand why the other did as he did. The Black man sings for enjoyment; the white man creates record companies for profit. Black people are the poets, white people the publishers.

A man in a cold environment has to order his entire life. Not only does he have to plan for necessities; he has to plan for enjoyment. His pleasure must be programmed into his life as much as his work is. This is one reason white people created prostitution; they could buy and sell it; and the chick doing it had to report on time. The Black man on the other hand could take the chance of meeting someone he wanted because he could get out to see people; if he missed today he could score tomorrow. When tomorrow is going to be freezing you have to score today, and the only way to be sure of scoring is to buy it—by contract (marriage) or extralegally. You just don't find prostitution in Africa or the West Indies aside from what white people have created. I mention this because even a white man born in South Africa whose family has been there for as long as or longer than we have been in America will manifest the same tendencies.

Let's take it another place. The Arabs created in the image of nature: their number system starts with zero and includes the ciphers 1, 2, 3, 4, 5, 6, 7, 8 and 9, which are quite simply the sun and the nine planets. Couple the sun with any of the nine planets and you find an infinite possibility. The Roman numerals on the other hand start with I and immediately are unusable because you have to go into an elaborate system to get ten. Ten in Roman numeral becomes X, an unknown. Ten in Arabic becomes 1 plus the sun. The Honorable Elijah Muhammad teaches us that the earth is ruled by twenty-three wise scientists who obtained their knowledge from Allah, the twenty-fourth. We find this in nature. There are twenty-three chromosomes in our bodies, and our sex, hence our knowledge, is determined by the twenty-fourth chromosome. But if the twenty-fourth chromosome enters our system we become mongoloids because one cannot contain God. To see God is to travel beyond our ability to articulate that knowledge. What I am saying is that the original man, the Black man, related to nature and tried to live within it. The white man tried to fight it.

Literature is one of the tools white people have used for survival.

The major invention of the white man in literature is the novel. The Spanish exemplar of the form is *Don Quixote*, a big, clumsily written book about a dude fighting windmills for the love of some chick who didn't dig him. It deals with chivalry and knighthood and stuff. In other words it describes the standard for a life style that no Western man could afford to live. It is quite frankly foolish. But it is long enough to take a season to get through. With a big novel in the court and someone to read a couple of chapters a week winter would pass. The modern counterpart is the soap opera. You get a little each day and tune in tomorrow—in other words, you delay your gratification. Black people come from an oral tradition. We sat by the fire and told tales; we tended the flocks and rapped poems. We had a beginning and an end for we didn't know what tomorrow would bring. We were prepared to deal with the unknown. Our laws were natural laws; they were simple and straightforward. Our laws were people-directed; the only don't was, don't kill anyone unless your tribe or community was at war. Whites' laws were property-directed; they made people property even before they had us. And it makes sense. If only so much land was fertile and was only fertile for one season, the more land you had and the more people working it, the better your chances of survival. We on the other hand had plenty all around us all the time; the land was there and we never thought to stake it out because it didn't have to be worked and it bloomed all year round. The women kept the common land and the men did the hunting and fishing. All shared. Still today if you go to a Black's house, even if he has very little, he'll share and be insulted if you refuse. Those of us from the North who worked in the South during the sit-in days were constantly surprised by the people's generosity. And their generosity was based not on some moral law but on the fact that wherever you find Black people they share and say to hell with tomorrow. That isn't negative; it's based on our collective historical need. Even a dude who doesn't want to is compelled to share. Call it an irresistible impulse. White folks say we are illogical.

Logic is the spiritual understanding of the subjective situation and the physical movement necessary to place life in its natural order. In other words, on some gut level we understand that we all will survive or we all will not survive, and my hoarding a little corn or your hoarding a little meat will not let us make it. But if we get together we can have at least one good meal, which may give us the strength to push forward the next day. A Black person will have one big meal and thoroughly enjoy it even if he knows there will be nothing tomorrow. He will be full for one day. The white man will measure out and starve himself or never be full forever.

We have been called nonreaders.

Blacks as a people haven't jumped into long books because they usually have proven to be false. White people write long everything—novels, epic poems, laws, sociology texts, what have you—because they are trying to create a reality. They are generally trying to prove that something exists which doesn't exist. We rap down on a daily level because we appreciate our existence. We had many gods, one for damned near everything we could get our hands on, while they had one (how many gods could one castle hold?) who was the most together dude of all. They were waiting on a messiah to solve their problems; we had no problems to be solved. We are the poems and the lovers of poetry.

Poetry is the culture of a people. We are poets even when we don't write poems; just look at our life, our rhythms, our tenderness, our signifying, our sermons and our songs. I could just as easily say we are all musicians. We are all preachers because we are One. And whatever the term we still are the same in the other survival/life tools. The new Black Poets, so called, are in line with this tradition. We rap a tale out, we tell it like we see it; someone jumps up maybe to challenge, to agree. We are still on the corner—no matter where we are— and the corner is in fact the fire, a gathering of the clan after the hunt. I don't think we younger poets are doing anything significantly different from what we as a people have always done. The new Black poetry is in fact just a manifestation of our collective historical needs. And we strike a responsive chord because the people will always respond to the natural things. We are like a prize stallion that Buffalo Bill thought he'd tamed. Then the free horses (they call them "wild") came by and called, and without even knowing why, we followed. And those who couldn't follow, like any caged animal, whined and moaned and then began to kick the door down. The call has been made and we are going to be free.

We don't know who our great poets are; we have no record of the African poems before we were set upon by the locusts. And like that dreaded insect they ate/destroyed everything in sight. Call them French destroyers. They started with the physical and went into the mental. I can well imagine a man sitting in a village watching the whites approach. He at first wondered what kind of insect was that large. He probably ran for the No-Roach, and then in a typical humane manner decided to wait to see if it was friendly. The insect presented itself as a man who wanted to learn. And he did. He studied at our universities; he lived in our villages. And in peace. We often make the mistake of thinking that the white man came and destroyed right away. In actuality he learned. He invited our scholars to Europe. We had an exchange. Then after he had taken, as all carbons take, the form, he began to destroy the original. But he didn't have the feeling. He didn't have the ability to create. He didn't have the essence. We spoke of personal freedom; he made it a law—with no emotional understanding of the simple fact that personal freedom cannot be made into a law. How can you order someone to be free? And even the most liberal of the countries, which was America at its inception, held it to be self-evident that all men were created equal, which meant that all men were entitled to life, liberty and the pursuit of happiness. But the earliest laws among whites were property laws, and even today the fight is still for control of land because they could not/cannot understand life and happiness aside from the ownership of real estate. And to them the realest estate has got to be the control of other men.

So we sang our songs and they copied what they could use and mass-produced it and banned what they didn't understand. We told our tales to their children and they thought we loved them. Just listen to "Rockabye Baby" and picture a Black woman singing it to a white baby—when the east wind blows the cradle will rock and down will come baby, cradle and all. Or Peter, Peter, pumpkin eater, put her in a pumpkin shell and there he kept her. They didn't know we were laughing at them, and we unfortunately were late to awaken to the fact that we can die laughing.

We have a line of strong poets. Wheatley by her life style was a strong woman intent on survival. And it's funny that all her poems talking about the good white folks are reprinted but not the poems about her hard life. I've seen only a few of her later poems and at that only once. They say her writing wasn't good after she married that Black man and had children. They say the same thing about Chesnutt. He was fine when he was publishing without anyone knowing that he was Black; after that they say his writing went down—especially in works where Black folks come out on top, like *The Marrow Tradition* and *The Wife of His Youth*. And we've got to dig on the whole scene because whites have been the keepers of records and they've only kept the ones they like. My theory is that the older we get as a people here in America the more we are going to check ourselves. There are many fine works locked away in trunks; there are many fine poems running in the heads of the old people. We should always talk with old people because they know so much. Even the jivest old person, in line with his collective historical need, can give a history of some movement or maybe just his block and the people on it.

The tales that we trade on the corners are taken seriously. Lives have been lost over one version or another, and it's not because Niggers just like to kill Niggers but because we have a duty—call it a religious calling—to record and pass on orally.

Black is a sacrament. It's an outward and visible sign of an inward and spiritual grace. A poetry reading is a service. A play is a ritual. And these are the socially manifested ways we do things. There have been Black novelists, Black writers of history, Black recorders of the laws, but these are not tools for the enjoyment of the people. These are tools for the scholars. And I am not knocking them. For when Black people have been recorders we have sought truth; when white people used these tools they sought dreams.

We hear a lot about the Black aesthetic. The aesthetic is the dream a culture wishes to obtain. We look back when we seek an aesthetic; whites look forward. In my opinion the search for an aesthetic will lead down a blind alley which will have a full-length mirror on three sides and at the end—we are our aesthetic. Given the definition of aesthetic, it already is the Black life style in whiteface. What white people are seeking is the removal of the pressure of the "real" world from their backs. The word closest to that in Blackdom is bourgeoisie. And Greer and Cobb call them dilettantes—a small group not worth worrying about. Most of us accept the responsibility of/for living. It's very worrisome when we find Black people committing suicide by dope, self-hatred and the actual taking of life. It means we have gotten away from our roots. This is when the poet must call. Brothers, brothers everywhere and not a one for sale. Jewel Lattimore calls it utopia. The poet calls in *Youngblood* when big strong Joe

Youngblood comes to take his wife. The poet called when Stokely said, "Black Power." The poet calls when Rap says, "Come around or we gonna burn you down." The poet called when Rosa Parks said, "no." We are our own poems. We must invent new games and teach the old people how to play. The poet sang "What happens to a dream deferred?" Or when the O'Jays summed up the sit-in movement asking, "Must I always be a stand in for love?" The poet called when Sterling Brown said, "The strong men keep coming." Or when Margaret Burroughs asked, "What shall I tell my children who are Black?" Or when David Walker addressed his *Appeal to the Colored People of the World with a Special Message for the Black People in America*. Or when LeRoi Jones said, "Up against the wall, motherfuckers." Or when the young men out of work asked, "What I wanta work for?" The poet calls with the cry of the newborn. "Get on the right track, baby."

9

The Beginning Is Zero

I've finally lived long enough to realize Black people are not fools. Many things, perhaps, but not fools. That Booker T. Washington could have a dream and excite enough Blacks in it to make the bricks that built the buildings is fantastic. There are many side arguments about the value and validity of his dream but Tuskegee is alive . . . it's a Black institution. You say *Ebony* is just *Look* or *Life* in Blackface? Try telling that to Mississippians who made a best seller of *Before the Mayflower.* We know better. *Black World* has never been *Reader's Digest* and SNCC has never coordinated. What we mean is, nothing starts from one. It starts from zero. In literature Charles Chesnutt is our zero. And we swim or sink on his accomplishments.

Chesnutt's first published stories are contained in *The Conjure Woman*. He began publishing them in the *Atlantic Monthly* because they thought he was white—just as many writers are published in it now because the *Atlantic Monthly* thinks they are Black. It's a question not of passing but of posture. *The Conjure Woman* puts Joel Chandler Harris and

Stephen Foster and all those dudes up to and including Styron in their places. Uncle Julius is out to win. And he does. He convinces the cracker that the grapes have a spell on them and are therefore better left alone. He shows what would happen if the white man had to live in the Black man's shoes in "Mars Jeen's Nightmare." And he keeps his nephew's job for him. He uses the white woman's natural curiosity about Black men to his advantage. She always sympathizes with him while her husband is prone to back off. He is a good Black politician. The cracker gives the lumber that is "Po' Sandy" to the Black church. Uncle Julius is one of Black literature's most exciting characters precisely because he is so definite about his aims. He intends to see his people come out on top. John, the white voice, thought he could use Julius while it was the other way around. And Chesnutt drops a few gems on us dispelling the romantic theory about slavery's charms. In "Goophered Grapevine," for example, a new slave eats the grapes and is bound by the terms of the goopher to die. "The overseer said on the first rainy day he would take the slave to see the Conjure woman." Well, if he is bound to die wouldn't it be worth taking him right away? Not if it is just a slave. And Henry is sent out and sold and resold to suit the convenience of the household with no thought of him. And Sandy of "Po' Sandy" is treated the same way. Rather than be a slave he'll be a tree and plant his roots by the river? But he is destined to be cut down anyway—unless he fights back.

Chesnutt's second collection was *The Wife of His Youth*. Charles Chesnutt was born of free parents in Cleveland, Ohio. His family was from North Carolina. Chesnutt began a saga-type tale which is still being used by novelists like Attaway and

Hal Bennet and which was and is the pattern of movement of Black people—from rural South to urban North. And this was in the 1800s to early 1900s. Naming his mythical city Groveland (after Grover Cleveland perhaps) he moves his newly emancipated Black men and women along the social scale. Mr. Ryder in the title story has come North and made his fortune in the post office. He is about to wed a lovely light-skinned young lady whom he loves when an old Black woman comes asking his help in finding her husband. He is that husband she seeks. He decides to acknowledge her, thereby giving up much he thought he wanted. Is this just a jive short story or wasn't it in fact exploring the historical relationship between Black man and Black woman when, after emancipation, he chooses to "better himself" and leave her behind? Chesnutt's main fault was perhaps his optimism. He accomplished in that story one of the goals we seek from literature— the truth and its ideal ending.

"Her Virginia Mammy" was the forerunner of that horrendous novel which was made into that equally horrendous movie, *Imitation of Life*, which had you know who crying in the aisles even after the third viewing. It's all in his story—the stereotypical self-sacrificing, self-denying mother and the child who should have a better chance. This is an important story because later his novels negate it. Who hasn't at some time thought it would be easier to be white? And how many have actually overcome that? Two of Chesnutt's best known stories, "The Sheriff's Children" and "The Web of Circumstances," both appear in *The Wife of His Youth*. Both these story themes have since resounded in white literature, from the *Ox Bow Incident* to *To Kill a Mockingbird*. Chesnutt, by making the Black man innocent and the white man his executioner, introduced Jesus as a Black man into the American context.

We can easily see that Charles Chesnutt set a tone for literature in America. What is clear is that they can praise you or damn you, but after a certain point they cannot ignore you. And we cannot ignore many people who preceded us. Surely E. Franklin Frazier was inspired in his classic study of the Black bourgeoisie by "Baxter's Procastus." Baxter, who belongs to an exclusive men's club, decides to write a book, which he then sells to all his fellow club members. They all tell him how wonderful it is and how much they enjoyed it. Then on a whim one of the newer members of the club decides to open the book. It is a sealed copy since sealed copies are more valuable than unsealed. He opens it to find all the pages blank, exposing the fact that the other members either did not or could not read. Baxter had a good laugh and the bourgeoisie suffered embarrassment. And yet they haven't learned, if a current observation is an indication. I recently attended a writer's conference where one writer began a question to another with "I haven't read your book but I understand it's salacious." That's a big word if the book wasn't read. But it's all in the story with the humor and love that only one who had been there and escaped could give.

Chesnutt's novels are deserving of much time and attention. He wrote three though I will touch on only the first two (the third is out of print)—*The Marrow of Tradition* and *The House Behind the Cedars*. *The House Behind the Cedars* was written first. It deals with a man who is passing for white and his sister. The brother has gone away and married well and is living a comfortable life. He comes back to the house behind the cedars to take his sister away with him. She would like to come but she really can't. She goes with her brother to live in his big house and be a part of his society; yet she is haunted by dreams of her mother and a man she has left behind. She cannot dance between the two worlds. Her roots are deep in the soil that gave her birth. When her mother needs her she tries to go home briefly, but to look back is to have the curse of Lot's wife upon you.

Chesnutt's view of the Black woman is remarkably accurate, even in the stilted language of his time. The Black woman historically has never been able collectively to move from her roots. Too many emotional strings are wound around her. It is man's place to go forth and conquer; it is woman's to seek the soft, warm places. Man expels; woman receives. Chesnutt resolved the question for all of them—from Lillian Smith to Alice Childress. There are two realities within the Black community and two within the white. One is the reality of men and the other that of women. Black men control the Black reality as white women control the white. We are what he is. Otherwise why this talk about manhood? They are what she is. Otherwise why the lynching and knighthood stuff to defend her honor? We now recognize that a bunch of misfits came to these shores to populate this nation. If white men were not successful in making those misfits into "ladies," their nation would never win the respect of the world. Look at Jackie Kennedy—a plain, ordinary, maybe even not bright white girl made out to be the epitome of grace and charm. And when she married a non-Westerner the nation went up in arms. Never mind what white men have done; it all turns on white women. That's why women in New Orleans spit on Black kids: they have a lot to protect. And before Women's Lib can convince some of us that we should be involved in the Movement, that act will have to be fully and carefully explained. Black women have always known where white society was weakest, just as whites have known that the way to keep the Black man under their thumb is to hold us down. The weight of Blackness ultimately falls on Black men. And it is their response which will determine our position. This is clearly outlined in Chesnutt's novel.

The Marrow of Tradition was the beginning of the end of white folks' love affair with Chesnutt. He checked his antecedents and thought perhaps David Walker had something in his *Appeal*. Chesnutt wrote the first race riot and the critics began grumbling that perhaps he had lost his touch. The plainer he made it the more they hated him. The old Mammy dies in the riot. The Black folks fight back. The crackers are milling around smoking their cigars, deciding which Black folks will have to die, while we are preparing for a siege. It's so real and so graphic:

In the olden time the white South labored under the constant fear of negro insurrections. Knowing that they themselves, if in the negroes' place, would have risen in the effort to throw off the yoke, all their reiterated theories of negro subordination and inferiority could not remove the lurking fear, founded upon the obscure consciousness that the slaves ought to have risen. . . . There was never on the continent of America, a successful slave revolt nor one which lasted more than a few hours or resulted in the loss of more than a few white lives.

—*The Marrow of Tradition*

Yet Josh and the men come to Lawyer Watson and Dr. Miller and ask them to lead. Each of the Black men has an excuse. One says it will blow over, the other that he will be killed. Josh and the men make the monumental decision that must be made by the masses when the bourgeois show their real lack of color—that they will lead themselves. They will not allow white men to continue this madness that the educated coloreds seem not to mind so much after all. Miller, the protagonist, goes off romantically looking for his wife and child. Watson flees for his life. But Josh and the men move on across town. That kind of truth in literature hadn't been done before and is rarely done now.

Chesnutt used what we now call dialect, but given our use of language it is more accurately termed slang. And since it isn't our language anyway it doesn't matter how he spells it. It is for us to define the positive in and the negative out of our literature. Chesnutt clearly showed in his all too brief career the limits of writing Black. LeRoi Jones has come under the same pressure in the same way. Jewish critics now say Jones "can't write" as the WASP critics once said of another genius, Charles Chesnutt. Once you write for your people others will judge that your quality is failing. And we find it regrettable that Black critics don't more frequently view works from a Black perspective. A true numbers system starts with the son (sun) and that would be Charles Waddell Chesnutt.

10

Black Poems, *Poseurs* and Power*

I like all the militant poems that tell how we're going to kick the honkie's backside and purge our new system of all honkie things like white women, TV, voting and the rest of the ugly, bad things that have been oppressing us so long. I mean, I wrote a poem asking, "Nigger, can you kill?" because to want to live under President no-Dick Nixon is certainly to become a killer. Yet in listening to Smokey and the Miracles sing their *Greatest Hits* recently, I became aware again of the revolutionary quality of "You Can Depend on Me." And if you ask, "Who's Loving You?" just because I say he's not a honkie you should still want to know if I'm well laid. There is a tendency to look at the Black experience too narrowly.

The Maulana has pointed out rather accurately that "The blues is counterrevolutionary," but Aretha is a voice of the new Black experience. It's rather obvious that while "Think" was primarily directed toward white America, Ted White could have taken a hint from it. We must be aware of speaking

*Reprinted from *Negro Digest*, vol. XVIII, no. 8, June 1969, pp. 30–34.

on all levels. What we help to create we will not necessarily be able to control.

The rape of Newark in the 1968 election was criminal. If revolutionaries are going to involve themselves in politics, they should be successful. And while I'm sure poems are being written to explain the "success" of the Newark campaign, and essays and future speeches are being ground out on brand-new ScotTissue in living color blaming the Black community for not supporting the United Brothers, I would imagine the first problem the United Brothers encountered that they were unable to overcome is that they were not united.

LeRoi Jones, for whatever reason, had no business appearing on a show with Anthony Imperiale issuing joint statements about anything at all because he (LeRoi) did not have equal power in his half of the joint. Joint statements and meetings with the Governor did not encourage the Black people of Newark to support the United Brothers. Because of the prestige of LeRoi, no Newark voice is being lifted to analyze what went wrong. In the all-Black central ward, of the people who turned out to vote only 50 percent voted for councilmen, period. They did not vote against the United Brothers but they would not vote for them either. In a year when Black people showed little to no interest in national politics the stage was set for massive involvement in Black Power. There was no opposition—the people were not involved in another camp. So what went wrong?

Militarism, for one thing. To enter the main headquarters of the United Brothers one had to sign in. This turned most people off. Then you were asked quite tersely, "What do you want?" And if you couldn't answer concisely and accurately you were dismissed. The extreme of this behavior at headquarters was reached when a man carrying $600 to give to the campaign was requested to sign in and then engaged in conversation by one of the keepers of headquarters. The man turned from the conversation to speak with someone else and was told by a second headquarters keeper, "The brother wasn't finished with you." When the man's response wasn't satisfactory they pushed him up against the wall and the brothers "guarding" him were told, "Do anything necessary to keep him in line." The man with the money finally made his way upstairs and complained to Karenga and LeRoi. He was told his treatment was "an honest mistake."

It was a disaster. If that kind of treatment was accorded a man with as much prestige as he had, I shudder to think what happened to those who just drifted in to see. They offered an apology to the offended brother but that missed the point entirely. The people of Newark became more afraid of the Black candidates and their organization than they were of the present scandal-ridden, Black-hating administration. This is too bad—to put it mildly. The contradictions are too great.

Revolutionary politics has nothing to do with voting anyway. But if we enter electoral politics we should follow the simple formula that every Black person is a potential vote and must be welcomed and treated as such, with or without dashiki, with or without natural.

The latent militarism of the artistic community is even more despicable—art and the military have always been traditionally opposed. We saw the epitome of the new alliance at the 1968 Black Power Conference at Philadelphia. Every artist worth his salt had a military wing attached to him. The conference had guards; the artists had guards; the guards had guards even. One of the highlights of the conference to me was Karenga's guards complaining about Stanford's guards. This is foolish because it has already been proved beyond a reasonable doubt—with the murders of Martin Luther King, Jr., and Robert Kennedy—that anybody the honkie wants to take off he not only can but will, whenever and however he wants to stage it. The artist-guard syndrome seems to center around the impression we can make with the various communities. The artist impresses the white community with his militancy and the guards impress the Black community with their power. It's a sick syndrome with, again, the Black community being the loser. There is no cause for wonder that the Black community is withdrawing from involvement with the Black artist.

On "Soul," which appears on educational TV in New York, the same simplistic crap has taken place. "Soul" is funded by the Ford Foundation and the Negro Ensemble Company is funded by them also. Yet the people on "Soul," after giving Barbara Ann Teer credit for founding NEC, put it down as not being Black enough. And the Last Poets, which is proba-bly a truer title than they know, performed *Die Nigga*. It's just not the same concept as "kill." It would seem to me that the most important and valid aspect of cultural nationalism would be the support of other Black cultural ventures, especially since one cultural function is funded by the same white folks who fund the group being put down.

Since Black people are going to look at TV they should look at "Julia." Diahann Carroll is prettier, i.e., more valid, than Doris Day any day of the year. And while the idea of cops is bad to me, period, and extralegal Black cops are even worse, if Black people are going to watch cop shows on TV then "Mod Squad" beats the other white vigilante shows. And if "I Spy" is indeed, as I've been told, the new Lone Ranger, then Bill Cosby, by becoming the new Tonto, should help make us aware that we are the Indians of this decade. The parallel institutions that we hear so much about must certainly have reached their apex with "I Spy." *For Love of Ivy* is as fine a movie as we've had since *Nothing but a Man*. And it's certainly more valid to us than *Planet of the Apes, 2001* and those other white things we are forced to watch. It would sometimes appear some elements of the Black artistic community are against popular success unless it's theirs. Sidney Poitier has moved into the area where we have said we want actors to go—only we didn't mean, and make money, I guess. Everybody knows *Guess Who's Coming to Dinner?* is a bad movie but it is neither the beginning nor the end of Poitier's career, and the righteous indignation we spout is really quite out of place. Black people will soon quit listening to us if we can't get in tune with them. I would imagine it's a question of wigs.

Everybody has done his wig poem and wig play. You know, where we put Black people down for not having taken care of business. But what we so easily forget is our own wig. While we put down commercially successful artists we scramble to the East Side to work, we fight for spots on TV, we move our plays downtown at the first chance we get—we do the very things we say are not to be done. Just because our hair is natural doesn't mean we don't have a wig. We are niggers-in-residence at white universities and talk about voting as a means to take over a city, and then we put James Brown down for supporting Hubert Humphrey. It's all a wig. We obviously have no concept of power because if we did we'd recognize that the power of Black people forced James Brown to go natural. Everybody can't come up through the civil rights movement because it just doesn't exist anymore. When Black boys and girls from Mississippi to Massachusetts write J.B. letters complaining about *This Is My Country Too* (or was that a John A. Williams book?) then we ought to rejoice that Brown changes his position. The people we purport to speak for have spoken for themselves. We should be glad.

And it's not as though—if we just like to complain—there isn't an abundance of issues to complain about. What was John Coltrane doing with music that made some people murder him? Why isn't Otis Redding's plane brought up from the lake? What about the obvious tieups in the murders of John and Robert Kennedy with Martin Luther King's death? What elements in this country conspired to murder both Richard Wright and Ben Bella? What did Malcolm and Nkrumah say to each other that caused one to die and the other to be overthrown? Why have so many Arabs and people of Arab descent been arrested for murder or conspiracy to commit murder? And I'd like to know what the cultural nationalists think about James Forman, living with a white woman who has borne his children, controlling and directing SNCC while Stokely, married to a Black woman, was kicked out. These are cultural questions—relating to survival. But it sometimes seems that the only thing that culturalists care about is assuring themselves and the various communities that they are the vanguard of the Black Revolution. They have made Black women the new Jews while they remain the same old niggers. We have got to do better than this.

Our enemy is the *New York Times*, not the *Amsterdam News*; it's *Look* and *Life*, not *Ebony*; and we ought to keep our enemy in sight. If we're going to talk about parallel institutions then we have to recognize the parallel institutions we have. It is just not possible to have a crisis in Negro intellectualism unless we recognize that Negro intellectualism exists. Young writers ought to recognize that an old writer can't put down other old writers for our benefit. It's sometimes better for a swimmer flailing around in a turbulent lake to be left to drown than for other swimmers to go under also in trying to save him. This may, however, be a personal decision.

One of the main points I'd like the culturalists to remember is that the Jews had more than 100 art festivals while in the concentration camps. The Warsaw ghetto itself became the cultural place to play until the Germans carted the inhabitants off. And while it pleases me to know that we are making cultural strides, it also worries me that we are failing to make political connections. Poems are nice, but as someone points out, "They don't shoot no bullets." "We must," as Marvin X says, "read our own poems." As a group we appear to be vying with each other for the title Brother or Sister Black. That will not get us our freedom. Poor people have always known they are Black, as Rap Brown pointed out, just as poor honkies have always known they are white. These are facts. We need to know where our community is going and to give voice to that.

The Onyx Conference in 1969 showed just how far from the community we had strayed—we didn't even want people there who weren't artists. We are in grave danger of slipping away from our roots. The new hustle, starting with Claude Brown and brought to its finest point by Eldridge Cleaver with his hustle of Huey Newton, seems to be who can get the ear of the enemy for enough money and/or prestige to float on a pink damn cloud to the concentration camps. Everyone who is breathing easy now that Wallace wasn't elected ought to check again—that's gas you're smelling, artist—and it will take more than a Black poem or your Black seed in me to rid this country of it.

11

The Sound of Soul
by Phyll Garland
A Book Review with a Poetic Insert

In the last decade perhaps the most beautiful soul sound, and certainly our choice for the number 1 all-time Black parade, is "Ain't Gonna Let Nobody Turn Me Round" as sung by Martin and the Freedom Riders, challenged only by Stokely and the Militants with their updated version of "Black Power" (the tune that made Nat, Sojourner and the Frederick—sometimes called the Black Rascals—so popular). Perhaps if negro writers (and we use the term advisedly) were more aware of soul sounds and less interested in the sound of soul there would be more clarity over what we are about. All the singers aren't on stage and few of the songs are protected by BMI.

The current run to do something Black, like eating soul food or dancing in the streets, did not create Black music. And we would think Black people, particularly here in America, will be singing those down home blues again very soon since the suburbs have pushed the price of chittlings to 40 cents a pound, greens up to two pounds for a quarter, and you can't find chicken feet at all. As Marvin and Tammi said, "Ain't Nothing Like the Real Thing, Baby." Janis Joplin never sang the blues. And we can only consider it a sign of our own continued self-hatred for her to be thought soul. Xerox Corporation makes an excellent copy but you wouldn't want to dance to it. Sly and the Family Stone said, "Thank You Faletinme Be Mice Elf Agin." Which is very deep because they're talking to us—not them. We've always been ourselves and are always gonna be. And it's amazing to us why negroes create unnecessary conflicts for themselves, as if they don't have enough to do just being oppressed. Black people must become the critics and protectors of Black music. A people need to have something to ourselves.

There are many loose ends that could have been tied together if a little more time had been put in. Nina Simone quotes a poem at the end of her interview. The poem is "Utopia" by Jewel Lattimore, a Chicago poet who we're sure could use the publicity. There is the overlong chapter on Stax and the nonexistent one on Motown. And we never considered sister Aretha, the top soul singer of the last couple of years, a "minister's daughter from Detroit." Something more needed to be said. B. B. King, whom we remember from way back, along with Jimmy Reed, was in our opinion done a disservice by the sly hinting that Albert King, a Stax come lately, is his brother. On a trip of his to New York I visited the show he was appearing in and asked him the "delicate question" Garland didn't wish to pose. Mr. King replied, "Albert King is my brother like you are my sister." Now, that wasn't so hard to find out. I would imagine it's difficult to do a book centering on the now, as Garland—*Ebony*'s New York editor—

has done. Yet there are many points that we feel simply should be brought out.

When a bright teenager began hanging around Berry Gordy, sometime songwriter for Jackie Wilson, wanting to do a tune, Gordy told him to GO GRADUATE. He did, came back and made "Way Over There." And the Motown sound was on its way. Then came Diana Ross and the Supremes, the Temptations and the scores of R&B stars who brought back the sound of Harvey and the Moonglows, the Clovers, Luther Bond and the Emeralds, Hank Ballard and the Midnighters. There could be no book on R&B without Hank Ballard. He was most definitely a forerunner of James Brown, talking about a "thrill upon the hill, let's go, let's go, let's go." And how can you overlook "The way you wiggle when you walk/ Could make a hound dog talk," a direct link to the old blues? Or "Annie Had a Baby, Can't Work No More"? "Work with Me, Annie" was stolen by bug-eyed Teresa Brewer, called "Dance with Me, Henry," and made lots of money for the insignificant others. Speaking of Brewer, she also stole Sam Cooke's song "You Send Me" (somebody really should have). And Dorothy Collins and "Your Hit Parade" was born. We have paid a high price for breaking into white time. I mean, Snooky Lanson? "The Bob Crosby Show" with Joanie Sommers doing "Most of All" "Sincerely." A high price.

And Garland doesn't even mention Harvey Fuqua and the Moonglows. "We Go Together." Harvey teaming with the former queen of soul, Etta James, for "My Heart Cries." (Actually the other side was the hit but that's what I dug since I'm a romantic.) Harvey now works for Motown. Etta James and Richard Berry were among the first duos to click. Mickey and

Sylvia. "Come On, Baby, Let the Good Times Roll" (I've forgotten their names but never the good times). These were forerunners of Marvin and Tammi. And the teaming of the Supremes with the Temptations. If one on one was good then more should be better. And could there be an R&B book without mention of "Earth Angel"? The Penguins were the first group to be named after animals. (We even lead in that.) Or the Moroccos singing "Red Hot and Chili Mack." That's a direct link. Or making sense out of the overdone "Somewhere over the Rainbow," saying, "Pardon My Tears, Pardon My Tears." The Flamingos singing "I Only Have Eyes for You," keeping a family tradition going—the lead singer is Bill Kenny's (of the Ink Spots) son. And where, pray tell, were the Dells? They are the only group to have hits in the 1950s ("Oh, What a Night") and come back intact in the 1960s ("There Is"). That's worthy of mention. The Chicago people were woefully neglected. Curtis Mayfield and the Impressions have been with us from "Gypsy Woman" through "We're a Winner" to "Mighty, Mighty (Spade and Whitey)," and Mayfield has other significance because of Curtom, one of the few Black record companies. His company has been instrumental in bringing younger groups along, most notably the Five Stairsteps.

I think Garland got hung up on the dream of integrating and ignored Black music for integrated music. Stax would certainly be allowed, if I ruled the world, to do what it wants, but a book on soul should deal with soul. The people who have been abused by the insignificant others are being abused by Garland also. Stax, like Motown, started in the Black community, one in a house, one in a theater. It was one man's dream, like Motown. People came in off the streets begging to be recorded, as at Motown. The main difference is that Stax started off white and Motown was Black. Now both appear to be white or extremely integrated. What happened to Motown? It's easy to see an insignificant other just plundering a good thing but Gordy knew what he was trying to do. Why didn't Garland dispel the rumors that the Mafia told Gordy he could have half of Motown or all of nothing? If the rumor is true then we can understand why Temptations puzzle people. We can understand why Florence Ballard would rather quit than fight. Why didn't Garland look into Ed Sullivan's connections with the people who rumor has it took over Motown? If Sullivan doesn't own a part of it now why didn't Garland dispel that rumor? Many important questions could have been cleared up if time had been taken.

Then there is VeeJay. Jimmy Reed recorded for VeeJay. The group that sang "Little Mama, I need your loving but I wasn't true to you" recorded with VeeJay. The Charms, among other groups, were recording with VeeJay. And it just folded— while Atlanta and its subsidiary Epic got fat off our sound. Why? And why did they all of a sudden just close Blue Note and auction everything in the building off? Why is Motown suing T-Neck and the judge (à la the Dred Scott decision) say, not only am I ruling against you but every other judge will too? That sounds a little out of order. Reminds us of the automobile accident the Impressions' band had where two members of the band were killed. Before verification could be made they were doing eulogies of the Impressions. (Could that have been the inspiration behind "Choice of Colors"?) And what happened to Volt? It used to be Stax-Volt (which despite the length of time spent on Stax Garland fails to mention). Redding's brother, probably because he was grief-stricken, accused certain insignificant others of Italian origin of murdering his brother. Of course some do consider it strange that the plane has never been exhumed. And that the radar was exactly three miles off (which put the plane in the lake rather than the airport). To say something about Redding and not mention the Voter Registration project he was doing in Macon is to do his memory a disservice. Not to mention the youngsters he was sending to school is to overlook a great part of his soul. And why was there no chapter or paragraph or even a tiny sentence on Macon? Redding, James Brown and Little Richard, to name the giants, are all from Macon. That town must put out some heavy blues.

The blues didn't start with Dixieland or work songs or Gospel or anything but us. It's really catering to insignificant others to try to delineate our music. The cadences heard in bolero are heard in the jungle, and we all know the Philadelphia Philharmonic hasn't yet appeared in the Congo. (That's what the war is all about!) Dvořák's "Fifth," commonly called "The New World Symphony," is nothing but our music, which Garland mentions. But she fails to mention that the "Fifth" is done but not Mingus' "Freedom Suite." She correctly calls "classical" music formal music but she doesn't state that it is formally Black. All music in the world is Black music. Or was until it was imported and, like good dough in the hands of a bad cook, kneaded and bent until it was too tough for us to handle. The blues haven't been reborn because they have never died. But the blues, like the sermons, like the colloquialisms that mark our speech, have always been just beyond the grasp of the insignificant others. The blues today are sung by Leon Thomas to Pharaoh's horn, are created in drum suites by Milford Graves, were constantly with Coltrane, and Shep sleeps with them probably every night. The blues were never popular as we deal with the mass media. Negroes were ashamed of them, didn't understand them, just as they don't understand Ornette, Don Pullen, the Aylers. And when Jerry Wexler or the unholy Stax finally learns a way to package it we will be off into something else. A people need to have something all to ourselves. The blues will be with us until we are free.

Garland, we think properly, gave the history of Black music over to LeRoi Jones. But the field she opted for herself is still largely untouched. Nobody deals with Aretha, a mother with four children, having to hit the road. They always say, "After she comes home." But nobody ever says what it's like to get on a plane for a three-week tour. The elation of the first couple of audiences, the good feeling of exchange. The running on the high you get for singing good and loud and long, telling the world what's on your mind. Then comes the eighth show on the sixth day. The beginning to smell like the airplane or bus. The if-you-forget-your-toothbrush-in-one-place-you-can't-brush-your-teeth-until-the-second-show. The strangers pulling at you because they love you but you having no love to give back. The singing the same songs night after night, day after day, and if you read the gossip columns the rumors that your husband is only after your fame. The wondering if your children will be glad to see you and maybe the not caring if they are. The scheming to get out of just one show and go just one place where some dodo dupadeduke won't say, "Just sing one song, please." Nobody mentions how it feels to become a freak because you have talent, and how no one gives a damn how you feel but only cares that maybe Aretha Franklin is here, like it's the new cure for cancer. And if you say you're lonely or scared or tired how they probably always say just "Oh, come off it" or "Did you see how they love you—did you see?" Which most likely has nothing to do with you anyway.

And I'm not saying Aretha shouldn't have talent and I'm certainly not saying she should quit singing, but as much as I love to see her I'd vote yes (if someone asked) to have her do three or four concerts a year, stay home or do whatever she wants and make records, because I think it's a shame the way we are killing her. We eat up artists like there's going to be a famine in three minutes when there are in fact an abundance of talents just waiting. Let's put some of the giants away for a while and deal with them as though they have a life to lead. Aretha doesn't have to relive Billie Holiday's life or Dinah Washington's death. But who is there to stop the pattern? She's more important than her music if they must be separated, and they should be separated when she has to pass out before anyone will recognize she needs a rest. And I say this because I need Aretha's music. She is undoubtedly the one person who put everybody on notice. Aretha sings "I Say a Little Prayer" and Dionne doesn't even want to hear it anymore. Aretha sings "Money Won't Change You" but James Brown won't sing "Respect." The advent of Aretha pushed brother Ray Charles back to singing the blues. Made Dionne quit fooling and stick to movie themes. Made Diana Ross get an Afro wig. Pushed Black singers who were negro into their negroness and all others into Blackness. You couldn't jive when Aretha said, "Woman's only human." The Blazers said, "Gotta let a man be a man." When Aretha took the stage the blues were "rediscovered." There has been no musician her very presence hasn't affected. When she told Humphrey to go fly a kite he pressured James Brown. They removed Otis because the combination was too strong. The Impressions said, "We're a Winner." The Black songs started coming from not only the singers on stage but the dancers in the streets. Aretha was a riot. Was the leader. If she had said, come, let's do it, it would have been done. And this was not unnoted by insignificant others. It should also be noted by us.

Two years ago John A. Williams published a novel called *The Man Who Cried I Am*, which contained two significant parts and one significant line. The line is "How should we do it [kill Max]? They can't all die of overdoses." And this means a lot to us when we realize the number of musicians we've lost in Europe to overdoses. But it also has meaning for us when we realize that John Coltrane died. Musicians have always been in the forefront of the Black experience. Long before the advent of the X seekers musicians were naming themselves with African names (Ahmad Jamal, Yusef Lateef). Music has been the voice of the Black experience most especially here in America. And an important voice was stilled. Many important voices one way or the other have been stilled.

Coltrane was easily understood if you understand Black people. Insignificant others recorded him and slowed the tapes to a crawl—they still couldn't chart how many notes he would hit with one breath. And I say John Coltrane played the blues because the blues are what we sing to ourselves. You can't hum *Ascension* all alone but a group of you can create your own salvation. That's all he's saying. And it comes through loud and clear. And if it's disturbing that's because the truth generally is. Coltrane isn't another kind of soul—he is soul. How can you separate food from thought? Sex from salvation? The mind from the body? They are all one. And John Coltrane brought them together. Garland continuously delineates, tries to say this is one kind of soul and that another or that isn't true soul. It's a whole bunch of foolishness because our music is Black music. Call it work song, Gospel, spiritual, jazz, R&B, Liberation music. It is Black music created by Black people to let other Black people know what we feel, what we are thinking. All the rest is about how white people react to our expression.

The last chapter, "The Sound of Soul To Come," is particularly weak because Garland ignores Liberation Music and opts for universal (whatever that means) music. She ignores Sun Ra's Space Music, which children really love. And sort of overlooks the crying need for the groups to come back. The youngsters are still harmonizing on the corners and our music will still be determined by our condition.

I'm sure *The Sound of Soul* will be read, as all books by Black people should be read. We've spoken recently a lot about the need for us to criticize ourselves, and this can only be done if we know what we are criticizing. We find Garland to be a little off base and hope that the book on R&B will still be done. Just as Cruse has accused the intellectuals of the 1930s of holding back Black people, we feel that Garland is saying, if we just had a few more white people singing the blues all would be right with the world. I'm sure if that were the case no singer would be without an insignificant other in his group; but that is not the case. The music was born because of our treatment by others, and the more they steal it the more they prove how little regard they have for us. The more we support their thievery the more we show what little regard we have for ourselves. Sly says, "Thank you for the party but I could never stay." That's a soul sound.

12

Convalescence—
Compared to What?*

In the beginning was the rape
And the rape was labored
And the embryo was cleaved
From the womb
And the painful journey
Across the ice
Began

Perhaps the biggest question in the modern world is the definition of a genus—huemanity. And the white man is no hueman. It's sheer stupidity for America to be in Vietnam—win, lose (which we are all doing) or draw—because only David can win when Goliath accepts the challenge. It's like men playing women in basketball; after all, they are men. But it's questionable whether the honkie has a mind. He is an illogical

*Reprinted from Mel Watkins, ed., *Black Review No. 1* (New York: William Morrow & Company, Inc., 1971), pp. 117–128.

animal. Animals in their natural environment have friends and enemies; live in a circumscribed place; travel by one or two methods—if they swim and fly they don't run; create little animal communities; live and die. The honkie has defied all this and forced us to defy it. Honkies can eat anything with impunity—witness pigs, snakes, snails, each other, their children. They have made one form of cannibalism a love act, which just has to be a comment on their ability to understand word meanings. It's difficult to define a honkie. We all remember zombie movies, the big, black, dead things under the bidding of the evil scientist moving around in the jungles of Haiti or some island (it is always an island) hating themselves for what they are but powerless to put their bodies down to rest. Generally an ugly honkie woman, which of course is redundant, comes along who is taken to the zombie hideout and Wild Bill Hickok in safari hat and bush jacket follows her, finds the secret of how to kill the zombie (how can you kill something already dead?) and runs back to civilization. Now, the zombie is a drink. You order it when you really want to tie one on. Wouldn't it be marvelous if we could run to the neighborhood bar and say, "Give me a double honkie on the rocks, Sam," and have the bartender pour something into a mixer and shake it up? Something needs to shake up the honkie. And a lot of negroes too.

When someone looks at the Watusi and thinks that's the totality of our contribution to the world we realize we are in trouble. Not that we are against the Watusi—personally we favor ass shaking under even the most mundane circumstances—but the Watusi is a religious dance performed ritualistically by the high priest and priestess of soul. And just as the Roeman Catholic Church will not allow the unanointed to partake of the blood and body we should set up the same standards. A people cannot accept as a sign of health nonbelievers practicing their service. This is the crisis Harold Cruse speaks of and a gross abdication of our duties. Those of us who have studied and feel compelled to speak on issues should speak the whole, not the hole, truth.

O ye of little faith and less knowledge, let us venture forth into the night, you with your Fanon and I with my twat in the hand.

In the beginning was the man and the man was Black and the Black man was a good man. In the beginning was the woman and the woman was Black and the Black woman was a good woman. They had children, planted, reaped, lived, died. Maybe drank a little bali hai, were late on the rent, probably had some kind of car, educated the children—were men and women. Black and proud, "Say it loud." They meditated on the sun and planets, created a number system; meditated on the earth and figured if they could get a lever they could tilt it. Figured out how deep was the ocean, how to mummify people, that Anacin was the best thing for a headache ("Butter? Butter? Bitch, you know we ain't had no butter since yo' daddy left us!"); charted the seasons, figured out astrology— the Sphinx is Virgo and Leo no matter what honkies say about their not going together; lived in peace, blended with the earth, had children . . . lived . . . died . . . continued. Then, Buffy tells us, a buzzard came along, sucked the eggs and changed the story.

Man can't separate the mind from the body, sex from salvation, food from thought—the supermasculine menial does not exist. There is no such thing as the omnipotent administrator—what is a superbrain? The pope is the queen of the earth. We are a complete people ready and able to deal completely with tomorrow. We are lovers and children of lovers. We are warriors and children of warriors. But we don't send children to war. No crusades to hold back the Muslim tides. No crusades to hold back the union forces. The child's place is in the home though we, as children, seized the initiative here in America. The Black family in America has never been declining. When the honkie speaks of the deteriorating negro family he's wrong on all counts. We are not negro. We are not deteriorating; our structure has always been the extended family—many generations living under one roof. Our structure has generally been matrilineal, though seldom matriarchal. What does the Black woman have to be powerful with/over? If ever you see a powerful nonwhite know that you are seeing a powerful negro. Then ask yourself . . . what's a negro?

The honkie is the best mythologist in creation. He's had practice because his whole wrap is to protect himself from his environment. After generations of lying he does it by second nature. And his first nature is so unnatural that we aren't surprised. "Fish gotta swim, birds gotta fly"—honkies gotta lie. I'm telling you why.

Black people are calypso singers; call us signifiers. Carolyn Rodgers and Larry Neal say Shine swam on. Rap Brown played ball in Central Park and Shine swims on. The ultrafeminine and the supermasculine menial—no good. I can't use it. "Try to make it real compared to what?" It ain't real—we can't even pronounce the words they and some of us are using to describe us. "What you mean, castrated? Oh, yeah. Well, I been that." Bullshit. Try to make it real. "My mother did what? Man, you better watch yo' mouth." Goddammit! Compared to what? (Un)Les McCann can't. Honk on, Pharaoh— that's for real. Compared to anything. Sock it toward me now.

Oh, we're so angry with you, America; ask Buck White. "I gotta live the life I sing about in my songs." Marion Williams and the sweet Inspirations. Electric Mud and the Dells saying, "Oh, What a Night." They were in Washington, D.C., April 5, 1968. Souls on ice, but "To be black," Don Lee says, "is to be very hot." The age of the cool went out when honkies learned to say "dig" with their eyelids lowered. All we got left is motherfucker. F(or) u(se) (of) c(arnal) k(nowledge). They can never get that together.

A slave is defined by his duties. And none of us is free. The guns should be toward the West. Nix(on) him. Spear o Agnew. Won't we ever learn? Elijah says we are what we eat. The time is overdue to close the doors. It's overdue time to say which nigger is our nigger. That's all that matters. Support our own. Look out for our own. Yeah, turn the system Black. Don't be afraid of Black folks. Don't be afraid of yo' mama. She ain't the one who put you in this trick. But she's the one who'll get you out. And we aren't speaking genetically. We are all fathers and mothers. Mother is the earth, father the tool to fertilize her. We/they go hand in hand.

In the beginning of the honkie the word was God and the word was white. The paper was white so the word couldn't be seen but only felt. Take away the damned and you get evil. DEVIL. Take away the damned. Some were taught the devil is Black. We're taught he's red. By any definition of devil *she's* got to be white. Only the devil could cause so much heartache.

> *Roaches are red,*
> *The sky is now blue.*
> *If you ain't gone by night*
> *We're gonna lynch you.*

The original white poem. And some Black folks think whites can write.

It's a cinch we didn't need to read their shit. Why would Dostoevski need to write *Crime and Punishment*? For the same reason Shakespeare needed to write—not to pass information but to pass time. There are no great honkies—anything that excludes our existence is not great. Anything that sheds a negative light on us isn't great. Faulkner was a racist. Not even a great racist—just a Southerner who had no useful skills. Didn't even write well. The best you can say for an imitator is that he copies well. For true knowledge we must go to the source. Camus and Sartre dig on existentialism because it relieves them of guilt and allows them to colonize Fanon and other Blacks under the name of philosophy. Without existentialism they would just be honkie colonizers. Existentialism became popular after World War II when it was obvious that the world had changed colors. German collaborators, honkies who refused to speak out for the Jews (though speaking out wasn't nearly ever going to be enough), Jews who refused to speak out for the Jews all turned to a philosophy that would allow them to be responsible for the world in general and nothing in particular.

Black groups digging on white philosophies ought to consider the source. Know who's playing the music before you dance. Someone's poem said, before you go to the water know who invented the beach. Brothers digging on class struggle ought to go check out African communalism. That warmed-over communism which allowed Russia to become a modern, industrialized, capitalistic state isn't for or about us. It's just an old way of colonizing us. "Pussycat, pussycat, I love you," and some of us are falling for that. Some of us seem ready to accept the essence without performing the act. Can't be done. If they had such great minds how come their country is falling apart? James Earl Jones notwithstanding—America is the great white hope. And she's building a country home in South Africa where the weather is cooler. And people talk about not accepting dirty money. All money is dirty. Dirty, lazy, filthy lucre. Money don't work. Money don't sing. Money don't dance. Can't keep you warm. Money is a leech. And we drain ourselves to obtain her. Have fallen in love with her. Will put no other god before her. Try to make it real. Compare the gold in Fort Knox in bars to the way our bodies used to shine with ornaments. Yeah, we are the body and the blood. We are the salvation. But we too need a transplant. Vital organs cannot survive in a decaying body.

Melvin Tolson says a civilization is in decline when we (they) begin to judge it. The Visigoths didn't destroy Rome; they just got there in time to claim historical credit. Who will get credit for America? That's what the struggle is all about. Some say niggers twisting will cause the decline; some say that will save it. But this old body is dying all on its own and we must decide whether we are going to take credit for giving it its last kick or for being the last group to try to save it. If I saw a sick old white lady on her way to a convalescence home I'd kick her in the ass and rob her of the twenty cents her dollar is worth—and be proud that I'd done it. No sense trying to save sick old white ladies. Try to make it real. Young white people will even kick an old, sick white lady on her way to the convalescence home because they want to take credit for being the cause of the fall. Compared to what?

There was peace after the fall of Rome. Roads fell into disuse. Weeds covered them. The aqueducts dried up. The soldiers turned their swords into plows. There was no central authority. There was no standard. Southern Italians were glad Rome was dead. They went back to drinking wine, having babies, educating children. Living. Dying. They spoke Italian. Roman mercenaries in France stopped collecting taxes. Learned French. Started drinking wine. People crossed the Channel. People moved into the Black Forest. The Visigoths moved on. And all was quiet on the Western front. Then some bright dude decided to write a book in vernacular. And in Italy the Renaissance was born. What had been a period of peace was deemed the Dark Ages. What had been a democratic period was called anarchy. The rich got poor and the poor got happy. And happy got his ass kicked for coming to the neighborhood. You see it now. The Black Renaissance is born. Joy to the world.

LeRoi Jones moved uptown. Wrote plays in the vernacular and a people found our voice. The idea and the essence had finally formed the man. But the separation was never mind from body. It was body from function. The mind always knew what needed to be done. It wasn't a stupid nigger that fucked with Nat Turner. It wasn't a stupid nigger that killed Malcolm. It's too easy to say how dumb we are. All we got is rhythm. Giving the twist to the world will not change that world. And it's far from what we have given. Our bodies—in fields, in offices, in laboratories, in beds, in Harlem, Watts, Accra, LondonParisRomeCincinnati—laid to sacrifice will not change the world.

Young whites deciding to get hold of our rhythm and fuck will not change the world. It's a physical change and chemical warfare is needed. We need to put a hurting on the world. And all our intellecting about changes are gonna come, "Yeah, baby, let me . . . let me, baby," will not change the world. Swapping sweat or spit, even wallowing in the shit together, may at best allow some honkies to try to sing the blues— which we would all do all the time if we knew what we don't want to know. The blues, Mae Jackson tells me, ain't what they used to be—done gone and got Americanized. And we know that's a shame. Come telling Mae to stay in school. Ain't that a bitch? Her what never went to no institution at all, telling her to stay in school, and the most tragic thing that happens in America is that there is an accident on the Pneu Jersey Turn-pike.

Ever think about waking up facing Lieutenant William L. Calley? Well, we'd better be thinking about it because they brought that cracker home as punishment for being so stupid. They're gonna force that cracker to listen to the Temps saying, "I Can't Get Next to You." And Calley'll be nodding, "You said it, nigger." It's all there in the big black book called *Whatever Happened to Cracker America?* Ruth ain't no Baby and her daddy would rather you not eat it—some things are just bad form. Squash it together and you get bath. Squash it at all and you'll need one. The biggest lie in creation is, you shouldn't try to keep up with the Joneses. LeRoi, Sandy, their mama and daddy are something to aspire to. The cracker will take everything away from you if you don't be careful. Woodie King is pure mahogany. The single most important theatrical event aside from Watts, Newark and Detroit was his production of *Slave Ship*.

It's so easy to deal off the top. Sly says dance to the music. A compelling call to do the freedom walk. But we're still dealing on the catch-up. Crackers have taken our blues and gone. Langston saw it a long time ago. Taken our blues and put long hair on it. Electrified it. They're gonna go in for electric dicks next. Gonna put them at thirty-three rpms. All they gotta remember to do is turn the heart up to "Excitement," turn the brain to "Profanity." Ain't gonna be much running off natural rhythm. Just like Anton Dvořák took our spirituals and put them in symphony, they're putting our blues in symphony hall. Yes, they is—saw the sign up in Newark. You see it now—the Grateful Dead—living proof. Of the Grateful Dead. Give a cracker a break—in the neck. And pan-broil it with Black eyes of sympathetic niggers; should make a good meal for the conjure man. Try to make it real.

Niggers got a natural twist, especially when we hanging from a wild oak tree. Ever hear a real Black person extol the virtues of nature? If you do you'll know it's a negro talking. Nature ain't natural here. Growing big Black niggers from trees. Running down country roads. Trying to make it to the swamp. Niggers love cement. And there's a reason. If little old men with eight heads came from Mars New Yorkers would send Lindsay down to see what they want. Absolute faith in the new politics. Rah-rah, Lindsay. Anyone Nixon hates has got to be good. Apollo got nothing to do with space; ask any Black kid from 110th Street to 155th. The Apollo now features Dionne Warwick with her love show.

Determined weakness will triumph over the most brilliant, strong-willed purist. There's something about weakness that always seems to make it prevail. Call it arrogance. Most strong people think they can reason with the weak—call it *noblesse oblige*. Most strong people think the least they can do is bend a little—call it illogic. Most strong people have no real knowledge of how their strength is used against them. The cracker is a weak being. So is the negro. Both sap the energies of Black people. The best anyone can do when dealing with weakness is to get as far away from it as possible. Learn to steel yourself against terms like *evil* (the weak always tell the strong it's evil to be strong). Learn to say, "That's true," when the weak say, "You don't love me." But mostly learn to deal with other strong people.

Jesus on the cross knew the weak have a league, a Thursday Night Weak Club, where they devise new and exciting ways to trap the strong. And we accept it. The weak have made *selfish* the worst possible name to be called. Couple *selfish* with *nigger* and there is no lower animal under Allah's wig. The weak have made cleanliness next to godliness and God a green faggot who fucked nature and set the world in motion. The weak have made weakness a religion. The weaker you are the more you have a right to drain the strong. The weak worship weakness. They thrive on it. They love it. Next to death weakness is all they respect. You are what you love. The weak have weakness built into the system. There's no way to beat the system. There's no way to change the system. Only you change. Only you begin to think it's not so bad. Only you become weaker because the weak have made strength mean ineffectualness, have made it mean exile, have made it mean jail, have made it mean loneliness, misunderstanding, negativeness. The only good strong person is a dead strong person and weakness kills us dead. God is dead. Jesus is dead. Allah is dead. King is dead. Malcolm is dead. Coltrane is dead. Dolphy is dead. Evers is dead. And we write poems to them. Sing songs to them. Pour gin libations to them. Miss them. Quote them. While we don't give a kind word to Mingus, the Aylers, Aretha, Ameer Baraka, Adam Powell.

Like we don't know what mess James Brown is going through. Like we don't know how A. D. King died. Like we don't like each other because we look alike. And like the book says, "Nothing black but a Cadillac." Niggers ought to be buried in Cadillacs because that's what's killing us. GM, Brooks Brothers, Lord & Taylor, VWs, Carrier air-conditioning, Philco "new color" TV with the works in a box—does your box work when you want it to? Get a Philco for your box. We've got to quit worshipping weakness. We've got to quit understanding it. We've got to quit accepting it. We've got to be strong. In a world where the weak function the strong must not function. We need togetherness to decide what we will do when they are gone. And we must help them go.

We need to devise a way to put Black teenage girls to work on the trains. Old Black people traveling on the East Coast take their lives in their hands. Are unable to make changes of trains. In the South and West buses are full of our elderly people. Why can't young ladies ride the trains/buses for the express purpose of helping these people? Why don't bus companies provide space for them and the state pay them to travel with our elderly citizens? It would help make the elders more comfortable. Why don't we have our young men with some kind of machine cleaning the subways? That could be a twenty-four-hour thing. The subs are filthy and unsafe. Why not put our youngsters to work for a four-hour shift with the state paying them to do it? New Yorkers will suffocate before the bomb drops. Why don't we close the streets, plant grass and leave only the avenues for traffic? We need to outlaw cars in the cities. Transportation could then be by bus with alternate avenues running up and down. You would never be more than a block from where you're going. Traffic jams would be no more. The air would be cleaner. Our children would have someplace to play. We need in all the big cities to have daily garbage and trash collection. We need to make the buildings we live in safe and habitable. We need to put our women to work sewing curtains, making quilts, cooking, keeping house. Our men need to repair, renovate, renew the neighborhood. We need to abolish by declaration private everything: housing, property, companies, clubs, you name it—it should go. Everything should be in trust for the people. And what the people don't keep up we don't need. We need to spend as much money feeding people as we do starving them. We need to spend as much time devising ways for people to live as we do for killing people.

Crackers invented Napalm, which is so hot it can melt your skin, but they can't deal with a decent ice defroster when it snows. We need a shift in priorities. And only we can bring it if it can be brought. And not by taking on their weakness but by building our own nation. And if a nation can't be built here, by preparing to live without the nonessentials, which we've never had and are better off without. We may in fact miss the refrigerator, but compare that to air pollution. It all goes together. The refrigerator you need today is keeping Nixon in office. Will put Agnew in office. This is the fall of America. The Kennedys were the Gracchus brothers; America is Rome. The end is the beginning. We must think small, organize small, do little things to chip away at this monolith, and Elvis Presley ain't gonna make it easier. We must recognize that most countries could fit into any American state. America is an unnatural city state run by unnatural people. We must huddle together in our similarities, develop our language, develop our life style, quit trying to impress the cracker and try to be happy. We must bring on the Dark Ages when Dark people rule. When, better still, there is no rule—only Black people living, giving birth, rearing children, dying, continuing the life pattern in a natural way. We need new definitions and the twist ain't got nothing to do with it. It's time to work to pull down the walls—yeah, it's time for Atlas to shrug so that Atlas Junior can live.

13

Gemini—a Prolonged Autobiographical Statement on Why

In the beginning, I'm told, earth was one with the sun. One bright hot ball in the middle of space whirling, whirling, whizzing around God like a smooth Bob Gibson strike. Then for reasons yet unexplained—maybe earth got bored with hot space balls—it pulled away and flew, as Mercury and Mars had done, from the mother sun. Since it was so young and inexperienced it didn't want to leave by itself so it coaxed Venus to come also. It settled in an all-white neighborhood between its brother and sister. Now, there isn't much a terribly hot planet can do all alone in space (being Christian and knowing incest is unacceptable) so earth cooled down. After a few thousand years it wanted something to play with so it invented man. I'm told on good authority by the Holy Ghost Company, Inc., one of our oldest census bureaus, that man was formed of many materials in different places at the same time. There were, however, three basic molds. The soil out of which the African was molded worked out to be the best. The standard was set by him. That's why mankind is called hueman beings.

The Oriental had a majestic manner and felt little or no need to involve himself with the rest of the earth. He set up trading with Africa and created an elitist mentality which wasn't necessarily imperialistic so God gave him gunpowder and explosives to play with. The European was always cold. All the time. He developed a gutsy quality which would help him survive almost no matter what. He learned to eat anything, go anyplace, and being basically mischievous how to destroy everything he didn't understand. God got a little bored with the antics of the Europeans and in the very first mass punishment of man sent the Ice Age to Europe.

The curse of the Nordics trailed them all the way to the northern tip of Africa. The first thing the Europeans wanted to know was, how come the Africans didn't have no ice age? And a very wise African guru who just happened to be visiting in the city at that time said, "Son, look at the Sahara Desert. We had a city there called York which was great and held many different peoples. It was a pleasant city run by a friendly mayor who could not quite get along with either the president of the republic or the governor of the province. The friendly mayor wanted more parks, more space, but trading was plentiful so more and more businesses went up and more asphalt was laid and more people from the surrounding countryside had to come in to work. Eventually they choked the land to death and the desert came in. This was a great tragedy and I am here to tell the Europeans of our loss."

The Nordics were so impressed and excited they decided to go to Africa to study and learn so that they would not make the same mistake. "May we go back with you to study and learn? Then we can tell our people." "But there are only two of you," the African replied, "and one is female." "Yeah, that's the only way we could escape the ice. They let one male and one female of each species on the great sled." "But how will you tell your people of what happened?" "Oh, don't worry," said the Nordic. "We have a thing called writing." "Writing? I have never heard of this." "Oh, it's a thing we learned when we lived in caves. We're a nocturnal people, you know, so during the daytime we began drawing on walls. Then we moved on to creating an alphabet. Now we write novels, poems and plays, not to mention short stories and legal documents, and we've invented a thing we call money. Fantastic! The best possible system for man to live under."

"Well, young man . . . and young lady . . . despite our being an oral people we have a method we developed during your Ice Age called hieroglyphics. It consists of—"

"Nothing like our writing. With our writing we tell our truth."

"But young man, you didn't let me tell about our hieroglyphics. Now, as I was saying—"

"Old man, it's nothing like what we have. We tell our truth. We are setting world standards of beauty, politics, love, literature. . . . We will control everything with our writing."

"Young man, you are rude and boorish. This 'writing' of yours will get you nowhere. If you would mind your manners and respect your elders you would go farther."

"You wait and see, Sage, we're going to change the world. You may think you have something like it but you don't. We're telling our truth. You tell yours. Our writing will get us over.

Just you wait and see." And unfortunately it did. And for a long time. Which is primarily why I became poetically inclined.

People always write you and ask how you got to be or how you became a writer or a poet. And sometimes I'm in a really good mood and I say, "Because I have no other skills," and they always, I mean always, laugh and say, "Yes, but how?" And that's the truth—I can't do anything else that well. If I could have held a job down in Walgreen's I probably would have and would have fantasied myself into believing that selling that perfume somehow made the world a more perfect place. I was always that kind of salesman. It's like starting out in your life with the idea that whatever you do is so crucial to the world. . . .

Emperors, heads of state, beautiful, chic ladies all came to Walgreen's on Linn Street to have me sell them the correct perfume. Then when they moved me to the front cash register I was a princess from a foreign country, not Europe or Asia but somewhere deep in the Afro-Carib or something, and my parents had sent me to learn about this America. It was at times a bit dull, at times very hard work but the test was, could I get through it? Could I, a being from almost another planet, communicate that it is all in good hands, I am here checking you out of this store? And I would laugh and talk, giving, as I thought a princess should, a little sun on an otherwise dreary day. And sometimes when I was tired or a bit lonely or afraid I would be tempted to turn to my bagger and say, "This isn't really me. . . . I'm a princess and my parents are testing me by having me in this city in this store and one day you will all know who I really am." But that's like getting the big end of the wishbone and then telling the wish. The real task was not the work but my identity. Could I maintain my silence? Could I alone keep myself intact? And I tried to perform to the utmost.

I did have a friend and people would say, what you are doing for Claudia is wonderful, and I wanted to say, but she's doing me a favor, because I didn't have many friends and have always been truly grateful for those few I have. And she went on to finish high school and my mother would say, you have really helped Claudia, and I would say, without her I would have gone insane. Which is more or less true because people or at least I cannot live without someone. That's one reason my son means so much to me. I finally have someone who knows me and isn't awed or afraid and I can love him completely and not feel that I'll be abused or misunderstood. Most people go through life never daring to say just one time, "Fuck it, I'm going to love you." And I can really understand why because the minute you do you open yourself. And sometimes you say, that's all right; if he takes advantage of me, so what? At nineteen that's cool. Or maybe at twenty-three. But around twenty-five or thirty you say, maybe men and women aren't meant to live with each other. Maybe they have a different sort of thing going where they come together during mating season and produce beautiful, useless animals who then go on to love, you hope, each of you . . . but living together there are too many games to be gotten through. And the intimacies still seem to be left to his best friend and yours. I mean, the incidence is too high to be ignored. The guy and girl are inseparable until they get married; then he's out with his friends and she's out with hers or home alone, and there is no reason to think he's lying when he says he loves her. . . . She's just not the other half of him. He is awed and frightened by her screams and she is awed and cautious about his tears. Which is not to say there is not one man or one woman who can't make a marriage—i.e., home—run correctly and maybe even happily but it happens so infrequently. Or as a relative of mine in one of her profound moments said, "Marriage is give and take—you give and he takes." And I laughed because it was the kind of hip thing I was laughing about then. And even if that's true, so what? Somebody has to give and somebody has to take. But people set roles out, though the better you play them the more useless you are to that person. People move in conflicts. To me sex is an essence. . . . It's a basic of hueman relationships. And sex is conflict; it could be considered a miniwar between two people. Really. I think so. So I began to consider being a writer.

I used to spend time in Indianapolis when I was younger. It was referred to by us as Naptown. And saying I had spent the weekend in Nap always made me feel I had done something. Then too my aunt, unlike my mother, was socially aggressive so we always knew the really in people . . . and even if I didn't no one knew that I didn't. So I could continue my fantasy about who I was and what my purpose was without going through the hard fact that somebody would know. What I regret most about modern children is that their imagination is stifled so early. City living is barely fit for adults and surely must be considered unfit for children. Where do the dreams be born? Where do you go for privacy? If a city child walks the streets alone what mother in her right mind wouldn't be worried? Not that the crackers in the suburbs or on farms are any different. Theirs is the ugliness that makes our cities unsafe and I would imagine it affects them.

When I was little we had an outdoor toilet which I only vaguely remember, but I do know sitting on the john was hip. I clearly remember that. Sitting and daydreaming about all the important heads of states and movie stars waiting for me, an essentially poor sort of muddy-colored colored girl, to emerge. I could hold the whole world up if I so chose. But with power comes responsibility and my grandmother, who was one of the world's greatest women, taught me my responsibility to my people. I would emerge to give Cab Calloway his turn or mostly Nellie Lutcher or Billy Eckstine, since they were the big favorites. Sometimes after we moved to a better apartment it would be Jimmy Edwards. I vividly remember *Home of the Brave.* Mommy got my sister and me all dressed up to go to town. I got sick on the bus to my mortification and everyone else's discomfort and had to be recleaned. I had a blue teddy-bear coat, a white muff and three plaits—and I was going with my mama and my sister to the white show downtown. We made it. Mostly the movie is foggy but Jimmy Edwards was a soldier coming home from war and he was beaten up. Mommy told Gary or maybe no one at all, "It's a damn shame." And Gary was crying. I remember Jimmy Edwards staggering probably home and I was in a rage. Then we left and had dinner at Mr. Patton's barbecue place on Ninth Street and came home. It was a fabulous muff and I loved the coat. But the rage stayed with me.

And when I was a little girl with mostly big eyes and high-top shoes people would come up to me and say, "Nikki, can you read?" And I'd proudly answer, "No. But Gary can." And they'd say, "Nikki, can you sing?" And I'd let my chest swell a bit and say, "No. But Gary can." Then they, I would imagine laughing at me though I didn't know it then, would say, "Nikki, can you play the piano?" And I would lean back on my heels and smile as if I had this one clinched too and say, "No. But Gary can!" And it really knocked me out that I knew someone who could do all those marvelous things they asked about. And sometimes someone would think to ask, "Well, what do you do?" And I'd say, "I'm Gary's sister!" If I hadn't been taught to be respectful to older people I would have added, "Dummy." I was Gary's sister and that really was quite enough. And I don't think I could have survived without that as a buffer. I watched the world through her eyes and saw what she saw and what I saw. And the family would say, "You're a fool about Gary. She's gonna use you." And I never understood that to be bad. I mean, if you must be used it should be by someone you love. So I would always say, "Just to keep the record straight, if I had eight pints of blood and Gary needed ten I'd take two from you and give her my eight." It seemed perfectly logical to feel that way about your sister. Mommy always told us we only had each other. Maybe that's why Gary's been married five times and I none.

I don't think I idolize her as much anymore. As a matter of fact our relationship hit a mature high when in the fifth grade she beat me up for wearing her clothes. I decided then and there we would shift to a sounder base. I would cease wearing her clothes and she would cease beating me up. I was badder than she anyway so clearly I let her win. That level of dishonesty can destroy any feeling so we drew a line in the room defining her half and my half with the vow never to cross it and settled down to be friends. I still dig Gary more than anyone outside Tommy. And recognizing that love requires careful nourishing we keep a safe distance, coming together to share happiness and sadness but never making judgments or giving advice to each other. "You ain't got no sense when it comes to her," even my grandmother used to say, but of course I did—I decided to feel about her and her life as she wanted me to and to do what she wanted me to do, and she gave this to me. What else are your people for?

We had to deal with Mommy's reaction to her own value system. Gary and I had a tendency to close her out. I think fathers are generally a little jealous of their children and mothers skirt a twilight zone between loyalties. But mothers give a lot to their little ones and are quite naturally closer to them than fathers. Mothers say, "If you don't buy the kids new skates for Christmas I'm going to find someone who will," and things like that to threaten fathers and then mothers turn around and find out that the very people they have gone down behind are closing them out. It must be a tremendous blow. That's why I don't believe in altruism. Nobody in his right mind would do anything unless it was better for him because the minute you try to go against your feelings to help someone you get shitted on. So I would slyly hint from behind one of those history books I used to be hung up with that it's best to do what is best for you and then you never have to expect something back because the something was inherent in your action. And Mommy would look at me and say, "I have given my life for you children," and I used to take it to heart and pledge my life to her until I understood that what she really meant wasn't what she was saying and what she really wanted us to do was to produce great, beautiful grandchildren and leave her the hell alone with our father. That's why it's dangerous for Black people to take English too seriously.

My fantasy life went on with a different personality emerging all the time. But I was always grand in my cowboy boots or grinding in Johnetta's rathskeller at parties. I was always just a little secreted away with the thought that one day I would be understood. This is probably a main reason any artist emerges.

I've been slow to make evaluations. My life style was that I read about fifty books a year and absorbed them and then related them to another level. And I tried to read Black books. I remember reading "Annie Allen" and being pleased for the first time with poetry. But I didn't pursue it. I went on to Pound and Eliot because it filled an empty spot in my head while not upsetting my emotions. I felt at some point I would probably have a nervous breakdown; then I recognized how aesthetically unattractive that was so I divorced reason from feeling and moved on. Mommy asked me to read three books, one of which was *Black Boy*. I took it to school in the seventh grade and the nun called it trash. Which was beautiful. Because I could intellectually isolate all white nuns as being dumb and unworthy of my attention. I fell madly in love with a Black one, however, which probably just testifies to my hopeless hopefulness that there is some validity in everything. And I was really turned on to Greek and Roman mythology— the gods and goddesses towering over everybody in their exclusive god club. And I would think if ever I was a goddess I would take it all seriously, and not eat pomegranates or fall in love with anyone other than a god and I would bear proud sons and train them correctly. I would learn from mistakes and if not eradicate them completely then at least create new ones. It seemed only reasonable.

And one thing I recognized quite some time ago is that no one makes a mistake. Yeah, you can show someone 1^1 plus 1^1 equals 2^2 or something like that but even scientists are reluctant to assert the earth was never flat or the molecule was never the smallest particle of matter. And I think we are in error when we begin with the assumption that we can show someone—anyone—the error of his ways. It's like with parents. No matter what a fuck-up goof-off you turn out to be they only have two reactions available to them: (1) there is nothing wrong with you or (2) they did their best. Mothers of murderers, rapists, thieves, psychopaths, corporate executives, presidents all say the same things. Tell your parents you're sick. They will finally, if you really beat them down, make one of those two statements.

Same with white folks. We started out thinking if we showed them how hurt, sick, misused or abused we were they would change their ways. Their response has been (1) there is nothing wrong with colored folks or (2) they did the best they could. It's only natural. And what we have to decide is whether we want to make them face the truth as we see it or to control our lives for our own goals. Those are two different objectives. One is for losing; one is for winning. Because it really doesn't matter, if you want to control, whether they understand or not—parents or white folks. It only matters that their behavior changes. And the way some of us conduct our lives we'd be at a loss if anything happened to our antagonists, you know? If all the white folks disappeared tomorrow a whole lot of us would be lost—but it shouldn't matter.

Same with kids who act out their parents' sickness. So you're twenty-five years old and were too severely toilet-trained. It's already happened. And you can run it down from every angle but it's your life and even if your mother says she's sorry you have to live with reality. Or worse, if they die you have no antagonist. You/we all must learn to live for ourselves.

In a rational system this means living for our people. But with the realization that we are our people. I'm always amazed at the Julia–Diana Ross discussion as if we would somehow become "free" if they somehow became "Black." So we spend a lot of time knocking people who perhaps don't go along with us as opposed to helping people who do. It's like the plain Jane who just has to have the football hero—not that she can't get who she wants, you understand, but why climb over five guys who want you for one who doesn't? Or negroes who need crackers to say, "Well done." Same syndrome. Why not try to deal with the folks who want to deal with you? It's self-hatred always to be chasing after what never was.

I never wanted to be Ralph Ellison. The piece James MacPherson did on him in the *Atlantic* was pitiful. He's not worth it—and when we have to give up an issue of a vital magazine to explain the one book he wrote it shows where we're coming from. Especially when there has been no issue on John Killens (four books) or John Williams (eight books) or James Baldwin (nine books) or any of the people who are continuing to write and take chances. The only single book worth that much space is the Bible and it's an anthology. In so many subtle ways we do ourselves an injustice. If Ellison's book was that great he should have won a Pulitzer Prize (Harper Lee did). If he wrote all that well he should keep writing. But he didn't. Which is the main basis on which I judge his work. As a novel *Invisible Man* is good; as a writer Ellison is so much hot air, because he hasn't had the guts to go on writing. But he can put us down and say we are not writers. Us—the Rodgerses, Marshalls, Reeds and others who are persistently exposing our insides and trying to create a reality. And I don't think all the writing out there is so dynamite. But I respect to the utmost the chances taken. Any one of us could pick our best work, present it and lay back. But we didn't/have not. We've gone on to write bad poems as well as other good ones, to write copout novels as well as stirring pieces—we've gone on to create a literature, to be hueman in our failures as well as glorious in our successes. But mostly we've continued. And I think that's what counts.

For whatever reason—one I hope to understand before I evolve into a turtle (my next form)—Black folks always seem to think there is one answer for one problem. Not only is that ludicrous to me but generally the right question hasn't been asked in the first place. Mankind is a morass of mistakes. His intellect has always outstripped his emotional growth. For some reason people still seem to find it easier to hate than to love, easier to kill than to help live, easier to control and abort than to allow and nourish.

And I believe the white man is a natural man, that his anxieties and fears are the anxieties and fears of natural men, because I watch us going into the same syndromes. I'm forced now to admit the white woman is obviously a natural and perhaps superior piece cause I have watched and am watching our men go ape shit to get it. Panthers coalescing and Communists communing are still talking about getting a white piece. And if it costs them their lives as it has been costing our men their cultural, emotional, spiritual and physical lives, that appears to be a small enough price to pay for it. Black men are having a prolonged love affair with white men. Check out James Baldwin's books—that's what he's talking about. Because Black men refuse to do in a concerted way what must be done to control white men. Since Black men are dying anyway I can't believe they are afraid of death. I think they don't want white men mad at them. I really do. And we watch white women really get into what they're all about with their liberation movement. The white woman's actions have been for an equality movement first of all and secondly have been patterned after Black men's. Only if she's asking for equality, the white man has given her everything by making her superior. She has the world at her feet, including, if you want to deal with it, all the Black men she wants; maybe not as much as they want but most certainly all she wants. And the only thing that has been denied her has been the Black woman. Check out a white woman going with a Black man and making a beeline to the first Black woman she spies to explain it. She didn't want the dude in the first place—she wants what stands behind him. If she's after my man she doesn't need to say anything to me at all; she got him. But white women and Black men are both niggers and both respond as such. He runs to the white man to explain his "rights" and she runs to us. And I think that's where they are both coming from. Probably any one of you knows a mixed couple—check it out. And the young white man doesn't know who he wants to be. He grows his hair long like his woman's; he dresses like our men and tries to run his home as Black women have.

We Black women are the single group in the West intact. And anybody can see we're pretty shaky. We are, however (all praises), the only group that derives its identity from itself. I think it's been rather unconscious but we measure ourselves by ourselves, and I think that's a practice we can ill afford to lose. For whatever combination of events that made us turn inward, we did. And we are watching the world trying to tear us apart. I don't think it will happen. I think the Lena Youngers will always survive and control in that happy sort of way they do. I don't really think it's bad to be used by someone you love. As Verta Mae pointed out, "What does it mean to walk five paces behind him?" If he needs it to know he's leading, then do it—or stop saying he isn't leading. Because it's clear that no one can outrun us. We Black women have obviously underestimated our strength. I used to think, why don't they just run ahead of us? But obviously we are moving pretty fast. The main thing we have to deal with is, What makes a woman? Once we decide that, everything else will fall into plan. As perhaps everything has. Black men have to decide what makes a man.

I'm sure it's easier for them to try to define us, which they frequently do in terms of white women because they frequently think of themselves in terms of white men. But if they ever would decide to define a Black man in Black terms I think they would have different expectations of us as women.

I went to the opening of an African exhibit at the Brooklyn Museum and noticed only about a dozen Black men in a crowd of at least 200 people and I thought to myself, how odd—no Black men. Then I looked at the exhibit piece by piece and began to think I understood something. There was a beautiful door, from the Congo. And looking at that door I saw a man, a woman and several children in the yard and this cracker saying, "Your door is an excellent example of the Kishana people's art and I must take it back to Amsterdam." And this beautiful African, barefoot, with perhaps a single ear-ring in his left ear, replies, "But this door is the door to my house and it is not for sale." And the woman, sensing some-thing, stops the grinding of grain and begins gathering the children around her while the cracker goes on with "I must have the door. The museum needs it and I can make 50 dinars on it." And the African rises to his full height on his long, lithe legs, tribal markings dancing slightly on his face, eyes clear and hard, saying, "My family needs the door. It is mine. My father left it to me, as did his father to him. You may not have it. It is not for sale." And the cracker turns in rage to leave. Then two, perhaps three days later the missionary comes up saying, "My son, your door is needed in a great country far away from here. You will be blessed by our Heavenly Father if you will give your door to the merchant." And this magnificent African, stooping by his doorway, playing with one of his chil-dren, shakes his head. "I would be cursed by my ancestors. Go now. Go away and leave us in peace." Then in the night the soldiers come with guns; the African responds with a spear. The fire ack-ack-acks from the barrels, the woman screams, the children scatter asking what is the matter, the man is stretched out in a pool of dark, murky liquid and the door is taken down, hoisted upon the shoulders of the Black mercenaries ("Don't know why Ododo wouldn't sell that door . . . could have made another"), walked to the sea and freighted back to Amsterdam so that it can be borrowed by the United States to show how the Kishana people lived in 1582.

And I began to understand why so few Black men had come, because it was not a door at all but dead ancestors murdered in their homes that they would see. Not a statue from Nigeria but a raped woman, a slit throat, a burned village. And even as I saw that I knew I would never really understand the reality of being a Black man. Men grow beards to protect the throat, have hair on their chest to protect the heart, have Afros to cushion the head blows; and these things become aesthetically acceptable, if not preferable, but they always have groundings in survival. My man and I can walk down the street together and if some other guy says something out of the way, it's an insult to me, it could be his life. I can walk away from words and gestures and still be a woman; he cannot and still be a man. So little of a Black man's existence relies on his acts. His women—mother, sisters, lovers—control his life and generally so irresponsibly that it can be frightening . . . it has frightened me to realize it. And sometimes Black women aren't very nice—for a lot of reasons; and sometimes we use our "power" against him—for a lot of reasons. I think some of the hostility is real and must be related to as such. We're angry and so are they but it's only when we admit it that we can get anywhere. All the poems dedicated to our brothers and the poems to our sisters are good but we should take the time to say to each other what we think we need, and we should do that honestly. I don't think a woman cares where she walks if you'll let her walk with you. And I don't think a man cares that she talks if she'll talk to him. And if we really understand we are born men and women and it's our choice whether or not we stay that way, I think a lot will change. But no one likes to admit, "Yes. I'm really put out with you." So the hidden hostility remains. And we cannot afford that. I don't think we can. I think we can do better. If now isn't a good time for the truth I don't see when we'll get to it.

Because I don't want my son to be a warrior. Or to go to some school where some insensitive bitch asks him why I'm not married, or where some cracker thinks he can run my son down anytime any kind of way he pleases. I read George Jackson's letters and I don't want my son to be a George or a Jonathan Jackson. Everything George has touched has turned sour. Everyone he has loved is now dead or dying. And this man must find a reason to live each and every day. We need some happiness in our lives. Some hope. Some love. No, I don't want anyone to be George Jackson. That much feeling bottled in a cell, in a prison, in California, in the United States. Something more definite must be settled. I didn't have a baby to see him be cannon fodder. I am cannon fodder. Something more definite must be decided. If it's a real war then he must be brave and true. If it's a mental war he must be Black and proud. But if it's a wake-the-people-up war Martin Luther King did it. Malcolm X did it. Stokely Carmichael did it. Rap Brown did it. And if the people aren't awake then perhaps the dreams are too good to be disturbed again. Perhaps Black people don't want Revolution at all. That too must be considered. I used to think the world needs what I need.

But perhaps it doesn't. Because if it did we would relate to things like John and Robert Kennedy's assassinations. Those weren't individual acts that murdered them. All white people need to be taken out of power but they all clearly are not evil. If we were real we would relate to Angela Davis and forget the Commie hype. Most of the American Communist Party is FBI anyway. Didn't you read or watch *I Led Three Lives*? We would see Jimi Hendrix and Janis Joplin's deaths as part of the same thing. And we could dig where Renault Robinson is coming from. Because we all know nobody sells what ain't being bought.

And I decided to be a writer because people said I was a genius and then would ask what I would become. And I couldn't see anywhere to go intellectually and thought I'd take a chance on feeling. I didn't want to get married, buy a five-room house in Madisonville and have lunch at Caproni's as my big event of the month. I could see becoming a bored, alcoholic social worker with a couple of kids I didn't want by a man I barely spoke to. And wondering at thirty-five what I'd done with my life. The second greatest thing that happened to me was getting kicked out of Fisk because I had to deal with my life. I could go back, join Delta (as all the other women in my family did), marry a Meharry man and go quietly insane; or I could go on to live. After knocking around and sponging off my parents for a while I went back to Fisk as a woman—not a little girl just being good like everybody said.

And I owe whatever mental health I possess to the care and devotion of my patient family and three mother surrogates—the Black nun I adopted, Theresa Elliott and Blanche

Cowan. My father, my grandmother and those mother figures kept saying, "Don't look back." And my emotional growth I consider to be almost the sole product of Barbara Crosby. That's why I almost became a social worker. I wanted to do for someone what they have done for me. But I couldn't take graduate school when I realized the minute you institutionalize a problem you don't intend to solve it. Of course my grandmother did not live to see any of it. She had told me when I reentered Fisk she was just living to see me graduate. I, being young and not taking any of it to heart, graduated in February 1967 and she died in March. She was really a gas. She was the first to say and make me understand, You're mine, and I'll stick by you no matter what. Or to quote her accurately, "Let me know what you're doing and I'll stand between you and the niggers." And sometimes I look at my son, her second great-grandchild, and wonder what she would say about me. And sometimes I dream about coming into her home and her having practically a list of questions for me— "What is this abstinence they talk about for controlling birth?" or "Have you learned the flowers yet? Lord, I do so want you to be a lady!" And all the other little changes grandmothers carry you through. And I think I wanted to be famous because my mother deserves to make the world notice her existence. And my family has worked too hard to be ignored. I don't think I would have much cared if it weren't for them. But they deserve more. Other people put a lot of time and energy into me and they too deserve something.

And I understood that words have an innate reality, like noon is always noon, front or back, twelve o'clock or midnight, and *live* spelled backwards is *evil*, which white folks say we are, or *genesis* equals *gene*, which is the beginning. And love means nothing unless we are willing to be responsible for those who love us as well as those whom we love. That's one reason I am always cautious in personal relationships, because people don't just love you out of the blue—you let them. And people have loved me when I needed to be loved so as an adult I must give that love back to those who want it, or it all will have been for nothing. I think I am no different from any other colored girl who has to grow up and make and live by decisions. I think we are all capable of tremendous beauty once we decide we are beautiful or of giving a lot of love once we understand love is possible, and of making the world over in that image should we choose to. I really like to think a Black, beautiful, loving world is possible. I really do, I think.

SACRED COWS . . .
AND OTHER
EDIBLES

1988

For Lillian, DST, and Jackie,
aka my friends,
who will always be with me

On Spam, Used Cars
and More of the Same

On Spam, Used Cars
and More of the Same

I just went out and bought myself a pair of designer jeans—two pairs actually—and two designer T-shirts to go with them. Sure, I know I can't afford them, but being Black carries a special responsibility in this recession. I got a new car too. "What the heck," said I. Folks in Detroit could start pulling in their belts on poetry if they just wanted to be practical; then where would we be? It's not easy to be a proper consumer. People like to think, "Oh, anybody can spend money," but it's not true. Non-Blacks tend to ask the rate of return, the longevity of the product, its tax deductibility. Blacks, for the most part, make economic decisions on the first law of capitalism: "I Want It."

Look at what happened to the housing industry the minute we finally said we wouldn't have a home in the suburbs if they changed the stop lights to red, black and green. Construction fell off—that's what happened. Look at automobiles for that matter. They laughed and laughed at us and our big cars. We finally said, "Fine. Chrysler can take a New Yorker and do what is physically impossible with it." Of course with the General

Electric sponsorship of Reagan we turned to Japanese electronics. The yen is solid; the dollar continues to fail.

I really think America should strike a special medal for the veterans of the sixties. This country, unique among the industrialized nations, has not experienced a war on its shores since 1865. What would our cities look like if Blacks hadn't had both the foresight and the courage to burn them down? Look at the money non-Blacks made with the commissions, studies, designs, constructions, reconstructions we made possible! For that matter, how many extra policemen were hired and drew overtime to contain us? How many social workers? Look at the button and poster industry in the sixties and compare that to 1982! All those people gainfully employed on Black Power buttons (with a panther in the corner), and MAKE LOVER NOT WAR posters, are now filling our welfare rolls. Take a peek at publishing. All those books to explain Blacks to Negroes and other non-Blacks. We, in fact, made California wines since liberals had to have parties for us and didn't want to serve their good German whites or French reds (and knew very well not to even chill their Portuguese rosés)! Doctors—and dare I mention them . . . lawyers! So many people were physically and mentally hurt, their numbers have more than doubled and their salaries quadrupled. A medal is not nearly enough. Guaranteed income is more like it.

If white Americans think about it they owe us a lot. We kept the Constitution alive by constantly testing it. We kept the country mentally united through the fear of The Riot. (When will It show up in your neighborhood?) Did they think it was easy? Fun? No! It was our sacrifice to the belief that They were better people than they thought they were. It was our own contribution to compassion. Since we have been afraid for two hundred years we helped them be afraid for a decade and we thought some good, some communication would come of shared concerns. But they seem determined to show us that once again we are wrong. They want to prove they are petty, ignorant and indifferent to the human condition. I must say this to my fellow and sister Americans who are not Black: Blacks hate a white person with no class. You sometimes think the kids on the street who are menacing you hold your color against you. No. It's the lack of class this nation is showing. It's the stupidity of always picking the wrong team to cheer for. It's the smallness of telling the young and old, the poor and dispossessed to go take a flying you-know-what. I mean, you just can't have your drunken daddy working on WPA and hate the poor. That is no style at all.

But the question is: Is it too late for America to regain Black confidence? Do we really care to sacrifice for these people again? I'm still doing my part. Not only do I use my Visa, which keeps the merchants busy; I have to be billed each month; I have to be called several times by one woman; I get a letter from someone else reminding me that I have not paid; I get a phone call from another man. That's five people right there who are working solely because of me. Lord knows I'm trying. But then, I appreciate and understand the level of sacrifice. When the rest of the country understands that money ought to be in the hands of people like me who have the faith, the courage, the willingness to spend even when we don't need and can't afford, then this recession will ease, the economy will turn up and Blacks, the consummate consumers, will regain our rightful place at the table of plenty. Otherwise, it's Spam, used cars and more of the same.

The Cincinnati Series

On Handicaps, Seat Belts, Risks and Reason
Part I and Part II

Part I

Recently, a friend of mine, through no lack of sensitivity, on a rainy day in Florida, pulled into a handicapped parking place. Well, the parking space wasn't handicapped, it was simply so designated. She's hardly the kind of person who would lie to a blind vendor, passing a one-dollar bill off as a five; she'd never, ever, under any circumstances take pencils from the street vendor and not pay. Hey! I've known her all my life; she's well bred. She, when she was without automobile, rode the public buses and always gave her seat to the elderly, disabled and pregnant. I've never known her to push ahead at the super-market when an older patron has left a gap in the line. She has a teenage daughter whom she is rearing, which in and of itself should be a ticket to heaven. She uses her lunch hour to take her daughter to work, meaning no food, no rest, no break. She picks up her daughter at 11:00 P.M., meaning no kick back with a beer after work, no letup. She's uncomplaining. Yet she got a hundred-dollar ticket for parking in a handicapped place. Somehow it seems so unfair. If a Black woman rearing a teenager alone isn't handicapped, then I don't know who is. She didn't roost in the spot, she parked: prudently turned off her motor, took her keys, ran in, picked up her paycheck and came out to a one-hundred-dollar ticket. I've never seen the physically impaired ticketed for parking in a spot designated for the temporarily able-bodied. I'm not necessarily against being sensitive to the needs of others, but I shop at the new Krogers several times a week since I have recently become quite inefficient and have yet to see eight handicapped shoppers' cars parked in the designated spots. I toyed with the idea of having a sticker made of my day. You know, just little time blocks: 5:30 A.M. me letting my dogs out/ 5:45 A.M. me wiping up the floor after Wendy, who is fourteen and incontinent/ 6:00 A.M. me calling teenage son, starting breakfast, letting dogs back in, getting morning paper, starting load of laundry in washer, trying to pour cup of coffee, struggling to keep eyes open, heart warm, manner calm. I think my mornings qualify for something. Is there no compassion for the ordinary?

I noted recently Gay Power is asserting itself for a special school for young gays in New York City. In Louisville a white worker was granted workmen's compensation because it made him nervous to work with Blacks. I guess we can look forward to the city council single-handedly taking the entire board of the Ohio Public Employees Retirement Fund hostage until they change their stock portfolio! Life seems so unfair lately to those of us who are ordinary. Ordinary people who saved their money in places like Home State so that they could take a trip to Greece end up being hijacked by people they never heard of for a cause they hold no feelings for or against. I mean, whatever happened to fair play?

But hey. We were discussing designated handicapped parking. At the risk of sounding a bit cold—if they can drive, they can take their chances along with the rest of us. Or I'm going to ask James Meredith to initiate a march demanding designated COLORED parking spots. Then, of course, the militant gays will demand designated gay spots, though everyone who laughs may lay a claim to those places, then white people will want designated white spots, then child abusers, then abused children, and dammit, there won't be any spots in town where normal cars can park, which is what it's all about anyway.

Otherwise we may as well dust off the old Black laws of a hundred years ago and begin the new loving, sensitive segregation instead of, I suppose, the old mean, evil kind. There must be a difference, but right now it's the forest and the trees to me.

Part II

Don't get me wrong. My interest in dying is right up there with my desire to see Beirut, save with Home State or have Reagan's new tax package passed. Excuse me. Reagan doesn't have a new tax package, he offers us a Revenue Enhancing Plan that will actually save people like me thousands and thousands of dollars. That one for sure is sitting on the desks of folks who say Divest Now and and earn millions or join the people who win at the New Ohio State Lottery. Naw, I'm being unfair. The New Ohio State Lottery gives you some chance, if not of winning at least of being happy you played, which is more than can be said of the others. But that has nothing to do with our topic of the day.

You see, I'm from Lincoln Heights, a small community about fifteen miles north of Cincinnati, directly across the expressway from General Electric. If the Feds hadn't built I-75, Lincoln Heights could make a good case for owning the land upon which GE was built. I mean, if Kentucky could sue Ohio over ownership of the Ohio River we could probably *win* our case. Those of us who are paranoid see the expressway as a part of the continuing policy to deprive those of us who settled the valley of our rightful wealth. Though, in the spirit of fairness, I should also acknowledge the tales of mayors who sold Lincoln Heights out. We in Lincoln Heights, lest we stray too far, are a rugged individualist community. We believe in doing it for ourselves.

You see, I think the new seat belt policy rates right up there with the missionary position. Something you do if your mate insists, something you may in fact have reason to want to do sometimes, but never the sort of thing that's designated by law. Even, and this pushes me, even if the insurance companies said, "Well, OK, if you have an accident and your seat belt was not on and you are hurt, your deductible will go up," I could maybe see it. It's still coercion, but it's a gentle coercion that allows me to feel I have some choice in the matter. I have heard testimony from friends and total strangers who swear by their belts. I'm glad. I want all who like being strapped in to swear by it. But it's funny, isn't it, if *Hustler* magazine ran a cover with a grown woman strapped in a car with a policeman standing over her saying, "Good girl," every born-again would howl. Now, yes, I know, someone will say, "Hey as much as

you fly, how can you take that position . . . er, ump . . . stand?"
I put my seat belt on in an airplane because it obviously makes
the pilot feel so much better. Do you honestly think that I or
any other passenger believes, as we roar off at approximately
500 mph, if we have to abort those little jokers won't cut us in
half? We know damned well they will, which is why we pray,
chant or distract ourselves with thoughts of the coming meal.
If you think I or any passenger believes we will survive a
plunge from forty thousand feet to planet Earth because we
are strapped, you also think Close-Up will get you a boyfriend,
Downy will make your kid write you from summer camp, and
eating fiber will protect you from cancer. Hey, I know. I see
the letters coming in right now: "I've been eating fiber for
forty years and am still cancer-free." I'm glad. I want the
world to be happy, healthy and sane. But somehow, I also
want to get into my car, pop a cassette into place and drive off.
If I speed, please stop me; if I'm drunk, please get me off the
road and into jail; if I fail to stop at a stop sign, please ticket
me; if I cause an accident or hurt someone, please, please
charge me, but don't make me wear a seat belt by law. When I
strap in, it ought to be by my own choice, or my desire to
please my pilot.

Citizen Responsibility
Hey! I'm Running for Office!

I'm thinking about running for Cincinnati City Council. "Idiot," I hear out there, "you can't run for Council. You don't even live in the city!" Well neither does Sy Murray's secretary; neither will the new chief of police. Hey, lots of folks probably don't even live in Ohio who are working on the Cincinnati Convention Annex! Some folks, I'll bet, aren't even citizens who play on our baseball team. Why not a representative from Lincoln Heights? You'd get a fresh perspective from an ordinary person for a change.

OK, so I know someone is saying, but hey, what about Reading—Norwood—Woodlawn—Winton Terrace, for Christ's sake? It's not the same, that's why. Only Lincoln Heights and Cincinnati have a council where most members feel they are gods. Lincoln Heights and Cincinnati both have had to make drastic cuts to cover up for past foolishness. Neither area has adequate police and fire protection. That alone gives me a leg up. Plus I'm fun.

My platform?

1. Annex northern Kentucky. All the way to the Florence Mall. It would stop all the petty criminal activity of purchasing liquor and cigarettes from another state. Newport and Covington are as nice as any other suburb on this side of the river, and it could smooth the transition for Appalachians making their way to the big city.

2. Annex Hamilton County. Let's face it: If Cincinnati gets a cold the county sneezes. Annexation will stop all the discussions about who lives where, not to mention overlapping taxes and underlapping services.

3. Annex Kings Island and the Jack Nicklaus Sports Complex. Sure Butler County will be upset, but so are the residents of Over-the-Rhine, and who listens to them?

4. Turn Union Terminal back into a transportation terminal. Greyhound and Trailways would move into the terminal. Keep it open twenty-four hours a day. Sure we'd need security, and by God that's a fine point. People can get work again. Use it for a bus pickup and drop-off for the airport. Keep the cab lines at the terminal and reduce the clutter downtown. People will need food and drinks while they're waiting. Hey, it could be a bonanza!

5. Consider public school teachers and all our librarians public servants of the highest order. Give them exactly twice the pay and all the benefits of police and fire people. Sure . . . sure, it'll cost in the short run, but in the long run we just might come up with a civilized populace. Run school twenty-four hours a day, eliminating that I-don't-have-time-to-attend excuse. Make ignorance a choice, not an excuse or defense.

My pledge to the voters: I will look out, to the best of my ability, for the good of the citizens of Cincinnati even at the expense of not making dumb headlines and occasionally at the risk of doing nothing. Sure I'm being a little hard-nosed, but hey, these are hard times! NIKKI—INFLEXIBLE AND UNFAIR has a certain ring to it, don't you think? NIKKI—A MADE-UP MIND IS A TERRIBLE THING TO WASTE. Now that's a class bumper sticker. I mean, what more honorable a pursuit for an aging poet than to serve the city that nurtured her? NIKKI—WHY NOT THE ORDINARY?

On Holidays and How
to Make Them Work

A proper holiday, coming from the medieval "holy day," is supposed to be a time of reflection on great men, great deeds, great people. Things like that. Somehow in America this didn't quite catch on. Take Labor Day. On Labor Day you take the day off, then go to the Labor Day sales and spend your devalued money with a clerk who is working. And organized labor doesn't understand why it suffers declining membership? Pshaw. Who wants to join an organization that makes you work on the day it designates as a day off? Plus, no matter how hidden the agenda, who wants a day off if they make you march in a parade and listen to some politicians talk on and on about nothing.

Hey. I'm a laborer. I used to work in Walgreen's on Linn Street. We were open every holiday and I, being among the junior people, always "got" to work the time-and-a-half holidays. I hated those people who came in. Every fool in the Western world, and probably in this universe, knows that Christmas is December 25. Has been that way for over a thousand years, yet there they'd be, standing outside the door, cold, bleary-eyed, waiting for us to open so they could purchase a present. Memorial Day, which used to be Armistice Day until we got into this situation of continuous war, was the official start of summer. We would want to be out with our boyfriends barbecuing . . . or something, but there we were behind the counter waiting to see who forgot that in order to barbecue you need: (1) a grill, (2) charcoal, (3) charcoal starter. My heart goes out to the twenty-four-hour grocery people, who are probably selling meat!

But hey. It's the American way. The big Fourth of July sales probably reduced the number of fatal injuries as people spent the entire day sober in malls, fighting over markdowns. Minor cuts and bruises were way up, though, I'll bet. And forget the great nonholiday, Presidents' Day. The damned thing could at least have a real name. What does that mean—Presidents' Day? Mostly that we don't care enough to take the time to say to Washington and Lincoln: Well done. But for sure, as a Black American I've got to go for it. Martin Luther King, Jr.'s birthday has come up for the first time as a national holiday. If we are serious about celebrating it, Steinberg's will be our first indication: GHETTO BLASTERS 30% OFF! FREE TAPE OF "I HAVE A DREAM" WITH EVERY VCR PURCHASED AT THE ALL-NEW GIGANTIC MARTY'S BIRTHDAY SALE. Then Wendy's will, just maybe, for Black patrons (and their liberal sympathizers) Burn-A-Burger to celebrate the special day. Procter & Gamble will withhold Clorox for the day, respectfully requesting that those Black spots be examined for their liberating influence. But what we really want, where we can know we have succeeded, is that every Federated department store offers 50 percent off to every colored patron who can prove he or she is Black in recognition of the days when colored citizens who were Black were not accorded all the privileges of other shoppers. That will be a big help because everybody will want to be Black for a Day. Sun tanneries will make fortunes during the week preceding MLK Day. Wig salons will reap great benefits. Dentists will have to hire extra help to put that distinctive gap between the middle front teeth. MLK Day will be accepted. And isn't that the heart of the American dream?

I really love a good holiday—it takes the people off the streets and puts them safely in the shopping malls. Now think about it. Aren't you proud to be with Uncle Sam?

Reflections on
My Profession

In Sympathy with Another Motherless Child
One View of the Profession of Writing

Writing is like any other profession—breakdancing, ninth grade, doctor of philosophy, surgeon—it's what I do to justify the air I breathe, the food I ingest, the time I take up on earth. I'm ever and still amazed that any artist considers himself God or in close proximity thereof. It's not like a double 0 number—it's not a license to kill, no excuse to not exercise normal courtesy in human relations, no copyright to bigotry. I suppose there is, or at least there appears to be, some human need to cull from the general stock those who should be exalted. I don't trust that instinct at all. The more you are in public life, the less likely it is that your life will be worth living, unless you exercise great care to be sure it's your life and not what someone wants your life to be that you are living. I feel as sorry for the modern politicians and rock stars as I do the Roman Claudius, who was told by his Praetorian guards that he had one of two choices: "You will be emperor or we will kill you." Ass-kissing is not a normal human posture for the kisser or the kissee.

I am not at all sure that forty is the proper age to look at a career. At forty, first of all, the body changes. No one in his right mind would ask a teenager to write or evaluate his life, because those who have been through adolescence know that every day there is another major change, another crisis, another reason to feel life sucks and there is nothing that can be done about it. I'm not sure that at forty we know much more. At sixteen we can feel there will be another sixteen and another and another; at forty you pretty well know there will not be another forty; you are pleased to think there might be another ten, and depending upon the rate of body deterioration you can hope for another twenty with the coda: If I'm healthy. Most Americans are medically indigent; I know I am. I have instructed my mother to sign nothing should I be struck with any disease more serious than cellulite. I'm probably going to die anyway and there's no point in her, my son and my dogs going into bankruptcy to stave off the inevitable. Can we talk? It's not at all that I'm interested in dying. As a matter of fact I think life is one of the more interesting propositions offered on earth; it's just that I have lived through a terminal illness and have seen.

I like my profession. I hope the telephone operators, the hamburger turner at McDonald's, the pressure checker at Kentucky Fried who sees to it that those spices and herbs get really deep in the chicken are proud, too. I know some degree of incentive is necessary to my profession. Writers are the world's biggest procrastinators and the second biggest paranoid group, being bested only by politicians. I know that we have to get some kind of seed in our craw to write, and then we only write after we have washed all the windows, cleaned the

oven, weeded the garden and are threatened with either bod-
ily harm by our publishers or imminent bankruptcy by our
creditors. I have a dear friend who invites me each summer to
come to her home to write. "You'll have lots of privacy," she
always points out, "and there are the swimming pool and the
tennis courts when you need to take a break." What she has
also figured out is that her closets will be both straightened out
and waxed, her silver will get polished, all repairs will be made
on the porch furniture, all doorknobs will be tightened. I'm
very handy. In fact, I'm a joy to have around! I paint, stain,
rescreen, file crystal; the only thing I don't do well in a house is
electrical work that requires the box to be turned off. I'm terri-
bly handy with plumbing and have been known in my mother's
house to repair roof shingles. Of course, we seldom mention
that the books don't get written. . . . To tell the truth, my secret
desire is to open my own Nikki's Best Handy Girl Service. Hey!
If this poetry doesn't work out, I've got my second career all
planned. As you may have guessed—I'm compulsive.

Ecclesiastes teaches us there is a season and a purpose for
everything under the heavens; what it fails to mention is there
is a place. I really can stand dirt since in my mind there is a
purpose for dirt; I cannot stand disorder. I am stupefied,
amazed, that people haven't alphabetized their books and rec-
ords, that clothes in the closet don't hang on proper hangers in
color and length categories. An unbalanced closet is the sign
of a sick mind, much more indicative of the true personality
than a cluttered desk, for which there is at least one excuse. It
used to be that you could tell all you needed to know about a
woman by the way she kept house; the same is true of men
these days. Chalk one up for the ERA.

Rage is to writers what water is to fish. A laid-back writer is like an orgasmic prostitute—an anomaly—something that doesn't quite fit. I have been considered a writer who writes from rage, and it confuses me. What else do writers write from? We are not, after all, songsters who put together a ditty because the bride is not a virgin and the groom is impotent. Can't you see the new Broadway musical—*Come Together* (a musical experience based on the songs of John Lennon and Paul McCartney with five—count them—new songs!)? As their mutually exclusive problems come to light on their wedding night, this scene unfolds:

HE [*Stage right in a bolero-cut smoking jacket and red bikini underwear. The orchestra strings hit high C*]: Ohhhh—I'd love to be able to screw you . . . [*in That falsetto country tenor he's so noted for*]

SHE [*On the bed center stage, butt naked, though the audience can't tell because her long tresses are covering her*]: I need your dick tonight . . .

HE [*Flicking his braids and rising to tiptoe over the bed*]: But since I can't pursue you . . .

SHE [*With that famous lip pout, pointing her toes in that gymnastic move so popular last year on the Sri Lanka tour*]: And we can't get it right . . .

BOTH [*She rises from the bed; he moves stage left and offers his right hand, giving full view to the audience*]: Let's get funky, funky, funky . . . [*They break out in a series of twirls*] Let's just screw the best we can . . . [*Both kick leg high in opposite directions*] Let's get funky, funky, funky . . . till we don't give a damn . . .

Of course "Funky, Funky, Funky" goes on to be the number one hit on the Pop charts and number three on Soul (according to *Variety*). "The Original Cast Come Together" stays at number one for thirty-two weeks in a row, setting a new record for Broadway musical albums. Forget that it says nothing and doesn't even rhyme; the writer, Dave "Mr. Rock Steady" Cummings, is on all the TV talk shows, and the artistic world hails his shocking innovations. It did more than add to his body of human knowledge, it did something more important than helping people grow and understand their problems—it did the most important thing a song can do . . . it sold!

A poet couldn't get away with that. Sure, I know Bob Dylan, as well as Lennon-McCartney, are considered poets, but that's only because we want to pay them a compliment. If Francis Scott Key and the man who wrote "Trees" hadn't had their poems set to music, no one would even think to listen to them today. I mean Dr. J. is poetry in motion, too, but we don't put that in stanzas. And as weird as Dylan has become lately, he hasn't become that weird. Why, someone would cart him off the stage into the nearest state-run mental hospital, because if he's that gone why waste the money? "I will now read from my song . . ." No. A poet has to say something. A poem has to make some sort of sense; be lyrical; to the point; and still be able to be read by whatever reader is kind enough to pick up the book. Certainly there are poets who deliberately use language to obscure the fact that they have nothing to either share or convey, but we aren't discussing them. Those would be the academicians who write for each other and, let us not forget, to impress the department head. I have even gone so far as to think one of the duties of this profession is to be topical, to try to say something about the times in which we are living and how we both view and evaluate them. Relevance will lead to either critical ridicule or total dismissal. One of the most severe criticisms of Rod McKuen is that people read and enjoy him. Imagine! What nerve! Poetry isn't to be read and enjoyed. It's to be difficult, dark, full of hidden meanings, allegorical, with strange images in even stranger words about some other poet no one ever heard of. If Black writers write about slavery, we are told it's parochial, no one is interested in this stuff; but when Jewish writers write about their history it's called the Old Testament. When women write about the reality of our lives, it's called too dull; when white men write their lives, it's called heroic. The ultimate literary confrontation will be the Old Testament Meets the New Holocaust vs. Deliverance of the Man in the Gray Flannel Suit. You the reader are invited to compare these two marvelous anthologies by some of our greatest writers. You can use the coupon at the bottom of this page to check your preference for the work of the millennium, and while you're at it we're sure you will want to buy these two black glove-leather–bound copies for your children. For only $5.95 down and $5.00 a week for the next 250 weeks we will put these right on your bookshelf. And if you order now and mention Joe sent you we will give you free of charge this marvelous bookmark blessed by three living rabbis and two popes. Don't miss This opportunity to help hubby get ahead and the kiddies do better in school. Phooey!

I think a lot of the Black poets because we honor the tradition of the griots. We have traveled the length and breadth of the planet singing our song of the news of the day, trying to bring people closer to the truth. As the written word became both possible and accessible, poets such as Dante, Milton and T. S. Eliot carried on the African tradition. Though some people were as unhappy with our "motherfuckers" as in other times some were shocked by Chaucer's eroticism, some people were simply born to be shocked.

On a scale of 1 to 10 I have to admit literary excess is about 380. Whether it's done smoothly or crudely; whether it's the ravings of *Mein Kampf* or American Unionists in 1852 clutching *Uncle Tom's Cabin*. It's neither *The Klansman* nor *The Strawberry Statement* that causes action; it is action that gives life to literature. I do confess to being shocked. I am not, nor do I recommend a state of, blasé that accepts any and everything. But what is shocking to me will never come from the lips of Prince on a record but rather from the lips of the New Bedford men *for* the record who stated she must have really wanted to be raped on a pool table or else why would she have needed a pack of cigarettes after the 7-Eleven closed?

I am totally shocked by the Cincinnati father who raped his five-month-old baby while his wife was out shopping. Guess that will teach his wife to ask him to baby-sit. I'm shocked that child molesters now simply open day care centers to which unwitting parents take innocent children. I'm shocked that people, estimated in the millions, will die of starvation on this earth; that people sleep in the crevices and corners of the streets in our major cities; that mass murderers and attempted presidential assassins get to plead mental anguish. Talk about a headache! I'm disappointed that Ronald Reagan thinks trees pollute and that the Democratic party nominated Walter Mondale. But hey! Who asked me? I'm sorry that every time I like a television program it goes off the air. That kind of thing makes you feel like you are a one-woman Nielsen. ("What does Giovanni like this season? Well, get it off!")

How we as a world got into book censorship is well beyond my powers to understand. It's really funny in a way. We can get *Little Black Sambo* off library shelves because Black Americans may be offended and it isn't even about Black Americans, but we support *Penthouse* and *Hustler* because of First Amendment protections. I'm not shocked at pornography, but it's awful. And what makes it so awful isn't naked women in totally absurd positions, but rather that somebody needs to make someone else submissive. But I attended a colored college, so I may have missed something. Maybe some reader will be kind enough to explain it to me because all I see is a married man angry because his mistress was unfaithful. The Miss America pageant gathers together all the winners of the fifty Miss State contests. They come to Atlantic City, which used to be just a playground for the rich and others who liked saltwater taffy and maybe an occasional Monopoly freak. They have never in their fifty-six-year history picked a girl of sturdy character, high intelligence, fluid articulateness who was ugly. They have never picked a girl who declined to participate in the swimsuit contest. They always say talent is important, but if what I see on-screen is what they call talent, either I am crazy or they are deaf. But hey! I'm not going to intimate that perhaps the true talent contest takes place in another arena and that the inability to properly judge that contest is what really cost Bert Parks his position. No. I will stick to my question. What is the difference between Bob Guccione and the other old pimps who make up the Miss

America pageant? What is the difference between how any of them are using women to earn their living? In every issue, in every contest, both, like the butcher, look for fresh meat. What continues to make men think they have a right, first dibs actually, on the bodies of women? I like Vanessa Williams. Nobody would even ask me to pose naked, nor pay for the photographs should I insist, though my doctor just informed me I am at my optimum weight and for a woman of my age in pretty good health. Oh, I'm sorry. We weren't discussing health, were we, but rather looks.

I think it must be awful to be beautiful. No matter what anyone says, I don't think people cheer for beautiful people; I think they are jealous. It's bad enough being intelligent or truly talented, but at least you can hide that a lot by just not talking. But beauty is a walking billboard to every bimbo who has eyes. More than being delighted that Williams was chosen Miss America, it made my day. She is cute and seemed to have a lot of moxie. And, let's face it, it was damned boring to have all those little miss blondies paraded before us all the time. It was time for a radical change, and the pageant had one of two choices: an ugly white girl or a beautiful Black one. They made the right choice. Of the two Black women in the running I was pulling for Vanessa because she had a glint in her eye. I love a risk-taker; I liked her existential approach. Though she appeared to be happy she didn't look as if her whole damned life depended upon being chosen. She was cool. As it turned out she is still the best choice because she's been a thoroughbred all the way. Until the mess with *Penthouse* no one had anything other than praise for the way she handled herself, and even when they all crumbled Williams faced the print press and the television cameras with style. She never backed down; plus, as much as people don't like to deal with it, it's her body. If she would stand on the stage for the judges of the contest, why wouldn't she have posed nude for her boss? She had no more an obligation to mention the photographs than they did to acknowledge she was their ticket to ride. But maybe there is something else that bothers me more than the shabby treatment panicking old men meted out to a young woman. They reminded you, didn't they, of Alexander Haig when Reagan was shot. All panic and no purpose. Call a press conference! Sweat like Nixon! "I'm in charge here!" Denounce Williams. Sort of Rumpelstiltskinish ("The witches have told you my name!"), flailing wildly about for an anchor ("It's all her fault!"). They were pitiful. What happened to that "grace under pressure" of which Hemingway spoke so well? What happened to "Let's give her a chance to explain"? No. They looked like the first Lite Beer camping trip when Rodney joins the party: It's the creature! Which was not Vanessa Williams, but their own veneer so neatly stripped. It's the mirror Bob Guccione held for them and they, like Dorian Gray, saw who they really are—old, gray-chested men with ten tons of gold around their necks from which hang fifty-six little skulls (fifty-five ivory, one ebony), their prissy little mouths sprouting prissy little platitudes while the Poli-Grip worked overtime. The pageant men and Guccione did what some would have thought impossible—they made a compassionate man of Hugh Hefner. They made a graceful, articulate, caring man of the granddaddy of them all. And let us not forget their first pronouncement after demanding the burning of Vanessa was that the second runner-up is busy with her own career and obligations so we will go to the third. In other words, "Let's get a real white woman in here. Louisa will save the day yet." In walks Little Miss Muffet, though, to save the spiders from the curds and whey.

I saw the photographs. I am one of those who rewarded Guccione as I had previously rewarded John Dean and Jeb Magruder. Tacky would be a good word for both occasions. Naïve would be another. Having also viewed the work of David Hamilton (*Sisters; Country Cousins*), I found it highly credible that pornography passes as art; that someone who thinks her looks are the entrée rather than the appetizer would easily be persuaded to expose herself. I simply won't buy the this-is-a-fantasy-of-hers bull. Chaipel didn't tippy-toe into his studio with his Kodak Instamatic and catch two girls off guard. These photographs are obviously posed. And, frankly, had they been properly cropped, wouldn't have been too bad. What's wrong with naked women, as opposed to naked men, is that women don't pretend shock at the sight of a photo of a penis; men are always upset that another man will see what he "treasures." It's time for men to grow up. Sex isn't dirty-dirty or nasty-nasty. It's time men quit using the anatomy of a female against her; it's overdue that men quit using the penis as a weapon. But the most disgusting statement on the Williams situation that I read was in *USA Today*'s Opinion, in which a 20-year-old Black woman from "Hopeless," Georgia, said Vanessa had "let the race down." Little chipmunk-cheeked Bryant Gumbel leered the same question on the *Today* show. Then, in his role as Mr. Compassion, he wanted to know, "When do the tears come?" A friend of mine said Vanessa should have said, "Nigger, please!"

There were too many people who wanted to pretend that the sight of that young woman without her clothes on had set the human race back to the Stone Age; the American people closer to nuclear confrontation with Russia; Black people back to head-scratching and "Yessir, boss." I mean, what did she really do other than mistakenly believe she could utilize her own self? While Little Miss Muffet Charles (was "Do Dah" her talent entry?) tells the world she has no secrets. That's admirable. One in every four girls and one in every ten boys have secrets by the age of twelve. Three out of four people have halitosis. Some have even known the heartbreak of psoriasis. I join with Marvin Gaye in a salute: Right on. There is no reason to think Miss Charles understood she was chosen only to make sure Vanessa was not shot down by some crazy American. She thought the pageant had made a mistake in overlooking her in the first place. There is no reason to think she would accept the pageant's offer not to disrupt her schedule. ("But I have to follow the white rabbit," said Alice.) There was certainly no reason to think she would simply decline to participate in the humiliation of Vanessa. Oh no. She was the understudy whose moment had arrived. I alone raised the value of Excedrin stock that week. It all gave me a headache.

Actually, I'm not in a rage frequently. For some reason, after all these years, meanness and stupidity still get to me. I work on it, honestly. I understand not everyone has had the advantages I have enjoyed of being able to both read and digest material and apply the lessons learned. I'm told by my young friends that experience is much more important than books. Of course Ben Franklin had something to say about experience and fools, but even Franklin thought that a fool would learn by his experience. That has proven false in the modern world. Some people are simply unwilling to learn under any circumstances, which maybe, even then, wouldn't be so bad if they weren't so damned proud of it. Doesn't it just make your skin crawl to hear somebody spout off about what they don't do and how they're never going to do it? It makes you cheer against the human race. I'm sure to be a crotchety old lady, assuming I have not yet achieved that state, because things like refusing to eat oysters will drive me up a wall. Stick one of the damned things in your mouth; then you can say, "I don't care for oysters, though I have tried them." This argument does not apply to cocaine or other hallucinogenic drugs; the experience of other people will do just fine. Isn't that the purpose of people living and sharing? So that others will at least not make the same mistake, since we seldom are able to re-create the positive things in life.

I guess one of life's experiences that I have always wanted to avoid was bitterness. Yes, I know I wrote a poem on bitterness and I know that earlier in this career critics thought I was bitter, but I am not nor was I. Just sick and tired of the same song and dance. The bitter people are as bad as the drug people because they seem to descend to a place from which no light ever emerges. I had an experience with the Interracial Council on Children's Books that pushed my bitter button, though. There is a book, *Jake and Honeybunch Go to Heaven*, which is illustrated by Margo Zemach, a white woman. She had taken the old Black folktale and placed it in the thirties. Jake and his mule, Honeybunch, are killed by a train because the mule wouldn't move out of the way. Jake gets to heaven first and, in his attempt to adjust, runs into trouble. He picks up two left wings, he sees a jazz band, there is a big fish fry . . . all the usual things. He finally meets God, who is a Black man with a white beard who tells him he'll have to leave because of the disturbance he is causing. Jake just misses Honeybunch, who has finally arrived in heaven. If Jake was a disaster, Honeybunch is a blind man with a pistol. No one can control the mule, so God sends for Jake, who promises to both control his mule and do better himself. God gives Jake the specific job of putting the stars and moon out, so if you look at the night sky and there is only darkness, just know that Jake and Honeybunch are probably off fishing and forgot to do their work. A really rather harmless story that has been around, for anyone who knows her folklore, for ages. From the same place as the modern-day "People Get Ready (there's a train a'coming)" to "Oh Pray My Wings Are Going to Fit Me Well."

There were literary complaints that God was both male and Black, though I had a difficult time picturing Jake being greeted by Sheena of the Jungle or Marilyn Monroe. Some said one of the illustrations, which showed a Black man sleeping in a Pullman, wasn't real, but neither is the idea of the L. C. Greenwood and Bert Jones exchanging letters. Some didn't like the food Jake saw being cooked and consumed. I just had a difficult time trying to see Jake enjoying lox on an onion bagel. Some didn't like the jazz band in heaven. Mostly what none of them liked was that a white woman illustrated a Black folktale. Why, they cried, couldn't a Black illustrator have done it? Because a Black illustrator didn't, that's why. It neither added to nor subtracted from the book that was before us to ask that kind of question.

Anyway, the council decided to wage holy war against Jake

and began lining up its Black pawns. My mother took a message for me to call the council. I returned the call and was told that the Jake situation was racist and something should be said about it. Being familiar with the council, though not its tactics, I asked if they would send me the book. I recalled several years ago they had accused *Sounder* of being racist because the book was named after the dog and the characters weren't given names. Since I hadn't been offended by *Sounder* I was at least cautious.

The book arrived the next day. I read it and looked at it carefully. After dinner I read it again. Since my mother is a much better folklorist than I could hope to be and since she has a special interest in children's literature, I asked her to read it for me. I called a librarian at the Cincinnati Public Library and asked her for an opinion, which she was unable to give because she had not seen the book, though she did supply me with additional material. I read the additional material. Neither my heart nor my mind could find any racist intent in *Jake and Honeybunch*. I could see why some people might not want to purchase a copy for their children, but that's hardly the same as condemning the book. Many people don't want to purchase *Slaughterhouse-Five, Catcher in the Rye*, all of my books, but that doesn't mean a full-scale literary war should be raised. Books are self-censoring agents. First they have to be written, then they have to be published, then they have to find their way into the homes or hands of readers, then they still have to go the extra mile of being interesting enough to be read. I figure books have a hard enough time without the added pressure of false information leaking out about them.

I sat down and wrote the council a letter that ended, "I do

not find *Jake and Honeybunch* racist," which was a simple statement of what I thought about the book. I don't like *Charlie and the Chocolate Factory* because I didn't like the way the "Oompa Lumpas" were characterized; I really thought William Styron's *Nat Turner* was just a total waste, but Dahl and Styron probably don't read me either. I would not be disappointed to find that is so; I would be disappointed to find that they demand the removal of my books from the shelves. I wrote the council a long letter explaining my reasoning since it was more than obvious that *Jake* was going to get reamed by most writers. I thought it the honorable thing to do.

When the council's newsletter came out that fall, responses to *Jake* ranged from, "Yes, it is racist and should be removed from the shelves" to "Yes, it is racist but should be left alone" except for one response—mine. Maybe I wouldn't have burned so much if the council had published my whole letter or at least given some of my reasoning. Since I was the only voice who spoke up for *Jake*, it seemed to me only fair that a fuller explanation was needed than "On the other hand," which listed me as saying I did not find *Jake and Honeybunch* racist. What was the great fear? That the reasoning would be so persuasive that all others would repent? No. The great fear, I think, is that one Black writer decided to say what she believed. This little soldier didn't join Nixon's army, neither would I start banning books.

About ten years ago James Earl Jones starred in an Off Broadway production of a one-man show on Paul Robeson. Friends of mine and people who knew Robeson were very upset with the portrayal and decided to take out an ad or something in the *New York Times* to protest. A friend called me and asked if I would join them. He explained their point of view and I said, "Yes." I did say to him that if anyone asked if I had seen the production I would be forced to tell them I signed out of friendship. The ad ran and I *was* asked about it by CBS local. James Earl Jones then said in the *Times* the next day he was disappointed with me because he expected more of me. I was actually ashamed. I had not even thought about James Earl or his feelings. I had only thought that I was helping out a friend. I knew I never wanted to feel that way again in my life. Not like a fool, because I have been a fool enough to know that doesn't matter one way or the other, but insensitive. If you're going to hurt people's feelings, it should definitely be because of something you believe in. In that way that people are when they learn something I'm glad James Earl expressed disappointment, otherwise it would never have crossed my mind again, and though I don't think my friend was exactly using me, I also know I seek no concurring opinions of my own beliefs.

When I saw the newsletter I felt compelled to write the council to tell them I thought they abused my good offices. Their response was to send me a Xeroxed copy of another book they didn't like. As fate would have it, the *Jake* controversy started with the refusal of the Milwaukee librarians to purchase copies for general circulation. The *Jake* publisher had accused them of censorship; they retaliated with racism. It just goes to show how wars get started. I had a speaking engagement in Milwaukee that fall. At the post-reception I had the pleasure of meeting one of the librarians. She asked me if I had seen the newsletter and I sort of went off on her. Then she said, "You know, I did additional research, and the book is basically sound." "Are you going to write the author to let her know?" "Oh no. I still don't like the book," she said. "But you do see that not liking the book isn't the same as saying the book is racist?" "Yes. Well, but it's probably best to let things alone." I have an unshakable affection for librarians. I'm sure, because she was a charming lady who probably meant no harm, that there was some unstated reason like, "My job would be at stake"; "Nobody was really hurt"; "The Devil made me do it." Aren't those the traditional excuses we seek? The lessons of Nuremberg have yet to be learned. But at least we are all trying. Each in her own way. I hope.

Mine, like most families of writers, lives in absolute terror that one day I shall tire of contemplating my own navel and turn to theirs. The most at risk in this situation are, of course, children because we, the writers, can sign a release for them, the minors. I look any day now for the family of Erma Bombeck to file a class-action suit and take away her tennis court. I'm luckier than Ms. Bombeck because I don't have any tangible assets. They can only hope that I will one day peck into a megaseller, then bingo! They can pounce. Of course, this will never happen because I'm a poet.

But then, there are advantages to having a poet in the family. I write marvelous little thank-you notes with just the right touch of both joy and humility at receiving a present. I do nifty invitations. And Ma Bell or, rather, the new AT&T Regionals, owe me one because I have raised the art of letter-writing to the point that very few people in my family will write—they generally just reach out and touch.

The only one who has successfully escaped my poetic intrusion is my girl dog, Wendy, though I did, of course, dedicate a book to her because I got tired of her bitching that she was left out. Dogs are funny. If you write about them they accuse you of exploitation. Look at the heartache Lassie and her family went through—always having to do a heroic number to keep the affection of her owners; look at poor Rin Tin Tin, galloping across the plains leading the cavalry . . . then having to listen to Black Beauty and the others complain that *he* gets all the glory. What's even worse is that sexism is ever present. Lassie was played by a male, though of course you can't get away with that with horses. So I have low-keyed it with Wendy. She's a really marvelous cairn terrier with a highly developed sense of self and duty. Truth is, she would give her life for me. She's a great watchdog and will let you know when anything is awry. Her desire to protect me got her into trouble in the house because she would always bark at my father when he got up to go to the bathroom in the middle of the night. He would curse her and say clearly, mostly I think for my benefit, "Damned crazy dog!" I naturally had to support Wendy so I would get up and pet her and say, "Good girl." My mother would by that time have stumbled out of her room to see what the commotion was, which always woke up Bruno, my boy dog, who then had to go out himself, which meant someone had to wait on him since he never, in rain nor snow nor dark of night, could just go out and pee; he always had to patrol the entire backyard. Tommy slept through it all, which was just as well as he usually had left his TV running and would have been reamed at two o'clock in the morning for the waste.

Bruno, by the way, is worthless. If I ever hit Lotto and get a big house and new car and buy a lot of nifty things people would want to steal, I'll have to find a new home for him. Nothing on earth should be as friendly as that dog. He sucks up to repairmen, telephone guys, the Orkin man, anyone who comes to the door, no matter how menacing or strange-looking. My mother, when we moved back home, at first said two dogs were too much, but every morning while she worked her crossword puzzle he'd climb over her feet to put his head in her lap. Bru has her convinced that he is actually of help with some of the words. My cousin Pat, who lives in California, has Bruno out each summer, and he's such a nerd that she reads fairy tales to him before he goes to bed. He ignores me completely. If I just need something little, like help with getting a twig out of the way, he will pretend to be busy. The only thing I do that really delights him is make ice cream but, as I always tell him, I'm on to his tricks. He and Tommy like to wait until they hear me go "Uumph! UUmph!" knowing those are the last couple of turns, then they both come bounding over. I always give the dasher to Wendy 'cause she'll stick with me through the whole thing—to hell with that sometimey dog and boy. Mommy says I ignore Bru but it's his own fault. I'm the one who bought him and his food; who takes him to be groomed; who sees to it he has his shots. And who does he suck up to? Everybody else.

Now, as far as children go, I have no special insight into teenagers, save this: The fourteen-year-old personality was invented to give ulcers to otherwise calm mothers; to cause normally tranquil, proud, loving parents to snarl, growl and threaten; the fourteen-year-old personality was created, in other words, to drive forty-year-old mothers to the nuthouse.

Everyone says babies are difficult; it's just not true.

Changing diapers, wiping pabulum from chins, heating bottles in the middle of the night are a snap compared to picking up your own telephone that you pay for every month and never hearing a familiar voice, either friend or relative, but rather a barbarian girl or boy demanding, "Tom home!" I was at first annoyed by the question and then by the tone, but I've trained myself to respond only to the question asked: "Why, yes, he is. How kind of you to call and inquire. I must go now." I then hang up. The barbarian response next was, "Can I speak to Tom?" to which I replied, again, as sweetly as possible: "It appears you are quite capable. I hear you very well. I must go now." Finally they reached the desired question: "May I speak to Tom?" which, unfortunately, elicits "I'm sorry, dear, but Thomas may not use the telephone until his grades improve." I don't add "Or hell freezes over."

Whichever comes first. Hell will surely win.

Why, sister mothers, do children want to fail? Is it the new high? Is there some sexual charge experienced when our ninth-graders come home with report cards full of F's and I's? What sado-psychological satisfaction is gained by them watching our hearts leap from our breasts, our eyes involuntarily tearing over, our breaths coming in short, unnatural spurts? What kick do they get standing over us watching our lives pass before our eyes? All my friends have marvelous children who clean their rooms, excel in extracurricular activities, pass their classes, get honors and awards. I've even taken, and I don't mind admitting it, to avoiding certain parents of perfect children, though I have not been a competitive parent. When little Billy Bob joined the Boy Scouts, climbed a twelve-story building and rescued a blind, paraplegic unwed mother from raging flames I never said to my son: "How come you never do anything worthwhile?" No. I smiled at the parent, congratulated the child and dutifully went back to pinning Tom's socks for the laundry and picking up the comic books that are spread across the floor, making his room a hazardous area. When little Sally Mae, in just the fifth grade, was invited to Athens to address the Senate in her fluent Greek on how stability could be obtained with Turkey, I said to her mother, my friend, "You must be very proud." I did not say to Tom, "Why is it that that little snotty-nose twerp is hailed the world over while you refuse to write a simple essay for English *in* English about the Alaskan cruise I had to mortgage the house to take you on?" I didn't even heap abuse when he replied, "Alaska wasn't so much." No. I calmly said, "Dear, I sincerely think you can improve this Incomplete by turning in your assignment." I am, however, about to be convinced that kindness, civil tone, and logic have no truck with teenagers. My son had a classmate last year who was spanked every time she brought home a B or less. Tom was appalled. "But dear," I pointed out, "look at your grades and look at hers. Surely I am the parent in the wrong." "Well," says Mister as he makes his way to the freezer to get a pizza and pop it in the oven, "she hates her mother and I love you." If this is love, folks . . .

My son, I do believe and have had demonstrated, has a lot of character. He has never lied to me. I'm told by friends with perfect children that that is because it's all the same to him. He doesn't lie because he knows I won't go off on him or stop him from doing anything he wants to do anyway. I like to think that's not true. I like to think he is truthful because (1) I *will* go crazy on him if he lies; but mostly because (2) somewhere inside that pickled fourteen-year-old mass that commonly is called a brain he has absorbed some of the values I've been trying by example to teach him. When I am hasty in my judgments or just plain wrong about something I don't mind apologizing. When I don't know something I don't mind admitting ignorance. When I don't want him to go somewhere or do something for no particular reason other than I think it's not right for him, I explain, "Mother is making an arbitrary judgment that has no logic or reason. You are right to be angry about this. I would feel the same way if the tables were turned." It may not be any easier to take, but it's honest.

I've also seen Tom come through a situation that would be difficult for a stable adult. My father developed bladder cancer following a stroke, which is the reason we moved from New York back to Cincinnati. Those years could not have been easy, living with someone who was, in fact, dying. My father was brave in the face of his impending death and so was my son. Neither complained of the burden or the pain. The night my father died Tom, my mother and I were the only ones at home. My sister was coming in from San Francisco. My nephew from Seattle was not contacted until the day after. The hospital called that Gus had died. I had to go out to pick up his personal property and sign for the autopsy. Tom, who was then twelve, said, "I'll go with you." He went to the hospital, viewed the body, got his grandfather's walking cane, stayed while the other arrangements were made. That night he came into my room and curled up next to Wendy, my dog, and slept on the floor. The next morning we had to pick a casket. "I'll go with you," he said to my mother, my sister and me. He put his tie and jacket on and sat through the funeral arrangements.

He stayed by my side as the family made calls, placed flower orders, took care of the kind of base-touching a funeral requires. For two days he looked after us as best he could. On the morning of the funeral he asked: "Mommy, when is Chris getting here?" Meaning, I think, that he had gone as far as he was capable. It was more than caring . . . it was character.

Last year we visited a boarding school of note in the East. He and I stayed three days and he loved it. My child would prep in the ninth grade. I, too, would have something to brag about over beer and barbecue. As the three of us, Tom, my mother and I, talked over our fall plans I started outlining how he could have his own MasterCard, how to check his bank balance, the numbers to call to reach me wherever I might be, the numbers for Grandmother. Tom looked up and said: "Wait a minute! Where *are* you going to be?" "I'll be out working to pay for your tuition. That's why I'm going over these plans with you." "Well, where will Grandmother be?" "She'll be here a lot but she may want to travel, visit her sisters or anything else she wants to do." "You mean I'm going off BY MYSELF?" Eyes getting larger. "Well, yes, Tom. That's what it means to prep. You go off to school by yourself." In that let's-get-this-straight manner he says: "You're not taking an apartment in Wallingford?" "No." "Well I sure didn't think you were kicking me out" with just a touch of the indignant in his voice.

He went to public school. And turned fourteen. Since I know the school system is one of the best in the country, since I know he has the ability, I can only blame it on fourteen. My grandmother, Louvenia Watson, used to baffle me when she said, "I'll be glad when you get off Fool's Hill." I never used to know what she meant. I certainly do now. He'll turn fifteen this year and I, who was supposed to turn forty-one, will turn 103. As they sing in the coffee commercial with all the winners sitting around smiling: Hold on tight to your dream . . . Actually, though, I am a very hip mother. I was into Prince and Michael Jackson before Thomas realized what he could be in life. Yeah, sure, you'd like a kid who could pronounce perfect and not "purrfect," but I think the way Michael says it is cute. I know "Thriller" is in the *Guinness Book of World Records*, but there will always be a special place in my heart for "Rock with You." I haven't quite adjusted to parachute pants, but I'm into ties and boots—what I call my Tina Turner look, though I have an Afro. We can't all do long hair. I tend to be a bit old-fashioned, and nothing, absolutely nothing, will get me totally out of my elephant bells. I mean, the big chill may have settled on the rest but I'm going forward. The sixties stood for something.

I shall always remember the joy on my grandmother's face when she came back from the mass meeting to tell me I *could* march and how proud she was. She and Grandpapa caught a cab to come see me. I actually figured I was on my way to meet my maker, but one must have a sense of social responsibility. When I enrolled in Fisk University the following fall one of the things I most looked forward to was sitting in. There was a sort of style to it. Assuming you weren't actually molested, it was cool. You sat on the stool and watched the white people panic. Dick Gregory has the best story. When he stopped at a diner the waitress said, "We don't serve niggers," to which Gregory replied, "I don't eat them." You always hoped someone would say something to you to let you be cool. Mostly you were scared. I was home alone the Sunday the little girls were bombed in Birmingham. I remember the news flash saying they were dead. And it was enough to make you want to kill. Like all southern youngsters I went to Sunday school in a big church with a basement that could have hidden anything. It seemed so damned unfair.

Our personal tragedy in Knoxville was the bombing of Clinton High School. It really made you wonder about the people we lived among. Racism is at best boring. When I was younger it was frightening. You always felt someone was trying to kill you. Or hurt your feelings. Now it's just tiresome. Who really wants to be bothered with it anymore? It's dull to hate, though I doubt that my generation will ever be able to graft new emotions to the scars. Emmett Till; Schwerner, Chaney and Goodman; Nina Simone said it best: "Mississippi God-damn!" The summer of '64 was frightening. All else became a release and to many a relief. And when you look at Miami where the police are back to shooting Black boys down or L.A. or New York, and anyone unfortunate enough to be arrested is committing suicide in jail, you really have to wonder, when will we learn? It's just so unworthy and spirit-sapping.

I do think we have been deeply touched by the past de-cade. Even the little things. We couldn't, in Knoxville, go to the movie theaters downtown or to the amusement park. I do like movies, but to this day I won't go to any amusement park. Cincinnati was no better. Coney Island, the local southern Ohio place to play for white kids, had to be sued before Blacks would be admitted. It's boring. Gwen Brooks and I shared a reading in New Jersey a few years ago and in the Q and A someone asked about racism in America. Gwen gave an intel-ligent response; I said it was boring. At lunch Gwen said,

"Boring?" Well, what else do you call it? It can't be a sickness 'cause the cure is known. It's not a condition 'cause the times they did a change. It doesn't make anybody happy. I mean, I never ran into a hater who said, "You know, this hating business is really good." "It makes my day to deny a job to some Black man or woman." "I really love flunking the Black kids I have to teach." Or, "Yesterday I dumped my Black neighbor's garbage on his lawn and I just want you people to know how pleased I am with myself." We used to laugh at the Klan, which liked to think it was the sheets that frightened us. Hell, it was the men in the sheets, and we knew that all along. One of the sure signs that Blacks and whites are coming closer together, which is not necessarily for the good of this earth, is Black people have begun sneaking around doing murder for no reason, committing real suicide as opposed to the over-drinking–bad driving–fight-picking way we used to and standing around making reasonable-sounding excuses for our failure to live up to what we ourselves know to be our emotional potential and moral obligation. But hey, what does this have to do with autobiography?

I took a test recently in one of the popular magazines. I, not surprisingly, find myself quite an attractive personality, though my test score indicated that people find me opinionated and perhaps pushy. Not bad traits for writers. I know this profession does not easily lend itself to friendships. Our friends are either deathly afraid we will write about them or terribly bored at hearing the same subject discussed from all possible points of view. It's what writers do—talk. I think I am pretty ordinary. I think if I was looking for somebody to hang out with I'd be the last person I'd choose. There is a mirthful side to my personality and I basically like to laugh, but mostly I take things pretty seriously. A friend of my mother's was having dinner with us recently and we began discussing movies, which frankly I think of as a pretty safe topic. I kept saying, "What was the intent of that scene?" and she kept trying to tell me why she laughed. She finally said, "I know your problem! You're an intellectual!" Not really. I just think things should mean something and I get confused when there is no meaning to be found. We waste too much, we humans, because we refuse to recognize that there is a possibility of order and things making sense and we as a planet doing better.

I really don't know what to say about myself. I like music. There is something very special about capping my headphones and drowning in a vision of sound. Someone once asked me if I played an instrument and I replied, "My stereo." It's not surprising that man's first musical instrument was a drum; the image of the heart had to be manifest. The African people made use of the ability of the drum to both inform and incite; for over two hundred years of the American experience drumming was outlawed. A people, though, are rarely stopped in their legitimate desire for either knowledge or pleasure. Whether the Eighteenth Amendment would outlaw alcohol or the Miss America Pageant would desire the clothing of their Black Venus, a people, through individual risk or simply aesthetic innocence, will bring word of a new day.

It is sheer folly to assume the various African cultures were without stress, frustrations, discriminations. It is only our desire to escape the challenges of our own times that leads us to envision some African Eden with fruit dripping from every branch, fish jumping in clear cool ponds, women willing with no discernible persuasion, men strong, beautiful and capable after undergoing some variation of initiation into "manhood." If the human species alone among the mammals is capable of dreaming, we are also alone in our capacity for fantasy. America did not invent the blues for Africans—it simply made us sing them in English.

The giraffe alone, among those who are warm-blooded, is without a voice. All other mammals, most insects and, as we have learned to listen to the ocean, not an inconsiderable number of fish make some sound. Among those on earth the chirping of birds is universally considered pleasant, the howl of a single wolf on a mountain ridge the most mournful. We howl with the wolf not so much in imitation of his sound as in sympathy with another motherless child. The African slave bereft of his gods, his language, his drums searched his heart for a new voice. Under sun and lash the African sought meaning in life on earth and the possibility of life hereafter. They shuffled their feet, clapped their hands, gathered a collective audible breath to release the rhythms of the heart. We affirmed in those dark days of chattel through the White Knights of Emancipation that all we had was a human voice to guide us and a human voice to answer the call.

Anthropologically speaking, humans were divided in the workforce by gender. The men became the stalkers of prey; the women tended the fire, garden and children at the home site. Men learned at a very early age the value of quiet; women learned the necessity of talk. Men learned to compete for the best spot, the biggest share; women learned to cooperate, to socialize. If there was a benefit of slavery to the slaves it was that it broke down gender barriers; men and women shared the work, learned the songs, began and ended the day together. If there was a benefit to white people during the Great Depression it was that men learned how to deal with enforced idleness; women learned having a "good marriage" would not protect them from the reality that everyone has a right, if not an obligation, to do productive work.

It is historically considered that there have been two American revolutions: the one against the British for the right to tax ourselves and the one against the South to free chattel slaves. The revisionists consider there was perhaps a third revolution: the recovery from the Great Depression to meld compassion with free enterprise. Those of my generation know there has been a fourth: American youth, not with fife and bugle but with drums and boogie, headed for the twenty-first century with the battle cry: "Oo Whoop Baba Loo Boop Oo Whop Bam Boom!"

The Coasters said they'd been "Searchin'," and once again an African–Afro-American ritual—the Stomp—was being practiced. Anytime that song hit the airwaves Black youngsters would pour from their cars to form a big boss line. James Brown begged "Please Please Please" and the Midnighters informed us "Annie Had a Baby." Sam Cooke intoned "You Send Me," but the Dominos were only a "Sixty-Minute Man." Jesse Belvin said "Good Night My Love" but the Dells asked "Why Do You Have to Go?" The Brown decision was rendered by the Supreme Court and Eisenhower had a heart attack. In the heart of Black America it finally was made clear that no matter what we did, no matter how much we abided by the rules and regulations, no matter how straight our hair, correct our speech, circumscribed our behavior, no matter *what*—we were, in the words of Moms Mabley, "still a Negro."

The advantage to a people who have clearly defined an issue is this: The individual is relieved of the burden of carrying his people forward. He can dance upon his own floor in his own style. Though white Americans would try to this very day to make Black Americans responsible for each other, Black people recognize that just as individual accomplishments open no doors, individual failures close off no avenues. The Right Reverend Ray Charles said it best: "Tell the Truth!" We no longer were ashamed of being Black; we no longer wished to hide our love of chitlins and hog maws; we no longer wished to pretend we cared. Rosa Parks in Montgomery said "No!" and Chuck Willis asked "What Am I Living For?" Johnny Ace, who allegedly shot himself backstage at Houston's City Auditorium, went number one in England the next day with "Never Let Me Go"; Jesse Belvin's car blew four tires, killing him after he played a dance in L.A.; Chuck Willis died; Sam Cooke was murdered in L.A.; Frankie Lymon left the Teenagers to begin his involvement with drugs; Little Willie John was arrested for murder and died in prison; Otis Redding's plane crashed. Don't send me Murray the K as some kind of friend, let alone god to rhythm and blues. We paid for that music. Mr. K changed his Cleveland station format because Black and white kids were tuned to WCIN in Cincinnati, WDIA in Memphis, WDAS in Philadelphia and all night long WLAC in Nashville where "Randy" played and packaged the hits.

Black people had some place to run! We, like Max Schmeling, lacked a place to hide. We went "Dancin' in the

Streets" behind Martin Luther King, Jr., behind Malcolm X, behind mighty mighty Sly and the Family Stone. If they snickered when Little Richard brought his painted lips, mascaraed eyes, hair piled high on his head out of his closet, they were silent when Cassius Clay echoed, "I'm Black and I'm proud." Otis Redding cried for "Respect," a coda to Chuck Berry's anthem, "Roll Over, Beethoven." And in case the message was missed, Aretha covered both Redding and Sam Cooke: "A Change Is Gonna Come." But Lady Soul, ever the lady, softened it with "A woman's only human." The Intruders replied, "Gotta let a man be a man."

I'm an old unrepentant rocker who joins with Bob Seger in demanding "Old-Time Rock and Roll." I've never been asked to do a commercial, but even if I were I couldn't demand "my MTV." No way. I like my music in my head and, when I was younger, my foot on the pedal. One of life's great thrills is putting Little Richard on the auto-reverse cassette in your car and heading from New York to Cincinnati. You don't even see the Jersey Turnpike. You pull over in Pennsylvania just before the first tunnel and get an orange sherbet ice cream from Howard Johnson's and you don't tune down until you creep through West Virginia. I liked being young and I like being not young. At the risk of being very, very dull I agree that "to everything there is a season." I think I would classify myself as happy. Which in no way means I don't go off on people, myself, situations . . . but more, that given a choice there wouldn't be too much too different in my life.

I'm finally old enough to know it would be nice to have money, but it's not all that necessary. I think I'd be a good rich person. At least I know I would enjoy my money. Nothing galls me more than somebody who's come into some sort of fortune or been born to one bitching that life is hard. I'm sure life is since the end of life for all of us is death. It just seems unfair when you keep hearing people who can call long distance and talk as long as they like, who don't worry how their children's tuition will be paid, who don't fear for their health since they are properly insured going on and on about life's difficulties. It's tacky. The very least the rich can do for the rest of us is either enjoy or shut up. But what does that have to do with what I have written? Nothing.

I can think of nothing less interesting to me than to walk slowly through my poetry and say ". . . and then I wrote . . ." The books stand on their own. They will either live or die. I hate that pretentiousness of writers who think people are too dumb to understand what is being discussed. I lecture part of the year and it's a great joy to me. I like to meet people and I like to talk. I don't like to fly, but there are few college campuses that will agree to come to Cincinnati so I grit my teeth and go. The one thing I'm very conscious of is not going over very old ground. I'm a space nut so I do talk about space a lot; I'm into the Global Village, but mostly I try to bring the best of me to my audience. Even if it's not good it's honest. I simply refuse to believe the public has nothing better to do than come out on a cold night to hear me read a paper that could have been slipped under their door when the morning milk was delivered. The whole point to being "Live and in Person" is that you bring a live person.

Academia is such a controlled situation, people like me cause problems. I think speeches and fruit should always be fresh. I know, sure I do, that there are those who will say,

"Well, what about dried fruit? I like dried fruit." This is not against dried fruit. A little Stilton on dried apricots is one of the taste treats of the world. Maybe a bowl of hot garlic soup followed by a roasted lamb shank and hey, you've got something. Yet one should always consider that fresh has its charm.

I'm just not a star. I think about it a lot. I say to myself: "Giovanni, be demanding. Make them put Perrier on the platform. Refuse to sign autographs when Saturn is in the house of Mars. Be peculiar. Get your makeup together. Need to change several times during your appearance. Demand a better dressing room. Keep people away. Work on your sneer. Practice hurting their feelings. Need special foods. Do something so folks will know that you know that they should know that you are special." Yet I distrust in the human species the need to exalt. Writing is like any other endeavor. I hope I am always able to bring my best to any audience that is kind enough to share an evening with me. I'm not humble. This is no Nikki Washington Carver. I believe in myself. I believe in what I do. Yet people need both gentleness and a challenge. Our college students especially need someone to talk to them as if they had sense.

I would remind any program chairman that it's *your* program. While it is unreasonable to ask your speaker to go to bed with you, it is not a burden to ask your speaker to have dinner with the committee. Your speaker has a right to be picked up on time. You have a right to a press conference. If your speaker is a funny eater, he should provide the food he needs. You provide what you can. And I'm not saying be sloppy. I don't care for McDonald's or Pizza Hut, but if that's what you can offer, then my job is to help you feel good about it while refusing to eat. I'm only your speaker for a short while. I will not try to change your habits if you don't try to change mine. I smoke. Anyone who picks me up after an airplane ride will find themselves facing cigarette smoke. That's because I don't drink. If you hate smoke, do not pick up your speaker. But hey, Miss Manners covers all this so much better than I. Your speaker at her best is there to serve you. If you are positive, she will be. If you are clear, she will relax and trust you. Should you also happen to know what your speaker does for a living ("Are you going to sing tonight?") you will win her affection ("No. I don't sing"), and pretty please don't decide to be honest ("Frankly I was hoping they wouldn't invite you") because that will depress your speaker ("But aside from that, Jackie, how did you like Dallas?") and she will become very closed instead of very open. Recognize that she is a human being whose dog may be sick, whose son has a science project due, who had water in the basement this morning when she left for the airport. Assume that she wants to be there and let her know you are pleased. Happiness is just such a nice thing to share. Try it. It may just make your day, too.

I date all my work because I think poetry, or any writing, is but a reflection of the moment. The universal comes from the particular. I like the nuts and bolts of life. I want to know everything. Sometimes, especially in the fall, if you're a morning person you wake up around five-thirty in the morning and start your coffee. The dark is just beginning to lift and in my backyard the birds come to drink and bathe. Soon they will not come so early because it will be too cold. But now they come and chirp. There's a big German shepherd that roams the neighborhood that is usually passing. But mostly you hear nothing. The sun rises in my eastern window where I am growing African violets and I just like to watch the red break and wonder about all the world. There is an ad concerning space that asks, "How long do we have to look at an organism before we recognize it?" How many little boys chunked the Rosetta Stone into the Red Sea before someone recognized that that was the key? And if there is never an answer, the quest is so worthwhile.

I like lace handkerchiefs. I like to look at those my grandmother passed to my mother; they are beautiful. Someone, perhaps Louvenia, perhaps my great-grandmother Cornelia, hand-embroidered them. They are as delicate as a spider web, as strong as a silkworm's cocoon. I cry when I watch *Little House on the Prairie*. I like to be happy. And other than an occasional response to an infrequent query I don't contemplate my work. I do try to be a good writer. I believe that I bring my best when I try to share. It's an honorable profession. There are so many pieces to my puzzle, I have no interest in trying to judge what I have done; but only to try to do more. I like my awards and honors. I love it when people say they have read my poetry. I never make the mistake of asking if they understood what I was *really* talking about or if they *really* liked what I did. I just thank them because whether I disappointed or delighted them they took the time to be involved in my effort . . . to explore with me . . . to extend themselves to me as I have extended myself to them. It's lonely. Writing. But so is practicing tennis or football runs. So is studying. So is waxing the floor and changing the baby. So is life. We are less lonely when we connect. Art is a connection. I like being a link. I hope the chain will hold.

An Answer to Some Questions on How I Write
In Three Parts

Part I

It's always a bit intimidating to try to tell how I write since I, like most writers, I think, am not at all sure that I do what I do in the way that I think I do it. In other words, I was always told not to look a gift horse in the mouth. Melvin Tolson said it much more poetically: A civilization is always judged in its decline. One reason that America has, I believe, always preferred its writers dead is that not only can it then be determined what we wrote and why we wrote that way, but we are not there to change our minds or correct any misgivings. A writer like W. E. B. Du Bois will always create problems for the critical establishment because he lived too long. Just think of the great joy that would have attended his death had Du Bois had the good sense, if not the actual kind disposition, to die after *The Souls of Black Folk*. He would have been hailed as a great seer, a prescient individual; all schoolchildren, black or white, would have been required to read his books. But Du Bois lived on, and wrote more and more, for almost all the next century. He is now dismissed by the white establishment as a Communist, and the Black critical establishment, which at least pays lip service to him, can't make up its mind which *one* of his books it ought to read. Writers are not rewarded for a body of work. We all seem to prefer one or maybe two books from a writer. After that we begin to hear disclaimers about how the earlier books were better, more passionate, or whatever. Ralph Ellison is probably the prime example. He has become, by virtue of one book, "the dean of Black writers"; yet a Chester Himes who continued to write was ignored. Though when Himes was kind enough to relieve us of his great talent we will all in time stand around giving memorials to him, decreeing the awfulness of the establishment that it failed to recognize him. We too have failed. But then, the Black writers seem no more able to overcome the green monster than any other writers. We fail to cheer for one another for a variety of reasons that have nothing to do with the art of writing itself. The conflict is not in the doing but in the talking about . . . which is also why my speeches are in prose and my poems in poetry. I was taught you never send a green frog to do the work of a Black princess.

I'm not sure I have any moral or political compulsions. I have habits: I smoke cigarettes, I drink an incessant amount of coffee and I do pick my nose when I'm afraid. It's gotten so bad, in fact, that I now know that I'm afraid because I find myself picking my nose. I think that emerged from my fear of airplanes. I love to fly. In some lone masochistic way I would love to go to the moon. I certainly would actively seek and never pass on a chance to at least circle the planet. I have been religiously saving my money to take the SST, and each time it becomes affordable for me the dollar drops again. There seems to be no limit to the ends of racism in this country. I'm totally convinced that any Black woman who consciously circled the earth, let alone landed on another planet, would have a very different view of the heavens as well as the meagerness of earth. I think Black people, and Black Americans especially, are the only people to really view earth from its proper perspective since we have no land that we can in any historical way call our own. I think at this bisection of time and space we are the ones uniquely prepared to accept life on another planet. I believe the poets are the proper people to send since we see love and beauty in the blooming of the Black community; power in a people whose only power has been the truth. Maybe that's a compulsion. I like to tell the truth as I see it. I hope others do the same. That's why literature is so important. We cannot possibly leave it to history as a discipline nor to sociology nor science nor economics to tell the story of our people. As I understand "obviates," nothing obviates the political because the political embraces all the desires and history of the people. Perhaps someone will say, "Well, I think the history obviates the political." And I shall reply, "The only way you even know the word 'obviate' is that Mari put it on her questionnaire." If the politics of a people is only Democrat, Republican, Socialist, or even the Black political ideologies, then our people can be said to embrace no politics. Our politics have been the standing for that which is right and good; for the desegregation of society; for the equitable distribution of goods and services; for the free movement of a free people; for the respect for the old and the love of the young. Electing a few white boys or Black boys to office cannot be serious politics. Nothing significant changes whether the majority is white or Black, only the view. I support a Black view but let's not fool ourselves. The ideas and ideals that inform the Black struggles must always be the integrity of the human spirit. Can we really picture Martin Luther King, Jr., as a white man? White Americans have to go all the way back to John Adams or George Washington, and even they could fight their revolution with guns against soldiers who traveled thousands of miles across the sea. Our general had to use words against an enemy who lived next door. In the battle for peace the word will always be the winner. And we who are Black can never develop a love for rockets and planes and marvelous Titan missiles that go boooooom! in the night because a wrench fell on them. We must hunker down into that love of the spirit of Black Americans that allowed a janitor to be a deacon in a church or a washerwoman to sing that perfect note. We must, before we, like many an endangered species, become extinct, rediscover that we are Black and beautiful and proud and intelligent. I don't think everyone has to write the way I write nor think the way I think. There are plenty of ideas to go around. I just think that in life all things are political. What we do every day and how we do it. It's nice to love the people but it's necessary to be a friend to someone. Fanatics are, for one thing, boring and, for another, unreliable. They tend to burn out just when you need them. That's generally because they were, in essence, summer soldiers. When winter came they expected to be back home. I'm not against summer soldiers; they're better than none at all. But we need some long-termers too. All our enemies won't be as difficult and as easy as the Bull Connerses or the old George Wallaces. Some will be like Jimmy Carter; others won't even be white.

I don't feel besieged. I'm ever amazed at the idea that I am or can be anything other than what I am. If I'm not a Black woman then where is the real me? There used to be that old expression that you have two strikes against you: one as a Black and two as a woman. I never could quite understand what would make me strike out under those circumstances. I've always been a Black woman and I shall always be. I recognize the possibility that I may not always inhabit this body, since matter is neither created nor destroyed, leaving us all to understand that we are really nothing more than recycled matter from some other decaying thing. But why should I be different from any other thing on earth? What the plants expel, we inhale; what decays into the ground gives forth fruits and vegetables; when the glaciers pass, the lakes are formed. We don't ask the sun to consider the pleasures of the moon; why should female and Black humans be constantly asked how we feel about our essence? Those who ask are, in effect, trying to assure themselves that they are inherently better off to have been born male and preferably white. That's just so much tommyrot. I wouldn't be other than what I am because for one I can't; I can only fool myself into thinking that I can. And for two: I like myself.

Part II

My first nationally published article appeared in the now-defunct *Negro Digest* through the intercession of the late David Llorens. Either he thought I showed talent or he was being exceedingly kind to a young Fiskite and he purchased my first article. It made my day. There are probably no words to describe the joy you feel when you see your first words in print. There's a story that I probably shouldn't share about John Killens, who was at that time the writer in residence at Fisk, and me. When my article in the *Negro Digest* debuted John took me and the rest of the writing class out to dinner to celebrate. John had just purchased a new car. I left my copy of the magazine on his seat when we all got out at the restaurant and John went to park. When we came out John couldn't remember where the car was parked and, as he tells the story, my first words were, "Oh my God, my article is in the car!" John was, understandably from his perspective, more concerned about his new automobile. My point of view was, however, not wholly without merit. Your first published article is indeed quite precious. My first published book was done by a few friends and me. It was the book *Black Feeling, Black Talk*. I formed a publishing company, borrowed heavily from family and friends, and hired a printer. Luckily there were a number of Black bookstores around the country to which you could just send books: Ellis's in Chicago, Micheaux in New York, Vaughn in Detroit, and one in San Francisco. All were very kind to me and all paid me promptly. Then came the second wave of bookstores in the middle sixties, so it wasn't very hard to at least get a hearing on the merits of the writing. Now, of course, there are just too many chains, whether in bookstores or with publishers. The independents are all but gone and even those who hang on find distribution a major problem. I don't know if it's necessary for me to say, and those who are already aware can skip this part, but with an estimated twenty million Blacks we could control the best-seller list. There should be at least several books on the fiction and nonfiction best-seller list every year. I was so happy when *Song of Solomon* was acknowledged but also should have been *Just Above My Head*. I happen to write in an area where we are not charted so it's not at all personal. But Black writers are the only ones telling anything near the truth in either fiction or nonfiction. If Studs Terkel can make it so should *Drylongso*. But we all know Blacks don't like to purchase books. Though we should. The literature tells so much about our people. I hope the poetry too. I think we as writers don't have a true sense of our profession . . . that we are there to cheer each other on . . . to expose our people to and interest others in our works. There is, quite simply, too much jealousy in the profession . . . and we all suffer from it.

Every time I sit down with my typewriter I am beginning to write. The "beginning" cannot be told until I know the ending. I am, however, a writer very much grounded in my sense of place. I need my own coffee cup, my own chair, but most especially my own typewriter. I had a steam pipe burst in my apartment and my typewriter was uncovered and thereby ruined by the steam. I had had that typewriter since college. It was almost a year before I would even begin to touch this one. I think, by the way, that every intended writer should learn to type. Most of us have a poor handwriting, and thinking on a typewriter is different from thinking on a yellow pad. The sooner you can think on a keyboard, the less room you have for procrastination. And all writers are great procrastinators!

A more legitimate question might be, is there any room for white men in literature? Black women on both sides of the

Atlantic are keeping traditional Western literature alive. We have, in Africa, Bessie Head, who with *When Rain Clouds Gather* and *Maru* has proven herself one of the great African writers writing in the English language, and, of course, Toni Morrison in the United States. Compared to what? Norman Mailer? Philip Roth? Be serious! *Roots* was of course a great popular success, though marred by the various controversies. I would hope each and every woman who ever thought she wanted to write would at least give it a try. It's not a ladder that we're climbing, it's literature we're producing, and there will always be someone to read it. The difference between young Black women and young Black men, as I see it, is that young Black men don't feel they will lose face if they say they want to write whereas young Black women aren't at all too sure that writing isn't too aggressive. What you hear a lot is: Can you write and be a good wife too? That's not exactly the question but that's what it amounts to. And the answer is probably no. Writing is a tough mistress, according to the men who've written about it, and I would submit it's no easier a paramour. But I'm not the best woman to ask about the blending of art and traditional married life because I think traditional married life is for traditional people. Or as they say in the Daily Ohio Lottery, "If you got it, go get it." I really don't think life is about the I-could-have-beens. I could have been a professional ballplayer but I met your mother; I could have been a professional dancer but my mother didn't want me to go to New York; or any variation of the theme. Life is only about the I-tried-to-do. I don't mind the failure but I can't imagine that I'd forgive myself if I didn't try. I don't have a life-style, I have a life. And I've made it a point not to analyze myself. I'll tell a story or confess a weakness but who I really am keeps surprising me. There's so much to learn about the species. I think it's foolish to determine what your life will be before you've even had a chance to live it.

Part III

Like all people who pry, I resist questions about my own work. I like to think that if truth has any bearing on art, my poetry and prose is art because it's truthful. I say that while recognizing that every time a truth is learned a new thesis, synthesis, antithesis is set in motion. I like to think I've grown and changed in the last decade. How else could I ask people to read my work or listen to me? It would have been pointless for a girl born in Knoxville, Tennessee, reared in Cincinnati, Ohio, to have lived in New York and traveled the face of this earth not to have changed. That would be an ultimate betrayal of the trust people put in any writer. I should hope there will be a body of work by Nikki Giovanni that's not just a consistency of unformed and untested ideas that I acquired somewhere in my late teens or early twenties. I seek change for the beauty of itself. Everything will change. The only question is growing up or decaying. We who are human have a great opportunity to grow up and perhaps beyond that. Our grasp is not limited to our reach. We who are writers live always in the three time zones: past, present, and future. We pay respect to them all as we share an idea. I loved my profession well before I joined it. I have always been a lover of books and the ideas they contain. Sometimes I think it is easy for we who write to forget that that is only half the process; someone must read. Now someone will say, "See, you have to cater to the audience!" But it's been my reading of history and understanding of politics that there is an audience for everything. If there is truly a sucker born every minute then perhaps we must wait the hour or the day for the wise one, the compassionate, the sensitive, for truly, the greater of the species appear to be in short supply, and yet they do come. There is always someone to remind us that there must be more to living than what we currently see. And that unusual person is what we seek. The bright, the concerned, the capable, are a part of our audience also. Someone said in the next century everybody will be famous for fifteen minutes. Who cares? We live now. As best we can. And we encourage others. We write, because we believe that the human spirit cannot be tamed and should not be trained.

About a Poem

As a child of the sixties I well remember when our movement began to sour. It isn't difficult to pinpoint. Some people would like to say we soured when violence came into the community and we began burning down our own homes and businesses. I don't think so. We, both Blacks and whites, are a violent people who throughout the American years have burned both our own and any other available community. We kill each other, we Americans, at a very high rate, whether at the stockade or the stock market. We, as an African people, have a bloody history of war. When I used to hear speakers of the sixties stand up for Black Power I always considered it one up for a library card because obviously they had just discovered something. Any cursory reading of African history teaches us there is not now nor has there ever been a dearth of warriors. The fact that a battle or a war has occasionally been lost does not detract from the ferociousness of the battle. There are some missing years because our African ancestors were either unable or unwilling to protect the great libraries of Timbuktu and Alexandria. More likely, given the human components, those who were not allowed to partake of the knowledge refused to die to perpetuate it. But that is speculation on my part. What we do know and can easily see is for those of us who are Black Americans, both our African mother and our European father have never hesitated to use any and all destructive weapons—whether food or shelter; whether napalm or Agent Orange; whether selling a captive into slavery or keeping him as a POW in a tiger cage—to have their way. No. It could not have been violence in the late sixties that tempered the gains of the fifties and early sixties. Rap Brown teaches us "Violence is as American as cherry pie" and he could have added as African as the Click Song.

We did, however, learn something interesting about violence during the sixties. It doesn't work. Violence is like money in the bank; it's only helpful if you don't have to use it. Any of us who have any kind of little chicken-scratch bank accounts know exactly what I mean. It looks good to say, "I saved five hundred dollars during the past year." Now that's not a lot of money but it projects a certain image. You look a little more solid than the person who has saved nothing. If you play your cards right you can parlay that into another $500 and pretty soon you look good enough to get real credit. But if you have the money and take it out, even if you try to put it back, that withdrawal stands and folks from whom you want to borrow need to know why you took it out. The worst thing that can happen is that you have to close the account because you are below the minimum. Violence is like that $500. Once you use it you have nothing to fall back on and you have to start resaving and rebuilding. Our community had nothing to rebuild with, and a few loud mouths refused to understand that we had no additional funds. The Black community, as we look at the eighties, has had our account stamped "Closed." We are still trying to spend what we earned and had saved during another era. Were we formerly rich and decadent we could sit and discuss the "good old days," building poems and plays around our lost innocence. But we were just hard-working people who fell into a Black depression and have not allowed ourselves the time and energy to discover the "why" of our condition, therefore depriving ourselves of the tools to bring ourselves out.

We soured, this Black community, when we turned our backs upon who we are and who we could become. We have not been, historically, a community that has received help from the majority of our fellow citizens. We are really hard-pressed to find a time that the majority was committed to us. Sure there are statues to Abraham Lincoln but we didn't build them. If we were building statues we should seriously con-sider a railroad engine, for I much doubt that slavery would have had to go had it not been for Western Expansion. I know that's depressing to some people. Some of us want to think that people do the right thing for the right reason, but there is no history of mankind showing that. People do the best thing for the most expedient reason, and should there be a benefi-cial side effect we are all glad. It's just sad to think that some-where in some big city or on some rural farm there is a gather-ing of Black folk wearing their pointed-toed shoes and little green caps agreeing with Peter Pan that they should never grow up. The reason we grieve when a child dies is not that we miss the child but that we mourn for the potential. Everybody should have an equal opportunity to grow up . . . and grow old. It's not promised—tomorrow never is—yet it is adulthood that we seek. Somewhere during the sixties, Magic came into our movement.

People began to believe that if they wished hard enough everything would be all right. If they only wanted it badly enough their lives would turn around and they would be happy. Somehow Freedom, which is clearly a list of responsibilities, became a list of wishes. We began to sour. I remember the speeches exhorting the audience to turn their backs on the Uncle Toms, the church, their parents. As if that which was denying us Freedom was outside ourselves. As if people could deny or grant Freedom. The community turned its back on the Freedom, since 1619, that we had achieved not only for ourselves but for the world. We, as a people, had so clearly shown that though our bodies were captured, our souls were free; that we could live with those who had so "dispitefully used us"; that though our bodies were tired "our souls were rested." The entire planet needs to take note of the Book of Black America because we rewrote the history of mankind when we neither fled our former captors nor sought vengeance. We showed that the human spirit had evolved.

But life is frequently like a chess game; for every step forward there are two to the side. We achieved true Freedom for those who had oppressed us and turned our backs on those who had freed us—the old men and women who had worked the fields; the young couples who built homes; the folk who insisted upon going into places where Blacks were not wanted; the students who studied to have skills; the businesspeople, both men and women, who not only serviced our community but employed our young; the old people who gave their dimes and dollars to build beautiful churches; the schoolteachers, beauticians, barbers, mailmen who through their Black Greek-letter organizations gave scholarships for young people to go to school; the men who did not abuse and desert their families; the wives who overlooked more than any woman should have to overlook. We soured because we failed to honor our forefathers. We wanted Freedom to be so much more than paying our bills at the end of the month; seeing our children grow up and go to college; retiring after twenty years on the same job. We wanted Freedom to be some kind of emotional lottery where when our number came up we would be rich and famous. We wanted Magic, and we soured because Freedom is reality.

I wrote a poem, *Nikki-Rosa*, in 1969 because you could see it coming. You could see the Government studies on the Black family and you could see the cavalry was on its way. My limited sense of Indian history taught me that any time the cavalry rides the natives had better scatter. You could see the "tender concern" for our Black youth and you knew: We would be the losers. The folks with the loud mouths and nothing in the bank thought they were winning: The Government was going to DO SOMETHING. Violent voices and violent acts thought they had carried the day. But nonviolence was never for the oppressor; it was for the oppressed. Martin Luther King's words were not to comfort the segregators but to teach us: If we can forgive them, we must then love ourselves. No one can be blamed for what he did not see, but we all bear responsibility for what we do not see. The magic of the Black community is ourselves. We held together when all others had fallen apart. We persevered as a community, in our families, when others turned their backs on us. We achieved from those segregated schools, diligently learning skills we had no foreseeable opportunity to use; gaining strength in those churches built penny by penny from folks who were insulted daily while washing clothes and floors, hopping bells in hotels though they had college degrees, being called "boy" though the gray in their hair belied the summons. We had dignity in segregation and we must achieve dignity in Freedom. I fully recognize a poem is not a response to a report by the United States Government. I know a few words scribbled on a legal pad cannot turn anything around. Yet I wanted to say, as the old gospel song so aptly expresses, "It is well . . . with my soul." I wanted to say that an outhouse, that a lack of some toys sometimes did not destroy my family. I wanted to say, for those of us whose fathers took them for Sunday rides in the better communities, that knowing there is more in life does not mean we were less. We had each other; and we had our dreams. And we knew our dreams were not and could not be separated from the "each other." I wanted to say, in 1969, because you could see we as a community were missing something, that "Black love is Black wealth." And the riches we gain, having not been given by man, can never, by man, be taken away.

Four Introductions

A Ribbon on the Maypole
For Paule Marshall

We can explain the generosity of the sun . . . by talking of
expanding gasses . . . We can chemically legitimize water . . .
as the union of hydrogen and oxygen . . . We can see a defi-
nite . . . undeniable . . . urge for flowers to turn to any source
of light . . . But that is only observation of behavior . . . We
also know slaves . . . identified with masters . . . that Jews . . .
cloved to authority . . . that women still love men . . . So much
of knowledge is not only empirical . . . but axiomatic . . . Yet
the scientific gathering of data speaks exclusively to craft . . .
There must also be art . . . if we are to yield reason

    Anthropologically speaking . . . we are incorrect to accept
the concept . . . that human male stood . . . to weld and bran-
dish weapons . . . A more gentle data would allow us
security . . . in the reasoning . . . that human female stood . . . to
nurture and embrace . . . Psychologically speaking . . . we are
unimpressed . . . that human genes are the determinant . . . of
human responsibility . . . We would agree . . . rather . . . with
the American Constitution . . . that all peoples are created

equal . . . and are endowed with the inviolate right . . . to perceive the limitlessness of their possibilities unencumbered . . . by another's view of racial characteristics . . . gender responsibilities . . . or religious comforts . . . Law demands that we refrain from unacceptable behavior . . . Justice whispers to us the necessity of risk

We are not so different . . . we in this last quarter of the twentieth century . . . We congratulate ourselves on our military power . . . yet Alexander of Macedonia was bored . . . by his ability to conquer the known world . . . While debating issues of sustaining life or accepting death . . . it is the Oath of Hippocrates . . . to which our healers must adhere . . . We are justifiably proud . . . of our ability to penetrate the solar system . . . yet it was the priesthood of Egypt . . . which first calculated the position of Earth . . . in relationship to the stars . . . Our arrogance of opulence pales . . . beside the splendor of Pompeii . . . our libraries no more than an afterthought to the great storehouses of Timbuktu . . . Our indifference to human suffering was as obvious in Imperial Rome . . . as the futility of fighting machines . . . was made clear to eighteenth-century London

To those who ask . . . in this space-age . . . high-tech . . . fast-paced . . . materialistic . . . immediately gratifying society of ours . . . what is the purpose of art . . . We would reply cavewoman has answered that question . . . In defiance of damp cold and dark habitat . . . against men and animals who would make of her their evening meal . . . despite a lack of adequate tools or knowledge of their proper application . . . on clay walls . . . in tune with the rhythm of her crackling fire and crying babies . . . she took the time to sketch a sabertooth . . . to etch the power of a mammoth . . . to exhibit awe . . . that the sun warms . . . the waters flow . . . the winds bend trees

We turn to literature . . . for the emotional gathering of data . . . not to say that war still occurs . . . but to show the continuing human price for human impatience . . . Not to show that hunger still exists . . . but to exacerbate unremitting greed from human relationships . . . Not to erect signs saying: "Mine" . . . but to wrap a ribbon on the maypole . . . We turn to literature . . . because our greatest literature teaches us "in the beginning was the Word . . ." . . . And it is the word that will lift the ignorance of the dark ages from our spirits and cast our possibilities to the heavens . . . It is words that will set us free

"The Spiritual: Evolution of a Plaintive Message"

There are advantages to slavery other than to the slave master. The slave master only gets free labor, and "free" only in the sense that there is no monetary exchange. The payment comes when the master has to surrender his soul to say that the enslaved is not human. The oldest book in the world asks: What profits a man if he gains the world but loses his soul? But the slave, and I am not recommending this system, learns that he can do that which, in contemplation, he thought impossible. He can survive, yes, thrive in a system that puts his total being under assault. All too many young people today look at the outward restraints, without understanding the inner strengths, that our people have endured.

All systems require myths for their longevity. One current myth that is working to the group advantage is that all Asian immigrants are smart; that they excel in science and math. One current myth working against our group is that we are lazy; that we only want welfare and special treatment. The problem with myths is that they are believed by both those for whom they work and those whom they work against. No slave was ever lazy; for he would not survive. No slave ever shied from hard work; for he did as he was told. No slave was ever stupid—uneducated, certainly, but never stupid; for he not only had to understand what the overseer wanted but what he would settle for.

One myth that the American people like to perpetuate is that those who came to these shores, from the days of the ill-fated Jamestown settlement to the boat people from Haiti, came by choice. Hip liberals and sensitive conservatives like to concede that Black Americans are here against our will. That we are the only unwilling migrants to the New World; somehow putting us in a category that says since we didn't want to be here perhaps we would be better off somewhere else. If we are the only unwilling migrants, and the Native Americans the only natural inhabitants, then we both can be excluded from the American family. No place need be set at the table for the Black brother for as soon as he is able, he will go to his real home.

One is, of course, forced to ask what level of choice are we dealing with? Did the Black Plague of Europe constitute a "choice" when the options were death or migration? Did the religious persecution of the British and French constitute "choice" when a man was not allowed to follow the dictates of his heart? Did the rotten potatoes lying in Ireland's fields constitute "choice" when the options were starvation or migration? I suggest the Spaniard with the viciousness of the Inquisition had no more "choice" than the African captured by a rival ethnic group and sold to the slavers. No option, philosophy teaches us, makes the perfect choice. And imminent death presents no option.

We do not, and cannot, know what the African response to the New World would have been had we had different options. We do know that the Moors traveled to Spain and built some of the most beautiful buildings, stocked libraries, gave Spain the advantage of their mathematical prowess. We do also know America could not be the same without us. There are legitimate Black complaints that in the Middle Passage we lost our native language, our cultural roles, much of our ethnic identity. We also became a new people with a new song.

We worked together, showing both ourselves and others that ethnicity is not a necessary ingredient for human relationships. We accepted new gods and found unique ways of worshipping while building tolerance for those who believed differently and those who did not believe. We were slow to judge as we understood that the burdens of mankind weighed differently upon different shoulders. We cultivated the land, built the bridges, painted the portraits, laid out Washington, D.C., performed the first open-heart surgery, separated the plasma from the blood, made the first shoe lasts, and did more things with a peanut than anyone could imagine.

But more than our material contributions, which, like the Rock of Gibraltar, though still standing, is just sand, we stood firm and fast for the reality that every man is equal in the sight of God and must be respected under the Laws of Man. We know, we who labored under the lash, that though our bodies were tired, our souls were rested. We willingly gave the world our song, which Dvořák made into his *New World Symphony* and we made a daily part of our lives.

In this, the fifth year of the Spiritual Festival Competition, I am proud to join the Human Involvement Project in

celebrating "The Spiritual: Evolution of a Plaintive Message."
Five years ago, when the Human Involvement Project was
told its funding would be severely limited, that it might not be
able to go forward with its work of serving people, a vow was
made not to descend to despair but to climb to higher ground.
The Human Involvement Project reached deep into its soul to
rediscover that which had carried our ancestors over—a song.
A new song for a new day. We are now celebrating a dream
that was dreamed not on our backs, in our beds, with the cur-
tains drawn to shut out the light; but a dream that was realisti-
cally dreamed of determination and self-help.

I am especially proud to be honorary chair in this anniver-
sary year, believing as I do that "Without a song . . . there ain't
no love at all . . . without a song."

The Women's Alliance
Introduction to Mari Evans

The giraffe is the only species without a voice. We share with the dolphin identifiable laughter. We recognize and give integrity to the language of the apes, baboons, orangutans and other primates though we cannot translate it. We understand and appreciate the growls and howls of the wolves, hyenas, lions, tigers, our own pet dogs and cats. Yet human beings are the only species with codifiable language.

What joy that first human must have experienced when sound, reproducible sound, came from his throat. Did he howl in imitation of the wind; did he chirp with delight at a bird; did he laugh and gurgle like the stream? He probably pointed and made a sound. And someone pointed and made a sound back.

Language builds from necessity. Only recently have we invented microwave, electric boogie, radar, penicillin, supersonic transport, superstars. Our technology has afforded us a new lease on life, so terms like "death with dignity," "sexual preference," "artificial intelligence" and "single by choice" have become necessary to explain ourselves to ourselves. Most people recognize Acquired Immunity Deficiency Syndrome or herpes, though they react to those words as if it was still B.C. and thereby interchangeable with "leper." Mankind has learned a lot but we have not internalized the intent.

We have learned that separate is never equal and therefore cannot be separate. We have learned that quality education means young people can read, write, compute, and think with some logic. We have learned we cannot expect people to pull themselves up by their bootstraps then take the boots away; but those of us without shoes have also learned we must never cease marching forward—no matter what hardships we encounter.

One of the new terms is "role model." When people do not want to do what history requires, they say they have no "role models." I'm glad Phillis Wheatley did not know she had no "role model" and wrote her poetry anyway. I'm glad Harriet Tubman did not know she had no "role model" and led the slaves to freedom. I'm glad Frederick Douglass did not know he had no "role model" and walked off that plantation in Maryland to become one of the great oratorical fighters for freedom. I'm glad Thurgood Marshall did not say the Constitution prescribes me as three-fifths of a man therefore I cannot argue the *Brown vs. Topeka* case before the Supreme Court. I'm glad Martin Luther King, Jr. did not say but segregation is the law of the land and we cannot defy the law, but rather raised his voice in constructive engagement against the segregationist practices of our generation.

The power of speech, the freedom to engage our hearts and our bodies in dialogue is the most precious freedom of all. To secure all other rights granted to us by either our religions or our laws it is necessary to raise our voices. An idea inside our heads is, to our fellow humans, the same as no idea. It must be expressed if it is to have power. And the voice, the pen, is far mightier than any sword, any jail, any attempt to silence. Censorship is an anathema to a free people. We may not always like what we hear but we are always the poorer if we close down dialogue; if we abrogate free speech, and the open exchange of ideas.

A great part of the joy of being human is not that we think; many other mammals think. Nor that we communicate with our fellow mammals; all other mammals communicate inter- and intra-species; but that we have a history which is located in human memory and in books. We are not bound by the moment but can go back thousands of years to see how far we have progressed; and we can go forward in imagination to envision our future.

We with our history of slavery where native gods, language and drums were taken from us devised a language using the Christian tools available. They serve us well, giving voice to frustration; offering comfort to the aggrieved. Music is a universal language: The field hollers, the gospel calls to worship are universally recognized as a major Black contribution. Patience is universal: The faith of a mustard seed, the determination of one drop of water in the Grand Canyon, 'cause if Job waited on the Lord tell me why can't I? Love is universal because we recognize and accept the call to reconcile the irreconcilable. And books are our window to these worlds.

We are honored to have with us today a poet, a book maker, a window on the world. Ladies and gentlemen ... Mari Evans.

Stained-Glass Windows
For Bobbi Sterne

Patterns are usually found on material . . . making colors blend with colors . . . dissimilar patterns form . . . new patterns . . . creating new styles . . . new fashions . . . new ideas: of what is chic . . . what is acceptable . . . what will be the future . . . Patterns are the way most lives are lived

Quilts are traditionally formed from scraps . . . pretty little leftovers . . . sewn painstakingly by hand under candlelight . . . or kerosene lamps . . . a communal endeavor with the ladies bringing their own pieces to share . . . carefully laying her contribution in just the right place at just the right time . . . Casseroles are quilts . . . different dishes on the same table . . . making a complete meal . . . for all the guests . . . Politics are quilts . . . each piece offering comfort to the old . . . disabled . . . the needy . . . as well as new responsibilities to the young . . . the able . . . those who know sufficiency . . . Quilters teach there is no such thing as waste . . . only that for which we currently see no purpose . . . Quilters teach patience to a hurried . . . impatient world

Stained glass is a colorful quilt . . . of processed sand . . . formed to keep the cold away . . . while allowing the light to come through . . . This is woman's work we are discussing . . . those who can see . . . the beauty and majesty . . . of that which has been left behind . . . Those who know . . . with their hands and their hearts . . . that the little pieces need each other to make a different day

Even dark days . . . even cloudy skies . . . concede the majesty of stained glass . . . a creation of an individual who said, "Let us not close up this space . . . Let us also not let the naked wind blow through . . . Let us take these broken pieces and form a pattern . . . showing humans were here who used the leftover . . . who eliminated the waste . . . who did not throw away the scraps . . ."

Most artists . . . even in our modern times of WASHINGTON SLEPT HERE . . . and KILROY . . . and TURK 182 . . . are unknown . . . laboring more for love . . . than praise or money . . . Those whose minds . . . are more nimble than their hands . . . weave a human quilt . . . of little people . . . bringing them together to fend against the naked winds . . . of hopelessness . . . despair . . . a feeling of uselessness . . . We who have admired . . . the artistry of stern and patient weaving . . . stop now among the shattered glass to admire the old patterns . . . and to quietly . . . and persistently . . . pick up the pieces . . . to make new stained-glass windows where the old were blown away

The Sports Pages

Defend Yourself

Defend Yourself
Against
Your: Husband, Lover or Friend

Everything
you ever wanted to know
About Sports
but are too embarrassed
to ask

Nikki Giovanni
Famous Sports Fan and Poet will teach you
Terms—Tone—Techniques
to sound like you know what
you are talking about

A California Woman writes:
How do you know which sport
is being played?
Giovanni Answers:
If they are in their underwear—it's Basketball;
if they have on their pajamas—it's Baseball;
if they wear helmets—it's Football.

Don't YOU want to know Something
about Sports???

My Own Style

I want to be a modern woman. I still have a nostalgic Afro, though it's stylishly short. I apologize to the hair industry, but frankly I like both my kinks and my gray strands. Plus being a sixties person glowing in the dark carries negative implications for me. The cosmetic people get my fair share. Most of my friends do base, pancake, powder, eye, lipstick and always keep their nails in perfectly oval shapes with base, color, sealer and oil for the cuticles. Do I use these things? No. But neither do I put them down or try to make them feel guilty for not being natural. There is something to be said for improvement. I've been known to comment: "Wow, you look really good. Who does your nails?" Why, I even have a dear friend who is a few months younger than I who uses a night cream to guard against wrinkles. Do I laugh and say, "You damned fool, you have no wrinkles"? No, ma'am. I say, "Well, your face is very very smooth," which (1) makes her feel good about her efforts and (2) keeps the friendship intact. All of life is a compromise anyway.

My major contribution to cosmetics is soap. I love soap . . . in pretty colors . . . hand-milled . . . in interesting shapes ... with the name of good perfumers on them ... preferably French. No one in my immediate family, and few who have ever used my bathroom, ever wonders what to give me for my birthday, Christmas, Valentine's Day, Mother's Day, Fourth of July, Labor Day, Martin Luther King, Jr.'s Birthday or Lincoln Heights Day. The way I figure, ask for what you want. I used it to, of course, bathe with, but it's also so pretty on my open shelves, plus it smells good and when properly arranged is more or less a living sculpture.

I really like useful things. You never know. Take candles. I really like a candle. I'm a Democrat so I have a donkey. I'm a Delta so I have an elephant. I'm a woman so I have an apple. Well, I have an apple candle; maybe I don't have to justify it. I also have candle candles. Just tall pretty candles in little holders. If the house gets hit by lightning I'm ready. Like all modern women I like to be ready. Without raising a hair on my chinny chin chin I can turn three cans of anything and a quarter cup of dry white wine into a gourmet meal in fifteen minutes flat. Give me an ounce of Cognac and I really raise hell. I've been known to make the most wicked bean soup with warm croutons and garlic zwieback (the secret is a dapple of sherry) the world has known. People say, "How can you be a full-time mother, full-time professional and still cook like this?" I smile sweetly, indicating that perhaps the very best is yet to come. Or as the old folk liked to say, "It ain't what you do, it's the way that you do it." In observing the younger women, that seems to be the one thing that they are missing: the ability to take nothing and make everybody think that something is there. You know what I mean? The younger women like to brag that they can't cook, as if that makes them modern. What is really modern is that you can throw it together from cans and frozen food and pretend that it was easy. Half of life is not avoiding what you don't like but doing it with no sweat.

I must congratulate the twentieth-century woman on her internationalism. You go into practically any house these days and they have Nigerian art, Egyptian cotton throws, French water, Hawaiian fruit, Japanese televisions, California wines, Polish crystal, Haitian lace curtains, Lesothan rugs, Dutch flowers sitting on their grandmother's handmade quilts draped across an Early American table. I think it's neat. There are no limits to our imagination. My house is a mess, too, so that means I qualify. Or as the lady who came to sell me draperies said: "It's not too many people who will put a print on a print." Well, it works. Mostly because I want it to work. And since it's my house . . . It's the little things that make the difference. I remember when you could go by the apartment of any guy of any relationship to you and find stale beer in the refrigerator. Nowadays even their places are perking up. Everybody wants to make a statement.

Oh sure, I've heard all the jokes about BUMPS (Black Upwardly Mobile Professionals), but I like a BUMP. Hell, I am one. Being laid back is a sexual term, not a personality description. We could use a little ambition in our community. Everytime somebody wants to trade their Toyota for a BMW that means they have to have more people to supervise; a bigger budget to spend; a larger program to implement. If they're in business for themselves they have to sell more, do more, 'cause everybody knows you don't get big in business by saving, you get big by spending, by expansion. I mean we are only fifteen years out of the twenty-first century! The Black community is 40 percent teenage unemployed, 53 percent illiterate. We are the most Social Security-froze, Medicaid-stopped, unwed, underemployed, unpromoted, not-appreciated-at-all community in America. Who we gonna call—Honkeybusters? No! We're gonna climb out on the BUMPS. The modern woman is a BUMP who is not a grind. We can do it 'cause we've done everything else. And hey, even though my body will be old sitting on a porch in some home, unless I can convince my son to let me live with him and his little wife (he does owe me, you know—I have given him right now fifteen years of my life and I expect the little bugger will be going around the block a few more times), I'll be surrounded by the good feeling that I am a modern woman 'cause even if I'm old I'm sure to be positive, and that's our ace in the hole.

Let's Sweat!

Like most poets, I carry a two-hole folder with me almost compulsively. It's not that I carry my ideas around so that should the occasion arise I can pull it out and say, in regard to some impending problem, "Oh well, a stitch in time saves nine." I do not have profound idioms at occasions of great distress so that I can intone: "It's always darkest before the dawn." No. It's just that like most writers I think I think best when I'm not actually thinking about it, so I carry a book that allows me to put either something I have thought up as being very clever or, most likely, something that someone else said that I would one day like to use. Steve Krieder, running back for the Cincinnati Bengals, once said in response to the question "Why do you think the fans came out in minus-twenty-degree weather to watch a football game?" "I think it's a failure of our educational system." I think that is neat. I love sports, too; but any fool who would sit in Riverfront Stadium in twenty below-zero weather to watch a game that was being televised anyway indeed has been let down by our public school system. I haven't found a way to work that into a poem, but with any luck and lots of persistence I will ultimately be able to achieve it. You don't see too many good poems on football. Baseball has "Casey at the Bat," but when you think sports, that's about it. Tennis needs a national poem. So does soccer. Any reader out there who's a soccer fan should really think about it because soccer is an international game and you could get a real chance to show off your Latin, Greek, Spanish, English, ancient Gaelic. It could be a real intellectual *tour de force*, as it were. I mention my folder because, in fact, I want to talk about sports. My folder, which is bright orange, has a mock license plate saying POETIC LICENSE, which is normal since I do poetry. But right below that is a white and orange circle that states: BODY BY SCANDINAVIAN. It's true. I've joined the Spa Revolution.

You may rightfully wonder why a forty-three-year-old woman would suddenly decide she can no longer get along without getting her body in shape. And that is exactly the point. If people know anything about the writing profession they know that all we do is sit and read or sit and write or sit and talk or sit on planes to go sit and do all of the above. I personally know writers whose legs give out if they have to go up one flight of stairs and now refuse to lecture at certain universities because the schools lack elevators. That's simply being in bad shape. Some writers have even given up smoking cigarettes, though I do not count myself among them, in the hope that they can avoid exercise. Dear young writer out there, you must sweat.

I guess you are wondering how I got into sports in the first place. I was visiting my father and mother one fall when a bunch of my dad's friends came over. Laughing loudly with beer and munchies they plopped themselves in front of the television and begin to talk in numbers and letters. RBI's 35; ERA 3.56; HR 15; only 21 percent against left-handers and other things I didn't understand. It seemed so unlike my father to have gone into the stock market. I went into the living room and asked what was going on. It was friendly. I mean, I wasn't meddling or anything—just curious. You know the look you get when people think you are not quite bright? well, five men turned to my father: "And that's the famous one, huh?" And they all burst out laughing. My father was mortified. "We're watching the World Series, sweetie," he said sweetly. That should have been my clue to go on, as he never called me "sweetie" unless I had done something extremely stupid and he was exercising great patience to not scream, "Lughead, what do you think is going on?" I then, with the smile, I'm sure, of the terminally stupid, asked, "Oh, who's playing?" The room literally shook with laughter. I, naturally, beat a hasty retreat. The Giovannis are a close but competitive family. I determined from then on that the next time I came to visit I would know the sport, who was playing and what all those little numbers meant. From then on instead of reading the front page I turned to sports first. I cribbed a *Sports Illustrated* anywhere I could. I even purchased *Sporting News* and, during Hagler's heyday (though the Marvelous One may think he is still in his heyday) read *Boxing News*.

Since I travel a lot I also made a great discovery. Alone in a hotel room on the road I would usually tune in *Tonight* or one of the talk shows. I can't stand violence and no lone woman in her right mind would look at *Hawaii Five-O* or any of those pictures where women are stalked and brutally killed.

I learned, and I'm lucky cable came in when it did, that I could catch the West Coast games live. I'll bet I know more about the Phoenix Suns during that period than any poet from the East Coast. I do have to confess I never became a Lakers fan but I kind of appreciate Houston—unless they're playing the Celtics. I could come back to a cold, empty hotel room in the middle of February and tune in something to cheer about. I could catch boxing, West Coast tennis, gymnastics—hell, fencing, if it came to that. I never did get into hockey because my major sports requirement is that I have to be able to see the ball, but I'm working on golf. Ahhh, but bowling. I love to watch bowling. You get a big, usually black, ball going down a clearly defined lane. I could sit and munch Planter's peanuts and cheer my little head off. I'm sure many a night my next-door neighbors, as I screamed, "Oh yes! Go for it! Put it in now!" were green with envy at the dull, rather pedestrian happenings in their bedrooms. Sports is fun. We expect the men to want to go shopping to pick out curtains but we don't feel the same obligation to understand why you punt on fourth down. We want the guys to marvel at the cleanliness of our homes but we don't want to know what a cleanup hitter is. Come on, girls. Let's be fair. It's time to quit being jealous of our jogging mates and join in. Since we sweat anyway, sometimes it ought to be on our feet as well.

Toward Better Human Understanding

OK, ladies, I'm going to help you out. I know I'm a poet and that poets are not supposed to be interested in these things, but let's file it under "Toward Better Human Understanding." That allows our subject to be considered either political or sociological. Men and women are different, and no matter what kind of data we uncover we will still see the differences . . . and sports proves it.

I'm not talking simple anatomy. Women, since the days of slavery, have been strong and physically capable, and we're not just discussing Black American slavery here. The Great Pyramids were as much built by female Jewish slaves as by male. The great Roman roads were laid by women and men. The stuff you see in movies and on television defies logic. The women were not simply lovingly dressed and taken into concubinage while the men gathered the straw. Both did bedroom duty; both did fieldwork. Black American slavery does at least openly admit women were worked like men, though I think the term is "worked like a . . ." (It's not, by the way, that

I'm against using certain pejorative terms, but when every comedian and left-wing politician thinks he can show he's hip and prejudice-free by using the term it's time for those of us who had a more familial connection to desert the field.) Anybody who thinks the women who went West in covered and uncovered wagons to open the frontier just stayed around the home fire fretting about the town gossip and baking biscuits is nuts, too. We shot Indians, marauding Mexicans and crazy white men who bothered us. We tilled fields, harvested the crops, fought weather, loneliness and sometimes our mates— the same as we do today. The myth of the delicate woman is very recent and very inaccurate. You had your historical crazies like the Chinese peasants who bound the feet of their wives and daughters because the Chinese rich did it. Of course, the rich did it to show that they were rich. The poor did it in pitiful imitation of the rich. Foot-binding is as sick as the cry for virgin women. It's simply a sign of men talking to men. "Hey man, I'm so rich my ol' lady want to go someplace I have Chester, here, to carry her!" "Babe, you too much. Do she walk to bed or do he carry her there, too?" (With a lot of eye-rolling and back-slapping.) Like soft hands. Some pitiful woman married to a normal factory guy or schoolteacher or policeman for that matter is expected to have hands that look and feel like she never washed a pair of socks or cleaned a greasy skillet or scrubbed the ring from around the tub. I mean, if you work with your hands, your hands will show it. And I say Hurrah. What a false sense of ego some men must have. How foolish of the women not to protest. All those overlong, splitting nails, patchy red-polished dishpan hands trying to make, hoping to believe, that Jergens or Palmolive or some miracle would make their hands be less red, less cracked, less dry. Scarlett should have said to Rhett, "There's a war going on, dummy. What the hell do you mean, what's wrong with my hands?" I'm simply trying to establish that women have used, and always will use, our bodies for real work. What we have been reluctant to use ourselves for is real play. Women don't like to sweat.

I do. I love sweat dripping from my chin or running down the back of my neck. I wear an Afro so I don't have to worry about my hairstyle. I can shower after a tennis match and wash my hair and go on about my business. In all fairness to the younger women, I'm also forty-three and figure what I haven't had I won't get. Athletics are fun. I've been totally cheered by the female bodybuilders. People thought they were nuts ("I don't see what they gonna do with all them muscles. No man ain't gonna want them"). Though those of us who have followed the history of men know men want any and every thing. My favorite sport is tennis, though as a two-pack-a-day smoker, I either have to win early or accept defeat graciously. I am, of course, very gracious. I bowl in the high 100's, of which I am very proud, and can run a quarter mile in fifteen minutes. I've even joined a spa lately, where I have been known on rare occasions to do ten sit-ups, though they are not my favorite. Aerobics. I like the music, the side-to-side motion, the look of my AMF red-velvet heavy hands flinging into space calorie after calorie, which are burned, incinerated, banished to that place where lost weight goes on hiatus until it finds another woman to descend upon. I've learned something else. Why men like to look at sports.

I need to take a minute to, if not explain something, then

at least admit it. Since turning forty I have found that I drift off the subject. Many's the year I had to hear that I was too direct, without humor, did not see the shadings. It never used to bother me until I turned forty. I never used to cry at commercials either. I never used to get choked up at poignant endings. Just a few scant years ago I would have torn apart a movie like *The Trip to Bountiful*. I would have found the son too weak, the daughter-in-law too stark, the mother too much a caricature. But I watched that movie and threw popcorn at the screen screaming, "Let her sing a hymn!" I just couldn't take it. I should have known it was coming because I used to get tears in my eyes watching that kid take the shirt from the football player in that Coke commercial. I mean, the kid looked so happy to have that sweaty shirt and it was so sweet of the player to give it to him. All right, I'll admit it. A tear or two fell when Pete Rose broke Ty Cobb's record. It was so touching. I had to be helped from the room when that Swiss female marathoner, Gabriele Anderson, limped crazily into the arena at the Los Angeles Olympics. "Don't touch her! Don't touch her!" I yelled until my mother, realizing I had once again been gotten to, put a steady hand on my elbow and took me into the kitchen muttering, "She'll be all right. She'll finish."

Unfortunately for me, my mother just loves *Little House*. Now, I can take the girls being blind and seeing again and all the fires and operations because I don't emotionally identify. But the show where the aging wrestler needs the money for his dying wife . . . well, I refused to look at it for the third time. It's just too much. I can't watch the *Highway to Heaven* where the actor ascends in front of the curtain to heaven after asking God to give him a sign that He understood the actor had tried to live a good life. It seemed that he asked for so little and it's only right that it be granted. And let's not even discuss *Star Trek*. The idea that Spock might die just broke me up. I had taken my son and two of his friends to see it and they all were horribly embarrassed by me. I got them back with *E.T.* Everybody heaved through that one. So I admit emotion has come into my life and, in many ways, I cannot control it. Honestly, I cried like a baby after amassing 346 points at Scrabble only to go down in defeat. But that's understandable. Most men like to watch sports because they refuse to admit they cry at commercials. They like to watch sports because they like to think that a group of men playing a game together are friends and really care about each other. They like to use terms like "Teamwork" and "I'll quarterback this" and "Let's run this up the middle" to get their subordinates to work harder. They sit around on Friday nights (fights), Saturday (college ball), Sunday (pro), and Monday (pro) wanting to believe that man does not struggle alone. That his fellows are there with him. That the team concept is alive and well. They cheer loudly and argue insistently about plays because it's also the only time they can show great and intense emotion without someone trying to analyze it. They can scream and holler and curse and thank the various deities without having to worry that someone will attach any deeper meaning. They watch sports, ladies, for the same reason you watch *General Hospital, The Young and the Restless, Dynasty* and *Dallas*. They need a fantasy. One other thing I should mention. They like sports because they are the undisputed master of the ERA, at-bats, percentages against left-handers vs. percentages against right-handers. This from a man who cannot remember his anniversary and occasionally forgets his wife's name (*"Honey*, will you bring me a beer?"). Something primordial and personal happens when a man watches sports. He doesn't have to talk to women.

Most women don't like to watch sports because we are jealous of the men enjoying themselves without our help. We hear the same animal grunts and groans, the same urgings to come on, to finish it off, as we hear in private moments, and women don't want to compete with the New York Jets for private moments. I'm surprised some mate has not reported his significant other as running into the room near tears during the Super Bowl saying, "But, Timothy, I thought that was our grunt." And in our genetic jealousy we seek, not understanding of our negative emotions, but excuses. "I don't like boxing," (with lips pursed) "because it's too violent." Have you ever been to a department store the day after Christmas? Have you ever been in any grocery store when 96-ounce Coke was announced as on sale for the next twenty minutes for 76 cents? Did you never seek a Cabbage Patch doll for your child or grandchild? How can women really discuss violence?

Boxing is a marvelous sport. Except for the heavyweights you have two wonderfully muscled men in the ring in shorts outpointing each other. Yes, I will admit that you sometimes find real hackers who are simply trying to hurt the other man, but real boxing—and we do have to look at the heavyweights now—is an art. You take Muhammed Ali who at the peak of his career raised boxing to liquid sculpture. No one would compare Ali to Sonny Liston, Joe Frazier or Larry Holmes, because they, as Ali liked to say, were just big bears. Sugars

Ray, both Robinson and Leonard, were a joy to watch. And Michael Spinks has shown it's not size but skill. Will boxing learn Michael's lesson? Probably not. But when you see a Lonnie Smith, who unfortunately lost his title, you see a man moving with a purpose. But mostly, whether you or I or the American Medical Association like it or not, boxing is here to stay. Men will always test themselves against each other. Someone is bound to say, "But we don't have to support it . . . it's barbaric." So is the stock exchange; so are interest rates; so are farm foreclosures; so is life. Most women don't want to think that someone could really enjoy hitting or getting hit by someone else. It's probably quite fair to say no one enjoys getting hit. Hitting . . . well, that's another matter.

Football is fun, too. My sister once asked me, "Why do they get up close to each other and scrunch down?" I realized right away why she doesn't enjoy the sport. She doesn't know what's going on. My answer was, of course, a very patient, "I don't know." Because I don't. I'm not only not a sport historian, I don't intend to become one. They line up because that's the way the game is played. A better question, and one that can be quite a conversation opener, is, "Why don't they throw on first down?" Your significant other will try to explain the importance of establishing a running game, which can take up quite a bit of time. If you occasionally ask something like, "Well, why don't they go for it on fourth down and inches? That front line isn't all that tough," you can talk all afternoon. Do not, I repeat, do not ask that if his team is playing against the Chicago Bears. You will look like the imposter you are. With any other team it'll do just fine. One minor thing you need to know: The object of football is first downs—not touchdowns, first downs. Your mate will be perfectly happy to have his favorite team lose if they get more first downs. Now that may not make sense but I'm not trying to make sense, I'm trying to save your relationship.

Shortly before the actual close of football—well, truthfully before the World Series is played—the NBA will raise its head. If your spouse is not a football nut you can count on losing him during basketball season. The trick to understanding basketball is calling the foul. You jump up and down saying, "FOUL! HE FOULED HIM! OH, WOW! DID YOU SEE THAT!" It won't matter whether or not a foul is called because someone is always fouling in basketball. You can always throw in a bunch of I-don't-believe-it-how-could-they-overlook-its and win the respect of every man in the room. Basketball, by the way, is the only sport where points are important. In the other majors it's the process.

Now baseball is called the American game and not for naught. It would take American ingenuity to come up with a sport that you do not have to be in good shape for, that takes all day, that you can get both mental and physical work done without interfering with your enjoyment of the contest. You simply must watch tennis and basketball to know what's going on. You need to see football replays so that you can talk about the tight end or nose tackle. It would help if you knew how the bowler was throwing in the first frame as compared to the ninth. A horse race isn't a race unless you are there when they say ". . . And they're off." But baseball . . . you can cook, clean, do your lawn work, read a book, play Scrabble, or pinochle. You can sleep, run errands, make love and still know what's going on. It's the perfect pastime because it demands nothing.

The men who play it climb into their pajamas, wad up their mouths with tobacco or gum and stand around spitting all afternoon. Everybody can play baseball. If it wasn't such an institution I'm sure women would have tackled it way before they tried to break into the NBA or football or boxing. It makes far more sense for an all-female team to play against men in baseball than any other sport. Billie Jean and Martina played and defeated men in tennis, and though Bobby Riggs is old, tennis is not necessarily a game that yields to age. Bobby was not in that bad shape. But baseball? My home team has two of the oldest players in professional ball and the Cincinnati Reds are still making a run for it. Have you seen the bellies on those guys? If baseball doesn't work out for them they can always go to Japan and try sumo wrestling. Ladies, what I am suggesting is that you've been intimidated by sports and for no good reason. You've been cowered into being weekend widows because you think sweat is sacred. Open that sports page, learn what a batting average is, pick a team, grab a beer and cheer. Just one PS here. Always take the underdog and points. Take the underdog even if you can't get points. I took the Dolphins over Chicago last year, and do you know that made me look like a genius? I was hot stuff. Always take the underdog, though, for another, more primordial reason. We're women. Somebody has to love the losers, too.

A Patriotic Plea for Poetry Justice
Or Hey! Play the Game!

Now that baseball season has ended, instead of being sad I'm mad. Not mad at baseball but the crap we have to go through to see a game. Baseball is already the world's most tranquil sport. It is probably the only active sport where you are not seriously required to be alive to play. Think about it. How would you really know, in the average game, if most of those players are alive? Oh sure, you're going to say because they spit; but do we really have any proof that a little spitting machine isn't installed in the position where the guy should be? Do we really know, except for the manager, that spit is coming from a human mouth? Now that a lot of the guys are blowing bubbles you can be sure a few of them are not human. I, for one, simply will not be convinced that Bill Buckner is any more than half human. I had a dollar, which in my conservative betting world is real money, on the Sox, and when Buckner went down for the last out in the sixth game, which would have clinched it for me and Boston, didn't I see a leg swing out at an odd and unnatural angle? I mean, if we can make a Stepford wife we can make a million-dollar ball player. Surely Ray Knight wasn't real. Here's a guy who hit every damned thing. That's unnatural, especially when you realize baseball is a game betting that you won't hit more than a third of the time. How can these things be explained? And poor Strawberry. Someone forgot his battery until the last game. Or as the announcer said, "When did he wake up?" I'm telling you a bunch of zombies and robots are out there. But that's not why I'm upset. I've had it up to my kister with "The Star-Spangled Banner."

OK. Let's start by admitting I'm a poet, and the purity of poetry is close to my heart. When Francis Scott Key wrote it, it was probably on the back of one of the envelopes Americans are famed for writing on. Key is out on a British ship watching the Stars and Stripes withstand one hell of a shelling. As dawn breaks he notices Old Glory is, tried but true, still standing. Hey, Key says to himself, this ought to be noted. Out whips the envelope, feather, penpoint, inkwell. "Oh, say, can you see . . . ," starting one of the best-known poems in history. He finally is brought to shore and probably shows it to a friend, who immediately says, "You oughta take this thing to the Government. We need a good motto." I'm sure Key tried to explain it's not a motto, it's a poem. "We're Americans," his friend says, "we don't get into poetry. But hey! I know a good old English drinking song that if you change a line here and there it'll go to." Poor Key. There was probably some reluctance about changing his lines, but if it was good for the country . . . well, who is one poet to stand in the way? I mean, does anybody remember Robert Frost's poem for Jack Kennedy? And that happened in our lifetime! So Key's poem and the

British drinking song were combined to make our national anthem. One reason it's so poorly sung, by the way, is you need to hoist a few before trying for those high notes, but that's definitely another discussion.

What irks me, as an American and a lover of baseball, is why do we have to hear it before each ball game? It's bad enough that we have to be introduced to the players. I mean, who really cares who's on the team? Are they going to play or what? If they're going to play, flash their position on the screen; if not, too damned bad. They just missed making the telly that day. If they want to be seen let them do something. But OK. I'm not being mean. Maybe we should let them be introduced. But honestly, I don't want it. I turn on the set, I want the game. I go to the ballpark, I want the first pitch. Not the ceremonial one; not the mayor; not someone who used to play ball in auk nine, but the guys who will actually do the game . . . that's all I want. We all know what time the game starts. If you can't get your beer and pizza before the appointed hour, too damned bad. You can always get it while the catcher is giving the pitcher his signs. But back to poor Francis Key.

He wrote a poem. I have no idea what is on Key's tombstone but it should read I WROTE A POEM. Have you actually sat through the concerts that are given before the game in the name of a poem? People start to sing "Oh, say, can you see" and in front of you literally lose their minds. They forget where they are and for what purpose they came. They begin to think that they are the show and try to make a statement. We should probably thank our lucky stars that Michael Jackson isn't a baseball fan or there would be no game at all that night as he moonwalks among the flashing lights hiccupping "OOOOOOOOSAYSAYSAY," with Paul McCartney and Stevie Wonder joining in. I could not believe Marvin Gaye the night he went on for five or six hours, only to be recently topped by Smokey Robinson, who combined *The Banner* with *The Beautiful*. This is baseball, not war. It was so much better when we the people sang it because somewhere around the second verse we would shout and scream for the game. You can even take it when the C & W people are called into action because they want a beer, but the rockers and the rhythm and blues people? Forget it. They want to make a statement. On a song that's unsingable. As if they didn't have concerts of their own. Let's see them have a bunch of ball players open for them. Yeah, that would be fair. Or, better yet, let's give *The Banner* back to the poets. Let's have it properly recited as Key conceived it. One person standing reading from one small envelope one little poem. Quickly. Concisely. With a sense of duty rather than feeling. I volunteer. Let's get those cards and letters going, campers, 'cause if we're not careful in the next year or two there won't be any time left for the game. Write your local newspaper and *USA Today*: Nikki—Quickly. *The Star-Spangled Banner*.

Or something like that.

. . . And the Loser Is . . .

OK. I've been pretty nice up until now. I have not actually by name called anyone a complete fool nor have I questioned the origins of their mothers' residence; yet it's got to be asked: Where do they get those sports announcers? Sure, the guys who write up the games are fools, too, but you don't have to read them. You can look at their dumb headlines and say, "I'm not going to read this fool today" and that's the end of that. But what can we do about announcers?

Tennis is the worst. I like tennis. In my younger days, and on one of my good, pain-free mornings I like to think if I didn't smoke, would work out and actually practice I could maybe have been a contender. I did join a spa and have been known to bench-press fifty pounds or so. I do three minutes on the LifeCycle and will, when all else fails, jog around the indoor track. I look good in athletic equipment. When I do the spa I, of course, have my shimmery tights on with contrasting color leg warmers. My towels are of imported cotton; I simply wouldn't be caught dead in a spa towel. I do my aerobics and, well, while I'm not in good shape I have clearly gotten no worse. I finish what I call a workout, sit in the steam, move over to the sauna, take a dip (as I cannot swim) in the pool, shower up and go home to watch tennis on cable. Sure it's all fantasy but it beats "adult" books and movies every time. I tune in and what do I hear? Bigotry. Pure and simple. A player is introduced: John Smith from Yugoslavia, number 114 in the world; last tournament the Cotton Grove, where he made semis. Then I have to see his earnings to date. Unfair. But mostly from then on he will be referred to as the Yugoslav, as if his, damned name is too hard to pronounce. It's bad enough when it's Davis Cup, with country against country, but in individual play . . . unacceptable. They do it to the Swedes. As if Wilander, Edberg, Pernfors, Nystrom don't have names. They do it to the Czechoslovakians to the point that *Sports Illustrated* had to finally say enough, no more Czech jokes. It's pathetic. Something in me cringes when I hear Hana Mandlikova called the Czech. I more or less expect Zina Garrison to be called the Nigger. Ninety percent of the commenting refers to the player's current home or the country in which he or she was born. When Noah won the French Open he became the Frenchman; when Hana recently beat Martina she was identified as "a soon-to-be Australian citizen." As if the crowd couldn't cheer for her because she's a great player. Becker carries all of West Germany on his shoulders, and it's some sort of national honor at stake when he plays Lendl, though of course the American announcers make a big deal out of cheering for Lendl since he (1) is a winner and (2) has a home in Connecticut. I have seen American crowds be downright ugly, and I can't help but think this is perpetuated by Bud Collins and company. Sports is supposed to be about the individual tuning his body to his highest effort then playing his best. But it turns into some sort of international substitute for balls. It's not fair to the athletes. Those of us who love tennis love it whether an American is in the tournament or not. John McEnroe didn't make tennis and he won't break it. He can only play for so long anyway. Yet their love of "Americans" rarely extends to showing Zina Garrison's or Lori McNeil's tournaments. The biases are pathetic. You can actually tune in a tennis match and listen to the announcers and never know there's a sports contest going on. We have to hear about and see the players' friends, their coaches, parents, everything but the match. Wimbledon is the best called because the British usually do it and they do the tennis. There is no other sport in which the players' origins play such a big part.

In football the teams are introduced and the players' college and hometown are listed. Then on with the game. In basketball the same. In both those sports the history of the player may come up as in "The Raiders traded him last year and here he is sacking the quarterback," but that's it. In basketball the same trading history is given and that's it. You would never hear an announcer say the Georgian or the North Carolinian or the Californian just upended the nose tackle or the white boy dunked the ball. The last time there was a racist remark on the air in football ("Look at that little monkey run") an immediate apology was issued, and it's not been done since. Yet tennis, the most international of all major sports, suffers from what can be called xenophobia at best and at worst—racism. It needs to be stopped. It's ruining our game and making no converts.

Why are announcers dumb? Maybe they were born that way. Maybe the fact that most of them used to want to think they had some sort of ability makes them so narrow-minded. The great players like O.J. Simpson and Bill Russell are great announcers because they know and love the game. And stick to the game in the comments. O.J. was the best football commentator on television. He predicted the right man and the right plays to watch, then you could sit back and watch what he said unfold. Bring back O.J. Bill Russell is great because he knows what is going on on the floor. Oscar Robertson was a great commentator, but the coaches didn't like him because he pointed out their mistakes. Bring back the Big O. We want people out there who will help us see what's going on; who love what they do. And who will stick to the game on the floor, not the one they wished had been. I saw Virginia play Villanova recently and all they could talk about was Polynice. Well, what about the five guys on the floor who didn't steal, who studied, who trained hard to play the game? And the bad thing is, Virginia was winning. All we could hear about was how they couldn't go to the final four without a dominating center. It's the scourge of American reporting. What is actually happening is not the news. The news seems to be what *will* happen. All those men sitting there with their mikes up close to their lips want to be fortune-tellers. They want to predict. Well, a sports contest isn't a place to predict. Just call the game. Keep track of the fouls, the yards, the score. Try not to miss the opening kickoff and try not to cut the game off before the clock goes to zero. Is that too much to ask? Apparently. Grow up, sports announcers. We really don't care about your old games and what you did and didn't do. If we cared we would tune in "Great Moments in Sports" from the Old Guys. We want the game at hand. We want a fair, impartial call.

Speaking of which, when are we going to pay the refs? From what I've seen recently those guys have to be on some kind of take. The worst calls get made, then stand. OK. It's only human to make a mistake. But the instant replay was made for mistakes. That should be an official time out. Or at least something sensible, like the guy who asks for the replay, if he's wrong, will lose a time out. It's not fair to have a better method of judging, then punish the people who use it. If the defense thinks the offense fouled, then the defense asks for a replay. If the offense did not foul, then the defense loses a time out. You'd have to be pretty sure before you wasted a time out challenging a call. We have got to do something because I cheer for the underdog a lot and it seems most bad calls go against the perceived loser. But all refs in all sports need better pay. Tennis especially. It's too hard calling a six-figure game on a three-figure salary. Just as baseball has its All-Star Game tennis should have some sort of tournament to pay salaries/benefits for the refs. At least the players and their fans could feel things were more professional and less emotional. I also have to say it: We need more Blacks and women in the announcers' booths. We need nonplayers, too. Most people watching a game never played the sport. The nonplayers look at things differently. I know I love a good effort. I am also a hometown nut. I like the Reds, the Bengals, the University of Cincinnati. I don't mind when we don't win so much as I mind when we don't seem to try. But a losing team becomes the butt of all those old, out-of-shape guys sitting there. I like a try-try-again mentality. And sometimes the home crowd could use a dose of compassion. In other words, guys, it's only a game. A game that pays a lot of money and a game that

makes a lot of money, but to those of us on the other side of
the tube it's fun, it's a hip hip hooray. It's a way of cheering for
something. Don't keep taking away from the effort on the
field nor the effort in front of the TV screen. We just want to
cheer. Since most teams are losers, as there is only one num-
ber one player, only one Super Bowl championship team, only
one World Series winner, most teams and most fans have
identified at one time or another with a loser. That's life. Most
of us lose, too. And it's not the worst thing in the world to say
"Well done." At a certain level of excellence we are all the
winners. And maybe the guys in the booth ought to think
about that. Or maybe the women in the booth will be sure to
mention it in the wrap-up.

Sacred Cows . . . and
Other Edibles

Sacred Cows . . . and Other Edibles

Well, OK, it seems to always fall on me to tell the truth and, hey, I don't mind. It's not nearly as bad a job as some people think. First of all, saying what you actually think energizes your mind for more creative solutions; not to mention freeing you from remembering what you once said and now have to backtrack on. It also allows you to offend everyone right away so that there are no false notions on either part. Now I'm not so truthful that if a, say, slightly overweight friend buys a dress with lots and lots of stripes going round and round I'll be the one to say, "God! You look just awful!" No. I am not cruel. Neither am I the sort of person who, visiting a friend with flu or something, will say, "Je-sus! You look like you're at death's door." I have been known to eat rubbery omelets that friends have made, exclaiming positively between munches at their unique texture; not to mention loving, absolutely lapping up every tender morsel my son ever cooked. I have, after all, been properly reared. But neighbors, I have to say it because no one else will. The rich have more fun than we do. I know that flies in the face of accepted wisdom. I know that there is an entire school of intellectualism which spends its time and energy trying to tell poor people how much better off we are than those with means. And I'm not talking about the working rich; I mean the filthy rich. The working rich, of course, have jobs that they have to go to every day. No. It's the filthy rich who come in for pity. People sit in their little, hot, about-the-size-of-a-decent-closet unair-conditioned apartments and pontificate thusly: "I wouldn't want all that money. It don't seem to make them happy." And folks, that's a lie. The rich are happy out of their fucking minds because they don't have to be in the hot, sweaty city sitting on their behinds contemplating the problems of the poor. They are not inconvenienced by store clerks who are insulting, traffic cops who stop them for seat belt violations, citizens who feel their one task in life is stopping you from smoking in public places. They don't have to worry with laundromats that take their quarters then refuse to dry the clothes; they don't get the nasty letters computers write asking, "DID YOU FORGET US LAST MONTH? . . ." Cars that break down with the very thing that just fell out of warranty; furniture that breaks before the second payment; children who tear their new clothes before church on Sunday—the shit in life that drives you crazy. The filthy rich don't have to worry about their health because they can afford doctors and surgery, but before they get to that they can afford proper shelter, good food; recreation . . . things that make life fun and worth living. They rarely have to worry about their sex lives, either, since everybody wants to screw them and they don't have to pay the pregnancy price since they can afford abortions whether they are legal or not. There's a conspiracy out there against us, the working poor. We are, as the sign says: Overtaxed, Underpaid, Not Appreciated At All. And we are expected to feel good about our situation because, after all, we could be worse off. Hey, we could be better off, too, but we are not encouraged to think that way. Sacred cows make hamburger meat just like the rest of them. We are being turned away from the very thing we need: a healthy dose of selfishness.

Now greed, as anyone will tell you, is a terrible thing. I know; I look at *Wheel of Fortune, Let's Make a Deal,* a couple of those shows almost every day and see people at lust for just one more spin, spin on things any fool should know. I saw one woman who hit the third-round $5,000 space two times, netting her almost $80,000 when she had:

The Th--ll of ---tory

The --ony of defe-t

The woman gave that smile of the terminally dull and said, "I guess I'll have to spin again." She hit bankrupt. My mother said the woman did not know the answer and I suppose if that's true she truly did not deserve to win. Yet how could she not know? Education is free in the United States. Compulsory, actually. Did she graduate from one of our fine Christian academies which did not want to burden her mind with quotations from anything other than the Great Book? Did she sit, her junior year in high school, dreaming of a White Christmas? I mean, how could she not know? But then, I have seen Monty Hall give people $1,000 cold cash and watched them trade it away for Curtain Three: two dead goats and a banana peel. *Let's Make a Deal* is the second all-time cheapest show on television. Anytime you get cash you should

take it and sit tight for The Big Deal. I know, you are wonder-
ing what is the all-time cheapest? I must confess I do not
often look at it because it upsets my stomach: *The All-New
Newlywed Game*. The last time I actually sat through it the
question was: "Name your husband's favorite fowl." And none
of the three wives could say chicken, duck, quail, squab,
turkey, capon, Cornish or guinea hen. I'm talking not even
Sally Rand, folks. Nothing with feathers at all. Which is only
comparable in my mind to the wife who, I hasten to add, is no
more stupid than her husband, answered "Potato chips" when
asked her husband's favorite condiment. We're probably lucky
she didn't say, "We're not using birth control." And what
makes these three couples expose their absolute stupidity five
times a week? Why, the desire for "A prize picked especially
for you," which frequently turns out to be an all new no-stick
ice cube tray. "Yes, Dave and Sue, *The All-New Newlywed
Game* has picked out for you your very own ice cube trays in
shocking pink. You can fill these trays with water for the next
two hundred years without fear of leakage. And what do we
have for the runner-up, Merle?" Or is Merle on another
show? That's greed. Though not greed for money but greed
for fame. Can't you see those people going back to Some-
place, Pennsylvania, asking their friends did they watch the
show? Many a young couple has probably gone into debt for a
VCR just so they could tape and maintain their appearance.
That show, neighbors, is grounds for divorce. "What do you
mean I'm so hot the water in the bed boiled?" (while hitting
him with the cardboard answer sheet). "Oh, honey, you were
all over me . . ." (while smiling sweetly because he knows we
know nobody in his entire life was ever all over him for any

rhyme or reason). Selfishness can be a terrible thing but I'm talking healthy selfishness . . . enlightened self-interest . . . let's call it "controlled ambition." Sure, a lot of people still prefer blame to responsibilities; excuses to explanations; desires to decisions. And that's pitiful. But let's face it, guys. We've got to start somewhere.

I've decided I'm sick of poverty. Sure, I know I'm not as bad off as some but, neighbors, let's be honest—I'm a hell of a whole lot worse than others. I see those *kids* running around in that little Mercedes-Benz that the last time I priced it was going for $60,000. Before you get the wrong impression let me explain why I was even on the Benz lot in the first place.

My mother purchased a Cadillac. A big, black Seville that did everything but make your morning coffee for you. My mother has always wanted a Cadillac. As you probably already know my mother is colored and it's not really that a Cadillac is a colored person's dream but, well, dammit, my mother wanted a Cadillac. It seemed a small enough thing to want after working at schoolteaching for five years at $100 a month, then working for the county for another twenty-six years or so at not a whole lot better. She and my father had sent two girls (my sister and me) to college, had purchased a nice but rather plain home in Lincoln Heights, and she just never did want a lot of stuff. Our furniture is comfortable but old: Mom dresses expensively but she never wears anything out and hasn't gained weight since my birth. It just seemed like a little thing to ask for . . . a Cadillac. When she started talking new car, which Lord in heaven knew she needed, I wanted her to look at the Peugeot, which is what I drove. It's not all that much, but it's nice and it looks good. Eventually she agreed and bought one. Everything was fine. She said she had purchased her last car as she was considering retirement and all she wanted to do was pay for it and quit working. Now, I don't know what you know about the French, and maybe I'm even bordering on some level of lawsuit, but the French are a strange people. They're moody. They make arbitrary decisions based on things like their pride or something. They also made a car that nobody can service but their own people. You can't even use a normal wrench to let the oil out for an oil change. No matter. We had the Peugeot dealer less than two miles from our home—until he started to sell the Datsun. The French didn't want him to sell the Datsun, or so we were told, and one thing leading to another as is wont to happen then bingo! He no longer sold or serviced the Peugeot. Not to matter: We found a foreign car place that had one man who could service the car—until he decided he was needed in Israel and went back home. Winter came and I probably don't even need to tell you the rest. Winters in Ohio are cold . . . very cold . . . freezing. Her car froze. Triple A could not get it started. Nobody could get it started. I called the hot line number for car service and was told my nearest dealer was in Dayton or Lexington. You've probably seen the ad for the Washington wine that has the French people sitting around at a taste test. They all just love that wine. It's great. "Where," one of the men asks, "does this wine come from?" He and another man walk over to a globe and the host says, "Washington," pointing to Washington State on the globe. "It appears to be a suburb of California." Of course, you and I would laugh; at least I laughed because the idea of Washington being a suburb of California is funny. But neither Dayton nor Lexington is a suburb of Cincinnati, either. How the hell was I suppose' to get a car that is not running to a dealer fifty miles north of me or one hundred miles south? The car had to go. And may the moody French never sell another to someone's unsuspecting mother again.

I have a theory about parents. Treat them like adults and they will respond. That's not always true of parents and grown children, which is one reason most parents and grown children cannot live together. Both want to treat each other as if they were children. Plus, folks, I had made a hell of a blunder recommending my car. My car worked because I had lived in New York City where it had had proper maintenance. I drove back to Manhattan enough to have it serviced on that end and hadn't realized the implications of owning a car that was not constantly on the road. I was, quite honestly, thankful that Mom never said to me, "I wouldn't be in this mess if it hadn't been for you." I don't think of myself as guilt-ridden but I do feel bad when things I recommend don't work out. I wisely decided to ask what she wanted in a car. "Well, Hortense and Willie have a Mercedes-Benz," she said. "Would you like to go look at one?" I asked. So we did. You know you're in trouble with the Benz when you walk on the lot and see the repairmen in jackets. Somebody has to pay for those clean hands. But hey. If you can't afford it you shouldn't be looking. I, in fact, have a friend who says the reason she drives a Mercedes is that she's poor and can't afford to replace cars either regularly or often. Makes sense to me. We took a test drive. The people couldn't have been any nicer. Then Mom asked how much. Mommy is by no means cheap. Frugal yes, but not cheap. She just was having the hardest time seeing a car that cost about twice what her home did sitting out front. No Sedan for her, no 190 either. "Well, maybe I'm interested in something smaller," she says, "like that one." She had pointed to the 450SL. I turned my head; the salesman perked up. He almost picked her up to carry her to it. That "little car" carried a price tag that said "$60,000." Mommy couldn't believe it. "For that little thing," she kept saying as I slowly, with as much dignity as I could manage, walked her back to the old car. She still hasn't really recovered. Even now she'll see one on the road and exclaim that that little car cost so much. I gave her space, then a couple of weeks later asked if she was still interested. "I want a Cadillac," she had decided. "Fine by me," I cheerfully agreed, and we went Cadillac shopping. There was really no question but that it was love at first sight. That 1980 Seville is one of the most beautiful cars ever designed. It's sleek, it's sexy, its lights turn on by themselves at dusk; if you have a heavy friend in the back, "level ride" will pump in to keep the car even. The sound system is great. You name it, the car has it.

She purchased a diesel. Mistake. For the first hundred miles or so everything was fine, then for no reason the car would die on you. I had it one day going to town and it died on the expressway. Folks, that's a lot of car to go dead on you in the inside lane. The final straw was when we went to the World's Fair in Knoxville. The Seville died in Lexington and I had to rent a Toyota to get us there. Ninety percent of owning a Cadillac is to show it off to your friends. Knoxville is my mother's hometown. If that car wasn't going to take her to Knoxville then she didn't need it. We pulled up in this Toyota. The next day I drove back to Lexington to pick up the Seville. It wasn't fixed. I drove back to Knoxville. The next morning I was scheduled to open the fair for Knoxville College Day. We are now into Sunday so I know Monday morning the car will be ready. I leave my mother and my son and his friend and drive back up to Lexington. I have by this time gotten to know the good folks of Raccoon Valley very well. We are friends. I stop in for gas and the lady is saying, "Still having trouble with your car?" I have made friends with the Wendy's people in Lexington where I get my coffee. "Car still not ready?" they ask, then whisper to each other. People all up and down that road see me going north and south and shake their heads. I can read the trucker's lips: "That poor woman's car ain't done yet, Jeb." And they blow their horns at me and give me the high sign. My mother did not become a Cadillac owner to have her youngest daughter become an object of pity. We do finally get back to Cincinnati and I immediately go get *Car and Driver* or *Road Worthy* or some book to tell me what the best car on the road is . . . Toyota! What is the purpose of a car? To get you where you want to go. How does it do that? You stick the key in and it starts. What are the side purposes? None. Fuck prestige. Fuck looking good. Fuck a friend that needs to see you in a hunk of steel that fucks up. I only in life, dear Lord, want a car that will run. But how to convince Mother?

One thing was becoming clear to me—I could not take this. I hate a moody car more than I hate a moody man. At least the slump of his shoulders or the scowl on his face will tell you when trouble is coming. With a car you never know. And like an unfaithful mate, once a car has let you down you never sort of trust it again. How to convince Mother? I called my sister. There are, I deeply feel, advantages to being an only child. I have an only child and would not change that for all the tea in China. But neither would I give anything for my sister. I guess Gary and I are lucky because we are not only kin, not only do we like each other, but we bring different skills to our relationship. I can easily whip Mom in shape by saying, "I'll have to call Gary on this." It's not that Mom is afraid of Gary but Gary takes no prisoners. The minute her mind is set on something it's got to go her way. Knowing how Mommy felt about the Seville I knew I needed more than a threat; I needed a body. "Can you come home?" I whined pitifully over the wire. "I need help." Gary, true to her giving nature, said, "I'll be right there. What's the matter?" I felt foolish. "We need to get rid of the Cadillac and Mommy loves it and I can't tell her what to do." "I'll tell her," Gary cheerfully volunteered; "get her on the phone." "No no. That can't be the strategy this time. You be on her side and let me insist. It'll be better if she's mad at me than you." "Whatever." When Gary got home a couple of days later she started praising the car and I knocked it. After two days of that Gary says to me, "Well if you hate it so much trade it." "Mom likes it," I reply as Mom is sitting there watching us go at each other. "Well if you knew what you were doing she wouldn't be having these problems," Gary says. "Mommy, why don't you come to California with me? Nikki doesn't know what she's doing." Mommy, I think it's fair to say, is fond of me. She also knows I would do anything to make her happy. I guess it's fair to say I'm fond of her. Gary starts insisting that we keep the car despite a "little aggravation." "If you come with me I'll keep your car running." Mommy has begun to panic. She doesn't want me to look bad in front of Gary. She still sees us as her ultracompetent older daughter and the nontalented, bad-skinned younger. She needs to protect me. Gary laid it on about how Mommy was right; I took one hell of a thrashing. Then the maternal instincts began to win out. "Well, I don't like that car all that much," she opines. "I've been thinking about trading it." Gary went into violent no's! "You love that car. Don't let her make you trade it." It was a masterful performance. Mommy insisted that she wanted to. By that evening we owned a beautiful white Toyota. Mommy for sure was upset with me because she never cared for that car all through summer and fall. But that first winter we had three or four days of zero weather. Our next-door neighbor's new Chevrolet froze; our across-the-street neighbor's brand new Chrysler corporation car froze. Hell! Triple A couldn't start one morning. But we did. "I really didn't like that car when I bought it," Mommy said, "but now I see why you wanted me to have it." "I? I had nothing to do with it." "Oh fiddlesticks," she said. "I saw through that dog and pony show you and Gary were running when you started." There is a moral to this story. In case you missed it I think I should explain: When you are poor nothing works right. I don't care if it's the top of the line or the bottom of the heap; it won't work right. Also, it is very difficult to fool your mother. I advise against it.

Being Black and poor is, I think, radically different from being anything else and poor. Poor, to most Blacks, is a state of mind. Those who accept it are poor; those who struggle are middle class. One of the saddest things that has happened to the Black community lately is that young people have begun describing their neighborhoods as "ghettos." We never thought of ourselves as living in a ghetto though very clearly we did. Another is that our young people are believing that white people control the world, that they have no control over their lives. When I was growing up if you flunked out of school, got pregnant, stayed drunk all the time, you were simply "no good." You had let your family and The Race down. Now you do that and worse and you are a victim. It's no surprise our communities are going to hell in a hand basket; Black leadership has finally managed to convince the young that it's neither their fault nor their responsibility. It wouldn't surprise me one bit if we ran a poll and discovered people *really* think if they change their hairstyle or toothpaste or deodorant that they will live happily ever after. The level of fantasy, unreality, is absurd. In the good old days when people finally got something, they knew it was well deserved, overpaid for and wouldn't last anyway. Today we have scores of youngsters, young men mostly, who are totally unable to accept success. There's something terribly wrong with being the number one draft choice of the defending NBA Championship team, then snorting cocaine and dying; there's something terribly sad about a bachelor party turning into death camp; there's something downright tacky about having several Super Bowl rings, then pushing drugs to buy your son a birthday present. Why can't these kids enjoy their successes? Because the current crop of what passes for leadership has said to them over and over again white people control your destiny and exploit you. Young men who get a chance to go to college on athletic scholarships feel exploited and demand more. Not more education, but more things. And find that they are still tacky thugs who sexually abuse women and still cannot read a book. Though it is agreed it is exploitation to put them on an academic track and, dammit, unfair to expect them to perform off-court as well as they do on-court. Young women who have an opportunity to participate in beauty pagents and model and all those silly girly things that a few years ago would have been unavailable are made to feel that they are being taken. Why? Because they believe in magical transformations. They believe they should be "happy" simply because they have used what few gifts they have. What is that old Moms Mabley joke: ". . . you are still a Negro . . . you were on your way to Cleveland but you fooled around with that Indian and missed your bus." I guess my age is showing but I remember when seeing *any* Black face on television was an event. People would call around the country, "There's a Black girl on *The Sixty-Four Thousand Dollar Question*," and we'd stop whatever we were doing and cheer for her. Despite its stupidity, whenever I need a quick Black fix I can tune in *The All-New Newlywed Game* because they always have a Black couple. Yes, making the same Black fools of themselves, but there, nonetheless. And why not? It's America and the whole country makes fools of ourselves. If America had style we'd never have come this far. Black leadership is tacky. And I guess that's American, too, but it's boring. Somebody needs to say to all of us: BEING GROWN IS NO DAMNED FUN. The Urban League's bumper sticker (which I don't have the slightest notion if they even do bumper stickers) should say LIFE SUCKS, 'cause it's true. But we live it nonetheless and hopefully find some fulfillment and a teeny tiny bit of happiness. The problems of the Black community are no different from any other communities: We work too hard; get paid too little; and nobody gives a damn. But that's no reason to give up and blame anyone else. That's the real world. If we could come through indenturement, chattel, emancipation, Black laws, segregation and just plain we-don't-like-your-kind-isms, we can come through "exploitation" that pays little boys millions of dollars to play games and pageants that pay little girls to walk around in swimsuits. But hey, I've strayed. Poor is a state of mind.

To state the obvious is not necessarily to agree with it. There's always some smart ass out there who'll say, "If poor is a state of mind then we should change our minds," then proceed to extol the virtues of some mind-altering drug. No. No. No. I'm even a bit beyond "Just Say No" into say "HELL NO." Drugs are death. No. If poor is a state of mind it must be embraced. James Baldwin, in one of his most beautiful sentences, says, "You must embrace what you fear." Makes sense. Again, age is probably a factor. When I was growing up nobody had cars. Everybody walked. The boys developed walks, took walking to a fine art. They dipped and swayed. You had no trouble telling what was going on by how they walked down the street. One walk for going to see the girls; another for getting together with the guys; a third for going to work; another for coming home. It was street ballet at its highest. Which certainly beats the whining we see today . . . which is infinitely better than the drooped shoulders and dragging spirits we encounter on the streets today. Black men used to walk with a "look at me" walk. Now they seem to walk within a shadow. They don't want to be seen and that's not good. When the men don't strut the women don't smile; and property values go down because nobody cares. The NAACP's new campaign should be "STRUT!" Aimed at young men. It should point out the significance of education, good health, responsibility. But why do I go on about leadership? I already know they don't talk to us; they don't live with us; their children don't go to school with ours; they don't work a real job. How could they know what's going on in the projects, communities, rural areas of the country? They are "national leaders," and if we have suffered from a spate of false issues, well that's obviously too damned bad. So what if every poll taken shows that Black leadership and Black people differ considerably on the issues? They are not so much leading us as they are making white people feel bad about our condition. And if those conditions have not and cannot improve with this leadership posture, well, that's too bad, too. If they changed they'd have to admit that we, the Black people who comprise the Black communities, are free. And a free people choose their representatives and spokespeople; a free people take joy in their responsibilities and experience sorrow at their failures; a free people set goals and map strategies to obtain them. A free people are, quite simply, free. And would therefore need no one to beg for us.

OK. I didn't really mean to get on Black leadership, but now that I did . . . I am fascinated. There seem to be two common denominators to leadership of color: They hang on until they are carried away in a casket; and they don't believe in any dissent. To disagree with "established" leadership is considered by those self-same gentlemen treason. This, despite the fact that they are supposed to be speaking for us. It would be laughable if it weren't so sad. They will accuse Reagan (the President) of not listening to them but they don't listen to anyone. The purpose of any leadership is to build more leadership. The purpose of being a spokesman is to speak until the people gain a voice. I am totally convinced the saddest thing that happened to Black leadership was the Civil Rights Act of 1964. If the people have civil rights then the next task is to exercise them. How do a people exercise civil rights? Individually. We have got to be the only community on earth that wants our people to do better but not the individuals who comprise our people. If that makes sense to you you are either a Black leader or I have a bridge I'd like to talk to you about. It makes no sense at all. Our people have fought a long, difficult battle for the right to be seen as individuals, and what do we find in 1986? Quotas that say we need so many bodies of such and such hues; so many male, so many female. It's no wonder no one takes pride in his work. He's not working; his color is. It's no wonder young people don't think they need to study for school; it's all going to be quotaed out anyway. Individual effort has been sapped, and we as a nation continue to pay for the lack of joy in individual achievement. Life is not a national lottery where chance controls the die. I'll say it again: LIFE SUCKS, but it's all we have and we ought to be joyful about the responsibilities we shoulder. Katharine Hepburn once said (if I may paraphrase), "Life is rough; it kills you." It doesn't just single out Black people for death; it doesn't just kill white people. It kills everyone. We don't need terrorists to take us hostage; we are all hostage; we don't need murderers to kill us, life will do that. Rich or poor; male or female; the proud and the profane alike. The Good Book teaches us, "Man born of woman will die" and if the prophets had been a bit more daring a couple of thousand years ago they would also have pointed out man conceived in a test tube will die. If you are on this earth you cannot get off alive. Fact. Fancy: Can you make something of your life? That's the question.

Can you turn off the people who deliberately use you for their own limited ends to make some sense, gain some joy, love somebody? Can you wake up in the morning with someplace to go and come back in the evening to somebody who cares? Unemployment must surely be the worst thing on earth. To know that you are not needed for anything, not even a menial sweeping the streets or stacking bricks or anything at all. Benefits can't take the place of work. Benefits are necessary to smooth the transition but we need jobs. There is no such thing as "make-work" because all work is made by somebody. All work is necessary. I don't have any trouble seeing why people become abusive when they don't work. They feel useless. And all the social work in the world will not make them feel better. They need a job to go to or be studying for. People need a purpose. I know I do. I know I would feel different if I had nothing to do all day. Even if I hit the Ohio Lottery (and I sincerely hope I do) I'll find something to do with my time. Maybe I'll be able to structure my week instead of my day. I'll know that I need to be at the library to read for the Children's Hour on Tuesdays instead of in the classroom at 8:30 A.M. on Monday; I'll maybe, even be able to say in March I take my annual cruise instead of at 7:30 P.M. I watch *Jeopardy!*, but it will still be an ordered life. I'll get to pencil shopping trips in the fall instead of when my dogs go to the vet; skiing trips at Christmas instead of reminders to get sidewalk salt. Hell yes, I would be rich and love it. No confusion here at all. No whining from me about how money has made me terribly unhappy. I can handle it! But I've deviated. It's got to be the most emotionally devastating thing to know you are not needed. It's not right. Whether it's make-work or make 'em work, people need something to do to contribute to the common good. When you think about the cave people, as I frequently do lately, what is absolutely striking is that someone, probably a woman, drew a figure on a wall. Why would she do that? To make her cave more beautiful? To say to future dwellers that humans were here? To communicate something within her soul? Why would she do that if it weren't important to her? To see the plains dwellers fashioning, in the dwindling light, a figure on a bowl . . . why would she do that? Why would primitive humans, despite all the dangers they faced, want to create something? I have to think it's because we all want to do what is expected of us and then a little more. Could we really be so different from our plains-dwelling-cave-dwelling ancestors? We all want to do our share and then some of us want to make it beautiful. Yet I remain puzzled.

Why don't Black people ever want to relinquish the reins of leadership? Why don't they have enough faith in us to step aside and allow new, local leadership to emerge? Why do we in the Black world mostly have to vote with a gun and not a ballot to make changes? Aside from the Communist/Capitalist wars of attrition, why haven't we built an infrastructure, a generation after colonialism ended, that gives us a score of leaders to draw upon? We have one man who probably at the beginning was very good and then he dies or gets killed and we get another man and, in the words of Stephen Bishop, ". . . on and on . . ." Whether it's the president of a country or the mayor of a city or a city councilman, you can bet your bottom dollar they will hang on and . . . God bless them . . . someone in the Black community five years after their deaths will still be voting for them. It's no wonder we stagnate, we have the same old tired ideas circulating through the same old tired leaders until finally there is nothing left to defend but the idea of leadership itself. Sort of like Nixon in blackface. "Don't criticize me because that's an attack on the presidency." Great Foolishness. "Don't criticize Black leadership because that's an attack on Black people." What does that sign say? WE THE WILLING, LED BY THE UNKNOWING ARE DOING THE IMPOSSIBLE . . . WE HAVE DONE SO MUCH FOR SO LONG WITH SO LITTLE WE ARE NOW QUALIFIED TO DO ANYTHING WITH NOTHING. It's the credo of Black people. Did I leave out the part about gratitude? Try being Black and doing something extraordinary and you'll learn pronto what ingratitude is. You are simply not allowed to be Black and happy about your success. It's taken as a sign of spite by Black leadership. No one ever wants to talk about how well we have done, especially under the circumstances. We always need to show our scars. We the willing led by the unknowing always have to apologize if we do well. It's the unwritten code of Blacks and, if I may, women. You are never to say "I DID IT." You are always to say how many people you have left behind and how if they had had your "breaks" they, too, would excel. Folks, a lot of people wouldn't excel if you gave them Heaven on tuna fish. They'd eat the damned thing. A lot of people, let's be honest, can't even answer a damned telephone the way you want it answered. They don't come to work on time and don't work once they get there. They have a shit-eating attitude and should their supervisor mention that to them they write him up with the personnel office on discrimination. A lot of people that you would want to network with and share little company secrets with will go to the company picnic and drink too much and say you said your supervisor is dumb. A lot of others will go to the Christmas party with their spouse, who then proceeds to discuss how despicable white people are and how its spouse is being exploited. A lot will not be able to write a decent memo and will charge they are being held back because of gender or race. And others will not go on out of town trips then be angry because they can't get promoted. But hey, you caught my drift. I just believe we are the masters of our fate. We may not get all we deserve but I don't know who does. At any rate . . . It's still tough being poor. It's still tough to look at the catalogues and know you can't order. It's still unfair that some have an awful lot and others have nothing. I just think it's a good thing to take control of your ambition.

Having shared all that, let me say I'm easy. It's true. I learned a long time ago, maybe before I even knew that I was learning it, to be happy with what I have. Not content as in I-deserve-this-bullshit but rather since-this-is-mine-I-may-as-well-make-it-what-I-want-it-to-be. No matter how rich I would have become, if I would have been rich I would not own a big house. My idea of both luxury and security is the top floor of the best hotel in town. I'd adore being rich enough to live in the Beverly Wilshire or the Plaza or the Georges V or any Continental or Hyatt. I want someplace to sleep, another area to sit, a bathroom and, of course, room service. It's not that I don't cook; I do. And I'm a very good cook. It's just so boring to wake up in the morning having to decide what, rather than where, to eat tonight. I only eat once a day and it depresses me to think about food the first thing. I really can't imagine how people manage who have to think of breakfast and lunch too. And you wonder why housewives drink. I don't. At the risk of a feminist picket line running around bookstores that stock this book, the hardest job in the world is the work women who stay at home do. This work can never be adequately compensated for by money, though money would help. Women's work is the pits because it's a limited audience for a show that plays every day seven days a week. Women who leave home have it made. They can easily explain their irritability by blaming it on the job; we who stay home have to rely on the premenstrual syndrome. Women who leave home can explain dull dinners and no breakfast or lunch at all by saying, "But I'm working so hard to give you things you need." We who stay home picking up smelly socks, making up tousled beds, cleaning dishes, dusting furniture, planting flowers nobody sees . . . we're just so much garbage giving both our children and husbands, not to mention dogs, cats or other pets, a false notion of our worth. There is nothing so undervalued as women's work. I'm probably as guilty as the next working woman in not understanding my sister mothers who stay home. Until my father became ill I lived in Manhattan, had a housekeeper, went to work every morning and returned to a clean home and occasionally dinner in the evening. I must say I made my own bed and counted my own laundry but I never thought much about the work of a house. When my father had a stroke I moved back to my parents' home. All of a sudden I found myself with time on my hands waiting for him to need something. The house itself is old and needed work. I began to work on it. Before we venture further let me say I know I should have bought a new house. It would have been, in the long run, cheaper and easier. But Gus didn't want to move and Mommy didn't want to move so that left bringing our home up to our standards.

Gus, my father, had obviously been sicker longer than we had noticed. We noticed when he was felled with a stroke but we probably should have noticed when little things that he used to do weren't getting done. I guess when you're married to someone for over forty years you don't want to notice things because that reminds you that both of you are getting old. That is probably poorly said but what I mean is I think it's hard to admit how much people change. Anyway, we had a slow leak in the bathroom, which had buckled the floor. Mommy said she didn't notice it; Gus was in the hospital so he could say nothing. The easiest thing to do was put another floor in. The problem is finding workmen. I never knew what my grandmother meant when she said, "You got to beg 'em and pay 'em too." About a month back home I found myself using that expression a lot. We got the new floor put in, though; I was totally pleased. Mommy said it looked nice. This is not about putting the floor in. Once you do a really big inside job everyone says it looks nice. This is about waxing the floor. I would wax the floor and no one would notice. We put in an oak kitchen floor next. Everyone said how great it looked. I would Murphy that floor and no one would notice. No one notices now and the floor is six or seven years old. Mommy does. I do when she Murphy's it. It got me thinking. I would dust the furniture then feed it with lemon oil. That furniture would shine, glow, come alive. My friends would say, "Your house always looks nice." Maybe so. No maybe, definitely. But Your-house-always-looks-nice does not respond to my inner need to have people exclaim over my work. I want each wood piece delicately examined and lovingly commented upon. I want each piece of crystal to be observed for the way the light bends through it; I want, dammit, the silver that sits out to be individually praised. If my glass was spotted and dull, if my floor was greasy and dirty, if my silver had yellow stains it would be noticed. But if you keep a clean house it's an "Oh, well. We expect that of you." It's not fair. When I get on my hands and knees to put Murphy's oil on that floor I want it noticed. And nobody does. I quickly understood that woman's work is noticed only on its absence. Even women who should know better will ignore your effort. If a man does any little thing at work, let alone anything extra, everybody goes to Hosannahs. But a woman is expected to do these things with no praise and in fact no notice taken. She will only hear about it if it's not done. No one says "Great dinner, dear." But you can bet your bottom dollar they'll all scream "What! Meat loaf again?" No one says "I love the new way you made up the bed." But you can count on criticism—"Marge, why isn't this bed made up?"—when he comes home. No wonder house-wives are skittish. They get nothing but negative feedback. I have taken to observing and commenting positively on any change that occurs in any friend or relative's house. I try to see how things are and what they are trying to do with it. I always like it because (1) it's not my house and (2) I don't have to live in it. I expect the same uncritical support. If we stay-at-homes are not supportive of each other all is lost. I also remind my working-out-of-the-home friends that the reason we stay-at-homes have better-looking houses is we have nothing better to do with our time. Otherwise we women are playing a vicious one-upmanship game with each other; both trying to prove we are right in a situation that is neither right nor wrong; just dif-ferent. Sacred cows make very poor gladiators.

Wait. Let's pursue that for a moment longer. There are two totally illogical things that people, more specifically women, do: (1) have children and (2) try to make homes. These are two thankless tasks and should be undertaken with extreme caution. I have friends, I'll be honest about it, who think I am good with children. I probably am because I do not treat them as children but as people. It always scares the bejesus out of me to hear a parent speak of "the baby" as if the child had no name, no personality, no individuality. Many people speak more personally of their dogs or cats than they do their children. You sometimes wonder why they have bothered to have children at all. Or you get that what I really think is sick situation where some parent drones on about how the child is his or her best friend. I never trust that. We go through entirely too much to have children to end up with only a best friend. Even though I do have a best friend I know there is a world of difference between her and my child. For one thing I'm not responsible for my best friend's bills. For another, though I rejoice when things go well, and am quite sad when things don't . . . I know it's neither my personal triumph over street thugs and indifference nor is it sad enough to make me question my values in life. Children aren't friends . . . they're joyful responsibilities. But it's illogical nonetheless that something that happened, in many cases quite by accident, and as a side product of something else entirely, can change your life. Just another little reminder that things do not always work out as we think. I don't so much like children as I like my child. There are reasons for this: (1) he's mine and I've paid for him; (2) he's a nice young man and (3) I know that no matter how this relationship ultimately works out I do not, nor does anyone else, own him. There wasn't a whole lot I was looking for in a child. I just wanted basic intelligence, some sensitivity and a hell of a whole lot of sense of self. I figured if I taught him not to take my shit I would have given him about all a parent can give a child. That will, I admit, occasionally cause problems with his algebra teacher or the vice principal but hey! He doesn't have to be perfect, just the best he can be. Houses, on the other hand, are freely chosen after much thought, many evaluations and every possible consideration. I'm sure there is the perfect house somewhere. I read *House and Garden, Architectural Digest, Home* among other things and I see perfect houses. I just don't know anyone who lives in one. I don't know anyone who ever has. And even when I look at those gorgeous mansions, lovely Manhattan pied-à-terres, charming little caves in Utah or somewhere I say to myself, "I'll bet that basement leaks," or "They probably have a termite problem," or "God! What their heating bill must be." It's not that I have the best house, it's simply the reality that there is no better. Like children ... or cars. No matter what you get someone gets something better and someone gets something worse. The whole trick to life is the simple recognition that "No option makes the best choice," followed by some variation of "But he's our rascal." STRUT. It's all we have left.

I have a sad tale to tell. It's not about my house because in reality I don't have a house; I live in my mother and father's house, but as long as I'm coming through the door I may as well wipe my feet. We're smokers, my mother and I. My father was a smoker when he was alive; my sister is a smoker. I don't mention this as any sort of pride in bad habits but as a reality.

Some people don't smoke because they don't like to. Some don't smoke because they were too old to learn by the time it became available. And a few assholes don't smoke because they think it's just the cutest thing in life to say, "I doesn't smoke. Please put out your cigarette." Or something of that nature. Nonsmokers have gone way over the brink about clean air. A more reasonable worry would be that the water we drink and the air in the streets is tainted by leaks and accidents of our industrial society. Of course they also think industry should be shut down, and what they'd really like is one day to wake up in a forest with nothing and no one on earth but them and Bambi. Hell, cave people didn't smoke; plains dwellers didn't smoke; Neanderthal man didn't smoke, to name a few of our ancestors of the last million years or so, and they lived about fifteen or twenty years. Not that anyone has to put up with my smoke; they don't. You just have no right to require me to stop. Prohibition was stupid in the twenties and it's stupid now. It's not really the nonsmokers who really tear my curtains, it's the ex-smokers. Nothing on earth is as righteous as a reformed prostitute. Little old ladies who hated their husbands for forty years of marriage wait until he dies, then get on the bandwagon. The only thing I know that makes me half as angry is to see a man walking a picket line against abortion. Especially a Black man. To see those hypocrites who could not honestly tell you their own children are well fed and well clothed—"well" here to mean fed and clothed at all—saying to some woman they neither know nor want to know that she has to use her body twice in the service of mankind: first to screw him; next to have his baby. It drives you nuts. To see white people talking against abortion when there is not one Black man, woman or child whose life and right to life they respect. What do they want us to do? Have babies so that the ghetto can continue? Do they warehouse children in their spare time? I mean, why the hell can't, couldn't a woman and in many, many cases, a girl choose not to have a baby? I won't even argue whether or not an embryo is a child; I think since it is in the female's body she is the one who should make the decision about bringing it out. Any man who doesn't like it can easily prevent his sperm from fertilizing her egg by any number of methods, first among which is abstinence. "JUST SAY NO" should be aimed at men the women are so obviously going around seducing. Very few guys are taken against their will; very few women run out of gas on dark roads; I mean when was the last time you saw a television show with some female stalking some guy in the dark and pulling him down in some alley? Give me a break. Abortion is about women having options and anti-abortion is about men taking them away. Hester Prynne should not have worn her "A" alone; there were two parties involved. But then I never believed Eve seduced Adam. It's illogical. I also reject the idea that sex is punishment. Psych 101 teaches us if you put two people, no matter what their race, religion, ideology, of the opposite sex in a room . . . sex will happen. We further learn from Kinsey to Masters and Johnson that if you put two people, no matter what their race, religion ideology, of the same sex in the same room . . . sex will happen. But further we know if you leave one person, no matter what race, religion ideology, etc., in a room alone . . . sex will happen. The rat, in other words, will cross the grail more for sex than for food. We ought to stop this foolishness of controlling or trying to control sexual behavior and be supportive of people's control over their own lives.

But we were talking smoking. Sorry. Since we all smoke our walls have to be painted every five years or so. I would imagine that even folks who do not smoke get their walls painted but I have never seen data on this. My mother and I live in a small house. I like to think of it as a cottage. If we were surrounded by a couple of acres we could put Heidi to shame. I like that old house. It's illogical, but I do. We had discussed having the house painted but like a lot of old ladies who live together we have accumulated a lot of things over the years . . . tiny little things like the elephants my mother collects and the hippopotami that I do. It's amazing how many elephants you can get once you are in a place for thirty years or so. I also collect Black memorabilia so there are a million little Black figurines. Not to mention little photographs of everybody, every occasion and everything. We are now, quite honestly, in a position to bring nothing into the house unless we are willing to take something out. I suppose there will always be room for one more family photo but I swear it's getting close. It's even becoming a pleasure to shop again because there is no possibility of purchasing anything. The standing Christmas rule for the last five years is: A gift may not be given if it's not consumable, usable (as in perfumes, lotions or soaps) or won't die soon (as in cut flowers). Painting is, and ever will be at my home, a pain in the ass. Mother kept hinting that perhaps the gook on the walls needed to be painted and since I would do anything to avoid the painters I would get my Big Wally or whatever that stuff is and ask, "Where? Where is there a spot?" That was working fine until the day my mother's bed broke. And this is the sad part. My mother's bed broke.

My mother is a small woman, four feet eleven inches, not

weighing quite one hundred pounds. I wouldn't say mother is undemanding because in her own way she is; yet she's not overbearing, and dammit, the bed broke. I was sitting reading in my favorite rocker with the game going when she brought it up: "My bed broke," in a very sweet, gentle voice. Well, nobody should have to sleep on a broken bed. How long had they had it anyway? There aren't too many things in life people are absolutely, unqualifiedly, unquestionably entitled to, and a bed is certainly one. She could not have picked a better time to have a bed breakdown than when she did because Shilito's was having a bed sale. Not to worry, I assured her. As soon as the game is over we will go to Tri-County and buy a bed. It was fall, the leaves were changing, yet not really cold. I put on my boots, she dressed as little old ladies are prone to dress for special occasions and we headed out to get a bed.

Sometimes when you wear boots that squeak and jeans that are, well, gamy, a sweatshirt that has seen a better day or two, salesclerks will ignore you. Even if you are with your mother who looks every ounce a lady. Not today. A very cheerful woman came practically running over to us. While she did not actually break into a sweat she was a bit winded as she asked to help us. I don't like to fool around; I hate pretending I don't care when I'm shopping. I like to tell them what I want and have them go get it. I have friends who say you will get a better deal if you feign indifference but I don't want a better deal; I want what I came for: "We need a double bed for my mother. Today. To be delivered on Monday." That put it square in the salesclerk's court. We look, finally deciding upon a cherry bed that was, really, quite lovely. "It doesn't go with my chest of drawers," Mommy whispered as the sale was being written up. "Hey. We need a chest of drawers," I said. Politely. But pointedly. It's sometimes necessary to spread a little guilt around since in fact we hadn't been asked about the chest of drawers. "Do you think," this little voice comes up at me, "I need a night table, too?" Now I'm really not a bad shopper. I prefer to antique if I'm going to do furniture but I really didn't care. What I wanted was happiness and to get back in time for the second game. Plus, honestly, I thought she really deserved and needed this bed so what could the big deal be? "Mother, get a bedroom suite. Please." My mother is a frugal woman. She needs you to persuade her to spend her own money. Even if it had been my money I would not have cared because, dammit, she needed a bed. "You deserve this, Mother. And it's beautiful. Should we get a new lamp? Rugs? I really do want you to have it all." She only wanted a double bed, chest of drawers and a night table. To be delivered on Monday. We went home happy. Now this is a sad story so how could we be happy? Because we were dumb . . . stupid even . . . definitely foolish if we thought anything could be that easy. How could it be that girl and mother purchase bed; bed is delivered; girl and mother are happy. No. Girl and mother are of color. Nothing could be so simple.

Sunday morning in an unbelievable, yes, even unnaturally good mood I arose, fed the dogs, started my coffee, stripped the ads from the Sunday paper, poured my coffee, then settled with my comics. I always read Miss Manners last figuring, rightfully so, that the Forum section (Week in Review for you *New York Times* fans) will depress me. She's right, you know. If simple courtesy were practiced more, if we were less inclined as a species to be boorish, selfish, vengeful, we'd be better off. MISS MANNERS FOR PRESIDENT. I don't read the *NYT* anymore since migrating Midwest. For one thing I don't care and for the *all* important *other* there is no comic page. I had subscribed to *USA Today* thinking they would eventually recognize the need for comics. I mean, really now . . . what's a paper without comics? How can you really begin the day without knowing what Opus is doing? Some people just expect too much of us—so I settled into my largely reduced paper to read my comics first, sports page next, Forum, arts & leisure, Lifestyle and wrap it up with the magazine gossip section (Didn't Dipsy Doodle, gorgeous star of *To Hell with You*, used to have a mole on her right cheek? I say yes but my husband says no. If he is right I have to perform an unnatural act on him. Worried, Standby, Missouri. Keep that tongue in cheek, Worried. Dipsy, noted for turning those quick phrases, did indeed have a mole on her cheek. She got rid of it when Vanna White made the cover of *Time*. "Who wants to be different these days when there's a fortune to be made?" Do *you* have a question about the stars? Write us. We have the answers.) Yes. Actually I am ashamed of reading things like that, but hey, who wants to be left out? You never know when something will come up in conversation. I had a young militant tell me recently that he disliked Magic Johnson because his (Johnson's) wife is white. There are reasons, I suppose, if you deal with that sort of thing, to dislike Magic Johnson. As a dyed-in-the-wool Celtics fan, though I wish Mr. Johnson no harm, his playing ability disturbs me. But because of his wife? I was proud to very sweetly say, since I read gossip, that "Mr. Johnson has no wife. He are single." Usually you may have noted when people have prejudices and you have information you have to repeat the information several times before they get it through their thick skulls that they are forming opinions on false information. "Well, his girlfriend is white." Now my son tells me I have become everybody's mother and that is probably true also but it pains me to hear hatred and stupidity coming out of young Black mouths. "Well, I want to thank you, young man, because I just learned something. I was under the obviously false impression that I watched Magic Johnson play basketball. I didn't realize tuning into the Lakers was some sort of validation of Magic's choice of companions." "Well I still don't like him" was the reply. "And neither he nor I give a shit" was mine. I gotta tell you this. He was a nice kid. After I got to know him better I understood his problem; he wants the Race to do better. By the way, I have no idea in 1987 who Magic Johnson dates, nor, at forty-three, do I care. I'm long out of the running. Plus, I like short men.

So Mommy gets up and I say, as we have a game at 1:00 P.M., "Let's clear your room out now." Monday I have to go to work and I don't want them coming to deliver the bed and chest of drawers and night table and be unable to since the union will not allow them to help a sixty-plus-year-old woman move her furniture. By getting the stuff out on Sunday, though, Mommy will have to sleep in the den. Not to worry. It is only for one night.

There is nothing so small as an empty room . . . nor so dirty. The walls looked like shit. A very quiet voice suggested—at third and long—that perhaps the room needed painting. At third and long you would say yes to a tour of hell in a beaver coat. What I really remember is the "Oh, goody" from the other side of the table and me trying to figure out why she was as happy as I that my team had made first down.

OK. So I hadn't wanted to have the house painted, but one room, which was empty now—how much trouble could that be? Monday I called to delay the delivery and she called a painter. He'd be there tomorrow. "You got to beg 'em and pay 'em too." Tuesday came and went. Our next delivery was Thursday. Wednesday came and went. Call to delay delivery. By Friday I have decided to paint the damned room myself.

Painting isn't hard. You purchase paint, paintbrushes, get a ladder and put the paint on. Mostly. Almost. Sort of? I miscalculated the amount of paint I'd need. No one told me you need semi-gloss. Flat looks like shit. And paint splatters. In your hair, on your clothes but mostly, neighbors, over your floor. And it will not easily come up. By this time I have to admit it. I am annoyed. It's been a week—the house is torn up and the paint job I did was not good. Mommy, having some idea of my limits, knew it was time to call somebody. Frankly, friends, as I look back on it all, I was about one aggravation from burning the house down. Tennessee Williams has always been one of my favorite writers, though *Streetcar* is not my favorite play, but in one blinding flash I understood Stanley. Of course you flip the dishes onto the floor when asked to help. You are at the end of your rope. Mommy's friend, Hortense, who already got Mom into the bind over the Benz, has a daughter who just married a very big (as in important) rock star and they were redecorating their condo and Van just loves her decorator. We finally snare him. "Why," he asks, "are you painting one room? Why the whole house will only cost you——" and he named a not cheap but not unreasonable figure. All righty. But I would have said yes to anything by now. As we stood there in the kitchen, someone, I can't really recall who, said, "The kitchen sure could use some new wallpaper and maybe a little tile over there where we fry all the time." Yes. And just one other minor point. Very minor. I had not noticed until Theresa had a stroke that our steps are high. For example, where the average sane person's home would have two steps, we had one. You can actually huff and puff coming up that step. The steps leading to the patio were in the same condition. Theresa Elliott is a dear friend to us and a great barbecuer. After her stroke she had to go out the side door through the garage to get to the patio to barbecue. I had called a contractor to put new steps in. He was delighted to do the work but he couldn't do it in the summer—he was busy. But by October first he would be there. October one, with her room empty and badly painted, the house torn up, the wallpaperer working . . . Skip sent his men. Without asking, having, in fact, no knowledge of the distress going on inside, they started that machine that tears up concrete. My patio steps to the house, my steps to the garage were all gone. I understood completely Scarlett O'Hara: NEVER AGAIN WILL MY FAMILY GO THROUGH THIS.

OK. It's time to fess up. I wasn't always able to be calm in the face of disaster. I used to, in fact, during my early college years, kick back with a beer or two. Then I got busy and just plain didn't like the taste of alcohol anyway and hey, I hadn't had a drink in maybe fifteen, sixteen years. I needed a drink. I'm teaching my writing class at the Mount and every morning my students look worriedly at me—How's the house coming? And I would share the latest. When I walked in that Monday, now into my third week of this mess, to say, "I have no back steps at all," uncontrollable weeping broke out. A wave of Oh my God's could be heard breaking over the back of the room. Women started beating their breasts—How much more can she take, Sweet Jesus? Even my younger students who have never known the sorrows of home ownership fought back tears. Is there anything we can do? Poor Linda, upon hearing of the steps and herself contemplating renovation in her own house; poor Linda who had already dissolved into pants and oversized sweaters from the neat little lawyer suits she always wore; poor Linda whose hair, generally tied into a neat little bun, which at the beginning of this saga was coal black, turned gray. To this day, dear friend that she is, she doesn't admit that my class did it. But I know. I was there. I then recognized there was only one way to get on top of this thing. I had to pretend, from that moment on, that it was not happening.

My world turned a hazy red—either sunrise or sunset—I was not sure and did not especially want to know. My two dogs, Wendy and Bruno, were being forced to defecate in the basement, which was beneath their dignity. I actually saw our Thanksgiving pheasant being cooked in my den on an open fire—the ceiling which Bobby and I had so carefully laid turning black from the smoke. I understood for the first time in my life why people cease trying—why folks give up, why we who are poor think there is no end to our troubles. How could something as simple as a bed lead me this low? Once before, with this house, I had been so tested. Once before I had seen on my floor little droppings that I knew had come from something eating at my foundation; once before I had been given more than I thought I could handle. We had termites.

Now really, I am aware of the food chain. I am, in fact, a strong supporter of the darter snail. I believe everything has a right to exist, should, in fact, be secure in its integrity, but neighbors—I hate an insect. They have not created the insect whose death does not bring rejoicing to me. I have been known, among my son's friends, to offer a bounty for the body of a wasp. Even now if they need a few pennies for gasoline I'm perfectly willing, for the body of a waterbug, to part with five bucks. Even the little bees that buzz my flowers can only escape my Raid for a brief period. Nothing will stop me in getting to kill a fly. I, in fact, hate them so much I do preventive spraying. I thought, and until I noticed that sort of powdery substance on my floor, that I hated flies the worst. But then I discovered termites.

First of all, what I actually hate about insects aside from them being ugly, crunchy, sneaky little teeny tiny sons of bitches is they are un-American. They're Commies. "Yeah, sure," you're saying, "ants are flag-carrying, Marxist-reading, Mao-suited Reds. Yuk. Yuk." But hey, look here. They are organized in cells, there is a hierarchy of work divided along the lines of what's good for the group; there is no possibility of changing your future or job through individual effort; and if you go away from your group you will perish. There is no thinking on your own, no innovation, nothing to mark that you were here and had a dream. They work so well because they keep doing the same thing over and over again. Those of the human species who think that neat, who say things like we ought to be united and each one do a prespecified job are looking to insects for leadership. And who in her right mind would want to be a drone? The humans advocating droneship intend, in fact, to be the queens anyway. They are advocating droneship for the rest of us. If I have to choose I much prefer the mustang free on the plain or the thoroughbred running a race . . . the lone wolf howling on the hill; the coyote still seeking a way to exist on the prairie. Not a fucking termite. Under any circumstances.

I'm told by my Terminix man that you cannot hear termites. They silently eat your house away. But I swear I can hear the little buggers digesting my wood and shitting it out. I hear them in my wall laughing at me. I hear them sliding toward my bookcase deciding they will take my favorite volumes. Forget the Stephen Kings, the Sidney Sheldons, the Jacqueline Susanns and Jackie Collinses. They want my Toni Morrisons, my James Cleveland records right below her, my dictionaries, my maps . . . my whole fucking life. I called the exterminator. "Oh," he says, "not a bad problem at all. We can handle it." But once you have been leered at you fear rape. "How do I know they won't come back?" "We can tent your house and nothing will come back. Everything will be dead." Actually it sounded good to me. "Everything?" "Yeah. Bees, wasps, ants, crickets—all the pests." Now wait, I don't want to appear to be vacillating, but crickets? I grew up with "Brownie and the Cook." It's not only bad luck to kill a cricket but honestly, how can you say Jiminy Cricket is a pest? Crickets sing and dance and don't hurt anybody. Willfully harming a cricket is right up there with clubbing baby seals. But those g.d. termites have got to go.

When everything deteriorates time changes; your life rolls slowly, slowly before you. You see your errors, you once again bitter-sweetly touch the sweet parts. You see yourself unable to make changes. Words, that have the power to change things, spew from your mouth only to be trapped in bubbles slowed down by molasses. The world goes in slow motion. How long have we been working on this house? Was it really November and my tile is still not complete? Would the bed, chest of drawers and night table ever get in? Would the concrete set? Would Wendy ever, ever forgive me for the indignities she suffered? One bright, though chilly morning, they all left. The quiet, like fog on the Ohio River, folded over the house. We were clean, tiled, painted, wallpapered, concreted, railed. I could not believe it. Broke but happy, my heart turned to Thanksgiving while my finger dialed Shilito's. This is called DON'T THEY EVER LEARN? Yes, neighbors. There is more horror coming our way. But first, let's take a commercial break.

I discovered something a few years ago. You cannot be (1) sane; (2) a female; and (3) look at daytime television. You can only do two of those things at the same time. From the 6:30 A.M. shows until 8:00 A.M. it is considered that the men are at home. That something, in fact, serious, can happen. You get your real news. (THE WORLD WAS BLOWN UP AT 1:35 A.M. EST. EVERYBODY DIED.) You get your real people. (THE PRESIDENT OF THE UNITED STATES AND ALL THE LEADERSHIP OF CONGRESS WILL BOTH BE WITH DAVID THIS MORNING . . .) You are, in other words, treated as a sensible adult. At 8:01 A.M. this all comes to a halt: *Screeeeech*!! And the attack begins. "Hate that gray? Wash it away." You haven't even combed your hair this morning let alone contemplated its color and texture. But wait, what have we here? "Some people call these 'age spots' . . . but I call them UGLY!" This is delivered to us by a little old lady in a house neat as a pin who clearly has been married for the last fifty years. Are we really to think he would leave her because of liver spots? Then we'll be gone. He should have split years ago, giving her a chance to find someone who valued her for more than her body. But if that doesn't drive you to drink, how about the woman sitting in front of the mirror talking to God knows whom saying, "John felt old when he saw the gray in my hair." Give me a break. John *is* old. And the color of your hair will not change his physical condition. She, of course, uses some product that not only keeps her marriage intact but the son of a bitch actually takes her out dancing! I hope she finds a better man. But now we see the morning mist in the background. A powerful car, its motor purring, is coming into view. Are we women finally to get a real ad? In the right-hand corner creeps the picture of a little cottage. If it weren't so obviously European we would say "shack." "Françoise! Françoise!" shouts the overjoyed woman in the seed sack dress with children pouring, like clowns from a circus car, out around her feet. "How do you manage to look so young?" Not hello. Not how are you? Françoise so obviously is rich that a more appropriate question would be when did you get your latest face-lift? Plus this poor simpleton, concerned about fading youth, is probably an abused wife. Anybody with all those children surely will qualify. Françoise not only is driving a great car, she probably is a single woman with an exciting career. She has probably spent the night with "Roger," who is pressuring her to make a commitment. Whenever she feels herself weakening she drives out to see this poor soul; be renewed in her commitment never to marry and returns to Paris quite content with her life. Porcelana indeed. Common fucking sense is more like it. But hey, if I was a guy I would resent some of these pitches obviously aimed at keeping woman in "her place." There is this ungrateful dummy who climbs into the shower with the water running. We could maybe overlook it if there was no water because maybe he didn't realize that little room with no windows and a spigot hanging down was the shower. But no. The water is running. After wetting himself he leans out of the shower calling, "Hon, get me a towel." No "please." Not even her name. She stops what she is doing, wiping her hands on her apron, and brings him a towel. Does he look sheepish for having forgotten it in the first place? Does he smile in gratitude at her bringing it? He sniffs. "Are you sure this towel is clean?" The answer to which is, "Are you wet or what?" This pitiful excuse for a human being is probably in middle management. He probably makes important economic decisions affecting thousands of lives—but he can't remember to get his own towel and is not appreciative when helped out. And that's supposed to induce me to buy fabric softener? I'd sooner shake myself. The world, of course, is incensed by Ring Around the Collar. Doesn't he wash his neck? Doesn't he know that if his hair is clean this won't be a problem? But, hey, it's no wonder housewives are crazy. By 8:30 A.M. your entire being has come under assault. Noting with guilt that you do, in fact, have yellow waxy buildup; looking with disgust upon your gray hair and wrinkles, you do what most people do. You stare at your hands. "DO YOU HAVE ROUGH, RED HANDS?" they boom at you. They do seem to always have these things perfectly timed. "THEN YOU NEED PALMOLIVE DISHWASHING LIQUID." I swear, one day somebody is going to kill Madge. Madge sitting there reaping a living off the misery of other people. Madge with the big mouth and smart-ass saying about hands. Hands that have washed diapers and floors. Hands that do dishes three and occasionally four times a day. Hands that have to wipe up dog shit and pick the paper out of the yard. Hands that haul cases of beer home so that his weekend will go smoothly. Madge is putting down these hands! Someone ought to lay reality on Madge and point out what her hands were like before she agreed to bear his children and keep his house clean; before she agreed to wash and iron his shirts in a washer that never breaks down with an iron that won't burn. These are not friends to women since there is never a break. The vacuum is not a friend to woman since our floors are supposed to be free of all signs that life has passed in this room. The dearest friend of woman in the home is the microwave, which frees her from watching the same sacred cow unthaw, cook and brown. We will be entirely free, sisters, when we see the ad with Bernard standing there: "Sure, I use the forty-eight-hour girdle. When Cathy met me my stomach was flat. I owe it to her to look good." Or Steven. "Hi. I just want to talk to the men. When Myrtle and I met I knew it was my hair that attracted her to me. So now I use Mr. Robin's Wigs. They look just like real hair. And when we go out no one says, 'Who's that old guy you're out with?' " We will know equality has sneaked in when Edward says, "I washed dishes. And I tried them all. No liquid could do what a servant can. I bought Ann a full-time maid. After all . . . we deserve the best." Of course, someone is asking about the maid's hands. Well, how about a dishwasher? If she's Black she'll whip that household into shape, toote sweet. And hey, we can't all be winners.

The bed was arriving in the morning.

I know how Charlie Brown feels in the fall. He is standing there, hopeful . . . pitifully so . . . waiting to kick the football

Lucy is holding for him. He knows, because he has been through it before, that she will snap it away just as he reaches it. But he wants to believe. I, too, wanted to believe the bed would arrive. And it did.

Cherrywood double bed, chest of drawers, nightstand. Beautiful. Put the chest of drawers here; the nightstand there; the bed in between. No. We ordered a double bed. I measured it myself. Yes, I do know how to read measurements. I, after all, successfully completed fifth grade. THIS IS NOT A DOUBLE BED. What do you mean beds come in one size to be double or queen!! If we had wanted a "queen size" bed we would have purchased and paid for it. Get this piece of crap out of my house! What does that mean: You don't take back, you just deliver. Calm down! CALM DOWN? C A L M D O W N ???

Clearly I was on the verge of hyperventilating. I went into my newly painted, wallpapered and tiled kitchen. Calm down, I started saying to myself. You knew it couldn't go smoothly. You are, after all, still colored. There are times when religion plays a big part. The only thing between me and a fatal heart attack was Job. I contemplated the rather horrible example God made of Job while showing off for the Devil. "Consider my servant Job." And I could see how a similar conversation could take place: "Consider my servant Nikki." And the Devil replying, "Well, certainly. Look at what you've done for her." Not that my life has been easy or anything—I think I could raise a tear or two for me. But on the whole, I'm alive, relatively sane, earn a living off my insanities, have a loving family, faithful dogs, a house that is, right now, quite beautiful, a car that mostly runs and good credit. Perhaps I haven't reached high enough but on the whole . . . it could be a lot worse. I thought, as I sat smoking, about my fellow humans going through the daily hassles and it occurred to me . . . I should do something. I should start the Society of Job. At first I thought to restrict membership to Black women, then I thought, "Naw." Sensitive Black men have the same kind of hassles. So, yeah, let's offer some comfort to the men. Then I thought of White, Brown, Red, Yellow women who were hassled by things out of their control. Then, of course, I simply had to consider White, Brown, Red, Yellow men. Should membership be restricted to the English-speaking? Of course not. And if not restricted to the English-speaking then how could we ignore the anguish of female elephants who watch their mates be murdered for tusks or young rhinoceri who watch their fathers, gentle males, vegetarians who would only attack to protect their families be shot down because of a superstition that their horns make human men screw better; how could we ignore the fears of female seals that their babies would once again be clubbed to death for their fur or the worry of all whales that they will be assassinated for perfume factories? I finally understood we are already a part of the Society of Job. It's only a question of who will force themselves away from our comfort by insisting upon their right to commit murder, rape, genocide, ignorance, indifference. I felt better.

I dismantled the bed and hauled it out to our garage. I wrote the president of the store a very nice letter detailing our affection for his company and a desire to have his very fine merchandise removed FROM MY GARAGE. I said lovingly, gently, though, I confess, with great firmness, to my mother, "Should you ever again in this life mention a bed to me I will have you committed. I do have grounds, Mother," I continued, "since only a clearly crazy person would ever in this life mention a bed to me again."

And what have I learned? The rich do indeed have more fun than you and I. I do believe it would have been just as difficult if I were rich but I would have been able to hire someone to be aggravated. I know, honestly, that I'm a better person for having handled everything myself for I learned to question everything. Nothing is easy; nothing is sacred. Somehow, you and I, the ordinary grunts who get up in the morning, go to work, make a little less than we owe, come home at night to a house that needs a little more than we are willing to do, to people we are periodically not sure we should be bothered with and on the contrary not at all sure we deserve, and we will lay down at night on our own mattress and box springs mounted on the little legs we purchased from our hardware store, say our prayers to a God we are not sure is listening and close our eyes to the howling of sacred cows on their way to the slaughterhouse. We may not know the truth but we've learned to question the suspect. And after all, neighbors, isn't that a beginning? Knowing we'll have fresh hamburgers in the morning?

. . . Film at Eleven

Our Own House Is in Disorder

The Civil Rights train, in 1965, pulled into the station for rest and refurbishing. It had been mightily battered but was still on track with Martin Luther King, Jr. conducting though his fireman, Malcolm X, had been, for reasons still unclear, shot down. Three years later the train was not so much derailed as diverted by the assassination of King. It was reassigned first to the Peace Movement, then to the Woman's Movement where it did honorable though still unfinished work. It has not yet returned to the inner city.

Our old are on the streets, sleeping in parks, being forcibily moved into prison-shelters (where a refusal to accept "help" is taken as prima facie evidence of insanity), standing in what has become the longest food line since the Great Depression, unable to make food stamps, welfare, Social Security stretch from the first to the thirtieth.

Our young are out of school, out of work, out of hope; unable to read effectively or write with clarity; imprisoned by self-hatred and institutional racism they prey, like the walking wounded they are, on the old, on the helpless, on themselves.

The New York Police Department tortured five suspects with electric prods; shot a sixty-six-year-old grandmother to death on an eviction . . . and there was no outcry.

A Los Angeles policeman murdered a seven-year-old boy because he was home alone watching television while his mother went out at night to work . . . and there were no sanctions.

The Philadelphia Police Department bombed a Black neighborhood, then a few months later that same city had to declare a State of Emergency because a Black couple moved into (and out of) a "white" area. And there are no marches.

Our Black college student population was reduced by a bit over 10 percent last year, as were the numbers of Blacks entering professional schools: doctors to heal us; lawyers to fight for our rights; teachers to educate us; future leaders to help us shape the twenty-first century. Our own house is in serious disorder.

Twenty years after the Voting Rights Act, twenty-one years after the Civil Rights Act, thirty-one years after *Brown* we are still separate and unequal. It is, I believe, good and proper to help others, yet I recall a line from the old Thanksgiving hymn: "Sing Praises to His name—He forgets not His own."

Pioneers
A View of Home

I don't own a class ring. Actually, I didn't graduate from high school, but that's not the reason I don't own a class ring. I was an "early entrant" to Fisk University but I am sure that, had I asked, Austin High in Knoxville would have let me purchase a high school class ring. It wasn't the lack of money, either. My grandmother, who simply adored any kind of ceremony, would have been as happy as a pig in you know what if I had wanted to come back to Knoxville to receive some sort of something with my class . . . and purchase a class ring in the process. Nor did I forget. Proms and class rings aren't the sort of things you forget when you're sixteen or seventeen years old. No. It just seemed foolish. What do you do with a class ring after you are graduated? Give it to a girl if you are a boy, but if you are a girl . . . maybe pass it along to your daughter? I know one mother who did that. Put it in your jewelry box? I know lots of people who did that. Lose it? Certainly. God knows it's a sign of a really sick mind to see grown people, adults with respon- sibilities, wearing class rings. I go so far as to submit you know a person is having a severe personality crisis if you see a high school class ring on a finger beyond the first semester in college. Male or female. It's a big sign saying NOTHING HAS MATTERED TO MY LIFE SINCE SENIOR YEAR.

I don't own a yearbook from college, either. I did pay my fees and really could have sworn that a yearbook was included but none ever arrived. A friend of mine recently went to live in Indonesia and left a copy of her yearbook with me. She thought, quite correctly, that I would want the book with the photo of me sleeping in the Honors Lounge. No one can tell it's me, though I happen to recognize the desert boots, but aside from those and a beige skirt that I actually hated, no one would know it's me. Still and all I admit pride that I made the yearbook one year. Maybe another year, too, but no one has stepped forward with another copy. I'm not against pride. Not at all. I'm just a little picky about what I take pride in.

There are actually people who take pride in their race. This is actually stupid. You would think, the way some people act, that there is a Babyland somewhere in which babies could select their parents: "I'll take the rich, white ones." "Well, I want the Black ones." "WHO'LL TAKE THE POOR? WE NEED MORE POOR Here." "Oh, hell. I'll take them. You been yelling for that poor family for over a week!" "WHAT ABOUT AMERICANS? WHO WANTS TO BE AN AMERICAN?" "I want to live in Nepal. Got any Nepalese who want children soon?" No. I rather doubt that it happens that way. More likely two people happened to meet, mated, and you were born. Not that anyone should be ashamed of his race, it's just that when you think about it you had nothing to do with it. Not your race, nor your age, nor your nationality. Not even your name, though some of us sneak and vary our names more to our liking somewhere between the fifth grade and college—with which I sympathize. No one wants to be called "Snookums" or "Boo-bee" through eternity. It's a question of style.

I was watching *Family Feud* recently on our rerun station. Some of you remember *Family Feud*: Two families squared off with really silly questions answered by the strangest one hundred people in the world ("We asked one hundred people to name a friendly neighborhood bird") and the families had to guess what these fabled one hundred had said ("Buzzards"), and whichever reached 350 points first ("The number one answer—27 points") then got the chance to name national products for $10,000. A Black family consisting of, if memory serves me correctly, a father, mother, two daughters and a son-in-law was playing a white family consisting of a father, mother and three sons in uniforms. As luck would have it, on the third round, where all values are tripled, the Black family answered and got to play for the big money. Richard Dawson went over to shake the hands of the white folks and thank them for coming. You remember that you win the money in front of you (*Family Feud* wasn't a cheap show like *Jeopardy*, where only the winners get to keep the money), and Dawson pointed that out and said he was sorry they didn't do any better. You understand, Dawson wasn't expressing regret, just being polite, when one of the sons piped up with, "Well, we still can fly." I guess they were in the Air Force, but mostly that was such a racist remark. You Blacks may know what one hundred people think but hey, we whites can fly. Totally unnecessary. And tacky. I don't object to the boys being proud of flying; hey, if I could fly I'd be proud too. As a matter of fact I'm proud of myself when I *board* a flight! I'd be snuff in a pitcher's jaw if I could actually make that thing leave the ground. No. It was the context in which the remark was made. As if, "Well, hell, after all we're still white" could make up for the fact that they lost. That's as bad as if the Black family had whipped out the old Red, Black and Green nationalist flag and proclaimed superiority for Blacks based on . . . *Family Feud*? In the words of Joan Rivers: "Oh, puhleeeaase."

It's so clear, now that we have photographs from the moon, and man-made satellites even farther away, that earth resembles nothing so much as a single cell in the human body. That's not my observation; it belongs to the biologist Lewis Thomas. I was never good at biology. You stood around in a room with lots of little dead animals in jars and you were expected to cut them up and discover things. Or you started with live worms or frogs and you killed them to discover twitching muscles and stuff. I don't deny the importance of Life under the microscope or scalpel . . . I just don't do it. But what a concept. That the planet upon which we live is no more than a specimen on a slide. We, who think humans are nature's greatest invention, may well turn out to be no more than the life we see swimming in an ordinary drop of water. What then is important? When Paul Tsongas, the former senator from Massachussetts, was told he had some form of cancer, he decided to quit the Senate. "No one ever died saying, 'I should have spent more time at the office,' " he pointed out. No one ever died saying I should have hated more; I should have had more guilt or envy in my heart; I should have beaten my wife; I should have been less educated; I should have stifled my personal urge to explore my world and my life more. No. Most of us face our fading years wishing we had been more open, more loving, more capable.

They say Home . . . is where when you go . . . they have to take you in. I rather prefer Home . . . when you could go anywhere . . . is the place you prefer to be. I don't think of a home as a house, which is another thing I don't own. Certainly, though, I do live in a house that I have made my home. I won't even pretend living on the streets, sleeping in public parks, washing up at the bus or train station, eating out of garbage cans is a valid alternative to bedrooms, bathrooms and kitchens whiffing good smells every time the furnace blows. But I also readily concede if there is no love a building will not compensate. The true joy, perhaps, of being a Black American is that we really have no home. Europeans bought us; but the Africans sold. If we are to be human we must forgive both . . . or neither. It has become acceptable, in the last decade or so, for intellectuals to concede Black Americans did not come here of our own volition; yet, I submit that just as slavery took away our choice so also did the overcrowded, disease-ridden cities of Europe; so also did religious persecution; so also did the abject and all but unspeakable Inquisition of the Spanish; so also did starvation in Italy; so also did the black, rotten potatoes lying in the fields of Ireland. No one came to the New World in a cruise ship. They all came because they had to. They were poor, hungry, criminal, persecuted individuals who would rather chance dropping off the ends of the earth than stay inert knowing both their body and spirit were slowly having the life squeezed from them. Whether it was a European booking passage on a boat, a slave chained to a ship, a wagon covered with sailcloth, they all headed toward the unknown with all nonessentials stripped away.

A pioneer has only two things: a deep desire to survive and an equally strong will to live. Home is not the place where our possessions and accomplishments are deposited and displayed. It is this earth that we have explored, the heavens we view with awe, these humans who, despite the flaws, we try to love and those who try to love us. It is the willingness to pioneer the one trek we all can make . . . no matter what our station or location in life . . . the existential reality that wherever there is life . . . we are at home.

RACISM 101

■ ■ ■ ■

1994

Foreword
by Virginia C. Fowler

"A real writer," James Baldwin says in "Alas, Poor Richard," "is always shifting and changing and searching," a fact that often creates an "intensity of . . . bewilderment" in the writer's audience. But despite this inconvenience to readers, reviewers, and critics, "a real writer" will indeed challenge attempts to pigeonhole her or his work because, Baldwin continues, that "work is fatally entangled with his [or, presumably, her] personal fortunes and misfortunes, his personality, and the social facts and attitudes of his time."

Baldwin's observations have particular relevance to this most recent collection of essays by Nikki Giovanni, "a real writer" by anyone's definition. The essays brought together here span the past five years of the poet's life; they project her view of the world that her new perspective as a faculty member in a large research university affords her. Readers familiar with Giovanni's earlier life and work—both poetry and prose—will not perhaps be surprised by many of her reactions to being a member of one of society's most conservative institutions, though they will perhaps find it remarkable that this most icon-oclastic and individualistic writer made a decision to accept a position in *any* institution. That the perspective afforded by this decision should find its initial expression in prose rather than poetry is hardly surprising; what *will*, perhaps, startle the reader of this collection is the decidedly poetic sensibility Gio-vanni brings to the many unpoetic subjects she addresses here. Emily Dickinson's famous dictum that the poet should "Tell all the Truth but tell it slant" is certainly true of many of these essays, which work indirectly and figuratively to delineate "the truth" about education, educational institutions, racism, writ-ing, and a host of other subjects.

The prophetic and truth-telling qualities that we associate with the poetry that came out of the Black Arts Movement of the sixties and early seventies are as much in evidence in these essays as they were in Giovanni's earliest and most "militant" poetry. But the changes wrought in American culture by the last twenty-five years are quite evident in the modulations of the voice that speaks from these pages. What is constant in Nikki Giovanni, from her first book of poems to this most recent collection, are the fundamental values that shape her vision of society, culture, and life itself: a belief in the neces-sity to fight injustice wherever it appears and in whatever form; a commitment to an historical perspective, to looking at the present with a fully informed sense of the past; a respect, often even a reverence, for the past and present struggles of African-American people; a desire to find underlying connections between and among people and events; and, of course, an abiding belief in the integrity and the power of the individual. Whether she is speculating about space exploration, indicting higher education for the inequities it perpetuates and its frequent failure to accomplish its mission, or offering her own version of a film about Malcolm X, these values inform her attempt to get at the fundamental core of the subject, the heart of the matter.

In form, most of these essays are like jazz compositions, relying on highly individualized improvisation to develop their themes. To reduce those themes to their essence is to miss altogether the meaning and significance of the essays, for Giovanni's *improvisatory performance* of her themes is what ultimately matters. It is also what constitutes the *art* of these essays. They are not the sort of academic essays we would normally expect to read on the subjects addressed here. No, these pieces are artistic expressions of a particular way of looking at the world, featuring a performing voice capable of dizzying displays of virtuosity. Like a jazz musician, she is both composer and performer, and the prose style she has created is as distinctive as a Charlie Parker's or a Nina Simone's.

Louis Armstrong once said that if you have to ask what jazz is, you'll never know. The same admonishment must be made to readers of this volume. Those who do know, however, should sit back and listen to the music.

Acknowledgments

I really suppose when you write a book like this everyone already understands that the ideas contained therein cannot help but belong to the author. Who the devil would write some of the things that I do other than me? Speaking of the devil, a well-known colloquial expression, I'd like to thank my son, Thomas, for talking over his concerns and my ideas with me. He is a good and patient listener and a forceful presenter of his own ideas. I must say I would not want to have had a son who would just roll over because someone older and with more degrees or something challenged him. Of course, he will never do well in life because he believes in truth, integrity, loyalty, and honor. Please buy this book so that he does not have to work for people who don't understand that.

I would also like to give my warmest thanks to the librarians at the Johnson Publications Company. They have been consistent and cheerful helpmates to me over the past couple of years, researching facts, ferreting out old articles, and offering leads for the few facts that I actually used in this book.

Obviously, without some editorial direction I would not

have been able to at least make sense enough so that the academy, among others, could disagree. For that consistency of logic that was achieved, I thank Ginney Fowler. Probably, outside of those who birthed me, lived with me since birth, or whom I birthed, she best understands what I have tried to achieve with my writing. I would be remiss if I did not thank her for both the foreword and for a careful reading of this manuscript.

I thank my sister for the world's most wonderful Lemon Tart, which kept me going when I was stymied, and my Mother, who made grits and oysters when I was needing my mother.

Nikki Giovanni

Author's Note
"It's Elementary, My Dear Watson"

During that very hot summer of '93, I grilled a four-bone standing rib roast. I had purchased it in late spring, anticipating a visit from relatives, and when they had to change their plans, the roast went to the back of the freezer. I don't know about anyone else, but I clean house and garage and shed and freezer during seasonal change. The roast came to the front, but there didn't seem to be any special reason to turn on the oven . . . and after all, a standing rib roast is special, so it kept not getting eaten. Finally, one day when a storm was brewing and it was too hot for the oven, I nonetheless decided to cook the roast. It was illogical, I know. I could have waited; I was no more special when I cooked it than when I was refusing to, but I soaked it in olive oil and soy sauce, sprinkled lots of garlic salt all around it, and packed the top with cracked pepper. I let the roast relax for almost three hours while I prepared the fire. I have a very basic Weber, so I was, by then, mentally prepared to throw away that piece of meat if my equipment couldn't do the job.

When my fire died to embers, I gently laid the roast on

one side. The flames flared for about two minutes, then I turned it over. Two more minutes and I turned again. Same for the last side. Then I halved a lemon and squeezed the juice over the blackened parts. Spraying the flames down, I put the top on the Weber and went inside the house to finish the last pages of the biography of Adam Clayton Powell that I was reading.

I mention this because some of you may want to know how I put together this collection; or why it's called *Racism 101*, when many of these essays ostensibly have nothing to do with race; or why I repeat myself and my themes sometimes. I think I owe you an explanation: Any woman who would grill a standing rib roast would write this collection.

Writing is a conversation with reading; a dialogue with thinking. All conversations with older people contain repetition. Some of the ideas mean a lot to me and others are, to me, just interesting, so I both embrace and attack the ideas because I found them . . . well . . . delightful. I hope you do, too. I tried to vary by subject so you wouldn't be reading the same idea either in embrace or under attack, you know? I just wanted to write an interesting book and look at the world I inhabit. I'm a poet; I believe that the image will reveal itself. If the *Racism* is confusing, the *101* cannot be. Sherlock Holmes says, "Elementary." I think, "Basic." And the recipe is free.

I

PREFATORY

"To Catch the Conscience of the King"
—*William Shakespeare*

Griots

I must have heard my first stories in my mother's womb.

Mother loved a good story and my father told good jokes, but it was her father, Grandpapa, who told the heroic tales of long ago. Grandpapa was a Fisk University graduate (1905) who had majored in Latin. As he sometimes told the story, he had intended to be a diplomat until he met Grandmother, but that is probably another story altogether, he being Black and all in 1905 or thereabouts.

Grandpapa loved the stars. He knew the constellations and the gods who formed them, for whom they were named.

Grandpapa was twenty years the senior of Grandmother, so he was an old man when we were born. Grandmother's passion was flowers; his, constellations. One needn't have a great imagination to envision this courtship: the one with her feet firmly planted on earth, the other with his heart in the sky. It is only natural that I would love history and the gossip of which it is composed.

Fiction cannot take the place of stories. Aha, you caught me! Fiction is stories, you say. But no. Stories, at their best, pass along a history. It may be that there was no Ulysses with a faithful Penelope knitting and unraveling, but something representative of the people is conveyed. Something about courage, fortitude, loss, and recovery.

I, like most young ladies of color, used to get my hair done every Saturday. The beauty parlor is a marvelous thing. Every Saturday you got the saga of who was sleeping with whose husband; who was pregnant; who was abused by whose boyfriend or husband. Sometimes they would remember the children were there, but mostly the desire of the women to talk without the presence of the men overcame their desire to shield us from the real world.

My mother's family is from Albany, Georgia, but Grandmother and Grandpapa had moved to Knoxville, Tennessee. We four grandchildren spent our summers with Grandmother.

At night, when we were put to bed, my sister Gary and I would talk and sing and sometimes read under the covers using our Lone Ranger flashlight rings. Of course, we were caught. Grandmother would threaten us and take our rings. We would sneak out of our room, wiggling on our stomachs, to reach the window under which we sat and listened to Grandpapa and Grandmother talk.

Sitting under that window I learned that Eisenhower was not a good president; I learned that poll taxes are unfair. I heard Grandmother berate Grandpapa for voting Republican when "Lincoln didn't do all that much for colored people." I heard assessments of Black and white people of Knoxville and the world. No one is enhanced by this. I'm not trying to pretend they were; there were no stories of "the African" in my family, although I am glad there were in Alex Haley's.

We were just ordinary people trying to make sense of our lives, and for that I thank my grandparents. I'm lucky that I had the sense to listen and the heart to care; I'm glad they talked into the night, sitting in the glider on the front porch, Grandmother munching on fried fish and Grandpapa eating something sweet. I'm glad I understand that while language is a gift, listening is a responsibility. There must always be griots . . . else how will we know who we are?

II

"Plighting Troth Beneath the Sky"
—*Countee Cullen*

Paper Dolls, Iron Skillets, Libraries and Museums

I used to cut out paper dolls, a thing I think no longer exists in the age of Barbie and Ken and those turtle things. My sister and I would sometimes draw our own clothes, color them, paste and glue wonderful accessories . . . but we never could get the tabs right . . . and the clothes fell off. Fortunately we were not easily discouraged, and Mommy always praised our efforts.

There are certain advantages to having an older sister. She took piano lessons first and played so well I knew it was pointless for me to try. Well, I tried but it was the kind of effort one gives when one knows one is doomed to second place. She also took French first so I learned the alphabet, numbers, and a few dirty words before I enrolled in school. Our father was a math whiz. Give him a few numbers and he'd see the sequence; give him a problem and he would solve it. Gary, my sister, inherited that trait from him. It's all I can do to keep my checkbook straight. All this is leading up to a point. I had to find things that I could do well. Kickball is not actually a sport by which one can earn a living; I was good at dodgeball, but my temper is not suited to being graciously hit. That left tennis and poetry.

Had I not lived in a world that had so little regard for the wishes of Black girls, I may have tried the tennis circuit. Althea Gibson had, after all, shown that it could be done, if one subscribes to role-model theories, but, irony of all ironies, my parents didn't like the travel. And anyway, I started to smoke in college, so that killed that. My task? To find something I loved that did not require me to change my physical habits while allowing me to grow emotionally and intellectually. No problem.

I've always loved libraries. Spending most summers in Knoxville, Tennessee, where I was born, I established a wonderful daily routine. Breakfast in the morning, tennis, shower, lunch, library. To be quite honest, I'm not now and never was a breakfast fan, but it would just break Grandmother's heart if you didn't eat, not something, but a bit of everything. I ultimately moved to Knoxville and attended Austin High. When I went to college I was, well, chubby. Three weeks after registration I had dropped twelve pounds and could actually see my cheekbones and distinguish my eyes. But then, being human, I missed Grandmother's breakfasts. Moral of this story: People complain about what they have until they don't have it; then they miss it.

I never envisioned being a librarian because of the math. Dewey and the others still confuse me. I, in fact, which I say without bragging, will dial 411 all day long because I refuse to keep a phone book that I cannot use anyway. I've always made friends with librarians so that they didn't mind getting the books I needed or wanted. I simply am a firm believer that if you have incompetence in an area, you should turn to people who have expertise. Which brings me to museums.

As a Black woman I never visited a museum until I enrolled at Fisk in Nashville. Knoxville didn't have any that Black people seemed to visit; Cincinnati, our hometown, had them but we never seemed welcome. Both my sister and I are collectors. Though neither of us had articulated it until fairly recently, we now realize that we grew up in museums. Because the Black community had no public place to deposit our memories, the churches and Colored Schools, the Masonic and other lodges, but mostly the homes in which we and our playmates lived, were museums. The photographs of men and women in the armed services from the Civil War to the present; the framed letter saying great-great-grandfather was entitled to a pension for his service to the country; the books signed by Booker T. Washington, Langston Hughes, James Weldon Johnson, W.E.B. Du Bois; the piece of silver or crystal from "the plantation." The needlepoint chairs, pillows that were embroidered, handkerchiefs with delicate work, the quilts . . . oh, the beautiful quilts filled with gunnysacks, old army blankets, bags that once held one hundred pounds of flour or coffee beans, which weighted you down when you went to bed. The Black community is a living museum. This Christmas Gary fried chicken in Grandmother's iron skillets. Grandmother had inherited them from Grandpapa's family. Those things can't be purchased today. It takes a generation just to get them properly seasoned. And a lifetime of love to understand that they are.

I Plant Geraniums

I plant geraniums each spring. It's not that I am a geranium lover or even a plant lover; it's just that at spring there should be an acknowledgment of something new, some rebirth, some faith in constant change. I don't particularly like grubs or Japanese beetles; I actually hate flying things. My allergies allow me to plant my tomatoes but not to harvest them. Something about the fuzz that were I willing and able to pay six hundred dollars, my dermatologist could explain exactly why I break out when I touch it. I actually don't care. I'm quite content, in fact, to press family and friends into tomato-picking service: "It's my allergies, you know."

I'm not a critic, though I have been known to write a book review or two. When younger, I actually thought my opinion counted. I have since learned. When younger, I thought one of the particulars of being "Homo sapiens" was to communicate. I have not learned not to, though I am cautious when I try. Life is far too serious to take seriously. All the important things happen without our knowledge, consent, or active, conscious participation. We are conceived. We live. We die. We have no opinion on these subjects. Most of us don't even get to name ourselves. We can lie about our ages, but on the Gregorian or Chinese or Islamic calendar we are a certain age. That old expression, I think they call it a social lie, that "you don't look it or would never have thought you are . . ." takes away one of the crowning achievements of humans . . . that you survived. Of course, some people commit suicide to control the time of their deaths, but the end result is the same. Granting all that, which is, after all, not so much to grant, I support the concept of human life.

Shakespeare is lucky. There is an old African saying: "You are not dead until you are forgotten." Many groups share that belief, including some American Indians. The Euro-American must believe it because he works so hard to keep his history alive. It's fine by me. I hope, like Shakespeare, to one day be a *Jeopardy!* subject. I hope high school seniors quake at the fact that they have to take Giovanni before they graduate. I certainly can see the controversy over who actually wrote my poems; why did I never receive a "major" poetry award? These things get many a professor tenured, keeping many a family fed. One might even win promotion to "full" professor with the lucky and unusual discovery of some obscure grocery list proving once and for all, until deconstruction, that I do have false teeth. These things matter.

But I don't think Shakespeare had to worry about it. I think he had to write plays telling the king, "You are a fool" while keeping his head upon his shoulders. He had to tell the people who scrimped and saved to see his productions, "You are jealous, small-minded idiots who will kill the one you love." He had to show his public that the savage was more

noble than their pretentious societies while making them
come back. He had to expose literal-mindedness for the fool-
ishness that it is. Shakespeare was a working artist.

How could he have known that five or six hundred years
later he would be required reading? Should he have foreseen
this possibility and tempered his judgments to match? Should
not he have considered the possibility that his words would be
difficult to read, and should he therefore have anticipated
modern usage? Shouldn't we hold him to the same standards
as the Constitution and Bible and bring him "up to date"? I
think not. I think we should leave him in the brilliance of his
expression. We need, we modern artists and critics, to do
exactly what Shakespeare did. Write for now. Think for now.
Express ourselves in our best possible vernacular for now. Will
we be remembered? I doubt it. Most people are not remem-
bered. And most people who would remember the people are
not remembered. We have no true concept of what "Homo
sapien" has forgotten, though surely some of it was good and
some of it was useless.

Shelley or Keats, I always mess up which one, talked
about tending his own garden. Or was it Voltaire? I plant gera-
niums. No one will remember that. I have an allergy to tomato
fuzz. No one will care. I write poetry and sometimes prose.
No one will know me . . . let alone what I thought I did. But
while I live, during this all too brief period between birth and
death, my life and work have been meaningful to me. "The
rest is silence."

Remembering Fisk . . .
Thinking About Du Bois

There were three things the children in my family, both immediate and extended, were expected to do: go to church each Sunday; clean our rooms each Saturday; and go to college. I never really gave a lot of thought to which college. I think I more or less had decided the lot of the toss would make my decision. My parents were graduates of Knoxville College; my grandfather was a graduate of Fisk University; my sister was attending Central State in Ohio. To some degree, like all younger people, I did not want to attend any school where there had been a previous person. I had spent entirely too much of my life hearing about being so-and-so's sister, so-and-so's daughter, so-and-so's grandbaby. I was rather looking forward to going to places unknown, forging my own path, cutting new ground and all that. I attended Fisk.

The Ford Foundation played a small but significant part in my decision. It seems, if memory serves me well, that they had sponsored a study about taking talented students from high school early, as early as the sophomore year, testing them for intellectual readiness, and encouraging certain institutions to accept them as college freshmen. I was a junior when either Miss Delaney, my English teacher, or Mrs. Stokes, my French teacher, mentioned the program to me. Most of us, it is fair to say, are bored in high school. I jumped at the chance.

I had gone, by train, with my grandfather to Philadelphia to visit my aunt and uncle. I remember Philadelphia being murderously cold. I was living with my grandparents in Knoxville, Tennessee, and, to keep the record straight, we had gotten Austin High's permission for me to miss classes for a week or two. Both Grandpapa and I had forgotten that the test was coming up. I hadn't been in Philly for more than three or four days when Grandmother called and said I had to come home. Frankly, I was a bit unhappy, but I have always liked travel and I have always liked traveling alone, so the thought of leaving Philly was balanced by a twelve-hour ride on the train. I went back to Knoxville.

The test seemed like a normal test to me. Miss Brooks, our school librarian, administered it. I remember she teased me about not having enough squares to fill in my name, "Yolande Cornelia Giovanni"; I left off the "Jr." The only question I remember was a true/false: Fifty thousand Frenchmen can't be wrong. I said false. The correct answer is true. I still think the majority should not rule, but that's a different discussion.

We also had to fill out the name of the school where we would like our results sent. I had considered Swarthmore as a college I would like and I had considered Mount Holyoke, but they were not among those listed. I recognized Fisk and, with one of these real devil-may-care motions, checked it. I didn't think I'd done that well, anyway. A few weeks later I received a letter and an application. Still cool, I filled it out. Grandmother and Grandpapa were pleased; we called Mommy to tell her. I know now her first reaction must surely have been, "How are we going to send two girls to school?" but she was cool and made very encouraging noises. My father was a bit disappointed, as he had planned to come to my graduation. Gus, my father, had not been to a high school graduation since his own. My sister Gary had finished early in the summer and was at Central State, and now it looked like I was going to Fisk. I did.

Fisk was beautiful then: the lawn around the library, the majesty of Jubilee Hall, the comfort and very waxy smell of the chapel. There was no way to not love it, which I did. There was no way not to rebel, which I did. There was a men's dormitory, Du Bois Hall, which had, in fact, a painting of Frederick Douglass hanging. Odd. But not really challengeable. I, as did all young Black people of my age, knew who Du Bois was. Knew that he was alive and living in Ghana. Knew that he had walked these halls; sat in some of these classrooms; studied in the very same library. You could even still meet people who had known him, could tell stories about him. It was thrilling. I have always been a book freak. To this very day I am seeking an autographed copy of *The Souls of Black Folk*. I wanted to go to the library and touch and read from the first editions, but being a lowly freshman with no stack privileges, that was not to be. Fortunately for me, paperbacks were available and I reread, in one case, and read, in the others, all that he had written.

There is a lot to learn from writers, if I may use a cliché. We learn the information they have to share; we also learn their style and methods of writing, but for someone like me we learn that they are . . . that they did what they thought they should do . . . that they followed the dictates of their own hearts and minds.

Du Bois was a fearless man. He was not intimidated by white or Black; he did not gladly suffer any fool. He worked at colleges and with institutions based on his respect for them, not on whether he needed a job. If there was any one thing I learned from him it was, in fact, a relearning . . . you must do, say, and write that which you believe to be true. What others think can be of no significance.

Du Bois has stood the test of time. Though his late-life disappointments overwhelmed his logic, though he let his love of America and its failure to return that love turn him bitter, he was an intellectual of action, a rare combination. He showed us all that matters is that we contribute what we can where we can.

When I returned to Fisk, long after my graduation, long after presidents, deans of students, boards of directors had come and gone, there was a statue of Du Bois standing at Fisk. I am proud of my alma mater; we finally had the courage to salute one of our great sons who was and will remain "ever on the altar."

The Sixties

A Review of *My Soul Is Rested: Movement Days in the Deep South Remembered* by Howell Raines

My personal problem with what is called "the sixties," roughly that period between the *Brown* decision of the Supreme Court (1954) and the election of Richard Nixon (1968), is that I think we won.

I was born in a small town nestled in the mountains of eastern Tennessee, Knoxville, and grew up in a midwestern city that prided itself on being the "Gateway to the South." I have vivid memories of WHITE LADIES and COLORED WOMEN signs from Knoxville; Cincinnati didn't have signs—it didn't have to—you were simply ignored. My mother tells the story of going Christmas shopping with my godmother, my sister, and me when I was a little girl. She and my godmother, Edna Westfield, decided to take us to lunch at Dows Drugstore. We sat at the counter—two women and two little girls—and we sat and sat. Mommy says I said, "I'm thirsty," and the girl behind the counter finally slid a glass of water to us. Slid—not served—not given. We understood the error and left. I don't consciously remember the incident, but then I am not knowledgeable about the memory of the gene. There is a drugstore in a suburban Cincinnati area called Glendale. In the village square you park your car and walk to the drugstore, window-shopping, maybe stopping by the train station—all those things a family does on a Sunday in the fifties. We wanted, as kids do, ice cream, so we went to the drugstore. My father, who was a very friendly sort of fellow with a great grin, asked if we could eat the ice cream there. The clerk said, probably quite nicely, "*No*." "Well then," said Gus, "we'll order five double cones" and proceeded to pick flavors. The clerk, most likely happy that an ugly event had been avoided, made up the order. When he finished, my father looked at him and said, "Now, eat them." It was a small rebellion as rebellions go—but it was a rebellion. I don't mention my parents because they led the march for equal rights. I mention them because the utter pain at being subjected to that level of unreasonable and incomprehensible humiliation was multiplied by parents all over this country and is still being faced by Black parents in South Africa. There is something radically wrong about being unable to shop and grab a snack, or take a Sunday drive and stop for ice cream—there is something insidious in your child's wanting to see *Snow White and the Seven Dwarfs* and your having to explain it's showing at the white theater—or in a parent's guiding a child to the colored drinking fountain or the colored toilet or the colored waiting room.

It's become quite fashionable to berate the sixties. "All you did was get a cup of coffee," they like to say. All the sixties did, in reality, was save the political entity we know as the United

States from self-destruction. That Jimmy Carter, a poor white boy from rural Georgia, sat in the White House is a testimony to the impact of the effort of Black people. And we seem to be the last to understand that. Linda Brown was a little Black girl whose parents sued the school board of Topeka, Kansas, for equal education. I have no idea, and won't until Linda writes her book, whether her mother or father was more instrumental in the suit. They sued and the Warren Court reached a unanimous decision that separate was inherently unequal. Rosa Parks was not just a little old lady with tired feet. She was a moving force in the Montgomery NAACP; she was an active club woman. She was also not the only person arrested for protesting bus discrimination. She was, however, the person known in the community for her work as well as for her temperament—she was known to be both dedicated and committed. She was a reasonable woman. If *Mrs. Parks* was arrested, the Black community, from the doctor to the desperate, from the most honored to the least secure, from the professional to the pimp, understood not that something was deeply wrong—the Black community from 1619 to 1993 understands something as being wrong—but that some resolution must be sought. Martin Luther King, Jr., being the youngest, most articulate, and to a large degree most neutral figure in Montgomery, began to speak for the rightful aspirations of not only Montgomery but Black America. Montgomery was not the first boycott, nor the first mass protest. It simply produced the leader who was able to place that small community in Alabama in a world perspective. The rightful aspirations of Montgomery were felt not only in the United States but all over planet earth where Black people were being held down by whites and ultimately where the powerful and rich are holding down the powerless and poor. *My Soul Is Rested: Movement Days in the Deep South Remembered* is in the best tradition of the sixties. For those of us who are Black writers, it's almost ironic that the spoken word, in journalism, sociology, historical remembrances, is playing such a prominent role. Oral tradition, when Black Americans, Africans, Indians, and Hispanics practice it, is used as evidence of our "lower cultural development." When oral tradition is practiced by white journalists and sociologists, it is considered a new and exciting form. I am glad, however, that whites have once again discovered we are right. We are right in our moral outrage and we are right in our expression of it.

Howell Raines, a journalist, took his tape recorder south to record recollections of the movement days. People who would never write a book but who are great practitioners of the oral tradition tell their story.

Martin Luther King, Jr., is a personification of the sixties. His face, open and unafraid—his words, clear, compassionate, yet uncompromising, led a people—the Americans—into an examination of its soul. Risking his life, and ultimately losing it, King proved that words speak as loudly as action; that this nation and perhaps this world, because of the cancer of racism, was incapable of reaching the Christian idea of love. And by showing the barbarity of that incapability, he moved us all to a clearer understanding that we ultimately all share the same desire to live. King at first was not the American ideal of a hero. He was short; heroes were tall. He was Black; heroes were white. He was articulate; heroes mumbled. He led those without hope; heroes moved alone. Heroes after World War II were existential; King was committed to clear ideas of right and wrong. He led the Montgomery Improvement Association to victory and formed the Southern Christian Leadership Conference. What was wrong in Alabama was wrong in Georgia and Florida, in Chicago and New York City. "If violence was wrong in America," challenged Malcolm X, "then it was wrong abroad." "Why are we sent," asked Stokely Carmichael, "to defend our Motherland but taught not to defend our Mothers?" King was the most important public man to disavow the war in Vietnam. He was the first public man to speak of the equality of women and youth. He was a Daniel in a den not of lions—for lions are honorable beasts—but wolves. The packs howled for his flesh. They bit at his spirit. There is an old gospel song that says, "I've been lied on, cheated, talked about, mistreated, 'buked, scorned, talked about sure as I'm born; up, down, almost leveled to the ground, [but] long's I got King Jesus I don't need anybody else." King embodied the gospel songs and lived the Christian life. He was, while from man, clearly not of him. He shaped this age as neither Eisenhower nor Kennedy; John Foster Dulles nor Robert McNamara; Richard Nixon nor Joseph McCarthy could ever hope to. He was not a leader like Hitler, who hated; nor a wheeler-dealer like Franklin Roosevelt, who could care; but he was the man who gave reason once again to why the earth spins on its axis or why the sunbeams play on the noses of little barefoot children. He gave to us all the life-affirming concept of redemptive love. It is so regrettable that Howell Raines, because King was dead, was unable to include his words. Yet all the words in *My Soul Is Rested* are in fact King's—from the title to the last embrace Ralph Abernathy gives King.

I first heard Martin Luther King when he gave the commencement address at Knoxville College shortly after the Montgomery boycott. He loved to tell the story of the old woman he saw walking down the street one day. "Sister, you are old," he said. "You don't have to walk. Everyone will understand if you take the bus." The old lady shook her head no: "Son, I ain't walking for myself," she replied. "I'm walking for my grandchildren. My feets is tired; but my soul is rested." She continued her journey home.

Like a newly paved road with no speed limits and no restraints, *My Soul Is Rested* encourages the reader to speed on. It's a smooth easy read into an area that is still not fully explored. There are many more people to talk with, there are many more stories to be shared. The old folks used to say, "The half ain't never been told." But we are beginning. The real heroes of all periods are largely unsung and untold. Howell Raines has talked with people who shaped a great period. No matter that the ignorant, the indifferent, and the insensitive deride the contributions of Black men and women—we have known heroes—and heroic moments. It is for us, the cultural conveyors, to continue to explore what was the problem and what is the solution. Nothing in the sixties takes away the problems of the seventies, eighties, or nineties, or alleviates the pain of the post–World War II era. The sixties, however, solved the problems of the sixties—overt and lawful segregation; lynching; bombing; the wanton and capricious murder of Blacks by whites. As long as there are human beings, there will be problems in relationships. As long as there are men and women who shared their lives with the movement and their hopes with the Howell Raineses, there will be solutions.

Life is not a problem similar to science or mathematics where solutions can be discerned and tested. Life is a process where people mix and match, fall apart and come back together.

Today's clouds can never deny yesterday's beautiful sunset. The inconvenience of today's storms can never turn us from tomorrow's harvest. We plant, we reap, we *try* because we are human. We hope, we continue. Our soul is rested, but it will have to get up in the morning and start again.

Black Is the Noun

It is late. The poet has just opened her second pack of cigarettes. The poet smokes like a chimney. She fears the day when the possession of cigarettes, not just their use, will be illegal. The light is on in her den, though her window blinds are closed. She did not wear her seat belt today. They know. She knows they know. Contemplating her fingernails, she notices, to her horror, a speck of grease. She has, once again, eaten fried chicken. It won't be long before they come for her. What should she do? Finding no answer, she ambles to the refrigerator, opens the freezer, and takes out peach sorbet. If she must go, she will go her way.

"I've had my fun . . . if I don't get well any more."
—J. McShane

I knew I was old when, one evening last spring, I was driving from Blacksburg to Princeton to attend a party. I had finished early but a friend was driving with me and she couldn't get off from work. We left about five-thirty in the evening, driving my car, a candy-apple-red MR2. We had on our normal driving garb, jeans and T-shirts. I am always cold, so I had on a sweat-shirt. We were short-coiffeured, medium-nailed, no-makeup, modern sort of women on a fun drive to a fun place. We stopped for coffee, smoked, munched the sandwiches we had made—were, in other words, going about our business.

Ginney has two talents that I not only do not possess but do not aspire to: She can spell and she can read a map. My idea of getting around is to go to the farthest point and make the appropriate ninety-degree turn. For example, in order to reach Princeton from Blacksburg, I would go to Washington, D.C., and turn left. But Ginney can read a map, so she angled us onto the Pennsylvania Turnpike, around Philadelphia, and into the New Jersey Turnpike. I don't like to be picky about things because I lack certain skills myself, but I do think it is not asking too much for employees to know where things are located. You know, you go into Krogers looking for, say, tomato puree. You would expect to find this in the canned vegetable section, only it isn't. It's located with sauces. You ask someone wearing a Krogers shirt and you should get that answer. You expect the turnpike officials who take your money at the toll booths to know which exit to take for something as well known as Princeton.

I have an aunt, well actually I have two aunts, but I only want to talk about one of them. My aunt, and I will not desig-nate which, has trouble with her night vision. She is not quite as blind as a bat but she . . . well . . . has trouble. And there are, possibly, these genetic transfers. I don't think I've reached that stage yet, but sometimes it's difficult to see what exactly the signs are saying. It had gotten quite dark, we had stopped for coffee several times, and I, as driver, was happy to be on a turnpike with large green signs. When we were handed off from the Pennsylvania to the New Jersey, I asked the woman in the booth which exit I should take for Princeton. Had she just said, "Honey, I ain't got no idea where no Princeton is. It's been a long day and nothing has gone right. My left foot is hurting 'cause I cut that corn, but it's not healing right and maybe I have diabetes. You know, when a corn won't heal, that's a sign of diabetes. My mother had sugar and she lost her whole leg right up to the knee . . ." or something like that, I would have been understanding. "Yes," I would have said, "I've heard that corns that won't heal are a sign of sugar. My mother's best friend, Ann Taylor, from over in Knoxville, was just telling me about it when I was passing through last June." And she and I could have visited a bit while Ginney looked at the map and plotted our course. But no, she says, with authority, "Take exit nineteen," and we set out with the confidence of the innocently assured.

We were lost immediately; there was nothing that made sense on that exit, it was three-thirty in the morning, and, worst of all, I began to despair. We turned the light on in the car so that Ginney could see the map, but, golly, those lines are very, very small and the car was in motion, and bingo! The blue lights were shining in the back of me. I pulled over, popped the Dells tape out of the cassette, ground out my cigarette, grabbed my seat belt, and waited for the highway patrolman. "Your registration and license, please." I had the registration with my gas card in the front, but my driver's license was in my purse in the trunk. I looked up to explain my problem when he turned his flashlight into the car. He saw two McDonald's coffees, an ashtray full of cigarettes, and us . . . two lost, tired, old ladies. "Where are you coming from?" he asked. "Roanoke, Virginia." I always answer Roanoke because nobody knows where Blacksburg is. "How long have you been on the road?" "Since about five-thirty. We're lost. We're trying to get to Princeton." "Well," he explained, "you're way out of your way. You've got another fifty miles to go." He gave us directions and said, "Drive carefully." "I'll get my driver's license now," I offered. "Oh no, ma'am. You all just get where you're going. Have a safe evening."

Something in me clicked. A few years ago he would have given me a ticket. A few years ago whether I was lost or not I would have been written up. But we were just two little ol' ladies in what he probably thought was my son's car in the middle of the night trying to get to Princeton. I turned to Ginney: We are old. He saw old women. You drive.

"Going to Chicago . . . sorry but I can't take you."
—W. Basie

In *Star Trek II: The Wrath of Khan*, Khan, a criminal Kirk was responsible for putting on some planet way the hell out of nowhere, finally makes his escape. He is living for only one reason: He wants to kill Kirk. Khan and Kirk fool around for a couple of hours while Khan tortures and kills people and . . . finally . . . gets the *Enterprise* in his grip. Spock, of course, sees the problem and goes to the rescue. The awful weapon is turned on Khan and he is killed. But wait! Khan will have the last word even after death. Khan has trapped the *Enterprise* and it will implode because the crystals it needs cannot feed the engine. They all will die, and Khan, the evil Ricardo Montalban, whom I actually liked in *Fantasy Island*, will prove that evil triumphs over good even when evil can't be there to gloat about it.

Spock knows the answer, but Kirk cannot bear to see his friend give his life. Spock understands that either he gives his life or they'll all give their lives. He sneaks away from Kirk only to encounter McCoy. He uses the Spock maneuver to knock McCoy out, but at the last minute whispers: "Remember." And does his mind meld. Spock steps into the chamber, feeds the engine, and awaits his death. By now Kirk is on the deck, upset, quite naturally, about losing Spock. "The needs of the many," Spock says, "outweigh the needs of the few . . . or in this case, the one. I will always be your friend." He gives Kirk the Spock sign with the split fingers and dies. The next thing we see is Spock's funeral service and the *Enterprise* pushing his casket out into space. By this time I am embarrassing my son by actually heaving in the theater. I cannot believe Spock is dead. I will not accept it. But Tom points out to me that Spock's casket is headed for the Genesis planet. *Star Trek III: The Search for Spock* will bring him back. I cannot see it. If he's dead, how can he come back to life? In all our myths only one man was able to do that. But Spock did tell McCoy something: "Remember."

I love *Star Treks*. They are nothing less than Greek myths of heroic people doing extraordinary deeds with style and wit. No one on the good ship *Enterprise* will ever be short of courage. The television series, which was actually quite short-lived, marked a new era in television by obliging audiences to respect—and even to admire—differences among people. They talked to rocks in "The Huerta" and spirits in "The Companion"; they came back to defy death at the O.K. Corral by not recognizing the power of bullets; they stopped a war between two planets by making them confront the reality and pay the price of the killing; they gave us television's first interracial kiss. But Spock said: "Remember."

The Search for Spock opens with Kirk and McCoy meeting Spock's father with a flag. Spock's Mom is Jane Wyatt, formerly married to Jim Anderson on *Father Knows Best*. No one ever mentions the divorce, but when you see how the kids came out you could easily see why she might have wanted to make her way to another planet. Mrs. Spock, Jane, is not seen. Since she is human, she's probably off crying her eyes out over losing her only child. Ambassador Spock, the Vulcan, is not emotional, so he stands to talk. "Where are his memories?" Ambassador Spock asks. He knows his son is dead, and he can accept that. But where are his memories? Kirk and McCoy have no idea what he is talking about. "My son was a great man," Ambassador Spock all but bellows. "His memories are valuable to us. We can store them so that others will learn from what he knew. You must find his body and retract from his brain his memories."

Star Trek perfectly epitomizes the sixties. You had a courageous white boy; a logical Vulcan; an Asian scientific transportation officer; an Irish, emotional doctor; and, the ultimate genius of *Star Trek*, Uhura, a Black woman who was the voice of the entire Federation. Toni Morrison once wrote: "The Black woman is both a ship and a safe harbor." Uhura proved that. Of all the possible voices to send into space, the voice of the Black woman was chosen. Why? Because no matter what the words, the voice gives comfort and welcome. The

Black woman's voice sings the best notes of which earthlings are capable. Hers is the one voice that suggests the possibility of harmony on planet earth. Scholars are now studying what made the slavers bring females on the slave ships. The slavers could not have been so stupid as to think they could get as much work from a woman as from a man. There is the theory that since the women ran the markets and worked the farms, the white man understood that in order for his agriculture to prosper, he would need the women. I think not. I think there was a cosmic plan; a higher reason. In order to have a *civilization*, the Black woman was needed. So that one day forgiveness would be possible, the Black woman was needed. I need not, I'm sure, point out the fact that the first Black child born in what would become the United States was a Black female. The first poet. But more, I believe the first voice to be lifted in song was the voice of a Black woman. It may have been the "faith of our fathers," but it was our mothers who taught it to us. And when that faith is transformed, what do we have? A half earthling/half other-world being, saying to the doctor: "Remember."

Like Alex Haley's ancestor, who preserved his past by passing along his name, the slaves told their story through song. Isn't that why we sing "Swing Low, Sweet Chariot"? Isn't that why we know "Pass Me Not, Oh Gentle Savior"? Isn't that the reason our legacy is "You Got to Walk This Lonesome Valley?" "Were You There When They Crucified My Lord?" To Du Bois, the spirituals were sorrow songs, perhaps because he saw himself as so different from the slaves who sang them. But the spirituals were not and are not today sorrow songs but records of our history. How else would a people tell their story if not through the means available? We made a song to be a quilt to wrap us "in the bosom of Abraham." "Over my head, I see trouble in the air. . . . There must . . . be a God, somewhere." We knew "he didn't take us this far to leave us." We brought a faith to the barbarians among whom we found ourselves and the very humbleness of our souls defeated the power of their whips, ropes, chains, and money. "Give yourself to Jesus." Not your money, not a new church that you will sit in with other white people like yourself, not a new organ, none of those things . . . yourself. And all we had was a song and a prayer. Who would have remembered us had we not raised our voices?

Had Spock been a Black American, his father would have gone to church to ask the Lord for help. And his help would have come like the strength that came to Emmett Till's mother: "I know that's my boy," when the sheriff asked what she could contribute to the trial of Till's killers. "I know it's my boy," Mrs. Bradley, Till's mother, said when she opened the casket. "I want the world to see what they did to my boy." Didn't she roll the rock away? Two thousand years ago the Angels said: *He is not here.* Mrs. Bradley said: "Here is my boy. Look." And the world was ashamed. Spock told McCoy to remember. And McCoy didn't even know what he had.

They went in search of the body and, movies being movies, they found a young Vulcan boy on Genesis and brought him home. But McCoy had the memories all along. He just didn't know what he had.

"Although you happy, you better try to get along. Money won't change you, but time is taking you on."
—J. Brown

Much evidence to the contrary, I am a sixties person. It's true that I didn't do tie-dyed T-shirts or drugs, and I never went to jail. I argued a lot in coffeehouses and tried at one point to be a social drinker. It didn't work. I can't hold liquor at all. But I was nonetheless a sixties person and continue to be today because I actually believe in the people. That was never just rhetoric to me, though it has often been my undo-ing. Believing in the people is dangerous, because the people will break your heart. Just when you know in your heart that white people are not worth a tinker's damn and the future depends on us, some Black person will come along with some nihilistic crap that makes you rethink the whole thing.

I was never more than a foot soldier and not a very good one at that. I observed and I wrote. And the more I observed, the more amazed I was by our need to deny our own his-tory . . . our need to forget, not to remember. The contradic-tions were especially evident to me, perhaps, because I attended Du Bois's school, Fisk University. How ironic that Fisk's Jubilee Singers kept the spirituals alive, yet the students at Fisk were anxious to deny that their ancestors were slaves; if people were to be believed, nobody but me ever had slaves in their family.

The fact of slavery is no more our fault than the fact of rape. People are raped. It is not their choice. How the victim becomes responsible for the behavior of the victimizer is well beyond my understanding. How the poor are responsible for their condition is equally baffling. No one chooses to live in the streets; no one chooses to go to sleep at night hungry; no one chooses to be cold, to watch their children have unmet needs. No one chooses misery, and our efforts to make this a choice will be the damnation of our souls. Yet such thinking is one of the several troubling legacies we have inherited from Du Bois.

Du Bois needed to believe that he was different. That if only the "better" white people would distinguish between "better" Black folk, "the talented tenth," then together they could make a "better" person. I think not. The normal ninety have to be respected for the trials and tribulations they have endured. They've been " 'buked and they've been scorned." They bore the lash while they cleared the fields, planted, and created in this wilderness. Am I against books and learning? Hardly. But just because my tools are words, I do not have the right to make mine the only tools. It is disturbing that word-smiths like Henry Louis Gates, Jr., can say to those of physical prowess, "the odds are against your [succeeding in professional athletics]" (in a recent article in *Sports Illustrated*). The odds are more against any young man or woman of color being tenured at Harvard. Gates was not deterred in his determination to succeed in his chosen field, and he does not have the right to discourage others. Those young men on city playgrounds know that, indeed, basketball is the way out. Without that skill no school would be interested in them . . . no high school . . . no college. The academically excellent can use their words to sneer, but the young men know that's the only open door. Is it right? I think not. I would like to see choice come into everybody's life. But there are not good choices on the streets these days. The conservatives don't care, and the Black intellectuals are trying to justify the gross neglect of the needs of Black America. The Thomas Sowells, the Shelby Steeles no more or less than the Clarence Thomases and the Louis Sullivans are trying mighty hard to say, "I am not like them." We know that, we who are "them." We also know that such conservatives have no character. We know they are in opportunistic service. The very least they owe is the honesty that says, "I got here distinguishing myself from you." Clarence is against affirmative action? Shelby is against affirmative action? Since when? Since the people fought so that neither of these men would have to die for their choice of wives? So that Yale would admit a poor boy from Pin Point, Georgia? When did affirmative action become an insult? Shortly after you were granted tenure at your university? You don't like being made to feel you can honestly do your job because affirmative action made someone hire you? There is a solution. Quit. You think life is hard for you because you're viewed as a group? Try living in Newark or D.C. or Harlem and knowing that you will never be allowed by what Margaret Walker calls "those unseen creatures who tower over us omnisciently and laugh" to realize your dreams and potential.

Am I blaming Du Bois for his children? You bet. The Black conservatives belong to Du Bois. Booker T. Washington, born in slavery, reared in the coal-mining districts of West Virginia, walked his way to Hampton, worked his way through the Institute, labored in the red clay of Alabama among some of the most vicious white folks outside of Mississippi to build Tuskegee; he tried to empower Black folks. Is there a quarrel with the Atlantic Exposition speech? Somebody, other than the Black conservatives, show me where this nation is not still "as separate as the fingers of a hand" and how we would not all be better off if we would "come together as a fist" for economic development. Du Bois wanted to vote? So do we all. Didn't Martin Luther King,

Jr., have something to say about "Southern Negroes not being allowed to vote while Northern Negroes have nothing to vote for?" Didn't Frederick Douglass ask, "What does your Fourth of July mean to me?" Washington and Garvey wanted Black people to come to the table with some fruits of their labor. Both Washington and Garvey knew we needed and need, again in Margaret Walker's words, "something all our own." Why did Du Bois fight them? What an ironic twist of fate that Du Bois was the beneficiary of Garvey's dreams. That DuBois was the Renaissance man who spent his last days in Ghana, a Black independent nation, under a Black president. How ironic that Louis Sullivan and Clarence Thomas are beneficiaries of the struggles of the sixties.

"You better think . . . think about what you're trying to do to me."

—A. Franklin

I am an american Black. Period. The rest is of no particular interest to me. Afro-American, African-American, whatever. I am not a hyphenated American, regardless of how others define themselves. They can be Italian-Americans, Irish-Americans, Jewish-Americans, or whatever hyphens they would like to use. For me, the noun is Black; american is the adjective.

I do not fool myself often. I laugh about definitions because laughter is, well, so much more pleasant. I am not a particularly well person. I have lived too long with sick people to think I have escaped their malady. Every now and then, for one reason or another, someone will ask to interview me or talk with me or I will skim back through what has been said of my work just to, well, more or less see how I am progressing. I have always laughed at the critics saying I am bitter and full of hate. Nothing could be further from the truth. I am not envious or jealous either. I am just me. And I do have strong feelings about that. I do not and did not and most likely will not ever feel that I have to justify that. I do not have to be a role model, a good person, a credit to the race. When I look at Phillis Wheatley, Harriet Tubman, Monroe Trotter, Frederick Douglass, Sojourner Truth, Booker T. Washington, George Washington Carver, for that matter, W.E.B. Du Bois, James Weldon Johnson, Langston Hughes, Nella Larsen, James Baldwin, and I cannot possibly exhaust the list but, hey, Malcolm X, Elijah Muhammad, Martin Luther King, Sr. and Jr., just to name a few, the race has built up a big enough account for me to charge whatever I'd like. Doesn't Toni Morrison have a character named "Stamp Paid"? Perfect. Black America is well in advance of the Sunday school tithing of the folks with whom we live.

I had the great pleasure of meeting Anna Hedgeman when she visited Fisk University during, I think, my junior year. She was talking to honors history class about Frederick Douglass: "Every time I see that statue of Lincoln sitting below the Emancipation Proclamation, I want to have a statue of Frederick Douglass standing behind him guiding his hand." I could see that. Lincoln was an interesting white man who did the right thing, finally, by freeing the slaves in the states where he had no power to enforce his decree. But hey, why be so picky? He did it. True. But not for me. Not for Cornelia Watson so that she could birth John Brown Watson in freedom and he could marry Louvenia Terrell and they could conceive Yolande Watson and she could marry Gus Giovanni and they could conceive me. No. Not for me. Lincoln didn't care about Cornelia Watson. Nor conceptualize me. Near the end of *Song of Solomon*, Morrison has Milkman finally review his life, and he realizes that it is the women who wanted him to live. Or, as the father in *Sounder* says to his son, "I beat the *death* they had planned for me; I want you to beat the *life*." Am I saying I'm glad we have President's Day instead of Lincoln's Birthday and Washington's Birthday? No. I like my holidays to have real names. But I also know I don't owe these people any great affection or loyalty. They do not love me or mine. That, by the way, means I live in a narrow world. Well, maybe not so narrow. Maybe a more accurate way of looking at it is that I will not have my world nor my worth determined by people who mean me ill. Unlike Du Bois and his latter-day children, I do not measure my soul by the tape of the white world.

"It's been a long time coming . . . but my change is gonna come."

—S. Cooke

Like most people approaching their fiftieth birthday (I was born in 1943), I have contemplated the meaning of my people. I have wondered why we were chosen for this great, cosmic experience. We were not the first slaves in human history, nor were we even the first chattel. We were, however, the first slaves who chose, after freedom, to live among our enslavers. That is about the only thing that gives me hope. If God could part the Red Sea for Moses, surely the Atlantic

Ocean posed no unsolvable problem. I have contemplated what life must have been like around 1865 or so when freedom became a possibility. Why didn't we seek boats to take us to Haiti, which was already a free, Black republic? Why didn't we start great treks, not just a few wagon trains here and there, to the uncharged lands of this nation? What made us determined to fight it out essentially where we were? Some books tell us we loved enslavement . . . we didn't have to worry about our care or our duties. Some books say we didn't know where to go. Some books tell us we believed the promises of emancipation that we would be given forty acres and a mule. Mostly I think it was cosmic. The spirituals show us a people willing to "wait on the Lord." Though "sometimes I feel like a motherless child . . . a long way from home," though we knew "the rock cried out no hiding place," though we had the "Good News" that "I got a crown up in the Heavens," we "were there when they crucified my Lord." We were chosen to be a witness. Like Job in his patience, like Samson in his foolishness, "my soul is a witness . . . for my Lord." And without that faith there is no foundation for this nation. America may not be the best nation on earth, but it has conceived loftier ideals and dreamed higher dreams than any nation. America is a heterogeneous nation of many different peoples of different races, religions, and creeds. Should this experiment go forth and prosper, we will have offered humans a new way to look at life; should it fail, we will simply go the way of all failed civilizations. The spirituals teach us that the problem of the twentieth century is not the problem of the color line. The problem of the twentieth century is the problem of civilizing white people.

When I was a little girl, you could still buy things at the five-and-dime. You could buy those paddles with the ball attached that you would sit and whack for hours; you could buy jacks and pick-up-sticks. You could buy spin tops that you pulled a string around and the top would go spinning off. If your surface was rocky the top would falter and fall; if your tip had a nick, it would jump and fall; if your release of the string was not smooth, it would jerk and fall. If you wanted your top to spin the longest you did everything you could to get and keep things smooth.

"You read my letter baby . . . sure must have read my mind."
—B. Eckstine

The poet lights her fortieth cigarette. She will go over her limit as she opens a new pack. It is her favorite time of the day . . . when morning begins fusing itself into night, bringing that nether light to the sky. The poet recommends life. She likes the idea of the human experiment going forth. She knows her people are more than capable. The worst blows have been thrown and parried. This is only the cleanup. Perhaps, she thinks, she should treat herself to something wonderful. Fish. Fried fish. The poet remembers her grandmother's joy at fried fish and extra salt. Yes. And maybe a cold beer to salute her mother. Good job, Mommy. I'm here; not necessarily crazy; looking forward to tomorrow. No mother could do more. Maybe, the poet thinks, I'll buy a lottery ticket. The forty-first cigarette is lit. First thing in the morning. Fish and a lottery ticket. Hey . . . we're going to make it.

His Name Is Malcolm

First we hear the drums. There are all kinds of drums. The drums are being beaten with sticks and hands . . . there is an incessant rhythm. There is nothing on screen, but we hear the drumming. The screen lightens up . . . HARLEM: 1920. We see the feet . . . run-down heels of men's shoes . . . polished but obviously well worn . . . a woman's foot comes out of a medium heel . . . she rubs it as if her corns hurt . . . we see the white shoes of nurses . . . the flat shoes of the young women. Then we move the camera up just a little bit and see an ocean of cuffs . . . neat . . . clean . . . pressed, and we pan up to the hems of the skirts and dresses of the women. The camera moves into the sky . . . a beautiful shot of the skyline of New York looking down Central Park across to the skyscrapers . . . we pan back to the tops of the buildings of Harlem. People are sitting out, men in shirt-sleeves or undershirts, women dressed like housewives, children happy and excited by the upcoming parade. Maybe some birds flutter by, a pigeon or so, then we move to a great, colorful plumage. Feathers are everywhere. The plumage is flung up and we recognize the headdress of Marcus

Garvey. Garvey steps slowly to the front of the gathered people. His flag bearer hoists the Red, Black, and Green. Garvey looks to his left, then to his right. The drum major high-steps, blowing his whistle. He turns and the parade begins.

The camera is now at face level. We see hundreds, no, thousands of faces marching with Garvey. As the parade goes down Seventh Avenue, passing known Harlem landmarks, the background dissolves to Chicago, then to the Cincinnati train station, showing soldiers and civilians disembarking from trains, coming up stairs, passing a sign that says, "Gateway to the South." The drums are still insisting while we hear the feet in a parade cadence, but we now see rural America, people standing in fields looking north as if they hear something. We change background again and see Jamaica and people looking north. Garvey's voice is now being heard. The Red, Black, and Green with the lone Black star is oversized. The camera pans down on Garvey explaining the meaning of the flag. The crowd is animated, clapping, assenting to Garvey's words. "Africa for Africans . . . at home and abroad!" Garvey proclaims and the crowd cheers and cheers and cheers.

In an office room overlooking the parade two men are watching from the window. They are Black. One is Du Bois, the other is a James Weldon Johnson–type figure; older than Du Bois and less agitated about the parade. "That man is dangerous," says Du Bois. "All our efforts to claim manhood rights are going up in smoke." "Oh, William. I've been all over the world. Even you were just last year in Paris with your own Pan-African Congress. People want something of their own." "But this is our own," Du Bois insists. "We are Americans. We have got to make our stand here." "But the lynchings, the burnings, the people just can't take much more. We've got to have something to offer them." "I agree," says Du Bois, "but this Garvey is as bad as Booker T. Why would we voluntarily segregate ourselves? That's half the problem. We need to work to show that we are good citizens, that we do have a valid culture, that we are men." "That, too, in good time." But the Johnson figure looks back out the window. "That Garvey really can rouse a crowd, can't he? He really has the people." Du Bois frowns. "He's in the way. We will never be free with that nihilistic philosophy. He's a danger to our freedom."

Now the camera moves into a big office. A pug-looking official in shirt sleeves is asking for the latest figures on the parade. "I wish we could send those jigaboos back to Africa," the J. Edgar Hoover figure says to no one in particular. "Garvey has over a million coloreds in this so-called Back to Africa Movement. He needs to be stopped. The good colored folks don't like it and neither does the president." Hoover looks up to the three or four G-men standing around. "He has to be stopped." End of scene.

Swirling snow is blowing. The streets have few people on them and they are moving quickly. DETROIT: 1930. The camera pans Depression Detroit, coming to rest in a small, indistinct room while a voice is saying: "We must carry on the great work. I have been sent to the Lost-Found Nation of Islam in North America. I cannot stay long, but I am anointing you to be my worldly representative." The camera comes full face with Elijah Muhammad. "Robert Poole," the voice commands, "are you ready to forsake your former life, your former associates, your earthly family, your name, and follow me?" "I am," he replies.

"I now greet you, Elijah Muhammad. You must carry my Word forward." We then see Elijah Muhammad meeting with a small group of men in a home; we see spring and Muhammad is standing, talking to a larger group; we see the white heat of summer and Elijah is going into jail talking with the men; when the colors of autumn come, Elijah has gathered a crew of men who are calling Him Messenger. End of scene.

We are now in a kitchen of a worker. The man is eating, the woman is serving him. There are many children around. The man is saying, "Louise, I know they think because they deported Mr. Garvey we will be silent. Well, Louise, I've been silent too long. I know I have to take Mr. Garvey's message to the Black Man. Did you hear about that lynching last week? It just won't stop until we stop it." The woman is tending to the children and trying to eat. She is loving but worried. "Earl, what about us? We've been burned out of one place. They won't quit until they kill you. Please think about the children." "Louise, what kind of life will they have if I'm not a man? What kind of life will they lead if I can't stand up?" Next we see Louise and seven youngsters huddled in a broken-down house. Louise has obviously left them for a better world. The children are trying to care for her, but it is obvious that they are not capable. A social worker comes and gently herds the children away. The younger ones are crying. The middle boy looks defiant. He is the last to leave the run-down shack. He pulls the door closed and there is a loud SLAM. We then hear another SLAM, and Elijah is seen, coming out of prison. Elijah looks back and we hear the third SLAM. Malcolm Little is behind bars. End of scene.

■

It is visiting day in the Charlestown prison. Malcolm Little is being visited by his brother, Roger, and his sister, Ella. Roger gives indication of being mentally delicate, as was his mother, but he is excited about what he has learned. He and Ella are telling Malcolm about "the true religion for Black people. Write Mr. Muhammad, Malcolm. Do this for me. I know I won't be with you long. I have dreams like Mamma used to have. I've been crying in my sleep. I know I'll feel like I've done my work if I can get you to know about this man. Mr. Muhammad offers us a way out. He was in jail himself, for refusing the draft. He won't let the devils tell him anything. You need to know about this." Malcolm looks at his sister, who is nodding her head yes. "Roger is right. We've found a peace I didn't know existed. After that thing with Daddy . . . and Mamma, well, Mamma couldn't take any more. . . . I never thought I'd have a family again. But the Nation has given me a family . . . and wants us to come to you. Do it for the family, Malcolm. You remember how Daddy was always talking about Garvey and nation building. This man, Mr. Muhammad, is building what Daddy wanted. Look into it, Malcolm." A prison guard walks by. The three look up. Roger says: "Everybody who's not dead is in prison. These books will help you come back to us." Malcolm takes the books and kisses his brother and sister good-bye. End of scene.

Now we see Malcolm working out. We see him in the "yard" walking with a book in his hand. We see him in his cell reading; we see him in the library copying words. He receives a letter with a Chicago postmark. Malcolm opens the letter and a dirty, much-used five-dollar bill falls out. Malcolm reaches for the bill. He is touched, pleased and smiling.

It is insulting to the Black community that we have to sit through almost an hour of gibberish to get to what Spike Lee has promised: Malcolm X. The only excuses for the opening of the movie have to be (1) to pad it out to "epic" length and (2) to get Spike Lee's face on screen. Perhaps some Americans aren't interested in the history of Black Nationalism and perhaps, even, some Americans think Malcolm X has to be "entertaining" in order to be a successful movie, but others of the Black community have kept Malcolm X alive for all these twenty-seven years not because we envision his dancing at the Savoy or kissing some white woman or robbing someone's home; there are thousands of people who do that and more every day, and we do not remember or honor them. We have kept Malcolm X alive in our hearts and our culture because he embodies our dreams of transformation and redemption. The story is strong enough to be told straight.

Malcolm X had to be a dream of Elijah Muhammad. Elijah was the brain of the Nation, but Malcolm X was the voice. When the two men first meet, Lee has Malcolm crying, but I can't accept that. As a Christian, if I met Christ, I would probably cry and He would probably touch me. Then I would ask: "Lord, what would you have me do?" Elijah Muhammad had to have charged Malcolm with a task. Malcolm needed to be shown performing it. There would be no task too humble for him. Cleaning the temple, serving that small band around Elijah, listening, learning. He would have to earn Mr. Muhammad's trust. Then Muhammad would have sent him out with a trusted minister. Again, Malcolm would have performed honorably. We need the scene when Elijah Muhammad calls Malcolm into his study and asks the others to leave. Muhammad tells Malcolm his dreams for Black people. He talks about his life in Georgia; about meeting Wallace Fard and how he was converted. He tells Malcolm about his own limitations, what with his asthma preventing him from being a great speaker and maybe even laughing about his height. He tells Malcolm how together they can build a nation; together they can galvanize the masses just as Garvey did. He asks Malcolm if he will follow him. Malcolm, like a knight of old, pledges his life and honor to Elijah Muhammad.

We need to see Malcolm X building a temple. A temple is a building made of people. We need to watch him recruit the Fruit of Islam (FOI). We need to see their drills, their workouts, their disciplines. We need to see others fall to the side and to understand how Malcolm, even though he has to put them out, holds out hope for them. When we finally get to the scene where Malcolm goes to the police station to inquire about a man beaten by the police, we need to see him put the FOI in motion. Each man calling another. We need to watch those men come from their homes, their jobs, stopping in the middle of their meals, putting their books down to answer the call. When Malcolm tells the police captain to look out the window, we need the camera to pan those faces: some mean, some scared, some excited but all holding themselves in check. We need to look at the shoes and the cuffs of their pants; we need the drums to start. After the man is taken to the hospital and the conflict is resolved, the policeman tells Malcolm to turn it off. Malcolm makes a physical gesture and the FOI march off. We need the drums, solemn and steady, to march them back home. Back at the temple we need to see some of the men celebrating their victory. Malcolm has to mount the podium to say there is no celebrating; they just did their job. We need to hear the mumbling that Malcolm is getting just like King: "... *next thing we know he'll be talking nonviolence.*" We need the laughter while Malcolm, who has overheard the remark, ponders the significance.

Slowly coming on screen is the brown grass of a field. The camera follows the grass over to a river. We hear the water running while the drums begin coming up. The camera shows an object that is unclear but bobbing. We see a big cotton-gin fan and attached to it the body of a boy. Over the drums we hear a woman's cry, "Emmett ... oh, Emmett." It is his mother who is sorely distressed. We see the crowds passing a coffin in Chicago, and we pan down on the horribly mutilated face of Emmett Till.

Next we are in Money, Mississippi, in a courtroom. People are drinking RC Colas and fanning themselves. The judge is charging the jury: "I'm sure every drop of Anglo-Saxon blood in you will give you the courage to free these men." The jury foreman returns the verdict: not guilty. We see the mother of Emmett Till saying: "I'm disappointed but I'm not surprised." We take a close look at the face of Mrs. Bradley; the camera holds it until it dissolves into the face of Rosa Parks saying, "Why do you all push us around?" She is sitting on a bus and refusing to move. The bus driver is asking her, almost pleading: "Make it easy on yourself and give me those seats." Mrs. Parks sits: "No." We see footage of King giving the first charge to the

Montgomery boycott. We see people running off flyers and distributing them. The buses roll on Monday and they are empty. We see the arrest of King and the booking, the photographing, the fingerprinting. We see King's home being bombed and King addressing the crowd, telling them to go home. We see Martin Luther King, Jr., walk to a desk drawer and take out a handgun. He walks to the back of his house and throws it away in his garbage can. King is speaking to Ralph Abernathy: "Ralph, we can't win this one with guns. If they have an excuse to kill us all, they will. We have to find another way." Now we see King picking up the books. He is reading about Gandhi. We see King at the closing rally after the boycott is won. King is holding up the papers on the Supreme Court ruling. He gives the speech on redemptive love. We cut back to Malcolm, who is giving a speech in the temple about the foolishness of loving your enemy. Malcolm is saying Muslims don't turn the other cheek. The camera turns to a church bombing; four girls are killed Sunday morning in church. King is saying we will stay in Birmingham; Malcolm X is saying we don't want to integrate with that pale ol' thing. We see the police dogs being sicced on the protesters; the camera cuts back to Malcolm saying, "Kill the dog! I say if they dogs attack us . . . kill the dogs."

Both young Black men were contending for the soul of Black America. White America had considered King radical until Malcolm's voice began to be heard. Our movie should show books and articles being written about the Black Muslims, television shows being produced. People are listening to Malcolm X and this, quite naturally, is causing some problems with the ministry in Chicago.

■

Cut to Chicago. A few ministers, maybe three, are saying to Elijah Muhammad that Malcolm is getting too big. Mr. Muhammad tells them to look around. Look at the number of temples that have been built; look at the membership and how it has grown. This is due to Malcolm. He assures them that Malcolm enjoys his highest confidence. In fact, he is sending for Malcolm and they will talk. He will have no more of this dissension.

Malcolm and the Messenger are talking in Mr. Muhammad's den. A very pretty, pregnant woman is bringing coffee or tea to both men. Malcolm is asking Mr. Muhammad if this is a wise move. What will their enemies say if they find out Malcolm is meeting with these men. "Malcolm," Mr. Muhammad says patiently, "look at our people. They are poor, hungry, in jail, or just out. Without money we can't help them. Look at our schools, our businesses, our newspaper, our restaurants. Do you think we can continue these things without money? Where will we get it? Do you think the government is going to give us a grant? None of these devils like us. Not the liberal devils; not the reactionary devils. They are all racists. We have to take the money where we can." Malcolm is shaking his head in agreement, but there is puzzlement on his face. "Messenger, I have pledged my life to you. I will always do as you ask. I just hate to think that we are giving a weapon to our enemies." "I'll do the thinking, Malcolm. I'll do the thinking for the Lost-Found Nation in North America." The woman moves some things from Mr. Muhammad's desk. She is fussing over him. Malcolm looks at her with questions in his eyes. He rises, goes to get his coat. "Good night, sir. I'll be leaving early in the morning before you awake." Mr. Muhammad absently waves Malcolm away. End of scene.

We see the skyline of New Orleans and two men, one Malcolm X, one white but obviously underworld. They are walking through the French Quarter. They are talking but we cannot hear their words. There is the faint sound of drums. The white man passes something to Malcolm, who takes it and turns a corner. We see the Gateway Arch of St. Louis. Malcolm is watching the Mississippi flow when a long limousine, black, pulls up and a white man emerges. The sounds of the river give way to the sounds of the drums. The white man hands something to Malcolm X and walks back to the car. We see the plane landing in Denver. Malcolm rents a car and drives into the country. He emerges after a long drive at a lodge. There are several white men to greet him. The drums are humming in the background. "Look around," one of the men tells Malcolm. "This is what your people need; some private place to train. Nothing but the best here." They take Malcolm inside. They all sit around the fireplace. "Give my regards to the Messenger," says one man. "He is the only colored person in America who knows up from down." Malcolm is clearly uncomfortable with these men. "That King, Martin Luther Coon"—they all laugh—"is causing all this trouble. Kennedy can't control him. Something's gonna have to be done soon. Now you people . . . you don't want to vote, you don't want our jobs, you don't want anything from America. That's a program we can get behind." They are all laughing and talking. Malcolm is very quiet. Someone announces that dinner is served. They all move to the table. There is ham and fried chicken. Malcolm

*has a cup of coffee, "Black," he says. "Strong." They all laugh
again. Malcolm is readying to go. The first white man puts a
briefcase in Malcolm's hands. "Now see to it this gets directly
to the Messenger, boy," the white man says with no particular
inflection. It is his way of talking. Malcolm looks at him
strangely and smiles. "Yes, sir," Malcolm says with a broad
grin. "I certainly will."*

*Malcolm is on a plane to Chicago. He is looking out the
window and it becomes spring. He sees Betty Sanders in the
audience. They meet. He begins to look forward to seeing her.
He calls her one day and asks her to marry him. She says yes
without hesitation. We see Malcolm deliver the briefcase to
Mr. Muhammad. He is anxious to get home to New York. Mr.
Muhammad is asking if he needs a larger house, now that the
baby has come. Does he need a new car? Is everything all
right? Malcolm assures Mr. Muhammad that everything is
fine. He is simply anxious to get home to Betty and Attilah.
Mr. Muhammad hugs Malcolm with a puzzled look on his face.
Malcolm embraces Mr. Muhammad with distaste. The woman
Malcolm had seen earlier is still around, fussing after the Mes-
senger. End of scene.*

I obviously am not a movie maker. I just wanted to see for
myself if I could at least construct a better film than that sick
joke Spike Lee entitled *Malcolm X*. I went to the theater
wanting very much to like the movie. A source I have highest
respect for said, "Well, you won't be embarrassed." But I am.
Had I possessed a piece of rotten fruit, I would have hurled it
at the screen. What was the purpose of Spike Lee's being the
first face on screen? Why did Malcolm look like a country

bumpkin waiting in the barber shop? Where did that doofus Malcolm come from? Why were Spike and Malcolm the only people in zoot suits, making them look like clowns? Why didn't Denzel Washington ever stand up straight for the first, laborious hour of the film? I think it's more than fair to say Spike Lee hates Black women. What was the purpose of having that white man pick up that Black woman, take her into an alley à la *Catch-22* and have her go down on him? What narrative drive was served by her humiliation? And I totally fail to understand why Denzel, being in bed with a woman whom he wants to humiliate, tells her to kiss his foot. Men have asked women to kiss many things, and "foot" has got to be the last of them. Spike chose the Black woman going down on the white man to "put her in her place" but did not dare risk showing a white woman doing the same thing to a Black man. As a Black woman, I grow ever more disturbed by Spike Lee.

In *She's Gotta Have It*, the young Black woman was attacked; in *School Daze*, Black institutions from the schools to the fraternities are attacked; *Mo' Better Blues* gave us a doofus musician who didn't know one woman from another and stupidly mounted the stage to play without ever realizing his lips had been permanently damaged; *Jungle Fever* is a case study in sexual harassment. Why couldn't he find a woman who was his equal? And all that talk from Spike about how he doesn't believe in interracial sex is disingenuous at best. What movie has Spike Lee ever made that David Duke, now that his bid for higher office is only a distant dream, couldn't make? *Do the Right Thing?* Spike, playing another diminutive male, working in a pizza parlor on the hottest day of the year, gives us an overworked song coming too loud from a radio and mur-

murs from the Black community as the police kill Radio Raheem. Don't let me forget we also get the longest *yoooooooooooooo* in the history of the world, but mostly, what happens to the neighborhood? Where are the people? What are the antecedents? We get stereotypical whites and stereotypical Blacks and signs—there are always signs in Spike Lee's movies, trying to explain what the movie couldn't.

Lee was not the director or writer for Malcolm. It is not X and that was not his name. His name was Malcolm. And whether he was rebelling against a teacher who tried to "put him in his place" or a system that tried to "put him in his place" or a religion that tried to "put him in his place," he fought for his individual dignity as a Black man. He picked up and put down many weapons in that struggle: nihilism, crime, withdrawal, belief in Elijah, belief in Allah, belief in himself, but he always fought. Malcolm X was an angry man. Malcolm Little and El Hajj Malik El-Shabazz was an angry man. If you liked him at the end, you liked him at the beginning. His goals were not always clear, and the ending, being what it was, does not speak to him ever being a "good boy." King, who certainly, and for no reason, got the brunt of Lee's venom, was a "good, Christian man" who was shot down, just as Malcolm, the rude boy, was. Both men gave their lives for the dignity and integrity of Black people. If Malcolm moved to "some white people are not devils," King moved to "some white brothers are sick." Did Elijah order Malcolm assassinated? Given the climate and infiltration of that time, he didn't have to. Neither did J. Edgar Hoover. All anyone had to do was restrict Malcolm's movements and incite some of the less stable young men. We see it today. When the Black community claims the white community is waging war against us, the white community replies, "You are killing yourself." Yet the young men in the streets neither make nor import the drugs or guns. Somebody is bringing them in. Would I like to see it stopped? You bet. But it takes more than good intentions. Elijah may have had his faults. I am not and have not been a Muslim, yet we all must concede that Elijah offered a program and a hope that has yet to be repeated. He was not some sickly, jealous man who coughed his godfatherly way into the Black community. He was a giant; a nation builder who, in Malcolm, found the voice he needed. You have to show Elijah as more than a delicate old fool. Were there jealousies in the Nation? Certainly! As there were jealousies in the civil rights movement. As Bush, in fact, hates Clinton, and Truman refused to ride with Ike. It is not unusual, in fact it would be extremely rare, if differences were not there. But the job of the storyteller, who is weaving the saga of his people, is to tell us why they were heroes; what they overcame in both the outside world and within themselves.

I hated the ending. If all it took to be Malcolm X is a doofus schoolteacher saying something and some doofus children standing up, then we would have another Malcolm X and another. Twenty-eight years would not have gone by without several other Malcolms coming along. If Lee wanted to show Malcolm's impact in Africa, he needed to show Malcolm addressing the Organization of African Unity on his trip home from Mecca. Lee needed to show African leaders from Egypt to Ghana receiving Malcolm as a head of state. And whatever happened to Cassius Clay? One of the main reasons he became an international figure, beloved the world over, was his conversion to Muhammad Ali, a conversion wrought by Malcolm's influence. Malcolm made an impact on the world. Yet where, in Spike Lee's film, do we see his greatness?

Lee has a marked inability to show historical antecedents. He is only good at attacking those parts of the Black community that we hold dear: the Black woman; our schools; our music; our neighborhoods; our families; our shining Black princes. This son of Clarence Thomas, this revisionist, this man who is not short in height so much as small in stature, needs to hear one of his own symbols: the bell in *School Daze*. Malcolm X was assassinated by Black men in 1965; but he is being destroyed in 1993 by stupidity and greed. The question about Malcolm's death is also the question about Lee's movie: Who gave the order? Whose interests were served in each case? Wake up, Lee. The drums are calling.

Shooting for the Moon

I was born in the Congo
I walked to the Fertile Crescent and built the Sphinx
I designed a pyramid so tough that a star that only glows
      every one hundred years falls into the center giving
      divine perfect light
I am bad . . .
I mean . . . I . . . can fly like a bird in the sky . . .

I wrote that poem, "Ego Tripping," over twenty years ago. And now, I'm so proud that on September 12, 1992, Dr. Mae Carol Jemison made history by flying *higher* than any bird in the sky. As the first Black woman astronaut, she rode the shuttle *Endeavor* into the space around the earth as a science mission specialist.

I'm a space nut. I remember thinking when *Sputnik I* took off in 1957 that now "we are earthlings." I've also been a Trekkie since the television series *Star Trek* began. I was intrigued that a sister, Nichelle Nichols, was Uhura, the communications officer. It was so right, it made such sense that the voice of the Federation would be the voice of a Black woman. Toni Morrison says, in *Tar Baby*, "The Black woman is both a ship and a safe harbor." Lieutenant Uhura proved that. So, while I was glad to see America's first woman astronaut, Sally Ride, go above the atmosphere, I knew what was actually needed was a Black woman: Mae C. Jemison.

I am at breakfast with Mae Jemison. I am, naturally, nervous. I am a middle-aged, cigarette-smoking, unhealthy and uninterested-in-health poet who has just snagged the opportunity of a lifetime. I get to interview Mae Jemison.

I would have liked her even if she hadn't said my smoking wouldn't bother her; I would have liked her even if she hadn't said, "Oh, I didn't get straight A's in school like my sister," with a devilish smile, "because I took subjects I was interested in." I would have liked her had she been arrogant and impatient with a poet whose view of space is metaphysical, not physical, but she was not only patient but kind.

"Aren't you bored a lot?" I was compelled to ask. I mean, she sits talking to people who haven't a hoot in hell what she actually does or can do. "A friend once told me: 'If you are bored, you're not paying attention.' I think he's right."

Over breakfast, Mae told me this story: "When I came home for Christmas, my first year at Stanford University, I had brought my calculus with me. My mother said, 'Why don't you ask your father to help you?' I thought she couldn't be serious. My father is a high school graduate, and I was this, well, hotshot at Stanford. But I did ask him for help, and he made it so clear to me. That one thing changed the way I thought about my father and myself."

There is something about Alabama men and numbers. My

father, like hers, was a mathematical whiz, and like hers, was from a little city outside Mobile. My mother, like Mae's, also taught school. But I grew up in Cincinnati, and Mae's hometown is Chicago.

"You know what my mother told me one day?" Mae asked. "I was feeling really good about some project I had finished, and she just sort of looked at me and said, 'But you're illiterate.' I was crushed. How could my mother consider me illiterate?" Mae laughs and shakes her head. She was so upset that she set out to learn more about Black literature and history. Her undergraduate double degree at Stanford was in chemical engineering and African and African-American studies. "But what made you decide to go to medical school after undergraduate?" I asked her. "Well," she ponders, "I could have gone into dance, which I love, or I could have gone to medical school. I just chose medical school." There is something wonderful about the way Mae phrases her choices. They are, well, logical. She doesn't feel special, just prepared to control her options.

Opting against a traditional career in medicine, Mae joined the U.S. Peace Corps as a medical officer in Sierra Leone and Liberia. I asked her if this has had any effect on her desire to serve others. Intriguingly enough, she bristled: "I don't believe in altruism. I've gotten much more out of what I have done than the people I was supposed to be helping. When I was in the refugee camp in Thailand, I learned more about medicine there than I could have in a lifetime somewhere else. I refuse to think those people owe me any thanks. I got a lot out of it."

After leaving the Peace Corps, she was a general practitioner and attending graduate engineering classes in Los Angeles when she was tapped by NASA in 1985. There have been four other Black women astronauts in training with her, but now she is the only one. Until her next flight, which is unscheduled, Mae spends her work days earthbound at NASA in Houston doing scientific experiments.

I'm the original little girl who wouldn't take biology because you had to cut up a frog. "Tell me," I bravely asked, "about your frog experiment." "We wanted to know," Jemison said, "how the tadpoles would develop in space, with no gravity. I hatched the eggs and developed the tadpoles. They showed no ill effects, and since frogs, like other life forms, take so much of their basic knowledge from their environment, we were curious if they would hear well, if they would turn out to be . . . well, normal frogs. When we got back to earth, the tadpoles were right on track and they have turned into frogs." Now I got to ask an intelligent question: "If most of the learning of, for example, frogs is genetic, then won't it be the second generation which will show the effects of the trip, not the first? If, in other words, there is a mutation taking place, won't we have to wait at least until the next generation before we see the effects?" But what I—and I suspect, she—was most interested in is, How can space technology help us? If the second-generation frog shows some mutation that is the result of the stress of being born in space, what will this tell us about the second generation being born in, for example, slavery or the second generation that is homeless or the fifth generation being born into a racist world? Will the mutations be aberrant, or will they be the logical adjustment to a foreign, untoward pressure? And can we ever be the same once such a change has taken place?

"What are your thoughts when you're whirling in space?"

"The first thing I saw was Chicago. I looked out the window and there it was," she says, and adds that she also saw all of earth. "I looked over at one point and there was Somalia." She was in space while others were in the last throes of starvation.

"Space is so meaningful to earth," Jemison says. "The third world will be the ultimate beneficiary of space technology because we're moving away from infrastructures. You don't need to lay telephone wire to have phones anymore; that's what cellular is all about. We don't need old-fashioned generators for electrical connections anymore. The third world will be able to jump over the industrial age into the space age." It surprises Jemison that there aren't more Afrocentric people excited about space and its technology.

"You know what I took with me when I went up?" I did know, but I let her say it. "An Alvin Ailey American Dance Theater company poster, an Alpha Kappa Alpha banner, a flag that had flown over the Organization of African Unity, and proclamations from Chicago's Du Sable Museum of African-American History and the Chicago public school system. I wanted everyone to know that space belongs to all of us. There is science in dance, and art in science. It belongs to everyone. I'm not the first or the only African-American woman who had the skills and talent to become an astronaut. I had the opportunity. All people have produced scientists and astronomers." And though she bristles at altruisms, clearly all her interests are of service to humankind.

Was she afraid? "You are aware that you're on a controlled explosion; but I have confidence in NASA." Plus, you have to think whatever Mae Jemison knows about fear was left in her mother's kitchen.

Mae Jemison is a mind in motion. If that devilish grin and those piercing eyes could be stripped away, I think you would find pure energy in constant motion. We use *genius* very lightly. In the movie *Sneakers*, the geek had a license plate that said 180IQ; I knew Debi Thomas would not prevail when I saw that her license plate said SKATING FOR GOLD. It was too much pressure. Mae Jemison is enjoying her life and its opportunities. Single, thirty-six, and living in the home she bought in suburban Houston, she loves the music of Etta James, and she talks as easily to children as to scientists. She's comfortable with herself.

What's next? If she could design her ideal space trip, what would it be? Her answer: "Me in a clear bubble floating through the galaxy . . . shooting for the moon." Who would she want to go with her? "Sneeze, my cat. I think I'd like to have Sneeze. He came with me from Africa, so he's used to flying. Then," that grin again, "if some aliens came by and invited me to another galaxy—well, look for me on *Unsolved Mysteries*. I'm gone."

III

"Wind in the Cotton Fields"
—*Langston Hughes*

Annual Conventions
of Everyday Subjects

"... from among ten thousand women to make a five-minute presentation in New York on ..."

The poet had decided to accept the invitation to address the 372nd Annual Convention of Black and White Women in America. Sure, she'd be misunderstood by both parties, vilified and lied on by one; venerated and quoted by the other ... but hey ... what's life without a little spice? And who's to say which side would do what? The poet was, in essence, a gameswoman ... raunchy even ... but the world is a game ... deep and dirty. The poet knew all about games. She had studied the men. The Princeton men, the Yale men, the Marshall men, the technical men; the men with stomachs of jelly and backbones to match. The erected men who protested abortions, the religious men who sniffed women's panties, the athletic men whose balls weren't always on the field, yes ... she would talk to the women of these men because it was all so ... well ... silly. The women fight over these men and who gets to service them. Mothers fighting with wives over who cooks for the sons, wives fighting with mistresses over whose children are legitimate, every one of them trying to stay thin and young so the men will enjoy looking at them. Each one of them determined to infantilize the men to keep her place assured. It is all so illogical . . . stupid childish game . . . grown women unsure of their place in his heart.

As the poet began to prepare her remarks, she felt glad that she is a Black woman. She remembered her mother's friends. The women, Flora and Theresa, who would take time to listen to her, though what no child says makes sense. The women who would pay and praise her for cleaning their stoves and refrigerators, letting her know her work was valuable. The women who would exclaim . . . yes, exclaim . . . over how wonderful her hair looked when braided. The women who would counsel her on which sorority she should join when . . . not if . . . she went to college. The women who had plans for her. The poet contemplated her grandmother and her friends. How at church on Sundays they would ask about and expect a report on her grades. How her grandmother would give her books the book club was reading so that the grandmother and she could discuss them before Grandmother was due to make her report. How Grandmother would stop and listen to what the poet said, though in retrospect, the poet knows she brought no insight. Ahhh, the beauty of the games of Black women. They make you feel smart and courageous and brave. The poet contemplated her mother: four feet, eleven inches. The poet was an old woman before she realized her five feet, two inches, in the real world, wasn't tall.

Being a woman of education, the poet knew that in order to properly approach any subject, research is necessary. She went to her library, which was composed of the books bequeathed or given to her from the libraries of her grandfather, grandmother, and parents. She browsed the section containing great speeches: Frederick Douglass, Sojourner Truth, Mary Church Terrell, W.E.B. Du Bois, Marcus Garvey, Ella Baker, Rosa Parks, Martin Luther King, Jr., and Sr. No. Nothing sufficient on white women. She browsed sociology; political science. Sure, there had been great white women but they were exceptional. In law, there is an expression: "Hard cases make bad law." In life, exceptional people make poor generalizations. A white person could befriend, even love, a Black person and never change his/her attitude about Black people. A Black person will witness horrors and take a passing friendship with a white person to show "not all of them are like that." It's so . . . well . . . Christian . . . to hate the deed yet love the doer. The poet called the white women she knew . . . all three of them. "I have been invited to address the 372nd Annual Convention of Black and White Women in America," she told them. "This may be my only chance to reach this many people. What should I say?" She sighed. "Would it be fair to bring up the, well, hurt we felt when you spit on our children trying to desegregate schools? Or is the fifties too long ago? I guess I shouldn't mention the women in the lynch mobs as Black men, hands tied behind their backs, were hanging from trees. I suppose we shouldn't even talk about how the women's movement wouldn't listen to the Black women when we tried to say that the average white woman didn't understand her maid. I mean, when Lana Turner said to Annie, 'I didn't know you belonged to a lodge,' Juanita Moore replied, 'Well, Miss Laura, you never asked.' There was no *women's* movement; there was a *white* women's movement and Black women never were, nor felt, included. It's all been an *imitation of life* to us and *the long walk home* won't change that. Should I mention," the poet continued, "that we get tired of your impatience? That snappy white-girl way you have of saying something to us? That . . . well . . . debutante way you have of thinking what you have said is significant and important and must be responded to right away? Or is that too petty?"

The poet wondered if she should even consider mentioning how very tired she is, personally, of white women telling her what Black women are really like. And should she demur, those women going on to explain how the book they recently read stated a different reality. Should she say how tired she is of issues being "women" until it is a Black woman and then that very same issue becoming one of qualifications and philosophy? From the glass ceilings of business to the straw floors of academia there is always a reason not to pay or promote a Black woman. Should the poet say how tired Black women are of being used? How upsetting it was to us that Tawana Brawley, a minor who is Black and made a rape charge against white men, had her name, address, and photograph in every major news publication, while we had to watch a national television news program blue-dot the face of a grown white woman who picked up a man in a bar, drove him to his house, got out of the car with him, watched him undress and go for a swim, waited until he came out of the ocean naked and ready for sex, and then was protected from undue publicity? Should I even deign to mention the Scottsboro Boys or Emmett Till? Dare I ask how does it feel to have a horrible crime committed in your name?

But hey . . . maybe I should just stick to the basics. My friends suggested that I at least mention some things I like about white women. No problem. I like frontier women. Maybe I've been overly influenced by *Little House on the Prairie*, but I think it awfully brave that a woman, with her children, would go into the tall grass among natives who had reason to be very unfriendly, with a man she barely knew who had a dream of making his life better. Frontier man tried to conquer the wilderness; frontier woman tried to tame it. I like the white women who came south after the Civil War to man (woman?) the freedman's normal schools and colleges. And I like the white women who stood with us in the sixties. It's been a little disappointing in the eighties and nineties to watch the affirmative action men and white women turn in their love beads for brown shirts, turning their backs on the people's movement that made their positions possible, but hey . . . this is, I suppose, the real world. "Well," the poet's friends pointed out, "you don't want to be a downer. Say something funny. Give white women a challenge and a charge. But be yourself." The poet decided to take that advice.

Wanting to make a positive impression, though recognizing Black success opens no doors just as Black failure closes none, the poet had her long, blue skirt and white-with-pin-striped-blue blouse cleaned. On the occasion of her sister's graduation from college, the poet and she had gone to Paris. They had purchased two ties for their father that, after his death, the poet had had cut down to woman-size for each of them. The poet is not only sentimental; she needed the strength. Reaching for her wild winterberry lipstick, the poet made ready to face the podium. Her speech:

OK. I think it's important to admit, up front, that we don't always . . . well . . . get along. I know it grabs my very last nerve to be at any and all public events and have the blonde in front of me either fluff out her hair or actually . . . start to comb it. I brush and brush madly at unseen cooties on my skirt, my blouse, my blue jeans even because . . . well . . . there must have been some reason she started to comb her hair in the first place. Was it something living? Was it some itch indicating an infection? Some viral life form that will now come to my seat? Why on earth do white women comb their hair in public? It's bad enough in the bathroom where they hog the mirrors. All I want, honestly, is a little peek at my face, but I'm afraid . . . really, I am . . . to step into the jangle of blond, red, brunette, and whatever living color is flying around there. Then they leave all that hair in the sink. Maybe, OK, actually, I'm compulsive. I was always taught never to leave hair in the bathroom sink . . . not even my own. I'll even grant that the reason is our plumbing wasn't good. Whatever reason you may wish to ascribe is fine but . . . *I hate hair in a sink!* It doesn't just look unclean, which it is, but unhealthy. Admit it. You've never used a sink in a public place after a Black woman and seen hair. Maybe you are getting ready to say "Well, gee! You people hardly have enough hair to leave." But that's not true. I can uncurl a very long strand if I want, and I wear an Afro. We have the hair; it just curls next to our head. You could say it's well trained: It stays where it was originally put.

And speaking of originally put, *the poet neatly segued à la Marlin Perkins of* Wild Kingdom *fame,* you and I were originally put on earth for the purpose of furthering human life. We were originally put here to help each other and be a caretaker for those unable to care for themselves. Our original purpose was noble and proper. If Steven Spielberg can take up *Back to the Future,* you and I can go forward to the past. Human beings need each other. That is an honorable calling. I hope we can heed it.

The poet was finished. She lit a cigarette. She had done today's job today. She asks no more of herself.

Pioneers
A Guide

The first pioneers who were Black came to America as explorers. Though exploring is a pioneering adventure, they were simply considered men who sailed toward the unknown, seeking riches, dreams . . . something different. History has ignored them, tried to wipe them out, because the people who could have told their story didn't realize there was a story to tell.

The Africans who came to this shore from the second decade of the seventeenth century weren't considered pioneers either. No one sang songs of their journey, no one would be on shore to welcome them home. They came in chains on ships that would never take them back. "I'm going to fly away . . . one of these days . . . I'm going to fly away." They were the true pioneers. We talk, in American history, about the wagons moving westward, but we don't get the miniseries of *Middle Passage;* we get no weekly sitcom called "My Night in the Galley." The songs that were ultimately sung were sung by us about us. But the true pioneers were those whose hearts, hands, and souls made this land come alive. Black pioneers cultivated the land and Black songs cultivated the spirit.

You would think from our history books that Frederick Douglass and Harriet Tubman were just about the only Black people who were abolitionists, all other people of color being so very content just to be a slave or to be some sort of "freed man." I don't think so. The slaves who had to stay and the slaves who were able to leave were pioneers not only of Black freedom but of the American ideal.

The Harlem Renaissance brought us another pioneer, artistic pioneers. For the first time, the masses of people could not only create something but sign their names to it. It could be a poem, a play, a novel, a dance, a piece of music or sculpture, or the food on the table. In the 1920s, for the first time, a "signature" was meaningful to Blacks because we owned ourselves.

Throughout these centuries Black Americans have been breaking open doors that others would close, opening lands others stumbled through, finding emotional strength to carry on when a lesser people would have capitulated. Emmett Till found the strength to put his socks on before he was carried out to be brutally murdered; his mother found the strength to open his casket. Rosa Parks found the strength to stay seated; Martin Luther King found the words to define a movement.

But if there has been one overwhelming effort made by Blacks since the beginning of our American sojourn, it has been the belief in the need to obtain education. The laws that were made against our reading, voting, holding certain jobs, living in certain areas, were made not because we were incapable; you don't have to legislate against incapability. No one tells an infant, "You can't walk"; one tells that to a toddler. No one tells a six-year-old, "You can't drive"; one tells that to a fifteen-year-old. No one tells a man or a woman, "You can't read," unless there is the knowledge that if that person becomes educated, he or she will no longer be my slave; will no longer sharecrop my land; will no longer tolerate injustice.

Those of you looking now at colleges are pioneers, too. History may not record your struggles, but they will be there, and you, like your ancestors, will have to find a way to overcome. Education, higher education, graduate education, professional school—all these different ways of learning more and more will set you more and more alone . . . will make you stand out and become a target. But as you climb the education ladder, your ancestors hope you will "walk together, Children . . . and don't you get weary." Every pioneer looks at a horizon, and sometimes that horizon can look so far that it seems safer and easier to go back. Your ancestors are whispering: "Don't let nobody turn you 'round." College is a great, though difficult, adventure. Those of you who find your way there, like our ancestors on stormy seas, like our foreparents forging their way on the underground railroad, like your grandparents working against legal segregation, like your parents sitting in, kneeling in, praying in in the sixties, know that once again Black Americans are being called to be our best selves. Knowledge is power. May that force be with you.

This Has Nothing to Do with You
A Special Message to African-American Collegians

There is a photograph that I hung in my son's room. It shows a Black man, clearly emancipated . . . not a slave, standing behind a mule. In his right hand he is holding the plow; in his left he has a McGuffey *Reader*. I wanted that picture in my son's room because I wanted him to know, viscerally, who he is and where he comes from. I don't know that the picture made all that much difference to Tom. He would probably have preferred some busty woman in some lewd or obscene pose, but since I am grown and he wasn't, I won the first battle of the walls.

The need to read and write is genetically deep. Humans have drawn on cave walls, fashioned language from the animal and natural sounds surrounding us. The need to communicate is basic to humans. Education is still the key.

I would not be so naive as to say or think that without formal education people cannot survive or thrive. Black people, especially, have done both. When we were, as a group, forbidden to read and write, when our drums were taken from us, when our religious practices were forbidden, we couched our tales in the spirituals, saying, "Go down, Moses" when Harriet Tubman and the underground railroad were ready to roll; we sang "Steal Away" when we were going to run; we released our sorrow in "Nobody knows the trouble I've seen"; and we shouted our Good News in "I've got a crown up in the Heavens . . . ain't that Good News." No history course can tell me the slaves didn't leave a record. They sang, "Deep River . . . my home is over Jordan." They told us, "You got to walk this lonesome valley." They told us, "Wade in the water . . . God's gonna trouble the water." The slaves left a record; America just doesn't like the fact that "everybody talking 'bout Heaven ain't going there."

I guess I just don't understand why this generation is so lost. The young people who are dropping out of school could not understand the fight of our people for literacy. Could not understand that one of the main reasons you could get "sold south" was because you could read and write. The young people today must never have sat and read the Constitution, let alone the *Federalist Papers*, or they would surely know how essential the Black presence in the New World was. It's not just that Blacks supplied labor; we supplied the skills that made that labor necessary. What did Europeans know about planting? What did they know about iron and bronze? Only what we taught them. Who has pondered the illogicality of bringing women to the New World? Slavery had existed and still does exist on earth. No people in their right mind would bring a woman across the seas. The Romans never thought to bring Greek women. Look at slavery in the African continent.

You killed and enslaved the men. The women you left behind. Why? Because once you bring the female, you cannot breed the Black out. Look at the Moors in Spain, look at France, Germany, England. Look at Switzerland today with its "Turkish" problem and at what was once West Germany for the same situation. Why did they bring women to America? It's a question needing an answer.

But what has this got to do with you? If you knew that Liberia was founded in 1822 to send free and emancipated Blacks there, what does it mean that some stayed because they wanted to and others stayed because they had to? The solution was in the hands of the Americans. Why didn't they take it? How can anyone say the Civil War was not fought over slaves? Of course it was. Free labor cannot compete with slave labor. But why would poor white boys fight for a system that does not benefit them? Perhaps for the same reason Black men fought the Indians with the British, defeating the Black men who fought the Indians with the French. How can you be a Black man and not understand the great job the Black preacher did in getting the slaves one day off? I still hear people saying the preacher is nothing. Where is their sense of history? How would they like to be alive in 1750 or so, trying to convince a planter that on a pretty day, which just happens to be a Sunday, the slaves should be allowed to praise God? What kind of network would we have had without the preacher? What would have happened to our language if the preacher had not been allowed to study the Bible? How would our story have been kept alive if we had not found a song in code?

All I'm saying is this stuff today has nothing to do with us.

The drugs, the drive-by shootings, the pregnancies, the dropouts . . . these are not us. We have come through the fires. How can we now be tired? Isn't there an old song that says, "Walk together, children, don't you get weary"? And didn't we sing that in Montgomery, Selma, and all over the South? Why did we do that? For a cup of coffee? For the joy of voting for Lyndon Johnson over Barry Goldwater? We did it for the future. Why now, young Black men, have you decided to live in the present? What happened to the future vision of your grandfathers and great-grandfathers? Why now do you have to go to jail before you take time to commune with yourselves? Why do you have to be on death row before you decide to read a book or study law or heroically save someone's life? Your generation talks a lot about "roles." What "role" will you play in life? Try man. Try responsible man. Try forward-looking man. Try man who learns something the easy way (college) instead of the hard way (prison). Try doing the very difficult job of helping yourself and someone else by building something. Try honoring the very best in yourself instead of the very worst.

Am I picking on the men? I hope not. I hope I am reminding you that you have a job to do today. I hope I am reminding you that the people who produced you had little reason to dream; yet dream they did. They dreamed that one day you would be judged by the content of your character. They had no doubt that you would pass the test. Something has got to turn around.

Clearly the men are going to have to change. Malcolm X was fond of saying, "Show me how a country treats its women, and I'll show you the progress of that nation." We in Black

America have turned that around: Show me how men treat each other, and I will show you the future of those people.

Those of you, young African-American men, who are struggling in high school and college . . . you are our pioneers. Don't let people tell you it is "individualistic" to try to do something with your life. Frederick Douglass was "individualistic" when he walked off that plantation in Maryland; David Walker was "individualistic" when he wrote his appeal; Marcus Garvey was "individualistic" when he got on that boat in Jamaica and came to America, and the people he organized were "individualistic" in their desire to make a better life. A people can be oppressed, but it takes individuals to seek freedom.

It is a wonderful thing to be young and Black today. The world is in the process of redefining itself. Those of you who will make a positive difference are those of you preparing yourself for the future. Your sacrifice is worth it. The slurs you take are worth it. The racists with whom we live have nothing to do with us. We are about our Father's business. We know there are many mansions in His house. We are now looking for keys that open the doors. Don't get down on yourself. Don't let shortsighted people make you feel bad. There is something out there that only the sensibility of African-Americans can understand. "Don't let nobody turn you 'round." Know who you are; then you'll know where you are going.

Campus Racism 101

There is a bumper sticker that reads: TOO BAD IGNORANCE ISN'T PAINFUL. I like that. But ignorance is. We just seldom attribute the pain to it or even recognize it when we see it. Like the postcard on my corkboard. It shows a young man in a very hip jacket smoking a cigarette. In the background is a high school with the American flag waving. The caption says: "Too cool for school. Yet too stupid for the real world." Out of the mouth of the young man is a bubble enclosing the words "Maybe I'll start a band." There could be a postcard showing a jock in a uniform saying, "I don't need school. I'm going to the NFL or NBA." Or one showing a young man or woman studying and a group of young people saying, "So you want to be white." Or something equally demeaning. We need to quit it.

I am a professor of English at Virginia Tech. I've been here for four years, though for only two years with academic rank. I am tenured, which means I have a teaching position for life, a rarity on a predominantly white campus. Whether from malice or ignorance, people who think I should be at a predominantly Black institution will ask, "Why are you at

Tech?" Because it's here. And so are Black students. But even if Black students weren't here, it's painfully obvious that this nation and this world cannot allow white students to go through higher education without interacting with Blacks in authoritative positions. It is equally clear that predominantly Black colleges cannot accommodate the numbers of Black students who want and need an education.

Is it difficult to attend a predominantly white college? Compared with what? Being passed over for promotion because you lack credentials? Being turned down for jobs because you are not college-educated? Joining the armed forces or going to jail because you cannot find an alternative to the streets? Let's have a little perspective here. Where can you go and what can you do that frees you from interacting with the white American mentality? You're going to interact; the only question is, will you be in some control of yourself and your actions, or will you be controlled by others? I'm going to recommend self-control.

What's the difference between prison and college? They both prescribe your behavior for a given period of time. They both allow you to read books and develop your writing. They both give you time alone to think and time with your peers to talk about issues. But four years of prison doesn't give you a passport to greater opportunities. Most likely that time only gives you greater knowledge of how to get back in. Four years of college gives you an opportunity not only to lift yourself but to serve your people effectively. What's the difference when you are called nigger in college from when you are called nigger in prison? In college you can, though I admit with effort, follow procedures to have those students who called you nigger kicked out or suspended. You can bring issues to public attention without risking your life. But mostly, college is and always has been the future. We, neither less nor more than other people, need knowledge. There are discomforts attached to attending predominantly white colleges, though no more so than living in a racist world. Here are some rules to follow that may help:

Go to class. No matter how you feel. No matter how you think the professor feels about you. It's important to have a consistent presence in the classroom. If nothing else, the professor will know you care enough and are serious enough to be there.

Meet your professors. Extend your hand (give a firm handshake) and tell them your name. Ask them what you need to do to make an A. You may never make an A, but you have put them on notice that you are serious about getting good grades.

Do assignments on time. Typed or computer-generated. You have the syllabus. Follow it, and turn those papers in. If for some reason you can't complete an assignment on time, let your professor know before it is due and work out a new due date—then meet it.

Go back to see your professor. Tell him or her your name again. If an assignment received less than an A, ask why, and find out what you need to do to improve the next assignment.

Yes, your professor is busy. So are you. So are your parents who are working to pay or help with your tuition. Ask early what you need to do if you feel you are starting to get into academic trouble. Do not wait until you are failing.

Understand that there will be professors who do not like you; there may even be professors who are racist or sexist or both. You must discriminate among your professors to see who will give you the help you need. You may not simply say, "They are all against me." They aren't. They mostly don't care. Since you are the one who wants to be educated, find the people who want to help.

Don't defeat yourself. Cultivate your friends. Know your enemies. You cannot undo hundreds of years of prejudicial thinking. Think for yourself and speak up. Raise your hand in class. Say what you believe no matter how awkward you may think it sounds. You will improve in your articulation and confidence.

Participate in some campus activity. Join the newspaper staff. Run for office. Join a dorm council. Do something that involves you on campus. You are going to be there for four years, so let your presence be known, if not felt.

You will inevitably run into some white classmates who are troubling because they often say stupid things, ask stupid questions—and expect an answer. Here are some comebacks to some of the most common inquiries and comments:

Q: What's it like to grow up in a ghetto?
A: I don't know.

Q (from the teacher): Can you give us the Black perspective on Toni Morrison, Huck Finn, slavery, Martin Luther King, Jr., and others?
A: I can give you *my* perspective. (Do not take the burden of 22 million people on your shoulders. Remind everyone that you are an individual, and don't speak for the race or any other individual within it.)

Q: Why do all the Black people sit together in the dining hall?

A: Why do all the white students sit together?

Q: Why should there be an African-American studies course?

A: Because white Americans have not adequately studied the contributions of Africans and African-Americans. Both Black and white students need to know our total common history.

Q: Why are there so many scholarships for "minority" students?

A: Because they wouldn't give my great-grandparents their forty acres and the mule.

Q: How can whites understand Black history, culture, literature, and so forth?

A: The same way we understand white history, culture, literature, and so forth. That is why we're in school: to learn.

Q: Should whites take African-American studies courses?

A: Of course. We take white-studies courses, though the universities don't call them that.

Comment: When I see groups of Black people on campus, it's really intimidating.

Comeback: I understand what you mean. I'm frightened when I see white students congregating.

Comment: It's not fair. It's easier for you guys to get into college than for other people.

Comeback: If it's so easy, why aren't there more of us?

Comment: It's not our fault that America is the way it is.
Comeback: It's not our fault, either, but both of us have a responsibility to make changes.

It's really very simple. Educational progress is a national concern; education is a private one. Your job is not to educate white people; it is to obtain an education. If you take the racial world on your shoulders, you will not get the job done. Deal with yourself as an individual worthy of respect, and make everyone else deal with you the same way. College is a little like playing grown-up. Practice what you want to be. You have been telling your parents you are grown. Now is your chance to act like it.

A Theory of Patience

Sometimes it is good to state the obvious: We cannot have a republican form of government and illiteracy. We can have, and have had, a republican form of government and preliteracy, but illiteracy indicates a willful ignorance, whether by choice of the individual or of the state. This, in either case, is unacceptable.

I believe in public education. I believe this nation made the right decision when we decided education should be open to all. Each of us here, however, knows that there was a distance between the ideal and the practice. In the South, people my age went to segregated schools even after the Brown decision; even now. Precious time was lost in our region trying to subvert a correct decision to both desegregate and to integrate the schools. Though those are two different goals, either one would have been acceptable, since good intentions could be ascribed to either. We disgracefully and hypocritically tried to sidestep the natural, logical, correct decision that we Americans will be as one. Equal protection in fact as well as theory. It would be good if all that was so much water under the bridge, but we are still living with a lingering racism that acknowledges quite frankly, "We would rather be white than right." This is unacceptable.

We have raped and neglected our urban schools all across this country. We are still looking for a way to avoid facing the errors of the past and to head ourselves toward a more homogeneous future. If we are to maintain the freedoms this nation has articulated so well, we must be about the business of fully appreciating all the various contributions of the various people who make up the body politic we call America.

It is clear to me that if there is any one crying need in our educational system, it is for the humanities to assert themselves. The disgraceful legacy of racism has made the idealism of the humanities want to go hide itself under a bush. The humanities approaches itself with a fear and trembling, hiding under pseudoscientific methods and jargon. The result is that students do not know any of the ideas that inform our body politic; they do not have any context by which to judge either words or actions. Our young people, and we see it every day in the violence in our schools and neighborhoods, have no context by which to set their standards of personal behavior. They imitate what they see . . . violence, and a "might makes right" philosophy . . . imitating the impotence and ignorance around them. Only the humanities are qualified to carry us through this more difficult period of adjustment; only the humanities are capable of gentling the spirit of human beings, allowing a more serene patience to prevail.

I am only a poet and therefore have no training in educational theories. I know we like to blame television for the lack of reading skills and the lack of interest in books. Yet the stupid, insulting, dumb books that we give to students will turn them against reading on their own. Students will read if there is a good story; if there is a hero to admire and a problem to overcome. Whether or not the protagonist wins, the journey through the tears is worthwhile. We have neutered books, censored teachers who have tried to present good, interesting books, quarreled in higher education about which books students should be familiar with, and yet we continue to expect our students to be readers? I think not. In the universities we have seen white men declare time and time again that they cannot teach women, they cannot teach Blacks, they cannot teach Native Americans, because they do not have any "experience" in this area. Yet we who are Black and women and not white males are expected to teach literature written by them because it is "universal"? I think not. It is called education because it is learned. You do not have to have had an experience in order to sympathize or empathize with the subject. That is why books are written: so that we do not have to do the same things. We learn from experience, true; but we also learn from empathy. The colleges and universities want to *talk* about multicultural, but they do not want to *be* multicultural. I am not one who likes the term "role model," yet I believe that the greatest good higher education can do for primary and secondary education is to be a model of a multicultural society. As long as higher education remains all white, the message we send is in our actions, not in our words. As long as higher education considers itself "higher," with all of the privileges but none of the attendant responsibilities, then hypocrisy is the lesson our students learn. We in the universities and colleges must close the gap between what we say and what we do. Only then can we justify the citizenry spending time and money on us.

In elementary and secondary education, the most obvious need is for students to have their families involved in their education. The schools must be open to parents and, if I may say so, grandparents. If I could persuade my university to lend me out, I would love to start a pilot study on twenty-four-hour schools. I would have students in one part of the building in the day and their grandparents in another. I know that older people have stories to tell, and I know that we can more easily teach a storyteller to write than to read. The desire to put the story on paper can lead a generation that has shunned books into an acceptance of the need for help. A Black presence can also help overcome the older generation's fears of the different and the unknown. I would also want an evening program for the parents. The family workshops don't have to be scheduled every day, but they should be weekly. The parents should be in some sort of workshop where they interact with different people. I mention the need for writers' workshops because everybody has at least one story: his/her own. A great stumbling block to learning is the attitude of the family/community. We need to open the doors to our schools to everyone. We invite them to our basketball, football, soccer games. We want parents to come to plays and support other activities. Why not pay our teachers enough, and hire enough teachers to service the needs of the communities?

I am, of course, not being practical here. There are probably money considerations, and money is not to be ignored. Yet, if we do not ask, we will never know. Americans have risen to each and every occasion. I think our teachers will reach down and try once again. It is also fair to point out that as long as we pay coaches and administrators disproportionately to teachers, as long as we "reward" teachers by taking them out of the classroom and kicking them into administration, we are sending a message that teaching is not so very important after all. Money, by the way, would help. It would also help if principals and school boards weren't so quick to CYA (Cover Your Ass) when parents and others raise questions. Education, in other words, has to be more than just a job . . . it is a great responsibility . . . and the future is at stake.

The nation has been excited to reform colleges and universities, to make better college graduates and therefore make America more competitive, but if trickle-down doesn't work in economics, it doesn't work in education either. There is no effective way to reform colleges other than to reform and improve secondary education. Our colleges are servants of secondary education, not masters; we need to put the shoe on the correct foot. Our energy and money must first go to public schools, from preschool to high school graduation, encouraging the student, teacher, and community to be better citizens, more informed citizens, more productive citizens.

We must reclaim the humanities to remind us that patience is a human virtue; we must integrate racially to show ourselves fear cannot always determine human possibilities. We have a world to conquer . . . one person at a time . . . starting with ourselves.

IV

"But Common Things Surprise Us"
—*Gwendolyn Brooks*

VI

The Common Things Surprise Us
—Gwendolyn Brooks—

Coffee Signs

My grandparents lived on Mulvaney Street in Knoxville. For the longest time I sang, "Here we go 'round the mulvaney bush," being quite sure at that young age that others were mispronouncing. Is it that things seem so much better with age or from a distance? I'm sure I was bored many an evening as we three sat on the front porch watching the JFG COFFEE sign flick on and off . . . on and off. Yet it is a peaceful memory. I loved the sound of the train whistle. It always seemed to bring rain. Logic says the whistle blew at other times, and in any rational system I would know that it was only on rainy days that I was in the house to hear it. Yet even now a train whistle brings the smell of rain to me, the dark clouds, flashes of lightning, and the warmth of sitting in the living room listening to Grandpapa tell stories until the storm had passed. Nothing is learned until the spirit incorporates it; nothing has passed until it is forgotten. Knoxville and I may change, should change, but there will always be, for me, that porch facing the tennis courts of Cal Johnson Park and, at a forty-five-degree angle, the lights of JFG COFFEE flicking on and off . . . on and off . . . and the two people with whom I sat.

A Letter from Nikki

Dear Pearl,

I have wrestled with your letter most of the summer. As much as I believe all writers are navel contemplators and actually think on some days that we may, in fact, be egomaniacs, I find I have nothing new or interesting to say about myself autobiographically. I've looked at my childhood, the way I write, anything that I think can be interesting, and I am not finding anything. Not that I don't think I am interesting—just not all that interesting. And then I had the additional problem of trying to decide if I am inside or outside. I wander but I carry my world with me, so I couldn't decide if I am a dreamer or a wanderer. I think all writers are dreamers, because why else would we do this, yet if I could I'd take the space shuttle. My problem by now is becoming evident to you.

Plus my child reached his majority. I am about to agree with the folks who say that's a difficult time for parents. I used to think, oh well, the kid will be gone, but you really do miss the little buggers. I went out Saturday and bought myself a candy-apple-red MR2, which I do recognize to be arrested adolescence, but somehow youth cannot be recaptured. Though in all fairness to the car, an MR2 comes close.

So that's a long way of saying I'm having one of my infrequent, though nonetheless serious, periods of personality crisis. A name that I carried for eighteen years has been, not deleted, because I will always be his mother, but sort of not needed. I think I must be having some insight into how people feel who are forced to retire. Or even how people who are glad to retire feel. You like to think you've done a good job and all, but then you are saying, "Well, shit, what am I going to do with myself?"

Having sworn I would not give up my bell bottoms, I turned around about the end of August (just before he turned eighteen) and threw out all my pants. I think I am trying to be reborn in a secular sense. Anyway, you want to look your age (because I like my age), but there is still a need to make some change that says to yourself you'll be all right.

At any rate and in conclusion, as they say, I didn't do your essay because I can't quite figure out who I am right now other than a forty-four-year-old woman adjusting to a totally new and largely unplanned obsolescence that I am proud of but regret. So if you do autobiographical stuff after I figure out where I'm going, I'll be able to tell you where I've been.

Nikki

Memories Are Selective

Our first home in Cincinnati was at Glenview School, where my parents were headmaster and wife. I say "wife" because she, like the first lady, came with the territory and, while not being paid, was expected to uphold all the good and truthful standards of doing things correctly while, also on the side, providing love and inspiration to the headmaster and boys. I don't actually remember Glenview School. I've heard family stories about being there, though there is one memory that I think I own: I fell down the second-floor stairs, tumbling, tumbling like a slinky. Mommy thought I had perhaps broken my neck or something serious; I was worried about my doll, which, thank goodness, was rubber.

We moved at some point to Woodlawn, where I have memories of being bathed in the kitchen, a wonderful thing that has spoiled me to this day and made me yearn for a bathroom that is a room and not a closet. We had an outhouse that was wonderful because you could go out there and no one knocked on the door telling you it was bedtime or that they had to comb their hair or something. Recently I mentioned that when I hit one of the three state lotteries that I periodically play I would

build a round house with an outhouse because I thought they
were so neat. Someone asked me, "What did you do in the win-
ter? Wasn't it cold?" I'm sure I urinated in the winter, as it is
illogical to think I could get through a winter without doing so,
yet I have no memory of plodding through the snow and cold.
But I learned something from that question: Memories are
selective. If people tell us good things, we remember the good;
when they tell us bad things, we remember that. Freud is not
right: we don't, I feel, remember childhood so much as we
remember what we are told about it.

Our next home was in Wyoming, Ohio, a suburb of Cincin-
nati, at 1038 Burns Avenue. I remember my kindergarten
teacher, Mrs. Hicks, and my first-grade teacher, Miss Scott. She
was probably Mrs. Scott, but that isn't how I perceived her. My
sister and I went to Oak Avenue School, which later became a
YMCA and, later still, a police station, if memory serves me cor-
rectly. Mother says I was not happy to attend kindergarten, pre-
ferring to stay at home with her. She is probably right, since, to
this day, I prefer to stay at home with Mother rather than ven-
ture forth into a cold and indifferent world. By my fourth-grade
year we had moved to Lincoln Heights, where we still have a
home. My sister Gary attended South Woodlawn, and I went
with Mother to her first job at St. Simon's School.

South Woodlawn only went to the eighth grade; after that
children in Lincoln Heights had our choice of high schools. You
could take a test and, passing, go to Walnut Hills. A lot of our Lin-
coln Heighters went to Taft and Withrow. Gary chose Wyoming.

I don't think I had a conception of "integrating" at that
point, but Gary was among the first Black students to attend
Wyoming High. I know Beverly Waugh attended, as did Yvonne

Rogers. I think Jimmy Morris had gone some time before they did. I do remember thinking when I saw Wyoming High that it was a wonderful building. Once when Oak Avenue did not have heat we youngsters all had to go to Wyoming High for classes for a couple of days. Although I don't have any memories of specific events, I do recall that we did not know our counterparts, and they did not know us. At recess we did not play together. I know I was glad to get back to my own school. The Wyoming High that I remember is now the Wyoming Middle School on Wyoming Avenue. Gary had lunch at school, and that was exciting to me. They made a thing called "hamburger shortcake" every Friday, and the way Gary described it, it was heaven. There is a taste in my mouth that can only be memory of a succulent hamburger, covered with gravy served on a shortcake bun. It was just too sophisticated for words. I could hardly wait for Gary to come home from school to ask: "Did they serve it again?" And she would describe it once more. I've never attempted to make hamburger shortcake, since I know the reality would, of necessity, fall grievously short.

She made a friend, Jeannie Evans, who shopped at Jenny's. Mommy, never wanting us to lack what others had, opened a charge account at Jenny's that we still use. And Gary was hit in the face with a basketball in gym. There was no question but that it was racist. The girl who did it did it deliberately because Gary was Black. I remember her face was red in a round circle and Gus, our father, made one of his many trips to see Bradbury, the superintendent of schools. Everyone was shocked and saddened by the event. Apologies were made all around. But what I recall is that someone hit my sister for no reason. Her teacher in civics, a still-needed course that is no longer taught, discussed the Emmett Till case with his class. "Till got what he deserved," he declared. Gary and Beverly walked out, and Gus made another trip to see Bradbury. Apologies all around. Shock and sadness that this could happen. I was sent to Knoxville, Tennessee, to live with my grandmother when the Princeton school district was integrating. Our family had already given a soldier to the war to make white Americans better people.

I am an unreconstructed Trekkie. Man (read humans) was meant to fly. Sometimes we get confused and think flight is a physical thing: something to do with engines or wings made of wax. Everybody told Icarus that if he used those wings when he got near the sun they would melt. I don't really know if Icarus simply did not believe them or if he thought his wings could withstand the heat, but he took off with the instruments available . . . and he failed. Or did he? Didn't he, in reality, simply fall back to earth? And can it be a failure when our goal is to reach higher? I think not. Had Columbus slipped off the ocean into the darkness we probably would not know him now, but he would have been just as successful as if he had sailed right up to India. There are some things we do simply because the doing is a success. We try to treat people fairly; we try to live our lives with dignity; we try, in our hearts and minds, to "go boldly where no man has gone." And isn't that the ultimate contribution we make to the human experiment? We young writers raise the questions of our time. We seek to expose the unacceptable and to celebrate the wonderful. We seek to "kiss the sky," because earth is our home, not our destiny. Our destiny is a better universe where we can live together in peace and understanding.

November 22

November was clear though seasonably cool in 1963. I remember the sun was shining. Mother had purchased a white, convertible Nova that she let me drive. It was too cool to have the top down, but any University of Cincinnati student with a convertible would at least sport the windows, which I did. Morning classes went as morning classes do. Students half asleep; professors muttering to themselves that there must be a better way to earn a living. My classes finished around noon. I would leave campus, then go to my job at Walgreen's. Walgreen's Drugstore was a perfect job for me because it kept my mind focused on school. No one wanted to grow up to be a floor girl for a drugstore. As I was crossing the campus to the car, someone said, "Kennedy has been shot." A group of students gathered and the person, I don't remember whether male or female, said Kennedy and Connally were shot in Texas. I hurried on to my car, thinking, "If one of them has to die, I hope it's Connally."

I immediately turned the radio on. The early reports were muddled. Johnson was all right. No other news. By the time I got to Walgreen's, about a ten-minute drive, they were announcing Kennedy's death. We on the floor wore white smocks. I put my smock on and walked rather aimlessly around. I was waiting for Richard, our manager, to close the store. I could see no sense in remaining open. After an hour or so, Richard announced that we would remain open. Because I was junior on the floor, I had already worked the Fourth of July and Labor Day. I had worked Halloween, and on another job I had worked both Thanksgiving and Christmas. It wasn't work. I never minded working.

I don't remember having any thoughts that history was changing or that the country had taken an irrevocable step backward. I just couldn't see the sense in my trying to locate Sal Hepatica for some customer or sell perfume. I went downstairs, put my smock back in my locker, and punched out. Richard saw me as I came back upstairs. He had a rule against employees parking in front of the store, which I had a habit of doing. "You are supposed to be at work," he said. I said I'd be back later. It wasn't a challenge; I didn't care to discuss it. It just didn't make sense, on November 22, 1963, to stay at work.

Virginia
My View

I like rain. That has to be one of the main reasons I live in the southwestern part of Virginia. If I didn't like rain I'd have to move to Arizona or New Mexico or even back to Ohio because it rains all the time here. Well, not all the time . . . just more than not. I found out—not that it was a secret—the year after I moved from Cincinnati to Blacksburg that Virginia Tech was located in Blacksburg because it rains here more than in any other part of the state. Of course, when you're being recruited, they sort of forget to mention that. No one says, "Come to Blacksburg and experience our rain."

Actually, other than "Where do you live?" I only know one question that throws me off: Why did you do something? Where do you live? throws me off because I have room space from New York to Cincinnati to San Francisco. I have, in fact, found this a pleasant way to live. I never have to carry luggage; I only have to remember where I left something. My wardrobe is quite slight and duplicated, so that has not proved to be a problem through the years. Why I live like a nomad is more difficult. Well, not actually more difficult, because the answer is: It is convenient. You can hardly run a career, rear a child, raise a couple of dogs, and have any sanity if you throw in window washing, stopped toilets, gutters that need cleaning in fall, furnaces that need filters changed . . . the rather normal things that go with a house. I thought I'd try a noble experience of letting my son know that home is where we are . . . not a building nor a place . . . not things but a feeling. I had to work because I have never been able to get six numbers together for any lottery. If he and Wendy, our cairn terrier, went to work with me, then I could have my family. All the advantages of home and few of the disadvantages.

After we acquired Bruno, Tom's dog, things began to change. Plus Tom needed to go to school, so we became apartment dwellers, then condo dwellers, then we did the really intelligent thing and moved back to Cincinnati to live with my mother and father after Gus, my father, had a stroke. People, in their kindness, want to say what a wonderful thing I did to give up my home and independence to go back to my parents' home, but the wonderful thing for me was that two people I have known and loved needed me and I needed them. Being a grown-up in my parents' home was no problem. They told me what to do and I did it. Simple. Gus was sick; Tom was a child. My mother and I traded off, and the household ran very smoothly. Unfortunately, though not unexpectedly, my father died and my son grew up. Wendy, my dog, succumbed to cancer. That just left the two of us and Bruno. I was worried, not without reason, that Mommy and I would become two little old ladies in Ohio. I would continue to work; she would retire. We would hold our annual chitterling dinner and see friends, but we wouldn't be contributing to the world. It takes very little for me to close down. My profession is a close-down profession. If I didn't make myself go out and see people, I stood a good chance of becoming what a lot of writers are: insular and indifferent to the real world.

Then one late fall or early winter morning came a letter from Virginia Fowler, associate head of English at Virginia Tech, inviting me to apply for Visiting Commonwealth Professor. Mommy had never even stepped foot in Virginia. We knew the Blacksburg area because we are from Knoxville, which is four hours due west at sixty-five miles per hour, but she had never crossed that state line and wasn't that excited to do so until Doug Wilder became governor. Mom and Bruno went to San Francisco. Tom would soon be graduating from high school and, as children are wont to do, probably going on with his life. I'm not a great believer in the empty-nest syndrome, but Mom and I were facing it. I flew over to visit Tech and, I suppose, be looked over. Thinking Virginia was in the South, I carried nice summer clothes. First mistake. Southwestern Virginia gets cold and snow and rain. But Tech is impossible to dislike. Tech has the greatest youngsters in Virginia, a good faculty, a dean who looks like he would just as soon roll up his sleeves and bake a loaf of cinnamon bread. I actually wasn't busy, so I came to Tech.

Being a visiting professor is not like having a real job. I was teaching a literature course and a writing course. I've long known the most important people in any organization are the secretaries, but I had no idea that ours could cook, too. Leota and I exchanged recipes; Tammy and I argued over who made the best beans. I've got to say that for a white girl she's not half bad. Our janitorial staff was friendly. Maybe I put too much stock in support services, but when the support services are good, the institution will follow. I've never known an institution with indifferent grounds keepers that meant anyone well. It's easy for the top to be friendly—they are well paid and well benefited for it; the others speak from the heart. I met Tech's interim provost, John Perry, and one just simply does not say no to John. There are three gentlemen at Tech: Perry; Burke Johnston, who is retired; and Hil Campbell, who ultimately stepped down as English Department head. I've heard about the Texas gentleman and the Virginia gentleman and it's not that you can't say no to them; you simply don't want to. You talk with them a while and you feel smart and witty and charming and just ever so needed. I fell in love.

There is always a difference between courtship and marriage. I've gotten to know Tech a lot better and see our needs a lot clearer. If Tech is to reach its full potential as a great institution, we need to accept our regional challenge. We need to reach into Giles County, which has some wonderful elementary school children who should, right now, be involved with Tech; we need a Black presence in Vinton, which seems to need, to paraphrase T. S. Eliot, another turning of another stair; we need to understand that we do not compete with UVA but with Charlotte. People should be looking to Tech for more than football. A real theater would help; a real concert series would help; more national speakers would help; a jazz series; a country and western series; a recognition that we face biracial problems, not multicultural. We get along fine with international folk; it's the homegrown normal Black Americans who cause us to stumble or over whom we constantly seem to trip. Our white youngsters cannot be allowed to reach around the Black to the yellow and the brown. But these are details. Roanoke calls itself the "Star City," and it's poised to be so. Roanoke offers some of the South's greatest craftspeople; we have a symphony and ballet; we have Artemis for writers and performers. All the elements are in place for southwest Virginia. And we have those gorgeous mountains.

Sociologists ponder why people would stay in these mountains with the bad, rocky soil, with the winter snow and the spring floods. I don't. They are majestic. The mountains and the people make this area one of the hidden gems of eastern America. Just to awake to the fog lifting from the valley; to see the sun, on I-81 as you roll into Roanoke from Blacksburg, break the clouds. . . . No, I don't wonder at all why people chose to live here. Maple Anderson, a friend, colleague, and Democratic party stalwart, once ran for an office in the party. She and her husband had just moved to Virginia from Maine. Her right to represent Virginia was questioned by her opponent. She said: "All Black Americans come from Virginia. We all *landed* here. Some of us just went somewhere else for a while." I think she's right. I live here because it's home. And hey, even the predictability of the rain is less unnerving once you get properly outfitted.

Sisters, Too

Almost every Friday four of us get together to play bid whist. Three of us are mothers; all of us are aunts. One of us has sons and daughters; two of us have an "only," one daughter and one son. Three of us have nephews and nieces; one of us has only a nephew.

Maple and I were behind, nothing that a couple of no-trumps wouldn't eventually clear up, but Maple was distracted. She was leaving the next morning for Oklahoma City to pin her niece. I shouldn't say "distracted," because the proper word is *excited*. Her family tradition of Delta Sigma Theta would go on. I have only a son and a nephew. It hit me. I had not really considered it before. But I, by having no daughters or nieces, have no one to pass a tradition on to. No one who would love the tablecloths my grandmother had passed down nor the silver she had purchased one place setting at a time. No one to admire the crystal vase we had purchased together and into which we put the prize roses Grandmother had grown. My mother had two daughters, each of whom took different aspects of her personality. She could see herself in us, even, or perhaps especially, now that we were well into our middle age. We kept her things and had an affection for them. The world is so boy-prone that, having had only a boy, women rarely think, To whom will I pass my sorority pin? Who will drink from the glasses my grandmother saved from her mother's possessions? Who will iron and patch the old tablecloths? Who will air the quilts? I guess I have always understood man's love of his sons, but there is an equal, and compelling, reason women love our daughters.

I have always wanted to be a good daughter. I have wanted to make my mother and grandmother proud of me. I like to think I am a good mother; at least I know I did my best.

There is always the history of Phillis Wheatley writing the first poems of note published in Colonial America; there is the glorious history of Harriet Tubman leading slaves to freedom. There is the unsurpassed courage of Mary Church Terrell crusading with her pen for the abolition of lynching; of Rosa Parks having the vision of sitting down to stand up for what is right. Emmett Till's mother opened the casket to say to the world, "Look what they did to my son." Shirley Chisholm running for president. There is also the quiet courage of mothers counseling patience in the face of brutality; offering hope in the face of despair. The women who taught the little girls how to iron the sheets and shirts; how to darn a pair of socks; how to pretend, when they became mothers, that they didn't need a new coat or want a new dress so that their children could have a bit more.

It is an honorable calling: womanhood. And a wonderful thing when we not only take up the task of gentling the spirit but passing our faith along.

I offered Maple the pin my mother was pinned with. My father, for their first wedding anniversary, had replaced the original pin with a Delta Sigma Theta with pearls in the beloved Sigma. He could not afford that. But he must have understood that one day she would have daughters who would need the pin more than he needed whatever the money spent would have bought.

Mommy was tapped for one sorority; others have made different choices. What we do know and applaud is the community of women, whether Greek or not, who come together to say to the daughters—now you are my sister, too.

Three of us write. One is a poet; two are scholar-critics. One of us is a widow. Every Friday, almost, we come together, answering the ancient call Gloria Naylor so beautifully expressed: "Sister, you still here?"

My Road to Virginia

There always seems to be a Virginia connection. I didn't come to Virginia because I thought Doug Wilder would be elected governor, though I'm delighted that he was; and I'm not staying in Virginia because he'll probably go on to be at least vice president, though I'm delighted that he most likely, if this is a fair world, will be. My very own Ohio majority leader, Bill Mallory, is just as good a candidate, though not as visible. It's funny that race is less a factor in the former home of the Confederacy than in a free state. But . . . hey . . . times change or not, according to ebbs and flows I will never fathom. I came to Virginia because I was offered a job.

In a way I hate to look at the previous sentence. Someone is bound to say, "But you could get a job anywhere." I like to think that's true, too, but I can't. I'm a writer who does, I believe, know something about writing. I may even know something about thinking. I certainly know something about giving, but I don't know, and I'm proud to confess I have no interest in, what someone who never in this life had to face a public, thinks about what someone else, who did, wrote. Was that an awkward sentence? I'm not an academic who is contemptuous of the people and the judgment of the people. I don't believe my "higher calling" in life allows me to be an insecure professor who gets her rocks off by not teaching students. I do believe in service. I know, I know . . . someone is saying, "Well, what are you doing at a research institution?" I like to think, on a good day, that I'm helping others to recognize that higher education's gravy train not only is over but should be.

Teaching is an honorable profession. I, in fact, come from a long line of teachers. My grandfather taught Latin in Knoxville, Tennessee, public schools; my grandmother taught in Albany, Georgia, Normal School. Both my mother and father taught, third grade and eighth grade respectively, until their growing family forced them to look for higher-paying jobs. My aunts, Agnes and Ann, taught in public schools and college; my uncle, Clinton Marsh, was president of Knoxville College. There is no one outside my immediate family I hold in higher esteem than Alfredda Delaney, who taught English in my high school, Austin. Madame Emma Stokes tried to get me to learn French. Miss Delaney recently passed on, but Madame Stokes is still with us, and I still consider her a friend. Perhaps these are not real credentials, but I bring a high expectation to the profession. Our first job is to teach.

When I graduated from college in 1964, the only true credential I had for a job was that I was pretty good at picketing. As many have since learned, being a sixties person does not serve as a qualifier. It does mean, most times though, that you are a believer. I could add that being a history major also was not what would be considered an asset. Of course, business has since discovered that it is far better off with a good history or English major than a business or computer person, but that discovery missed my bloom. I was not opposed to being a writer, but despite the changes coming, color-wise, in America, there were and are very few Blacks in the newsrooms, magazines, or free-lance market; publishers were not interested in more than one Black writer at a time. Opportunity was limited. I applied to graduate school.

My dream, at that time, was to win a Woodrow Wilson Scholarship and attend the University of Chicago, where I would make startling and profound discoveries in history. I would follow in the footsteps of John Hope Franklin, my fellow Fisk alumnus, making important connections between behavior and history, perhaps even testifying before Congress as to the effects, historically and currently, of racism on both victim and victimizer. I would settle down in some small college town, read and write books, teach (and be a very demanding teacher) young people a new way of looking at the world. I had an Afro, however, and Mr. Currier, the head of history, didn't think I had the right attitude to succeed in graduate school. He was probably right. Fortunately for me, Blanche Cowan, the dean of women, was a Penn graduate in social work. She thought my crusading should be put to use, and off I went to Philadelphia.

I never did make it through grad school. My year at Penn was great because social work is a wonderful background for any humanities person. Dr. Louise Shoemaker thought I was more suited to writing and suggested I should give myself a chance in that field. I'm sure she could have put it more bluntly, but she was a friend. And why did I have a difficult time in the M.S.W. program? I'm not institution-prone. Most times, in any dispute between an institution and a person, I take the side of a person. The human has to be found seriously wanting for my vote to sway the other way. Obviously, you aren't going to go far in social work if you are unwilling to keep records on clients. I kept records. Some of my best young writing was done while I was in social work school with my agency placement records. I simply didn't want to put names and judgments in the records. They read like wonderful short stories—hardly what my social work professors were after. Columbia University . . . here I come.

I still feel that Columbia owes me an M.F.A. Our job, once we were accepted into the program, was, over a two-year period, to produce a book. We were allowed to take other courses, but they were not required. We were to meet, read our work, receive criticism, correct our work, and come back the next week to do it again. Within the first year I had finished my first book. Fearing, as I always have, rejection, I started a publishing company and produced my first book, *Black Feeling, Black Talk*. Was it a great book? I don't think so, but it was honest, clear, and perhaps a bit bold. My writing professor at Columbia invited me to his home, where he gently explained that I would not go far with my poetry. I should temper it and find my way in academia. Thanks, Richard. I refused that advice, dropped out of school, and decided to go for broke. Or probably, more honestly, admitted I was broke, had been born broke, and would die broke, and decided not to worry about it ever again.

Since I was now the head of a publishing firm, I needed to make a go of it. I had borrowed money from family and friends, which is, I think, different from borrowing from banks and institutions. The books sold. I did have the sense to keep a competitive price on them. I also took a page from Langston Hughes, who had died two years before I got to New York, and took my books to the people. Rutgers University was opening a new campus, Livingston, and I was recommended by Toni Cade to teach. I accepted. This was a time of great activism, so I think we were expected more to contain than teach students. I learned a lot about the failure of high schools in New Jersey and made a lifelong friend of one student, Debbie Russell. Deb, by the way, traveled all over the world with me, moved to Cincinnati when I moved back, married a wonderful man, has three robust children, and went back to college, after her Rutgers graduation, to polish her skills. Rutgers failed Debbie, but she had the strength and support to push forward. It failed many other Black students, also.

Like most New York writers, I've taught a course at the New School for Social Research. I taught in the SEEK program on Long Island. But I didn't really get back into a real classroom until I was a visiting professor at Ohio State. That was a great experience; the students were excellent. Not that other students weren't, but these students made the classroom a jazz band. Everybody already knew the music; we could play variations. English didn't have any regular, tenured Black faculty, and I was not interested in trying to become one, but it did put something on my mind. The College of Mount St. Joseph, headed by one of the great educators of our time, Sister Jean Patrice Harrington, took a courageous stand on free speech. I would not rest until I called Sr. Jean, and having no money to donate, offered my time. I taught creative writing for the Mount for two years and loved every minute of it. Most of my students were nontraditional, as they say; older would be the other word. Sr. Jean persuaded businesses to contribute to the Mount and have that contribution work toward tuition for an employee. It was a great program that worked well for the Mount, business, and the employees. The Mount had no Black full-time faculty either, and has now lost Linda Dixon, in academic planning, to Miami of Ohio. One does have to wonder. Between 12 and 14 percent of all Americans are Black. We couldn't all be that busy.

Virginia Tech called at a time in my life when I was no longer committed. My son was graduating from high school and going on, as it turned out, to two years in the army. My mother and I had lived together since the illness of my father. I thought it would do us both good to make a change of scene. Mommy held no affection for Virginia and she declined to join me in Blacksburg. I decided to come; and having come, to stay. By now there were certain things I had learned. Come as "full" professor or come "tenured." I came "full"; we would have to see if we liked each other enough to accept tenure. My colleagues were wonderful my first year. Everybody was so happy I was there. Then my second year it dawned on some people: If I stayed I would be the first woman in the English Department who would be tenured full. As a Commonwealth Visiting Professor, I was accepted; as a tenured full with a mind of my own, I was not. I was surprised to discover myself engaged in a struggle to remain at Tech.

Why did I agree to fight against those who so glibly dismissed my achievements—to whom my sixteen books, my honors and awards, my twenty years in public life, simply didn't count? I decided to stay and fight because I want the future to be determined by the best of Virginia Tech, a microcosm of higher education, and not by its worst. Virginia Fowler, associate head of English, led the charge. John Perry, provost, and ultimately when he took office, James McComas, president, wanted me to stay. I also know that it's important that somebody stay. For sure you can jump around to other institutions and improve, greatly I might add, your paycheck. But at some point the institution and the people who serve it must recognize that their failure to bring Black professors on board is a faculty failure to vote tenure. All Black people do not have the record of support that I had, but surely most, if not all, are as qualified as their white counterparts. Had I had the meager credentials that some of my tenured colleagues have, I would have been turned down. But . . . hey . . . it is not new to me that I have to be better than anyone in the club in order to be admitted.

Why is it important to get Blacks into colleges and universities? Because the biggest stumbling block to progress in America is still racism. Because we have to find a way to comfort young white people about the fact that, though they will never stride atop that wonderful white horse and rule the world again, they can make valid contributions to our planet. The world is not, and has never been, white. Less so today than previously. Privilege is anathema to democracy. And the professoriate is a very privileged group. I remember all too well, during the days of segregation, not being allowed in amusement parks, theaters, and restaurants. I thought they must be wonderful things. I was never fooled by the drinking fountains, dressing rooms in department stores, waiting rooms in bus and train stations; I knew those to be nothing more than a way of inconveniencing patrons of color. But schools. They seemed special, too. We would see the white kids on their clean, undented, new bus going to and from school, to parks, museums, the zoo. Always, it seemed to me, screaming from the windows, laughing loud, throwing things; behavior that would not for one moment be tolerated in us. I remember when East High got a computer and new science lab. Our physics teacher at Austin, though very good, doubled as basketball coach. Something was wrong.

The sixties have come and gone. The United States is no longer the preeminent power in the world; we're not even nice people. White boys and girls may have always been dumb, and without the racial component they might now not have an incentive to try to excel, or maybe they were cocooned and were having the bottom described by Black people. Those white boys and girls who were not successful went on to join the Klan or the skinheads or whatever Nazi organization is available to those who are free and white and still losers. I don't know. I do know that those who come to college need to be taught that there is a larger world into which they not only can but must fit. I do know that we who are adult must adjust systems to include those who have been artificially excluded. I do well understand that while I am tenured and full it is an unjust system that awards us for avoiding the very thing we are being paid to do: teach. What do I want? An end to the tenure system. Period. An end to research on campus. If business wants to hire a professor, let it hire him or her, but mostly him, and give him the salary and benefits it gives any other employee. An end to the professionalization of sport on campus. Let the NFL and the NBA create their own training camps. Stop the whoring for television dollars and get to—it certainly is not *back* to—the idea of coaching as teaching. Treat coaches as we do any member of the professoriate. Stop the absolute nonsense of creating a migrant class of workers called the "adjunct." Higher education has increasingly come to depend on "temporary" underpaid faculty to do much of the teaching of our children, yet they can stay full-time in an institution only a brief time because of the fear that they might have a claim, after seven years, on de facto tenure. The professoriate should be ashamed of itself that it allows this system to exist. These "temporary" faculty would have more job security for a job well done if they worked in a lettuce field. Stop the graveyards called "associate heads," "assistant deans," "assistant provosts." These have become the female position on campuses; they are dead ends. Recognize, despite everything I've said, that there can be no reform without faculty. Give faculty a reason to teach again. Reward, don't punish, faculty who spend time with students. Stop encouraging the production of dumb books on dumb subjects that no one reads and that drain library resources just so some professor can say, "I wrote a book. See? It's in the library." Bring all student services, from concerts to the commissary, under faculty responsibility. In other words, give the university back to the teachers . . . and let them teach.

How will this lessen racism among faculty? We will run up against something called competence. People will have to admit what they know and don't know. Intelligent people normally seek help when they are not punished for it. I need to believe that the world can be fair. I know it will not be as long as there is a social and financial incentive to be small-minded and vindictive. I need to believe my colleagues across this country will once again take as much pride in the students they have helped as they do now in the lines of dubious publication they have produced. If Virginia, the home of Thomas Jefferson, George Washington, Patrick Henry, Nat Turner— men who, though flawed, struck a blow for freedom—cannot accept this challenge, we are hard pressed to say where the leadership will come from. The nation looks to California for trends; it turns to Virginia for reason.

Long ago, not all that far from my home, Thomas Jefferson and others sat to chart a course for humans that would incorporate change as a constant. Virginia has stood up to the political challenge; she will accept the educational one as well. I live here because I have a job at Virginia Tech. I wouldn't want to be anyplace else.

V

"At This Lopsided Crystal Sweet Moment"
—*Carolyn M. Rodgers*

Architecture

There are some things that you love simply because you ought to: the Sistine Chapel; old English country homes; everything in the Louvre; the crown jewels; valuable things like that, which, while lovely and representing great achievement, are still quite removed from our everyday experience. There are other things you love because of the joy and comfort they bring: gospel music; the quilt your grandmother made; warm blackberry cobbler; things of incomparable worth that only the heart can judge. Since we all die, there is even a need to love every cemetery in New Orleans, and none can deny the majesty of the pyramids. Those of us who are education lovers bow to Thomas Jefferson's vision at Monticello, lamenting the loss of the great libraries of Timbuktu and Alexandria. One stands, in fact, in awe of the Constitution of the United States, though it is an idea and not quite a reality. No one can deny the power of Jesus, whether we subscribe to the various little people who have capitalized on Him or not. Ideas are structured and remain much stronger than most buildings. I love the idea of "Lucy" (the prehistoric skeleton unearthed by

Donald Johannson in Ethiopia). Were I God, starting an ecosystem, I, too, would choose to put a Black woman at the center of my world with the surety that she would get things off to a proper start. The basis of all human knowledge, and therefore human action, is belief.

Albert Einstein had first to believe he could postulate a theory of E by putting it into a relationship with *mc* squared; Columbus had first to believe the world was actually round before he could decide to sail west to reach east; Pasteur had to believe those molds could do *something* before penicillin could be put to use to save human lives from disease. Rumpelstiltskin, for that matter, had to believe he could forever hide his name from the miller's daughter, though he lost his bet. And you and I have to believe we can alleviate human suffering caused by accidents of birth and circumstances by applying our skills to make this life an easier passage.

Sam Mockbee used his skills as an architect to build a better dwelling for some families in Mississippi. Who wouldn't want to live in these houses? They were actually designed by humans for humans. We know, from basic studies of our own domestic pets and animals, how important environment is to life. Polar bears don't function well in rain-forest environments; whales, though mammals, cannot function out of water; human beings do not do well in hovels or shacks, or on the streets of our major cities. Snails, we recognize, carry their houses with them, as do turtles. Humans house a soul in an imperfect body; the body needs a majestic dwelling to encourage the soul to expand. We do know that nature hates a vacuum; gases will expand to fill all unoccupied space; the heart will shrink to the space available. The lawyers and lawmakers will, of course, quibble over the meaning of "majestic," but poets have no such problem. We know we mean that which is adequate to the job at hand, and beautifully, lovingly prescribed for that purpose. Our urban and rural poor need Sam Mockbee; Mockbee deserves to be needed.

The job of the architect becomes more difficult in this secular age. Where once he had a god to extol, he now has humans like himself; where once he had "he," he now has "she" and "they." His task is no different from that facing any other profession based on belief: medicine, teaching, poetry, among many, many others. Are we able to believe that other human beings deserve our best? That, I believe, is the central question. I believe we, like heat or cream, can and will rise to the challenge.

Black American Literature
An Introduction

A few years ago, *Voyager 2* crossed our galaxy heading toward the Dog Star. We don't know a lot about the light that earth sees, but we know the brightest star in the galaxy is beyond the influence of the yellow sun. Galileo would be proud. I'm a Trekkie. I like the concepts of both space and the future. I'm not big on the idea of aliens who always seem to want to destroy earth and earthlings. It's almost laughable that the most destructive force in the known universe, humankind, always fears something is out there trying to get us. Freud said something about projection ... and though I would hardly consider myself a Freudian, I think he had a point.

It's not really a question of whether or not E.T. is Black; his story is the story of sojourning. It doesn't even matter whether he came to earth to explore or was brought to earth for less honorable pursuits. He found himself left behind with neither kith nor kin to turn to. He depended, in the words of Tennessee Williams, "upon the kindness of strangers." E.T. didn't sing, but if he had he would have raised his voice to say,

"Sometimes I feel like a motherless child . . . a long way from home." E.T., had he taken the time to assess his situation, may have lifted his voice to the sky to say, "I'm going to fly away . . . one of these days . . . I'm going to fly away." When the men with the keys captured him, taking him to the laboratory to dissect him, to open him up in order to find what he was made of, he might have hummed, "You got to walk this lonesome valley . . . you got to walk it by yourself." But E.T., like Dorothy, had friends who came to his rescue. Dorothy returned to Kansas more sensitive, more aware of her world. E.T. returned to space having, I'm sure, a mixed view of earth. Black Americans settled here, making a stand for humanity.

It is an honorable position . . . to be a Black American. Our spirituals teach, "I've been 'buked and I've been scorned. . . . I've been talked about sure as I'm born." We maintained an oral tradition and created a written one. Phillis Wheatley, a slave girl, wrote poetry while others sang our songs. We did both because both are necessary. Hammer, while different from, is not in contrast to, Frederick Douglass. 2 Live Crew is in a direct line with Big Mama Thornton and all the other blues singers who sang what is called the "race music." (The "good" people would not allow it in their churches or homes.) But we have survived and thrived because of our ability to find the sacred in the secular. "Oh, pray my wings gonna fit me well," says the song, but whether they fit ill or well, we wear what we have with style.

Style has profound meaning to Black Americans. If we can't drive, we will invent walks and the world will envy the dexterity of our feet. If we can't have ham, we will boil chitterlings; if we are given rotten peaches, we will make cobblers; if given scraps, we will make quilts; take away our drums, and we will clap our hands. We prove the human spirit will prevail. We will take what we have to make what we need. We need confidence in our knowledge of who we are.

America is no longer a nation of rural people. We no longer go to visit Grandmother and Grandfather on the farm in the summer. This is no longer a nation where the daily work is done by the body; the daily work is now performed by the mind. The distance between families is no longer a walk or even a short drive. Families, for that matter, are no longer clear. Biology no longer defines whom we love or relate to. We are now able to make emotional choices. There is so much to be done to prepare earth for the next century. Humans, who are so fearful of change, are in such a radical transition. The literature of Black Americans can lead the way. As we were once thrown into a physical unknown where our belief in the wonder of life helped forge a new nation, we can help lead earth into an emotional unknown and seek acceptance for those who are unique. Our literature shows that humans can withstand the unacceptable and yet still find a way to forgive. Our stories, which once were passed sitting on porches after dinner, spitting tobacco juice at fireflies, as Alex Haley's grandmother did, are now passed through the poems, speeches, stories we have written and recorded.

While a bowl of navy beans is one of my favorite meals (with a bit of coleslaw and corn muffins on the side), I still enjoy a smorgasbord. Sometimes a bit of everything creates an appetite while satisfying a hunger. For all the trouble we now understand the voyage of Columbus to have caused, it must have been exciting to live in an age when we finally began to break into a concept of the whole earth. For sure, we have not done a great job, but we have done a better job than if we had stayed home. This century is rolling on to a close. There is both outer space and inner space to be explored. The literature of Black Americans is, in the words of Stevie Wonder, "a ribbon in the sky." We learn about and love the past because it gives us the courage to explore and take care of the future. *Voyager 2* will not come back . . . it has gone too far away. We will not return, we can only visit. But isn't it a comforting thought to realize that the true pioneer of earth is our people? Isn't it the ultimate challenge to accept responsibility not only for ourselves but for our planet? One day, some identifiable life form will come to earth and ask, "Who are these people . . . these Black Americans?" And we will proudly present our book containing our songs, plays, speeches and poetry. We will proudly say, "We are the people who believe in the possibilities."

Discourses
An Introduction

There are certain things that require celebration: Thanksgiving, Christmas, Easter morning, weddings, maybe even the idea behind the Fourth of July. Things that, well, make us happy for a moment or two. We would normally celebrate birthdays, but folk are so crazy to be young that, after a certain age, birthdays become a topic that intelligent friends sound out carefully before even mentioning. We cautiously ask, "Lost a little weight?" hoping the answer will not be a long recital on illness or, even worse, an entire lecture on blood-pressure numbers, the evils of smoking, and the joy of jogging five miles a day. Health is largely overblown. There are other, more private moments that touch us: a new moon at rise, the sun setting red across the sky, some private joy that we finished stripping the furniture, cleaned the shed, wrote a poem.

Writing is both a public and a private pleasure. We write alone, talking to ourselves, trying to explain the universe in a series of metaphors, hoping to be understood. We mostly put away our thoughts, satisfied that we have written them. Occasionally we take a chance comparable only to skydiving without a parachute: We say to family, friend or lover: "Look what I wrote."

Parents spoil children. Having been and, in fact, being, both a child and a parent, I remember the utter embarrassment of my mother taking my poor efforts and putting them on walls. Even yet she has things I wrote in my preschool days. I have done the same to my son. Little notes he wrote from vacations, stories from second grade, are neatly framed, gracing my walls. I don't think parents do that to hold on to the child; I think we do it to let the child know we are proud of the effort. The only thing more embarrassing than having to look at and be reminded that once we could neither color within the lines nor spell is . . . well . . . nothing. Where would we be if mothers didn't hold on to scraps? How would we know who we are?

Glasses
For Toni Morrison

Philosophically we are told the glass is either half full or half empty. I suppose the same could be said for a journey. We are either taking the first step toward or the last step from. Anyone tracing our steps will, indeed, find that our first step is her last; though anyone following in our footsteps may find it difficult to know when the journey began. People will, in other words, ask a poet, "How long does it take you to write a poem?" And the only answer that we can honestly give is, "all my life." People do the same to novelists.

I suppose the difference between the novelist and the poet is that the novelist sees an entire world; the poet only a slice of it. Sure, someone is bound to say, but how do you account for *The Iliad* or *The Odyssey* or *The Song of Roland* or any, in fact, of those long, epic poems that give us a hero and a world? Epics, however, today take the form of films or novels. By the same token, had Toni Morrison written during the age of Homer, *Song of Solomon* would have been recited around the campfires after a grueling battle; would have been added to and subtracted from as "The Saga of Milkman Dead" was told to groups of men reclining with an ale at some tavern; would have been used as an example to inspire young Black males struggling in The Gambia with initiation rituals. Milkman, the classic male, tries to determine his relationship with his mother and his father. His mother says: "What harm did I do you?" His father: "Here are the keys. Own something." His community: "Your day is coming." Isn't Ruth simply trying to complete herself, find the half that was lost when her father died, when she called Milkman into that room? Or is Ruth, by having him suckle at her breasts, trying to immunize Milkman against the evils of this world? Did some primal gene Ruth is hardly aware of tell her to take him to his mother's milk and with that milk immunize him from the hurts that men visit upon each other? He could not hate his mother; she and Pilot were the only people who wanted him to live. He did not wish to hate his father. He needed, in the words of T. S. Eliot, to be taught "to care and not to care . . . / because I cannot turn the stair."

Milkman's odyssey carried him to Virginia where he, in order to claim himself fully, had to lose the only person he freely loved, Pilot. And in the losing, Milkman gained the wisdom of Solomon: Only she who is willing to sacrifice is worthy of the prize. Milkman learned that only when you no longer need a safety net of Guitar, of his father, of someone to adore him, of community respect, of historical certainty, can you learn to fly.

Love, Morrison teaches us, is no better than the lover. Cholly loved Pecola. He was, indeed, the only person who would touch her. Yet his touch, like the touch of any free person, is deadly. Cholly impregnates his daughter, then flees, leaving Pecola to her madness. "A whistling woman and a cacklin' hen," the old proverb says, "come to no good end."

Cholly is whistling when we meet him, coming up the road. He has no particular destination in mind, no particular thing he is seeking. In other times Cholly would have boarded a ship for the New World, raped the native inhabitants, collected all the riches he could, then squandered them back in Europe. In other times, Cholly would have gone out with his native Masai to kill a lion, or be killed trying to prove his manhood. In future times, Cholly would have set upon a rocket that would either blow him up or carry him to worlds unseen. But Cholly Breedlove is a Negro. And he is not allowed to have dreams. Isn't Morrison answering Langston Hughes when he asks, "What happens to a dream deferred?" It does, indeed, "dry up like a raisin in the sun." Cholly himself festered, then ran.

I like to think that old Cholly, who is dead when the novel opens, in fact, made something of himself. He was ripe to go off on some affirmative action program, maybe to, say, Holy Cross. He continued to have confusions. He wanted to acknowledge his blackness, but it just didn't seem to, well, pay off. In order to justify his lack of control, maybe old Cholly, well, went to Yale Law. Yale had an affirmative action admission program, and Cholly certainly fit the picture of the pitiful Negro who would try very, very hard. Let's say old Cholly graduated and got a job with some senator, say from Missouri, where he hung a Confederate flag in his office to sort of say, "I'm all right, see?" In that office it finally dawns on Cholly that whatever it means to be Black, it is too painful to support. Cholly turns on Black people with a vengeance. He cannot identify with them. They are losers. Didn't he, after all, put his past behind him? Why can't they? Cholly goes back and reclaims his son. At one point, he even sells his sports car (that

the company is recalling) to pay the kid's tuition. Cholly likes
dirty movies, though. That is his only visible weakness. He
likes to watch them and he likes to talk about them. But only
to the young Black women in his office. Only to the women he
feels have rejected him. Only to the women he knows have
less power than he. Cholly goes around giving speeches,
laughing at his family. He has found his father and takes pride
in not speaking to him. He takes pride in his mother's not hav-
ing running water in her home. He rejoices and revels in his
sister's needing public assistance. He is the darling of the New
Right. Sure, he has to hear the nigger jokes and laugh. They,
after all, cannot be about him; he's not a nigger. He is a chosen
one. He marries Miss Ann. He, in fact, gets a nice dowry since
no other man would take her. And he doesn't mind so much
when, as they climb into their twin beds and turn out the
lights, she says, "Cholly, smile. So I can see where you are."
After all, he is her husband and has rights if he chose to assert
them. And hey, success costs something. Why don't those
other Negroes listen to him and try to understand?

Poor Cholly is rewarded for his faithful service. He is
appointed to the Supreme Court. All he has to do is shift his
eyes, shuffle his feet, and lie like hell about the one Black
woman who dared to say: "This man has no character." Every-
body loved the show. Highest ratings since the Nixon scandals.
Cholly loved humiliating the Black woman. That will show
them about turning him down. She should have said yes. His
white folks came through for him! That will show all the Black
women to mess with a Black man. Of course, the fact that
Black women had done nothing to him would never enter his
mind. Which he lost. As he stood to be sworn in on the White
House lawn when, instead of the U.S. Marine Band breaking

into "The Star-Spangled Banner" or "America the Beautiful" or "God Bless America" or any song that indicated how far Cholly had risen, the band played "Old Black Joe." The president was amazed. "I especially requested that song for Cholly," he said as he watched, with puzzlement, the little Black men in the white coats carry Cholly away. "He always had a such a good, wholesome sense of humor. I just don't understand." Pecola, in case there are some of you that haven't followed her career, went to Europe and became the "Queen of the Blues." She settled in Paris and was the toast of the Continent. Remembering the tragic circumstances of her childhood, she dedicated herself to adopting orphans from around the world. Pecola died on a warm day in August just as a younger singer named Aretha Franklin went number one with a cover of a song by Otis Redding: "Respect."

If Cholly was a free man to whom love was a weapon, Sula is a free woman to whom love will be a trap. The only person Sula loved freely and completely was Nel. They were, in fact, opposite sides of the same coin. Perhaps it is not fair to say Sula loved Nel; perhaps it is more accurate to say Nel completed Sula, who was always searching for her other half. "Pig meat," said a voice in lemon yellow pants. And Sula did not know why she responded. She knew she connected with Shadrack. They were both young people under fire. "Private?" the nurse implored. "Pick up the spoon." A spoon is primordial. We use a spoon at the start of our lives and at the end. "I have measured out my life in coffee spoons." Not coffee cups. Not teaspoons. Coffee spoons. How American. But why were they calling Shadrack "private?" Private, he thought, was something secret. Was he a secret? Morrison is telling us yes, of course, the Black man is a secret. And his secret is that he must organize death; must order insanity to appear once a year so that it can be controlled. Must be in control of the unstable desires of the people among whom Black Americans find themselves. The privates of the Black man are an open secret. Something to be taken from him and burned, dried up, hung out for everyone to see. Take the privates from a Black man, Morrison says, and white folks feel that they will be safe.

But there is *Sula*. How shall we control her? The novel portrays Sula as the force of evil. It is, the novelist tells us, the community's way of organizing its life. If there is a visible object to hate, then love will be possible. The people of Appalachia have or had a person whom they called the Sin Eater. At death this man would come around and eat the fruit symbolic of the sins of the deceased. Then the deceased could go to heaven. The Sin Eater is an untouchable. Much like the hangman; much like the untouchables of India. Much like any leper. If we are not like "them," then we must be like "us." Sula stands in for every white hurt the community has experienced. She and Shadrack organize the community by being themselves outside it. The good cannot do this. The good, the faithful, the intelligent, the kind, only inspire guilt and anger. It takes a concept of evil to unite a people.

I have, personally, always been amazed that in all of humankind's wars we have never fought over the devil. You can't even get a good conversation started about the devil. Everyone understands you and everyone agrees. But God? You can go off on crusades to slay the infidels; you can be put on racks and flayed to be made to accept a God in which you do not believe; you can be run from one country to the next in order to be free to practice your religion, but it never will occur to you to let others have the same freedom. God is an ideal, but evil is real. We do not always know the guises of God, but we always know the devil. Sula was fine playing the devil's advocate. She had a function. Until she met her true other half. She was an artist without a canvas until the canvas appeared. Then she became confused. She wanted to protect and define him. She wanted to own him because she wanted to have herself completed. Robert Frost teaches us, "Good fences make good neighbors." The same is true of love. Sethe learned to love a little bit so that there would be something left over for the next one. Sula loved as completely as she disdained. Like her grandmother Eva, Sula knew that to name things is to control them. Eva named the Deweys and changed not only their personalities but their physical characteristics: "Theys all Deweys to me." And Sula named Eva "old" and sent her to a nursing home. Eva named Plum dead and burned him up while he was still a man. Sula watched Hannah burn because she was "interested." But Sula could not name nor claim Ajax. He was a free man freely loving a free woman. When Sula was no longer free, Ajax left, leaving Sula with his license so that she could know she did not know his name. I love that. A Black man with a license. Who else to leave it to but the woman he would not license to love him? But Nel never got with the program. Jude didn't want her; he wanted to feel like a man. He wanted Michael Jackson's "Muscles." He wanted the sweat, the bruises, the injuries of a man. He whimpered off to Detroit to hang out in gay bars . . . and refuse to dance. Nel lost them both. Because one needed her; and one needed to use her. Sula and Jude defined themselves by Nel; but Nel's other half was Sula. "We was girls together. Girl, Girl, Girl," Nel cries for all the lost love. And all the time wasted.

Jadine is not a woman to waste time. Jadine wants none of it. Like Phillis Wheatley, Jadine recognizes that in order to live she must unshackle the past. Wheatley had to ask herself: Whom will I hate . . . the seller or the buyer? Wheatley had to ask herself: Since this is my condition, what have I gotten from it? Wheatley wrote a poem to George Washington wishing him well on his quest for freedom. Perhaps she, Wheatley, would never know that freedom, but she was in a place, called the United States, where personal freedom was recognized; where the Enlightenment was more than just a phrase. Where education was possible to order and control the prejudices and superstitions of humankind.

Jadine will not be a good daughter, a good colored girl, a good woman. She will go forth into a great unknown and claim herself. Son is hardly worth it. Certainly he had no appreciation of Jadine's need to claim education for herself. He can fuck like a star, but this is a man fighting the future. Jadine tried to be a good lover to him. Wanted "the brother" to shape up, but he was a Mandinka warrior who could not understand that the wars are over. He loves his first dime, never realizing the diamond he slept next to. Morrison tells me only her mother and I love Jadine. But *Tar Baby* is a perfect novel. Morrison said in an interview some years ago that "the language must not sweat." There is not a wasted word in *Tar Baby*. From the river that lost its way to the couples who live in its wake. The white couple and the Black couple are tied together. They know each other's secrets; but Jadine is an orphan. Like Cholly, like Son, like Sula. Only she will not play out her own destruction. If Son is all the world offers her, she will admit to being alone. And Son will go lickety-split into a place a blind woman takes him.

Morrison does wonderful things with groups of women: the women of Mobile; the women of New York. Such a contrast. The women of Mobile are prototypical women. They do the right things for all the correct reasons against their own better nature. The women of New York strut. Know that they own the city. Know they are making a place safe for themselves. We get the great line from the women of New York: The Black woman is both a ship and a safe harbor. What a wonderful thing to be. Everything. We all know "it's not the size of the ship, but the motion of the ocean" that completes the ultimate intimacy. Morrison says that the Black woman is both. That level of control can either destroy or create. Jadine flies. My students tell me, when we study *Tar Baby*, that Jadine will always be alone. That she will be lonely and by herself. Surely if you are a ship and a safe harbor, you can journey to places unknown. Jadine flies. She does not fool herself that the white folks love her. She does not fool herself that life will somehow become easier. She just remembers that bitch in heat in Baltimore that she tried to save. She could not save the dog, but she can save herself. Jadine flies . . . like a bird in the sky.

Birds, contrary to popular belief, are not free. If you cut down a tree in which a Robin has made her home, the bird will fly a pattern around the area until, exhausted, she falls to the ground. Birds have no ability to adjust because they are territorial creatures. Bound by their home and their space. Environmentalists tell us never to cut a tree in spring. It makes sense. Cut a tree when the birds are not there. Otherwise not only the tree but the surrounding critters and creatures will die. Waiting for its return.

When Adam and Eve left the Garden of Eden, the child they conceived was Sethe. Morrison conceived a Sethe to tell her story of slavery. *Beloved* looks at the "peculiar institution" from the viewpoint of the slave. Some slave sang a song about "Oh freedom over me . . . and before I'll be a slave I'll be buried in my grave and go home to my Lord and be free." "No more auction block for me . . . no more . . . no more." "Flee as a bird . . . to your mountain." Someone had already told the story of Sethe . . . but not in a novel. Morrison offers her biggest challenge to American letters with *Beloved*. If she has taken Sethe's point of view, who will speak for the School Master and his nephews?

It must be very troubling to be a white man. When one considers the fears and superstitions of the European male, it is, in the words of the king of Siam, a "puzzlement." You can see caveman with an erection. Something within him says, "I want a woman." He forces a strong, erect organ in, and out comes something skimpy and damp. You can see the sort of myths that would emerge from that initial experience. She must have done something to me. Why didn't I come out the same way I went in. You could also easily see the confusion when, some nine months later, she produces a child. Surely he had something to do with that. But what? Mankind continues to evolve. They notice that the women bleed at certain times. What could that mean? And if he forces his organ into her at those times, all he gets is blood and this skimpy thing. She must be unclean and unsafe. It could not be he. It could never be he. There must be a perfect man somewhere who did not have to be brought to us this way. There must be a perfect man somewhere whose mother is undefiled. There must surely be a possibility of virgin birth where God simply gives the word and we sinners will be released from the burdens of the flesh. European male, African male, Asian male, all sought

freedom from women. All consider woman inferior. All fear
the power of the vagina. Freud was wrong. There is no penis
envy; there is vaginal envy. The penis, no matter what the
myth, is an entity. No matter what its length or width, it is
finite. The vagina is a space. It knows no boundary. I have
never had difficulty with the story of Adam and Eve because I
have never believed it. Any snake in that garden had to be
connected to Adam. It was not knowledge but carnal knowl-
edge that Adam forced upon Eve that caused the troubles.
The uncoiled snake was somewhere south of Adam's belly
button. In a male effort to control, marriage was created. Mar-
riage is not a female institution because it does so little good
for women. It labels women outside the institution witches,
who are then ripe for burning. Whores who are then ripe for
sexual exploitation. It labels the women outside the institution
dykes who are then ripe for hating. And with such hateful
options facing women, it makes any male better than none. "It
cost me a lot but there's one thing that I've got is my man," the
song says. "Happiness is just a thing called Joe." You would
think the enlightened man would rebel at such images of
themselves. But if Susan Brownmiller was right that "all men
benefit from rape," it is certainly clear that all men benefit
from both the ideal and the institution of marriage. A woman
should belong to somebody. She is a prize to be won, spoils to
be taken; is a concubine to be visited.

The white man in America must have a special problem.
If the relationship of the male to his penis is alienation, then
the white American male faces a particular and difficult task.
What has this organ, which they freely admit they cannot con-
trol, produced? If someone tells you they have troubled skin
that they "just can't do a thing with," why, we offer options:

drink more water, eat fresh vegetables, don't pick your pim-
ples, use Clearasil. If someone tells you they have trouble with
their hair and "can't do a thing with it," we offer shampoos,
oils, brushing rituals. Hell, if your teeth fall out, we make you
new ones. If your eyes fail, we give you glasses. If you can't use
your arms or legs, we offer therapy. But if you can't control
your penis . . . we blame the women. The white American
male under the sway of this same organ had to reconcile the
unreconcilable. When he forces his penis into a white woman,
she produces a white child. When he forces his penis into a
Black woman, she produces a slave. How could one organ be
responsible for two such different entities? One human to be
cared for and nurtured; one a product, much like wheat or
corn or cotton, to be cut down to size and sold. How does the
white American male live with an organ that is not only not in
his control but outside the control of nature? There has to be
a great fury at himself for his lack of understanding. Why
won't his penis be consistent? The Black man always produces
a black child. The Asian, the American Indian—every other
man produces a human being . . . all the time: Why can't he?
And who will explain it to him? The greatest challenge of the
twenty-first century will be reconciling the human male to his
penis. Morrison has opened the dialogue with *Beloved*: Sethe
will not produce a slave. The white novelists must now take up
that crucible. And shoulder the responsibilities of all their
children.

The writer's life is, I think, a good life. Whether the glass
is half full or half empty, we do not cup our hands, letting the
essence of life dribble through our fingers. We walk boldly to
the fountain and drink deeply.

Miss Piersall

Miss Piersall. We were all afraid. Sure, some of the class felt confident, and Miss Piersall was actually a friend of my parents, but somehow fourth grade would be different. For one thing, she kept a long ruler on her desk; for another, it was said she didn't like recess. I wasn't too much worried about the work; the teacher told you what to do and you did it. You couldn't watch television or read your own books until homework was done. My mom taught third grade, but I usually beat her home. My homework was waiting for her, and on my days to do so the dusting and dishes were done; the garbage taken out; Duke, our dog, was fed. It's not that I was a "good" girl so much as I couldn't, and can't, stand being fussed at. And worse than the words was that "you've-let-me-down" look. I hated that look more than anything.

One day Miss Piersall had teacher's meeting. I attended St. Simon's Episcopal School, and the nuns liked to meet during the day. The instructions to the students were: no talking. I didn't talk, but the fourth grade could be heard all over the building. When Miss Piersall came back to class she was very angry. "I'm going to give each one of you a swat," she said. I raised my hand. "Nikki?" "I wasn't talking, Miss Piersall. I shouldn't be swatted," I said. "But you know who was, don't you?" Which didn't seem fair to me. Of course I knew. But I didn't tell. And I was given one swat.

I am a writer because I believe fairness should be accorded the individual.

Meat Loaf
A View of Poetry

Poetry, to me, is the association of disassociated ideas. I like clear simple images, clear simple metaphors, making clear simple statements about not-so-clear, not-so-simple human beings. In other words, I believe poets like Robert Frost are apt to be highly underrated. I want my students to tell me a story poetically. I am not especially interested in their love lives, because young people, in my mind, don't have love lives, they have lust lives and stressful social lives, but they are far too young to know, let alone knowledgeably talk about, love. I have seldom read an interesting poem about the discovery of raindrops, or clouds floating by, or sunsets either, so we eliminate these categories. I start my classes by asking the favorite poem of each student in my class. Surprisingly enough, there are a number of students who do not have favorite poems; who cannot even lie about it. I ask for favorite poets and run into the same problem. I then, quite naturally, ask the class why it is taking my course. The answers are heartening and dismaying.

Why, which is a real question, do we think we can teach people to write poetry? Why would we want to do that if we could? I don't think we can, and I don't think we should. It's not as if there isn't an abundance of poets running about—in fact, the market is saturated with them—but poetry is an art, not an academic exercise. Poetry is the way we look at life and the conclusions we draw. Mostly, if I teach anything, I teach my students to think and to talk about their thoughts. How, you may legitimately ask, do I teach them to think? I don't think thinking is an exercise. It is something that if we do it two mornings a week for one hour and fifteen minutes, the habit might stick. Most young people want poetry to be math or science or history. A subject. If they put the right metaphors in the right place with the right number of syllables to a line, they will have a poem. I don't think so. I believe if they put enough passion into a real subject, they may stumble onto a poem.

All poetry is written in the vernacular. The olden poets wrote of and in their times. We must do the same. Will that mean that some of our images are "That sucks"? I think so. Some will use "shitty," some will say "motherfucker," because that's a part of our vernacular. Will it offend? You bet. But poets who don't offend are not doing their job. There is no right or wrong in my classroom; only what works or doesn't work for the poet and the poem. That, I admit, frustrates my class, because the students are used to being told what to do and how to do it. I think it's unmitigated crap that anyone in school—elementary, junior, high, or college—can produce a writer. We can produce junior assholes who think they can write and are therefore exempt from the rule of general civilization; we can produce youngsters and teachers who form cliques thinking they are the best and the brightest and don't have to engage in the daily cares of the world in which they live; but I hope I don't do that.

I hope, by discussing sports and homelessness, race and current television, world news, scientific wonders, and anything else that comes to mind, that I am showing my students they must contemplate the world in which they live. I believe their responsibility as writers is to have as much sympathy for the rich as for the poor; as much pity for the beautiful as for the ugly; as much interest in the mundane as in the exotic. Meat loaf is a wonderful thing as worthy of a poem as any spring day or heroic deed. The exercise I try to instill is: Look; allow yourself to look beyond what *is*, into what *can be*, and more, into what *should be*. Poems are dreams. Dream. But dreams are conceived in reality. Meat loaf is real. Write that poem.

Earthlings
The Future Tradition

Growing up in the Western tradition, which isn't really so much "Western" as an amalgam of all cultures, one can't help but admire Jesus. As a Christian reared in the Baptist and Episcopalian faiths, I always did, and still do, love the story of the boy in the temple assailing the elders. One of my favorite songs is "Peace Be Still," which tells the journey of the ship on the storm-tossed Sea of Galilee. I'm especially fond of the story of Nicodemus sneaking around at night to let Jesus know he did, indeed, believe but . . . well . . . maybe it was too much trouble to say so in the light. Of course, Jesus was killed. He rose on Easter and we are all happy. But He did die and that was sad. I used to cry each Easter season when we did the Stations of the Cross. It just galled me that Peter denied Him. That the crowd screamed, *"Give us Barabbas!"* That Pilate was such a gutless wonder that he, like Lady Macbeth, thought he could wash his hands of it all. In *King of Kings*, the talkie version, there was always one voice in the crowd asking, "What has this man done?" I identified with that. I liked to think that had I been in the crowd, I would at least have cried out, "What has He done?"

Socrates was a great favorite of mine because he wanted to teach the young people. I know now that he wanted to teach the boys, but when I was told about him by my grandfather I always thought there were girls as well as boys there. I always saw a group of kids sitting under an olive tree, answering questions this wise man would ask. Of course, we killed him. The town didn't want the young people to know anything. I could understand that. Adults frequently changed the conversation when I came into the room, but no one, as far as I could see, was ever made to take poison because she slipped and mentioned a divorce or a pregnancy or someone "running around" with someone else's husband. Frankly, I didn't see why Socrates didn't just "had up," as we say in the Black community, hit the road. Find a better place. But I was a child. And children think you can move on; adults know better. So Socrates died a noble death and his star pupil moved on and we were told we were the better. I think not. The crowd, once again, was wrong.

It's impossible for me not to love Galileo. He was the first modern, true rebel. The Church said he was wrong, and he went: *"Fuck it; I'm wrong."* He recanted. He refused to die because people were too stupid to understand what he was talking about. He knew he was right. But so did Jesus; so did Socrates. Though only Galileo refused to die. It took about five hundred years before anyone admitted Galileo had been wronged, but a late admission is, I suppose, better than none. Guerrilla warfare began at that point. Whatever else Galileo gave us, he said clearly: It is better to live on than to die in fruitless battle.

I'm not trying to fight any sort of religious war here, nor do I fail to admire the deeds and aspirations of divine beings. It is simply that the lesson I learned from these three men was that the people are frequently wrong because they tend to follow stupid leaders who indulge the people in outdated and outlandish folklore and superstition.

I am a Black American poet. I am female. I am, at this writing, forty-eight years old. I am a daughter, a mother, a professor of English. I like grilled rack of lamb and boiled corn on the cob . . . Silver Queen when I can get it. I like television and sports. I love bid whist. I smoke cigarettes and, should the occasion arise, will have a glass of red wine, preferably Merlot. I like my mother, my sister, my son, and my dogs. I will drink any hot, black liquid that someone will call coffee. I hate diet soda, seat belts, anti-smokers, pro-lifers, and stupid people who think they have any right to tell me how to live. I have no need to control anyone and will not be controlled. I believe that if I keep examining my life and what I think and feel, I will have added one, teeny, tiny bit of truth to this planet I call home. It is inconceivable that I feel alienated from Western tradition; my people have contributed so much that is vital and good to it. I am alienated from the *people* who call themselves white, who think they own Western tradition.

Why I write poetry is still largely an unknown. It's something that I think I can do. What I absolutely know is that it had to be my decision. I remember writers coming to Fisk University when I was an undergraduate. Other students would, invariably, give copies of their work to the writers. What they were actually hoping for, I don't honestly know. To me, people who do things like that really believe Lana Turner was discovered sitting on a stool in a drugstore. They must really think there is something called an overnight success. That one day you were happily walking down the street, maybe going to the grocery store for some milk or a pack of cigarettes, when . . . boom! Some guy steps out and says, "You should be in pictures." Off you run to Hollywood and live happily ever after. Or you give a poem to Gwen Brooks or Langston Hughes. They return to Chicago or Harlem. Tired from the journey, they venture into the kitchen and open the refrigerator. Ah, they are in luck. There is cold fried chicken from Sunday's meal. And . . . gracious . . . a slice of apple pie. They put the coffeepot on and sit at the kitchen table. But . . . they have nothing to read. But wait . . . didn't that kid in Nashville give them a collection of poems, or was it short stories? They, on tired feet, most likely swollen ankles, walk back to their briefcases. Yes. There it is. "My Poems" by a kid. Why, hot damn, this is great stuff. Forget about eating. They curl up in their favorite armchair and read on. Dawn is peeking through the shades. How could the time have passed? They call their agent who comes right over to read for himself. Yes, this kid must be published . . . right away. The kid goes on to win the Yale Younger Writers Series . . . is asked to join the Society of Poets and represents the United States in the USA/USSR Poetry International Conference. And to think he almost didn't show his work because he was shy. Ahhhh . . . happy endings.

Except, I think not. I think artists have to take responsibility for their work. There is no magic out here. Only a lot of hard work and very little reward. The great writers whom we venerate today were hardly known in their time; or were, like

Shakespeare, wildly popular and therefore scorned by the scholars. Am I alienated from Western tradition? Hardly. It taught me that no matter what you are doing, some folk will like it and some will hate it. But mostly it taught me that the critics and scholars are wrong. Which means one must always be wary of praise and always put criticism in perspective. Since I have little personal regard for what are called "leaders," whether of the race or the muse, one must get to the people who might appreciate and understand what one is saying and beyond the leaders who would control and trap you for their own limited ends.

Preachers, of course, only preach to the saved. Each Sunday in every church they may rail and rally against the sinners, but they are preaching to the saved. Folk sit in church and k-n-o-w, "We are not like *them*," whoever them are. Up to and including, I should imagine, Baptists, Methodists, Catholics, Episcopalians, Presbyterians, snake handlers, holy rollers, and any other segment of their own religion, let alone Buddhism, Islam, Judaism, voodoo, animism, and other beliefs far different. Opera singers only sing to those who come to the opera. Certainly there are operas on radio and, occasionally, television, but let a good ol' boy hit *Aida* by mistake and watch that dial turn like a rabbit seeing a dog in the field. Quick. Poets are like that, too. We are listened to and read only by people who like poetry. Men have been known to turn down lewd and obscene physical acts on their bodies rather than come to poetry readings. And we all know men will do almost anything for a lewd and obscene act. I have wondered why poets get into these petty quarrels when there are so very few of us and even fewer folk who care what we think.

If it weren't so pitiful, it would be funny to hear human males discoursing on why women don't write poetry. Some of us believe that the creation of language itself belongs to women. While the men were on all fours grunting around in the fields, we women were drawing pictures on the caves, putting decorations on the clay bowls in the savannah, walking around holding our children, developing the hoe and the rake, collecting seeds and learning the planting seasons. I mean, it is so illogical to think that any system that intended to support life first created "man." However would it perpetuate itself? Female has to come first. I'm sure the first man who tried to appropriate civilization was laughed out of the village. I know the first times the Africans saw white people they thought the whites were dead . . . were ghosts . . . and the Africans thought them uncivilized. Just as we have now come to the point that some of the conservative men—George Will and Walter Williams come to mind immediately—despite all their male chauvinism, have to fight for the rights of their daughters, we can easily see how the human female fought, thousands of years ago, for the right of her son to read, draw, plant, and be privileged to the knowledge of medicine. Had she only anticipated T. S. Eliot and his arrogant exclusiveness, she might have had second thoughts. But I don't blame T. S. He had enough self-blame in his life to do without mine. We have this guy here, Eliot, from St. Louis. Already you can see the problem. The most vital parts of St. Louis are on the riverfront, which is populated by Black people. His mother wanted him to be a gentleman? Why? And if he was to please her he had to turn his back on everything that was exciting. He had to make himself into what he thought was a "Western" man . . .

and, having worked so hard at it, found the United States wanting and moved to England. This is a guy whose best friend and mentor is certifiably insane. Without Pound, where would Eliot be? And how does Pound fit into "tradition"? That same Pound was a fascist, or he didn't mind saying he was a fascist. I'm not against Ezra. Like an old woman selecting yams, Pound picked talent. And he found the strong, durable ones who would feed the family tonight and still seed for next spring. But is this Western tradition? White men mentoring white men to the exclusion of all others certainly is.

Deutschland über alles. But is this good? Is it right? I agree with the women who say no. Common sense would tell anyone, white men included, that when the natives begin to question the system . . . the system is dead. Melvin Tolson, that wonderful Black poet, wrote three lines that I will always remember: "When the skins are dried/the flies will go home." And, "We judge a civilization only in its decline." I was a junior in college when I was privileged to hear Tolson read; he died the next year, and those three lines jumped at me. Of course, I said to myself, of course. At the same conference Lerone Bennett, Jr., pointed out: "The last bastion of white supremacy is in the Black man's mind." I don't know if Lerone meant man and woman, but he said man. I know and I knew what my generation had uncovered. Rap Brown said it best: "The whole honkie situation is through." I like that. Not white civilization, not Western civilization, not even Eurocentric civilization, but the honkie situation.

To agree that the end is upon us is not, however, to deny the journey. Human civilization is composed of human cultures. Some of those cultures are worthy of emulation, as long as it is understood that we emulate the values, not the rewards, of that culture. The West has given the world the idea of the individual. For a variety of reasons far too numerous to attempt to explain in this essay, America turned away from tribalism to the rights and responsibilities of the individual. It has taken this Western outpost these many years to include white women, let alone people of color, under the banner of "these truths we hold self-evident." Simply because the practice falls short of the ideal is no particular reason to reject the dream. No, I am not alienated from Western tradition, because I am, and my people have been, too much a part of it. The writers may write, the politicians may legislate, the preachers may hope, and the scientists may try to prove otherwise . . . but whatever is Western, not to mention tradition, belongs to me. We can be read out of the will, but the deceased is still dead. As that oldest of Western traditions informs us: "The king is dead. Long live the king." Just as nature abhors a vacuum, humans resist change. Change will occur; vacuums will be filled. And Western tradition, which started in the East and moved west, will in westward movement end up in the East and move once again west. We are all a part of the earth . . . earthlings . . . and we will one day push so far out that we will reach the ends of this universe, this galaxy, this wonderful star and, instead of the arrogance, domination, and guns of insecure people, say, "Hello. I am an earthling. I am from the third planet of the yellow sun. It is traditional with us to extend a hand of friendship and welcome."

Appalachian Elders
The Warm Hearth Writer's Workshop

The year was 1964. It was a fine spring afternoon. Big white puffs of cumulus clouds floated in a clear sky of blue. It was a day to sit on a hill and chew on a blade of grass, giving vent to the muse if you were a poet; it was a day to haul old clothes, mismatched dishes, half-empty, dried-up paint in cans . . . junk . . . out of the garage and maybe clean some gutters if you were a husband; a day for frying whitefish with potatoes and onions and a few hush puppies on the side to go with the apple pies you had already baked if you were a mother. It was a day to drive your sister's brand new Fiat 1100 D. I was just a student then, not a poet. I drove the car.

I only wanted to go to Kroger's. Gary was home visiting for my twenty-first birthday. I didn't need to go far nor for much, but since I was going, Mommy gave me a list. Gary's son, Christopher, was too little to help, but since I was going could he ride? I insisted Mommy come with me, since it was her list and she hadn't ridden in the car. Gary stayed home.

Everything went as it should. I hadn't driven a five-speed in years, but I got safely out of first and on the road. We lived in Lincoln Heights, which does not have a chain grocery store, requiring us to travel to Lockland, our neighboring community to the south. I drove out the long way, taking Springfield Pike through Wyoming, cutting back to Lockland via Wyoming Avenue.* The car was wonderful. The 1100 D was like a little box. Hers was powder blue. We shopped and loaded the three bags onto the backseat. Chris was in the corner.

The direct way home is Wayne Avenue. I never did like to travel Wayne Avenue because there's nothing to look at. No significant trees, no opening vistas. But it was the direct route and the logical thing to do. Between Kroger's and home there is a stoplight at Wyoming and Wayne, a stoplight just in front of the funeral home, one 4-way stop sign at the gas station and new factory, a stoplight at Medosch, and a stoplight at the top of the hill. I cruised along at a decent speed, as the Fiat was not a fast car. Traffic flowed smoothly for a Saturday. It was way too early for the cruisers and drunks who turned Wayne Avenue into a strip after dark. I had just reached the top of the hill when the light turned amber. Normally I would have simply gone on around the corner, but my mother and nephew were with me and I didn't necessarily want Mommy to think I drove with abandon. I came to a full stop. Then I heard the most awful sound in the universe. A car that had not even been close enough behind me for me to have noticed it started hitting its brakes. I could tell he was not going to make it. I saw, clearly, his rubber on the pavement. I saw his crazed

*Wyoming, Lockland, and Woodlawn are suburbs of Cincinnati.

eyes trying to stop his car. I saw us being hit . . . and then we were.

He came dead-on at us, knocking the Fiat sideways into the two lanes of traffic. I could feel the car scrunch under the blow. The back just seemed to fold under. I remember turning the engine off and riding the impact out. It all took seconds. My first real thought was Chris. He was shocked and scared but all right. I turned to Mommy, who was shaken but unhurt. The left side of the car had caved in also, and my leg was trapped. The car was totaled.

All the normal things were done. Police were called. The driver who hit us was a drunk and from out of town. No insurance. We, however, were covered. My ankle was hurt and swollen, but I guess we were all so happy no real damage was done that we went home, filed the necessary papers, apologized profusely to Gary, and that should have been that. But it wasn't. I was never to wear a high-heeled shoe again. My toe had been broken.

August 1988 had started with a decision for me. I would have a foot operation. I can't say that I had truly forgotten about the accident, but it was not at the top of my mind. Through the ensuing twenty-four years I had had foot problems. Many times I simply had to take shoes off because the pain of having anything on my left foot was unbearable. I well remember changing planes in Chicago one winter and taking one shoe off, going from terminal to terminal feeling like "diddle-diddle dumpling . . . my son John." I had come to southwestern Virginia to accept a position as Visiting Commonwealth Professor in the English Department. I had been invited to stay another year. The dress at Virginia Tech is casual, which probably is an understatement. I had taken to wearing moccasins, whether in business suit or evening dress. It's time to deal with this, I said to myself. And off I went to a foot doctor. Surgery was recommended, but it was summer and I was busy. Since I would be teaching in the fall, why not August? Both my left little toe and my right little toe needed surgery. The good thing was I would finally be pain-free. The bad thing was more pain than I had known since I birthed my son . . . and no crutches.

I, quite honestly, had looked forward to crutches. I had even purchased a long, white, linen skirt that I thought would just flow as I bravely, determinedly made my way about. No. No crutches for me, just two weird-looking wooden shoes.

My foot surgery was done outpatient. You just kind of lie there while he chats with you and grinds your bones. I seriously tried not to think about it. If you've never had someone grind on your bones, I have no metaphor for the pain. The painkillers are only to make your surgeon feel better. They don't do a thing for you. I didn't whimper nor cry nor push him away and leave. I'm so glad we did both feet at once, because I would never have had the second foot done. A friend took me home, propped me up in bed, and made tomato soup for me. She also got my painkillers. I was to be in bed, off my feet, for at least a week. Most likely I looked pitiful. Mommy and Gary sent me flowers with a card that said, "Happy Trails to You." The department sent me flowers saying they missed me. Other friends sent flowers, too. I like to think I brooded among my flowers. That I achieved a sort of poetic angst while I lay in bed contemplating my bound feet. I think, however, that I whimpered. I think I was miserable.

My best friend in the English Department is Ginney Fowler. Ginney was associate head of the department at that time. She took a call from Warm Hearth Retirement Community asking if anyone in English would like to do a writer's workshop with retirees. I don't know if Ginney thought of me because I like old people or because I was laid up in bed and would have agreed to anything that gave me a reason to look forward to being on my feet again. The phone rang, at any rate, and I answered it.

Ginney had to drive me out to Warm Hearth. It is a beautiful collection of buildings set in a glen. The trees whisper to you. Rabbits scamper across the road while the possum ambles and the groundhogs just look up waiting for you to pass. There are birds all around, and some have seen deer. I went up to the third floor. I had not led a workshop of this proposed nature before. As I hobbled in, I noticed the canes and walkers of the people gathered. I was home.

The first thing I wanted to establish was that they did not have to accept me. I told them who I was, read some of my poetry, gave copies of my book to the Warm Hearth library, and asked them to think it over. I am Black and they are not. We agreed to meet the next week.

My thoughts, quite naturally, turned to my grandmother. She was born in Albany, Georgia, but had lived her adult life in Knoxville, Tennessee. She had belonged to the book club, the garden club, the bridge club, and a host of self-help organizations for Negroes. She was a lifelong Democrat, though my grandfather was a Lincoln Republican. I tried to imagine what I'd do if I were conducting a workshop with my grandmother, what would I do? The answer was simple. I would do nothing. I would listen and encourage. She would be perfectly capable of telling her own stories.

Our very first reader was Zeke Moore. His story was short and funny. The workshop rather shyly commented on it and, in what turned out to be a wonderful thing, started to say, "Why that reminds me . . ." We had agreed to meet for one hour each Wednesday morning from ten to eleven o'clock. To me, all time is a suggestion. The watch I wear turned around on my left wrist is a gift from my mother who, one cold, winter afternoon when I was supposed to take her to lunch to meet her friend Liz Armstrong, walked out to the carport and sat in the car while I finished my phone conversation. "You know we have to be on time," she said. "Liz has to go back to work." That was Mother's idea of a reprimand. Of course, I felt foolish realizing she was sitting in a cold car waiting for me to drive her, but why did she go out when I was on the phone? Mother, unlike her mother and my father, is not a nagger or a shouter. That Christmas she gave me a watch. It has no numbers on it.

I was late—a lot. But I stayed later. Lunch at Warm Hearth has two seatings. My group ate at noon, giving us a built-in extra time. We could gossip and chat and still get downstairs on time. The one question that kept popping up was, What did I expect of them? There were about twelve of us: two men and ten women. There has seldom been more than two men at one time. I don't understand why.

Some of us have been teachers, some nurses, a preacher, an explorer for oil, farmers, lots of landowners, many housewives, and almost all were parents. Most of us cooked and all of us ate, so I had expected food to play a very prominent role in our writing. Janie Kay wrote a narrative saying she never wanted to cook again; Francis Brown found her grandmother's recipe book. We wrote about our marriages, our lineages, old homes we once lived in, and great homes we visited. Anna Kenney was our only short-fiction writer; many of us tried poetry. Mostly we wrote about ourselves.

Gloria Naylor was our first real writer-visitor. She was peppered with questions about agents, selling to television, how she got started. Alex Haley stopped by for a minute and stayed a couple of hours. And brought the press with him.

The workshop had no true idea of me, though I think they liked me. They did, however, have family around the States who would send them some clipping every now and then about me. "Why, you're actually famous," Zeke concluded after he had received a press clipping from Florida. If I have done anything right with the workshop, it is that I started us on equal ground, which is how true relationships should start.

Just about the time my feet had healed, I had to have a hemorrhoid operation. "I am carrying this identification with the workshop too far," I declared. They all had helpful hints and lots of sympathy. (For future workshop leaders only: I am not recommending physical infirmities in order to help your workshop identify with and understand you. It just worked out that way. I also wear bifocals and have dentures. We had bonded.)

One day I was having a bad day, threw on my jeans and a sweatshirt, and went to workshop. "Are you going to a football game?" I was asked. I have dressed properly ever since.

At the end of our first year we had accumulated quite a bit

of work. I thought we should do some desktop publishing. Tammy Shepherd, who works with me in the English Department, had been typing our handwritten manuscripts onto a disc. We could have them run off for a minimum amount of money. We purchased folders and bingo! "The Warm Hearth Sampler" was born. The next semester we did the same thing. Then came the inevitable question: When could we publish a "real book"? *Appalachian Elders* is the name of our real book.

What have I learned in these three years we have been together?

To have an effective workshop, you must be patient and supportive.

The workshop should be noncritical. It's all too easy to fall into the habit of noticing how something is said and miss the wonder and beauty of what is said.

Everyone should be encouraged to write, and no one should be pressured.

As workshop leader I do not read my work; I am there for the group. I also read every story that is written and make comments on the copy I return. Some people are shy; it takes them a little longer to trust the group. I think those who need more time should be allowed to take it.

Some of the group does not write. All our members are valuable; both those who write and those who listen. We have also been fortunate in our volunteers. Some of our members cannot write because of arthritis, failing eyesight, and other things of that nature. Having someone to talk the stories to can make a big difference. Cathee Dennison and Connie Wones got us through a very busy first February. Kathy Dickenson started as a volunteer and has become a member.

I have wanted the Warm Hearth story told because all too often the workaday world thinks that world is both the only one and the real one. Too many people think older people have nothing to give. People have thought we were doing oral history. They had no concept that older people who had never written before could take up a new task. Some of our members type; two recently have learned computer; most write by hand. Becky Cox is our typist now, helping us keep track of our work. We have not created any miracles on Wednesdays. We have only come together to share. I am not truly a leader; I am a catalyst. We have had public readings, our annual lunch, one fun dinner party. My mother and aunt have visited us. One member has a daughter who has joined. We have one member who is not living at Warm Hearth. We have lost Charlie, who had been married to Laura for sixty-three years; Zeke, who had a sudden heart attack; and Mancy Adams, who was one hundred and one years old. Janie Kay moved and Francis lost James. But we still have a story to tell. The years and the wonder of life inform our sensibilities. We mostly write about ourselves.

VI

POSTSCRIPT

"FaLaLaLaLaLaLaLaLaLa"
—*Traditional*

Christmas will just have to hold its horses. I'm not ready. Oh yes, I know everybody is so used to my efficiency that this is shocking news. After all, I'm the one who has usually finished my shopping by late July and am ready to wrap shortly after Labor Day. Have I learned my lesson, you may ask, remembering the year I had purchased and wrapped but forgot to properly label the gifts? No. It was only minor that my father was given a lovely nightgown I had purchased in Rome and my son received a wonderful box of Cuban cigars I had legally purchased in East Berlin, though sort of illegally brought into the United States. Mommy would not have noticed the difference, since she likes checkers, if the whole computer had not come with the game. These things, after all, do happen. No. Christmas will have to wait, not because I'm not capable of being ready . . . I have chosen not to be ready.

Let's face it. I was awake last December 26 at 5:30 A.M. anyway. We have five dogs (one for each lap, as my nephew says), and someone has to feed them. I know some folks think dogs lead cushy lives lying around the house all day, only really working when the mailman or meter reader comes around, but I don't agree. Dogs have a hard life. How would you feel if you, once a proud canine of the wild who chased his own rabbit for dinner, who reared his children in the collective ways of the group, now found yourself with three old ladies and two boys, or rather young men, whose idea of exercise is turning over a log or two on the fireplace? How would you feel having your world be restricted by a high fence with ivy winding its way down, and the cats, who once ran at the very thought of you, balleting along the trellis, laughing at your attempts to get your teeth into them? Now don't get me wrong, I'm not against cats, though it does seem not quite right that dogs have to be leashed and cats run free. But the real question is, How would you feel if you had no discernible reason to be? No real job to do; no place that was expecting you to show up at a certain time and perform a real function? You know how you would feel. Terrible. We know enough about people not having real jobs and how that deteriorates the personality to know that our poor dogs must feel, on most days, positively useless. Yet, they forge through, keeping themselves clean and occupied days upon end, watching *Jeopardy!* and *Wheel* and an occasional murder mystery with us. Are they truly interested in these things? I doubt it, but that's their day, and they accept it with a grace we all could learn from. I am still old-fashioned and southern enough to think living things should start their day with a hot meal, so I am always up by five-thirty to microwave their dog food with whatever scraps I can find in the fridge. My sister, by the way, worries that they will get fat and die before their time; I worry that they will be hungry and kill us before ours.

So I am up in time to make the Macy's after-Christmas sale, is my point. I could, last year, actually have been first or second in line at the door. The previous year I was in the first ten and made some wonderful purchases on wrapping paper, ornaments, Christmas cards, and an electronic pencil sharpener, which also opens letters. I have chosen not to go that route again. Am I getting lazy, you may wonder? My son came home from the army to discover I had purchased a red, two-seater sports car in his absence. He was both delighted and perturbed. Delighted because, after all, there is a sports car in the family; perturbed because I was not letting, nor interested in letting, him drive it. He agreed one morning to go to the grocery store with me because "those bags can be mighty heavy," and as we were trying to get from our side street into the main road I prudently waited until traffic abated. "Gosh, Mom," says the now-mature but still-adventuresome I've-been-in-the-army-two-years son, "you've really lost your edge." Lost my edge? Because I won't go running out into the insane, nay, suicidal, driving of Virginia? "Well, I better drive back or we'll never get home." I felt my car give a shudder. I know cars aren't supposed to cry, but they do. Especially when they are purchased by little old lady poets and now know they will be given a real workout by a young man with no regard for payments, insurance, scratches . . . all the things that inhibit mothers from burning rubber. No. I have not lost my edge nor am I lazy. I just have begun to think that things should be savored, slowed down, really slowly gone through, in order to be enjoyed.

I have traveled for a living most of my life. It's only been in the last few years, after my son graduated from high school, that I could actually afford a regular job with medical benefits, life insurances, and whatnot. I have learned, working a regular job with regular hours in a regular office and classroom, why you need medical benefits, however. My blood pressure, which has been low my entire life, is now up. Seeing the same people every day is really a lot of pressure, but that's another discussion. When you travel a lot you have to get ahead of things, or most assuredly you will be behind. I had to get the birthday cards out early or I would forget; I had to have Valentine's Day candy ordered for my mother or I would find myself in the only town in America that does not have express wire service. I had to have my turkey for Thanksgiving delivered and in the freezer, and quite naturally I had to have everything ready for Christmas or I would find myself on Christmas morning explaining that I meant to get to the store to pick up the wonderful gift that could not be lived without. No more.

Last year we overdosed. Everybody got everybody everything that was ever mentioned. Obscene is not too strong a word. If one more gift had come into the house, we would have needed to reinforce the floor. Did we think the world was coming to an end? Did we foresee some tragedy? I don't know, but December 26, over coffee and the lightest dollar pancakes a sister ever made, we had a discussion. Next year we would make choices. We will only give one gift to each person. We will have a limit on how much we can spend. Each person can only cook one dish. Is this going to be rough? You bet, because now we all have to think; now we will have to make choices. Yet, that is, to me and, really, to the family, the essence of Christmas. Jesus was born to give us a choice; we humans could continue to be controlled by fate or we could accept the Savior and be redeemed. We humans may not always control the circumstances of our bodies, but we can control our souls. That's what is so nice about Christmas. I think I took it too lightly and treated the holiday as a job. Something I needed to get done by a certain time. This year my family and I are getting back to basics. We will be back to telling family stories; back to a half-empty tree with ornaments we have made over the years. The angel on top is the one I made of straws and spray-painted in the first or second grade. We're lucky because Mommy has kept these things. We're stringing popcorn and sharing it with the dogs. This Christmas will be our best ever because we are determined to turn back to the days when it was just us, happy to be together, grateful for the love we share. I shouldn't say I'm not ready for Christmas because I really am. I'm just not ready for the mall to start Christmas sales before the World Series has been played; I'm not ready for my favorite radio station to start the carols; I'm not ready to be told how many more shopping days are left; and I'm definitely not ready for the arguments about putting a manger scene in some city square. I am ready to slow down and be grateful for all the blessings that have been sent our way. I still like Santa Claus and will faithfully leave him some chocolate chip cookies. Only this year, I am taking the time to make them.

AFTERWORD

■ ■ ■ ■

Morgan Owes Me a Car

The first car that I bought was a 1960 Volkswagen. It was kind of orangey, with a sunroof, but that year was the year before the gas gauge came in. You had a "reserve" tank that held one gallon of gas. What you were supposed to do was kick it in, and use that gallon to go directly to the gas station and fill up. What happened, quite a bit in fact, is that you would kick it in; lock it back, so as to not forget and not have the "reserve" available to you; and drive on for another forty or fifty miles then run out of gas and kick it open only to discover you had been driving on "reserve." It's amazing, it's incredible, how many times this happened before you finally said to yourself: "Kick it in; go to gas station. Period." I, who have prided myself on never making the same mistake twice, took an unnervingly long time to learn that lesson.

I purchased that car because I was living in Wilmington, Delaware, working at a settlement house just after I had dropped out of the University of Pennsylvania School of Social Work, waiting for the fall semester at Columbia University to begin. I could actually walk to work, and being on the east coast, there were trains to take to Philadelphia and New York and points further east. But I'm a Southerner by birth and a Midwesterner by rearing, so I definitely missed a car.

Uncharacteristically, I opened the Yellow Pages to look up car dealerships. Uncharacteristic because I hate looking up things. I'm a poor speller and my grandfather, in trying to help me learn, refused to spell words for me. "Look it up," he would say, when I knew damned well he knew how to spell it. I would have understood him punking me off if it was something he didn't know and didn't want to admit he didn't know, but I knew he knew, and was just not being helpful under that kind of guise adults use when they refuse to do something. How, I always wanted to know, can I look it up if I don't know how to spell it? This could take hours, days. This could turn into some sort of archeological expedition. This was looking for a lower-level Rosetta Stone. This was pure torture, when all he had to do was spell it for me. Even today I can be very disappointed in my spell-checker when it says, *You have chosen a word that does not appear in the main or custom dictionaries. Do you wish to use this word and continue checking?* In other words: *Dummy, why can't you get your words right?* I never have a problem *understanding* words; I just have problems spelling them. Of course, this is what I tell my students now that the shoe is on the other foot: There is no such thing as a misspelled word; there are only words for which we have no definitions. In other words, if that's what you think you said you spelled it wrong. Ha!

I pulled out the phone book and went to Automobiles, then Used and Pre-Owned Automobiles, since there was no way I could afford anything else. I called a couple of places to no avail then lucked up on something like Sammy's Good Used Cars. Thinking *What the heck?*, I called and asked if he had any cars under a thousand dollars.

He said, "I have a 1960 Volkswagen for $600. It's in really good shape—"

And before he could finish his spiel, I said, "I'll take it."

"Why don't you come out to see it?" he started.

"Sir," I patiently said, "I'll take it. I'll be there in the morning." I gave him my name and phone number and went to sleep that night feeling like a new-car owner and not just someone who had bought a pig in a poke.

The car was great. Aside from the gas thing it also lacked a cigarette lighter, which allowed me to get to know truckers all up and down Routes 1 and 9. I'd pull up close to the truck, wigging a cigarette, and the driver would drop or try to drop matches down to me. When they made it through the sunroof, we'd both give an air high five and I would speed off. Of course, hindsight says I should have known to quit smoking when my first car didn't have a lighter, but then hindsight *is* twenty-twenty. And I, wisely, no longer smoke.

Now with wheels, I could go visit my Aunt Anto in Philadelphia. She lived in Germantown, to which, being directionally challenged, I went a different way each time I visited her. I would fling my car toward the west and see what looked familiar. I always gave myself plenty of time since I was always lost. But I made it. Anto and I like seafood, and we used to go to a wonderful little neighborhood seafood place and order the Captain's Dinner. Sometimes her kids would come with us and sometimes one or two of her friends. I also drove up to New York to catch a poetry reading or a play or a movie. New York was only two hours away and if money was not tight you could take the Pennsylvania Turnpike and make it even faster; Routes 1 and 9 are free.

Cars are not an asset in New York City. As it came time to move to New York the car was great, because everything I owned could fit into it. But that was probably the last good thing the car would do for me. Being a Columbia student is, or at least in my day was, a great asset. They helped you with apartment locations and you didn't have to pay a deposit on your telephone. Back in the day getting a telephone installed quickly in New York City was a miracle. Columbia University helped.

I got to Columbia because it was clear to everyone I would never be a good social worker. Luckily for me, two good social workers came into my life at really important times. Blanche Cowan, Dean of Students at Fisk, which had, under another dean, kicked me out, welcomed me back. Cowan was a graduate of the Pennsylvania School of Social Work. As I neared graduation from Fisk, she was asking my plans. Since I had none, she suggested social work school. Since I also had no money, I was needing beaucoup help. Dean Cowan, who became a friend and whose death from a brain tumor is still extremely sad to me, helped me get interviewed and ultimately accepted to social work school. Louise Shoemaker, who ultimately became the dean of the University of Pennsylvania School of Social Work, and who was the major reason I found myself on the Concorde twenty years later to be able to attend her retirement, took an interest in if not me then the papers I wrote. She took me to lunch to "discuss your plans," which usually means we are kicking you out but we would like to be genteel about it. Dr. Shoemaker said, "We all enjoy your papers. We pass them around even when we don't have to. We think you have a real talent and should think about an M.F.A. program."

"So nobody thinks I will be a good social worker."

"Well, nobody thinks you work well with authority," she said.

Which I knew to be a fact. I still hate anything that smacks of rules and uniforms and I'm-only-doing-my-job–type crap. I'm not a whiner but I couldn't see my head above that water, so I kind of blankly looked at her.

"Columbia University has a wonderful program. . . ." And my mind immediately went to *No Shit!* But I said, "Well, yes, I can see your point," trying to be grown-up about it.

"Nikki, we know you will need some help so we have arranged for you to receive this scholarship. Your papers did the work for you. I hope you don't mind that I didn't ask you but . . ." I was beaming! Louise had understood two very essential things about me: I was poor and I hate rejection. And she had managed to not embarrass me and she had helped. To this day, social workers are high on my list, right next to nurses, of people the world should not have to get along without.

Now I am in the city each and every writer wants to be in. I am in the center of the world. I can go over to the UN and hear world news in the making; I can see Broadway plays in rehearsal; I can eat early at the Rainbow Room; I can go to the Bronx Zoo whenever I please; I can even work my way into Brooklyn and hear great music concerts; I can walk any and every place, Murray's Cheese Shop in the Village, the Univer-

sity Place Bookstore on Twelfth and Broadway; I can hang out
in Harlem, eating at Small's Paradise; I can have chicken and
waffles at Wells; I can go to Micheaux's Bookstore all the time.
I can be free.

I moved into an apartment on Eighty-fourth and Amster-
dam. This turned out to be a great building. My apartment
overlooked a school yard, so I was not closed in. Downstairs,
almost directly under me, lived the guitarist Cornel Dupree.
George Faison, the dancer and choreographer, lived down the
street; Eugene McDaniels, the songwriter, lived down the
block; Gregory Hines lived right there in the neighborhood.
Sidney Poitier hung out at Mikel's. Across the street were Mil-
ton Graves and Don Pullen and a bunch of other musicians
who had "liberated" the building they were living in. Since I
was a revolutionary I was looking forward to the showdown
when the owner came to reclaim his property. I saw myself
manning, or I guess that would be *womaning,* a corner at the
top of the building to give the signal when *they* were on the
way. I attended all the meetings attentively, waiting to be
given an important job to protect my block. When the men
finally got around to giving me a job it was—to cook breakfast
for everyone. It was assumed that since I was a writer, I would
be available in the mornings to cook, since I "didn't have a
job." I was hurt. I had seen myself playing a much more active
role in the defense of Eighty-fourth and Amsterdam. I
learned from that experience. Make your own job for your
own revolution. And, by the way, the block was not taken. But
my next-door neighbor was Morgan Freeman and his wife,
Jeannie. A frequent visitor was Clifton Davis, the actor and
songwriter. Morgan was in an off-Broadway play, *The DMZ,*

and was beginning to do television. Jeannie worked. And as is always the case with writers, people would drop off their kids, saying "Nikki, since you don't work would you watch . . ." Nobody respects writers.

I can tell you this: The reason I lost my Volkswagen is I was pregnant with what turned out to be my son, Thomas. Back in my day, you didn't know the gender of a child until it came. I went to Cincinnati thinking I was not due until October. I had gone for my sister's birthday, which is September 2, which can fall on Labor Day. I thought it might be my last trip until after the birth. Morgan needed a car to get around, and I left the Volkswagen with him. All he had to do was put gas in it and move it from one side of the street to another for New York City's alternate-side parking. Failure to move the car would result in lots of tickets and a tow. How was I to know Morgan would get a chance to go to some-out-of-town something, and how was he to know that I would give birth in Cincinnati and not be able to return to New York City for six weeks?

Now before I go on, I need to share this about Morgan: like me, he is a bid whist player. Sometimes, when we were not chasing our dreams, Morgan, Jeannie, Clifton Davis, and I would play bid. Morgan says he and Clifton didn't cheat; I believe him. But Mississippi certainly plays a different kind of bid than Ohio. Where I come from, the cards are shuffled, dealt around the table left to right, a five-card kitty placed in the center, and bidding begins. Bidding is Uptown, Downtown, or No-Trump. In a No-Trump, the Joker is dead. But somehow we ended up bidding three-low-one which means three are high one is low, and things like that are tailored to make each hand a winning hand. The Joker, Morgan swore, is the best card on the table, and in a No-Trump if you get the lead and have the Joker you can "call" it, that is, make it anything you want. You see the problem? Not cheating, I'm sure. But certainly strange. Teasing the kitty, too. Things we had never done.

Anyway, the tickets on the car piled up. The car was towed. I know this: I was at Columbia University enrolled in the M.F.A. program for one year. That M.F.A. program was a two-year program, at the end of which you were expected to have completed a manuscript. I completed and published my first manuscript that first year. Columbia said it was a two-year program and they would not give me my M.F.A. My car was towed to some police yard never to be seen by me again. Morgan said he was sorry.

This is what I think: 1) Columbia University owes me an M.F.A. degree. 2) Morgan owes me a car.

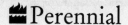**Perennial**

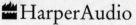